1989

Mental Health and Social Policy

third edition

David Mechanic

Institute for Health, Health Care Policy,
and Aging Research
Rutgers University

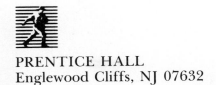

PRENTICE HALL
Englewood Cliffs, NJ 07632

LIBRARY OF CONGRESS
Library of Congress Cataloging-in-Publication Data

Mechanic, David
    Mental health and social policy / David Mechanic. — 3rd ed.
        p. cm.
    Includes bibliographies and index.
    ISBN 0-13-576034-8
    1. Mental health policy—United States. 2. United States—Social
policy.   I. Title.
    [DNLM: 1. Community Mental Health Services—United States.
2. Mental Disorders. 3. Mental Health. 4. Public Policy—United
States. WM 30 M486a]
RA790.6.M37 1989
362.2'0973—dc19
DNLM/DLC
for Library of Congress   88-2469
                                                              CIP

Editorial/production supervision and
    interior design: *Jenny Kletzin*
Cover design: *Baldino Design*
Manufacturing buyer: *Ray Keating/Peter Havens*

FOR LINDA
who has put these
ideas into action

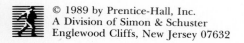

© 1989 by Prentice-Hall, Inc.
A Division of Simon & Schuster
Englewood Cliffs, New Jersey 07632

Printed in the United States of America

10 9 8 7 6 5 4 3 2 1

ISBN 0-13-576034-8

Prentice-Hall International (UK) Limited, *London*
Prentice-Hall of Australia Pty. Limited, *Sydney*
Prentice-Hall Canada Inc., *Toronto*
Prentice-Hall Hispanoamericana, S.A., *Mexico*
Prentice-Hall of India Private Limited, *New Delhi*
Prentice-Hall of Japan, Inc., *Tokyo*
Simon & Schuster Asia Pte. Ltd., *Singapore*
Editora Prentice-Hall do Brasil, Ltda., *Rio de Janeiro*

Contents ══════════════════════

3   *Psychological Disorder and the Flow of Patients into Treatment: The Study of Psychiatric Epidemiology*   45

4   *Conceptions of the Causes of and Means of Controlling Mental Illness*   61

9   *Central Perspectives in Formulating Mental Health Policies*   152

10   *The Social Context of Mental Health Practice: Ethical Issues*   184

11   *Innovations in Mental Health Services*   197

Preface

The mental health sector has been transformed in the past 30 years. The quantity and the diversity of mental health services available have expanded, the numbers and types of practitioners have proliferated, and the population not only finds mental health services more acceptable than in the past but they use them more commonly. In 1955, there were only 1.7 million patient episodes in mental health specialty organized settings, 77 percent involving inpatients; by 1983 there were some 7 million such episodes, and only 27 percent were on an inpatient basis. Mental health now accounts for about a tenth of health expenditures and consumes about one percent of the gross national product.

Many factors contributed to the growth and diversification of mental health services including the expansion of third party health insurance, changing social values and ideologies, and a growing psychological ethic. Advances in psychopharmacology made it possible to control severe symptoms of schizophrenia and affective disorders, and the availability of reimbursement for care in general hospitals and community mental health centers enabled the provision of acute care in more acceptable settings for those in the population who sought it. In terms of public visibility, however, no issue was more salient or difficult than deinstitutionalization and the failures to deliver on the promises of community care.

There are many troublesome policy issues in the mental health sector, but the critical challenge is to address the problems of the most seriously mentally ill and those patients who are most chronically impaired. Partly in response to demographic trends, partly as a consequence of shameful neglect of public sector services, the most needy among the mentally ill are increasingly on the streets with little of the necessary care they require. The fact is that we have the capacity to manage the care of such patients in a meaningful way but have as yet to demonstrate that we have the resolve to do so. Nothing short of a reorganization and revitalization of public sector services is likely to do the job. The policy issues are complex and the politics difficult, but to neglect these patients will only compound the growing tensions so apparent on the streets of our major urban centers.

The well-being of the mentally ill depends not only on psychiatry and medicine but perhaps even more fundamentally on such related sectors as social services, welfare, and housing. Because of the nature of serious mental illness, the boundaries between psychiatric and other medical and social areas are difficult to delineate, and policy-making in mental health requires expertise in financing, law, and welfare as well. Economics is always central, but to focus on such issues too narrowly neglects the devastating impact that psychiatric illness has on individuals and their families, on the healthy development of children, and on the capacity of people to maintain their functioning, work productively, and achieve a reasonably satisfying life. Examined in this context, psychiatric illness constitutes one of the most compelling problems modern societies face, deserving high priority in policy deliberations. And the economic accounting must involve a broad definition of costs and benefits of alternative pathways.

Coherent mental health policies must be based on careful comparisons of alternative modes of managing psychological disorder and on considerations of the roles of a variety of professions that work with the mentally ill. Much planning in the area of mental health takes place in a context of uncertainty resulting from the ambiguous boundaries defining mental illness and from the lack of adequate information on the success of alternative approaches to treatment and rehabilitation. The unknowns force us to make assumptions that are to some extent arbitrary, and we should be clear that these are assumptions often lacking a clear factual basis. Whatever the state of current knowledge, practicalities require that we define the public policy issues, explore the alternatives, and consider the probable advantages and disadvantages—given present knowledge—of following one course or another. This must be done with humility, however, not with dogmatism.

In reviewing the 1980 edition of this book, I had the opportunity to reflect on the major changes in the past ten years. When the previous edition went to press, the work of the President's Mental Health Commission had elicited a great deal of interest in improving the mental health services system, and there was considerable political mobilization around the Mental Health Systems Act. The Department of Health and Human Services was actively planning for the development of an integrated system of care for the most severely mentally ill, and the federal government was positioning itself to play a strong leadership role.

The election of President Reagan, the recision of the Mental Health Systems Act, and the new federalism philosophy returned the initiative to state government but with a reduced level of funding. Moreover, the crucial social and welfare programs on which the mentally ill depended—medical assistance, housing, disability—were either substantially cut back or did not keep pace with changing needs. Budget constraints at all levels made it more difficult for the most severely ill to receive the services they require, and homelessness became a larger part of the problem than ever before.

Things now look a lot worse on the streets than they did ten years ago. The problem is in part demographic; the baby boom cohorts are at ages of relatively high incidence of mental disorder, and there are many young people who critically need sophisticated services they are not now receiving. The public mental health services system, starved for resources and battered by political and organizational problems and growing public hostility, is in disarray. Deinstitutionalization is increasingly viewed as a failure, vividly described in influential media as "Crazy on the Streets," and "Rotting with One's Rights On." The tragedy is, as I will show, that it is possible to provide decent, humane, and meaningful management of chronic mental illness in the community if we only have the will to do so.

On the scientific side, despite a skewed emphasis, events look more promising. The neurosciences are progressing rapidly, and the technology of brain imaging and analysis have made impressive strides. Psychiatry has increasingly turned toward biology and medicine, and this has resulted in more rigor in diagnosis and investigation. Psychiatric epidemiology has emerged from the doldrums, and there is increasing research at the boundaries between the biomedical, behavioral, and population sciences. These advances have not come without costs. Psychiatry is now a less popular specialty among medical students than it was in the 1960s, and in its search for biomedical causes and in response to the economic incentives of reimbursement, much of the profession has turned away from its most needy and disabled clients who need sustained medical and rehabilitation services. Working with chronics is viewed as lacking intellectual interest, prestige, and sufficient economic reward, and the sophisticated psychiatry essential within the overall care of chronic patients is sadly neglected. The organized psychiatric profession and some of its most outstanding members have attempted to focus attention and commitment on the chronic patient, but this remains a rearguard action.

What has been said about psychiatry is equally true of the other mental health professions. Perhaps as a result of the current ethos of self-interest, relatively few students in clinical psychology, social work, or even nursing wish to address the problems of the most disabled mentally ill. The current preference among students is to become a psychotherapist and to practice independently, providing reimbursable services if possible. Their mentors also share these values, and few schools provide developed models of how one can serve the severely mentally ill in an effective and meaningful way. Without such models of care that give students appropriate experience and show them that such work can be effective and challenging, it is unlikely that young professionals will select these areas. My own institution, which has one of the most distinguished schools of applied psychology in the nation, has no one on its psychology faculty who has made a professional commitment to this population. This is the norm, not the exception.

On the positive side, the past decade has seen a significant growth of mental health advocacy, and the emergence of the National Alliance for the Mentally Ill and other mental health organizations on the local and national levels offers much promise for the future. Also, a number of innovators in the mental health professions have demonstrated and evaluated significant models of care and how they can be implemented, which establishes some of the important groundwork for the future.

As one looks ahead, it is apparent that mental illness services will continue to face difficult times. There seems little end in sight to fiscal constraints, and the growth of the elderly population, the AIDS epidemic, and other priorities will compete with mental health needs for attention. Although political trends are impossible to predict, it seems unlikely that vast new resources will become available for mental health, and the challenge will be to use the resources available wisely and with greater effect. In the absence of major breakthroughs in the biomedical sciences in treating schizophrenia and other devastating pathologies—and few anticipate them soon—the integrity of our services system will depend on the organization and vitality of public sector services. They leave much to be desired, and the sooner we dedicate ourselves to their reconstruction the better off we all will be.

ACKNOWLEDGMENTS

In this book, I define the major issues and questions that the mental health planner, practitioner, and researcher must face. I explore the ambiguities surrounding these issues and the research studies that help clarify at least some of them. While this book is written to be informative to the general reader as well as to the specialist, it is based on more than 30 years of active involvement in the mental health field as a teacher, researcher, and policy consultant.

We have an active mental health research group in our Institute at Rutgers, and a variety of friends and colleagues here and elsewhere have contributed to my thinking directly and indirectly. Four deserve special note: Linda Aiken, to whom this book is dedicated, is very special, and we do so much together that at times it's difficult to know where ideas originated. Linda coauthored with me one of the Handbook chapters noted below, as well as other papers, and inevitably some of her ideas are incorporated here. My friend, Alexander Brooks, a colleague of many years and a distinguished professor of mental health law, has taught me much of what I know about the law, and I am grateful for his astute suggestions about my discussion of these issues. My close colleague, Gerald Grob, one of the world's experts on the history of mental health, gives me a keen appreciation for the continuity of issues and dilemmas. Finally, Allan Horwitz, who co-directs the Rutgers–Princeton Postdoctoral Training Program in Mental Health Services Research with me, has been a particularly thoughtful colleague who keeps me alert to the extent to which the care for the mentally ill is part of a larger framework of social control.

Sections of the book were published elsewhere, and I thank the *Ameri-*

can *Journal of Public Health,* the *Journal of Nervous and Mental Disease,* the *Journal of Health and Social Behavior,* and the *Journal of Human Stress* for permission to incorporate parts of these discussions into this book. Also, some sections have appeared in *The Milbank Fund Quarterly,* in *Health Affairs,* and in two chapters prepared for the fourth edition of *The Handbook of Medical Sociology* (Prentice Hall), which will also be published this year.

Rachel McNally was particularly helpful in typing the manuscript and in assisting in details of its preparation for publication. Karen Orlando ably assisted me in proofreading. I am particularly grateful for their outstanding assistance.

David Mechanic
Rutgers University

Chapter One

Mental Health and the Mental Health Professions

Human feelings and behavior are extremely variable. The same people may be happy or sad, energetic or lethargic, anxious or calm depending on their environment and personal lives at the time. Many emotions and reactions fall within the normal range because everyday events evoke varying responses from us. To be sad when a loved one dies or to be anxious about an important but difficult examination is a normal response because such feelings fit the situation. Feelings of sadness, depression, or anxiety in themselves do not constitute abnormal responses unless they are dissonant with social and personal circumstances.

We usually recognize deviations from "normal" mental health in two ways. Persons sometimes engage in behavior that is strikingly discordant with their social circumstances and life situation; their behavior or expressed feeling states at such a time are so bizarre and difficult to interpret that we infer illness. It should be emphasized that the context of behavior is critical in making most such assessments. Although a person from a cultural background characterized by a belief system based on witchcraft might understandably be fearful of being poisoned or harmed by magic, a similar reaction from a person born and raised in Akron, Ohio, might leave us puzzled and concerned. Such an incongruity may suggest mental illness.

Another major way of identifying deviations from mental health is through recognition of personal suffering that is not justified by the circumstances of the individual's life. Although it may be normal for an unemployed person who cannot adequately provide for his or her children and who is objectively deprived and discriminated against to feel frustrated and angry, we infer that a person showing a similar reaction under favorable life circumstances and in the absence of any provocation may be psychiatrically disordered.

Bizarre behavior or profound suffering is not difficult to recognize. Much of our social behavior and most of our life circumstances, however, are not so clear-cut, and it is not always easy to ascertain whether a particular pattern of behavior or of feelings is inappropriate to or discordant with the social circumstances. Because extensive subgroup differences in value orientations and behavior characterize community life, it is often impossible to decide whether a person's behavior is bizarre or whether he or she is responding to a set of values characteristic of some subgroup rather than to the dominant or supposedly dominant cultural norm. Persons with counter-cultural life styles may appear bizarre to older and more conventional persons, but their patterns of dress and action are not necessarily discordant with the social scene. Similarly, many aspects of a person's life may lead to sadness or anxiety, but these circumstances are not always apparent unless we explore in some detail that person's real-life situation.

Attempts to define mental illness in some precise fashion have been disappointing. Although it is usually defined in terms of some deviation from normality, defining normality is not a simple matter. From a practical standpoint the persons themselves often become aware that something is not quite right and that their feelings, outlook, or state of mind is unusual or aberrant compared with their own previous experience or that of other persons. On other occasions, people define another's behavior as bizarre because it appears to be inconsistent with usual standards of normality or departs from that person's previous behavior. Because early definitions of mental illness depend on lay judgments involving varying criteria (Mechanic 1962), many behavior patterns are perceived as mental illness by laymen.

All of us may sometimes digress from usual standards of behavior and expression in a manner that appears strange to others, but these digressions do not lead to a diagnosis of mental illness. Such a diagnosis is ordinarily not considered unless the behavior is persistent or is so bizarre as to be unexplainable in any other terms. Although mental illness is identified by aberrant acts and expressions, the definition extends beyond these acts to implicate the person's entire identity and personality. When we define such behavior, we not only say that the person is behaving in a manner discordant with circumstances, but also that he or she is mentally ill or suffering from a mental disorder. This inference that the person suffers from some condition that permeates his or her whole being rather than from a more specific defect in learning or interpersonal relations has many consequences, which we shall discuss later.

From the perspective of particular value systems, the definition of mental illness in terms of failures in social adjustment or of lack of conformity to social expectations is inappropriate. Some psychologists have argued, for example, that neurotic persons who struggle psychologically and socially against the patterns of their society and may appear to be misfits in one way or another are more healthy than those who conform easily to all the mandates of their community (Fromm 1955). In this view, a person who conforms to a "sick" society rather than struggling against it, such as the Germans who obeyed Nazi mandates or those who applauded the Vietnam war, cannot be said to have a high level of mental health.

In trying to describe the characteristics of people with positive mental health, some clinicians and investigators have sought to define various persistent aspects of social character or personality that could be viewed independently of the social context. They emphasize such themes as social sensitivity, the capacity for environmental mastery, a unifying outlook on life, self-actualization, and self-acceptance (Jahoda 1958). However, such themes do not help us identify in any specific way patterns of behavior or feelings that indicate health. Social values and social expectations determine who is socially sensitive or who is achieving self-actualization, and the application of varying sets of values leads to different assessments. Although the concept of positive mental health is one worth keeping in mind, it is not very helpful in classifying different persons, groups, or populations.

Mental health professionals have specific conceptions of mental health and mental disorder; we shall describe these in some detail in Chapter 2. At this point, however, a variety of concepts frequently used in a confusing manner in the mental health field must be defined.

SYMPTOMS, DISEASES, AND REACTION PATTERNS

Those in the mental health field do not always make a distinction between symptoms and conditions. A *symptom* is a specific deviation from normality, such as high fever, lower-back pain, or apathy and depression. A *condition* is a constellation of symptoms believed to be typical of a particular underlying disorder. Such symptoms as fever, depression, apathy, and loss of appetite may be characteristic of a variety of different conditions; thus information on a particular symptom is usually inadequate for specifying the condition believed to be responsible for it. At times the same word is used to refer to both the symptom and the condition. The word *depression* describes a particular feeling state on the one hand and a general psychiatric condition on the other. Psychiatrists often find themselves in verbal binds, for example, when they maintain that a patient who does not evidence visible depression is suffering from a depressive condition. Such depression is often said to be masked or somaticized—that is, expressed through bodily complaints or behavior.

The concept of disease is an abstract one. The physician observes certain symptoms that appear to fit a particular pattern. He or she identifies this pattern with a disease label, which often serves as a theory and an explanation of the basic condition troubling the patient. The diagnostic process will be explored further in the next chapter; I note here, however, that, while some psychiatrists think the observable symptoms and signs suggest a particular underlying disease, others regard them only as a reaction pattern.

The term *reaction pattern* suggests that although certain symptoms go together, they need not imply any particular disorder. Those who view the behavior of psychiatric patients as reaction patterns rather than as the result of disease conditions point out that the same condition may manifest itself in many different ways, while different conditions may lead to behavior patterns that appear to be similar. Although this view is usually attributed to Freud, it has many roots. Vilfredo Pareto, an Italian sociologist who wrote in the latter part of the nineteenth century, differentiated the deep, persistent, and important aspects of the personality, which he called *residues,* from the more superficial and varying aspects of the personality, which he referred to as *derivations.* He maintained that the same residues might lead to widely varying derivations. For example, a love of pornography or a desire to legislate against pornography may be derivations of the same basic residue. Similarly, Sigmund Freud, in introducing the concept of reaction formation, posited that a basic human need might find expression through its vigorous denial and repudiation. Much of American psychiatry and clinical psychology has been based on the assumption that reaction patterns are not fully meaningful until their psychodynamics have been explored and their basic roots understood. In contrast, European psychiatry has placed much greater emphasis on the identification of underlying disease through observation of the patient's symptoms. In recent years, American psychiatry has been more biologically oriented and more sympathetic to the disease formulation.

DISEASE, PERSONALITY DISTURBANCE, OR PROBLEM IN LIVING

Mental health professionals differ considerably in viewing mental illnesses primarily as disease, as disturbances in the functioning of the personality, or as problems in living. Although these views overlap, emphasis may be put on one perspective or another. Those who view mental illnesses as diseases are most likely to believe that genetic and biological factors play an important if not prominent part in explaining the causes. Those who view mental illnesses as disturbances of the personality conceive of such problems as repertoires of behavior and patterns of feeling that have their origin in childhood social development and persist through time, even though they are inappropriate to effective social functioning and personal comfort. Some mental health professionals maintain that what is called "mental illness" results from other than genetic or physical factors or deep-rooted psychological disorders. They argue that such difficulties are problems in living that develop because of confusion in communication, maintenance of particular social roles, and enforcement of certain moral standards. Persons are labeled mentally ill because they fail to conform to certain social standards either because of their own unique understandings and viewpoints or because of their failure to develop certain social skills that others define as necessary. There is greatest agreement about the applicability of the disease perspective in the case of the most seriously mentally ill.

SOCIAL ADJUSTMENT

In addition to emphasizing bizarre behavior and personal suffering, psychiatrists and other mental health professionals frequently view illness in terms of the failure of persons to adjust adequately to their social surroundings or to fit into a recognized social group. They frequently assume that such adjustment failures result from certain biological or psychological deficiencies in the person. The basic assumption that failure to conform implies disorder leads some mental health professionals to regard all deviants as sick, and they attempt to explain such behavior by seeking its psychological or biological roots. In applying a psychiatric viewpoint to deviance in general, we often fail to appreciate the extent to which nonconforming behavior is a consequence of learning processes whereby persons within particular subgroups and social settings normally develop attitudes, values, and behavior patterns that are illegal or disapproved of within the larger society. No doubt, some deviants suffer from particular biological propensities and profound psychological disorders, but just as it is irresponsible to argue that all deviant behavior is acquired through normal learning processes, so it is irresponsible and shortsighted to conceive of all behavior we disapprove of as sick.

These conflicting views lead to defining a wide variety of conditions as mental illnessses. Some mental health workers treat only patients with specifically defined psychiatric problems; others believe in also treating those who are unhappily married, or fail to live up to their potential in school, or are bored and dissatisfied with life, or are criminals, delinquents, or prostitutes. Such multiple definitions of the responsibility of mental health professionals and the range of the problems they deal with make it difficult to describe their work clearly.

THE MENTAL HEALTH PROFESSIONS

Services for persons with mental health problems are provided by a wide range of facilities and professionals. When we think of the specialty mental health sector, we typically think of psychiatrists, psychologists, social workers, community mental health centers, psychiatric outpatient departments and clinics, psychiatric hospitals, and drug and alcohol treatment facilities. On an inpatient basis, care for psychiatric patients is provided, typically, in general voluntary hospitals, private psychiatric hospitals, and in county, state, and Veterans Administration hospitals. In the general hospital sector, psychiatric care may be provided in specialized psychiatric units or in scatter beds among other types of units. Despite this large specialized mental health sector, which we will examine in detail later, most persons with mental health problems either receive no professional care or obtain treatment from physicians with little specialized mental health training. The doctor of first contact is most typically the primary care physician (a family practitioner, general internist, or pediatrician), and such doctors see many patients who suffer from significant psychological symptoms or diseases compounded by high levels of psychological distress.

The best data presently available on these matters come from the Epidemiological Catchment Area (ECA) studies of populations in five areas of the United States, and we will examine this collaborative study in considerable detail later. These data indicate that mental health visits to general physicians constitute from 41 to 63 percent of all mental health visits depending on the geographic area studied. In New Haven, for example, where the number of psychiatrists is relatively large, people are more likely to turn to the specialized mental health sector. In Baltimore or Saint Louis, in contrast, people are more likely to depend on the general medical sector (Shapiro et al. 1984). Even these estimates of the use of general physicians may be low because many patients with depression, anxiety, and serious psychosocial problems do not define their problems in mental health terms and present primarily somatic symptoms and nonspecific physical complaints when seeking care. Estimates vary greatly on the proportion of medical visits that can be so characterized, but almost everyone agrees that such visits are highly prevalent. Since these visits are not reported as mental health visits by patients, they are typically not counted even if the doctor provides counseling or prescribes psychoactive drugs. In one study involving estimates from the National Medical Care Utilization and Expenditure Survey (NMCUES), the investigators noted that including such nonspecific complaints as "nerves" would increase estimates of mental health utilization by as much as 50 percent (Taube, Kessler, and Feuerberg 1984).

Beyond the medical and specialized mental health sectors are a wide range of agencies, counselors, and lay therapists who assist persons with emotional and psychosocial problems. Among these are clergy, family service agencies, and crisis centers. We know relatively little about the role played by chiropractors, spiritualists, and natural therapists, but they certainly play a part and, in the case of some cultural and ethnic groups, a major role.

In 1977 my colleagues and I collected data on the need for and use of mental health care from a cross section of persons living in north central Wisconsin. We asked the following question: "Sometimes when people have personal problems, such as with their feelings or marriage, they go someplace for help. In the past year, have you gone to any of the following for a personal problem?" Because the population area we studied had a wide range of services available, the responses to this question gave us some sense of the scope of the help-seeking network. It is essential to realize in examining the responses to this question that many people do not necessarily recognize depression, anxiety, or other symptoms as personal problems. The responses, therefore, tell us only what people who define themselves as having personal problems do.

First, we found that the lay network was the most prevalent source of help for personal problems. Thirty-three percent of respondents reported seeking help from a friend, and 28 percent reported seeking help from a relative. Professional sources of help reported in order of importance were clergy (6 percent), lawyers (4 percent), nonpsychiatric physicians (4 percent), social workers (4 percent), psychiatrists (2 percent), public health nurses (2 percent), social agencies (2 percent), psychologists (2 percent), chiropractors (1 percent), and mental health centers (1 percent). The possible source of helpers for personal problems was diverse.

My colleagues and I also carried out an epidemiological study of help seeking for personal problems among a representative sample of 1,502 students at the University of Wisconsin-Madison (Greenley and Mechanic 1976, Mechanic and Greenley 1976). Most students discussed personal problems with friends, relatives, and dorm counselors. Among more formal sources of help, 83 percent reported seeking one type of assistance in the three months before the interview, 15 percent reported using two services, and 1 percent, three or more services. The most common source of help was faculty members, followed in importance by general physicians, clergy, psychiatrists, and counseling services. Students with more serious problems used a wide range of helpers, however, including psychologists, T-groups, a women's counseling service, a telephone suicide prevention center, drug information centers, a community law office, a draft counseling center, and many others. The factors that influence the use of varying types of helpers will be examined in Chapter 6.

The four main professions that deliver mental health services are psychiatry, clinical psychology, psychiatric social work, and nursing. The psychiatrist is a medical doctor who has usually completed three or four years of a psychiatric residency that has provided intense involvement in clinical psychiatric problems. The clinical psychologist is not an M.D. but has had several years of graduate work in psychology, a clinical internship, and often holds a Ph.D. degree. The graduate program in clinical psychology is a blend of theory, practice, and research training. There is also a professional psychology degree (Psy.D.) for psychologists who have less interest in research. While the psychiatrist is more likely to have had intensive practical experience in handling different types of clinical psychiatric problems during the residency program, the clinical psychologist is likely to be better versed in psychological theory and research, to have a clearer understanding of the scientific bases of assessment and treatment, and to have a more critical awareness of research. The psychiatric social worker usually holds a two-year postgraduate degree. Graduate programs in social work have traditionally emphasized psychodynamic factors, social casework, and group organization. In recent years such training has become more diversified, giving attention to coping theory and crisis intervention, family therapy and behavior modification, the development of community care programs, and social administration.

Nursing plays a major role in mental health services, but there is large variability in training varying from nurses with a two-year associate community college degree to those with the doctoral degree in nursing or basic fields relevant to nursing. The best estimates suggest that of the 46,000 to 48,000 nurses practicing in mental health, approximately 12,500 have masters or doctoral training (NIMH Task Force on Nursing 1987a). Despite its numerical importance and its central role in care, nursing has not had a major leadership role in mental health policy. Other important mental health personnel include occupational and recreational therapists, mental health aides, counselors, and specially trained clergy. A common job title in mental health programs is the case-manager, but persons holding this title vary from masters-level social workers and nurses to individuals who have little specialized training.

Each of the major mental health professions reflects a somewhat different orientation and background, and each has its distinctive strengths and weaknesses. Although, theoretically, psychiatrists, clinical psychologists, psychiatric social workers, and nurses are able to work together as a harmonious team in which their distinctive skills complement one another, not infrequently their relationships are characterized by competition and resentment. Psychiatrists are usually on top of the heap, gaining dominance through their M.D. status, their monopoly over the prescription of psychoactive drugs, and their greater ability to be reimbursed for services under a variety of insurance programs. Clinical psychologists, having research and other technical skills often lacking among psychiatrists, have increasingly gained independence from psychiatric dominance and direct access to reimbursement for psychological and therapeutic services without working through a psychiatrist or clinic. Psychiatric social workers, the weakest politically of the mental health quartet, most often work through institutions or social agencies on a salaried basis, although they practice many of the same therapies as psychiatrists and psychologists (Henry, Sims, and Spray 1971). In mental health settings, such as mental hospitals, psychiatric units in general hospitals, and mental health centers, they often function under the authority of medical personnel and are disadvantaged as well by the lower prestige and power of social work in relation to its competitors. Social workers have been predominantly women, and discrimination based on sex and other cultural orientations have held social work back. Similarly, nursing has never wielded influence commensurate with its numbers and its central role in inpatient care. Nursing has traditionally been subservient to medicine in all specialties, but nurses in other areas have been more successful in defining sources of independent authority. In mental health, nurses compete with psychologists and social workers as well as with doctors. The political infighting for control of the mental health turf is active, and professional politics will have a major impact on the future organization of the mental health professions. The services that are and are not paid for and the conditions for reimbursement will greatly influence the power relationships among these professional groups.

Despite the differences among mental health professionals, there is considerable similarity in the background, value orientations, and attitudes among those engaging in psychotherapeutic work. One study has found that psychotherapeutically oriented psychiatrists are more similar to clinical psychologists and social workers than to their medical colleagues (Henry, Sims, and Spray 1971). While there are many political and economic divisions among the mental health professions, the common values shared by many types of mental health professionals provide opportunities for effective cooperation and team efforts.

Psychiatrists continue to have the most influence over the mental health sector despite their small numbers because of the prestige of their medical background and the advantage they have in being recognized by all payors as reimbursable providers. They also have the largest influence on care provided in medical settings. As of 1982 there were 30,647 psychiatrists in active practice (the number estimated in 1987 is approximately 36,000), and for a majority the primary health setting continues to be private practice (News and Notes 1986, pp. 1167–68), although many did some work in other settings as well. Most of their time was devoted to direct patient care largely involving psychotherapy accompanied by medication in approximately half the cases. Other major care functions included assessment and evaluation and management of medication. Only a small proportion of psychiatrists have their primary practice in institutional settings: medical schools and universities (12 percent); community mental health centers (6 percent); private psychiatric hospitals (4 percent); and other hospitals (3 percent). These facts are particularly significant in that they show that psychiatrists typically do not practice in settings caring for the most severely mentally ill and continue to play only a modest role in public sector mental health.

In recent years psychology and social work have assumed a much larger role in providing mental health services. While psychology has increasingly competed with psychiatry for office-based clients, social work has gained ground in mental health centers and other agency practice but has not become a major competitor in private practice because it is typically not covered by third-party insurance. In an analysis of mental health visits using data from the 1980 National Medical Care Utilization and Expenditure Survey, psychologists had reached parity with psychiatrists in mental health visits, each accounting for about one-quarter of all mental health visits (Taube, Kessler, and Feuerberg 1984). Psychiatrists continue to be greatly involved in outpatient care but are less commonly employed in mental health centers than previously, and social workers and psychologists provide the major leadership and most of the services in these institutions.

It is difficult to accurately count the number of psychologists providing mental health services. A thorough census by the American Psychological Association estimated that of approximately 102,000 psychologists in 1983, approximately 45,000 doctoral and 24,000 nondoctoral individuals provided or administered health and/or mental health services for at least part of their professional time (Stapp et al. 1985).

Estimates for social workers are even more difficult. Estimates for 1986, for example, vary from 460,000 to 480,000 by the Bureau of Labor Statistics to 110,000 to 130,000 Masters of Social Work (MSWs) by the National Association of Social Workers. The masters is the major professional degree for social workers, and of this total it is estimated that from 70,000 to 80,000 are involved in clinical work. However, many mental health agencies employ social workers without an MSW degree.

Another way of estimating personnel is by examining full-time equivalent staff in mental health organizations. This, of course, excludes those in private practice and significantly underestimates the involvement of psychiatrists and psychologists who are concentrated in private practice. It offers, however, a more accurate portrayal of the role of social work and nursing. In 1984, of the 313,000 full-time equivalent (FTE) patient care staff in mental health institutions, more than one-third had less than a B.A. degree. As of 1984, there were 18,539 FTE psychiatrists in these organizations. There were also some 21,000 psychologists at the masters level or higher, and some 36,000 social workers at the B.A. level or higher. These organizations also had approximately 55,000 full-time equivalent registered nurses (Witkin et al. 1987).

Data on the work of office-based psychiatrists come from the National Ambulatory Medical Care Survey, based on information recorded by office-based practitioners on encounter forms. It is estimated that from March 1985 through February 1986, almost 18 million visits were made to office-based psychiatrists, accounting for almost 3 percent of all medical visits. In some 8 million visits (46 percent), drugs were prescribed (National Center for Health Statistics 1987). The availability of psychiatrists continues to be concentrated in metropolitan areas and in particular states, although there is some tendency for the gap among states to be closing. However, in 1982, the ten states with the most psychiatrists, including, for example, Massachusetts, New York, and Connecticut, had ratios of from 16 to 40 psychiatrists per 100,000 population; the ten states with the least psychiatrists, including Idaho, Wyoming, Montana, and Mississippi, had between 4 and 8 psychiatrists per 100,000 people.

More detailed data on office visits to psychiatrists have not been published recently, but earlier data from the National Ambulatory Medical Care Survey convey the general situation. Most of the psychiatrists visited were in solo practice in metropolitan areas. While 73 percent of all visits to all specialists took place in metropolitan areas, 94 percent of all visits to psychiatrists were in such areas, suggesting the inequality in the distribution of psychiatrists (National Center for Health Statistics 1978).

More than two-fifths of the visits to office-based psychiatrists were for conditions diagnosed as neuroses. Other diagnoses in order of importance were personality disorders (14 percent), schizophrenia (11 percent), transient and situational disturbances (7 percent), affective psychoses (5 percent), and nervousness and depression (4 percent). These are the psychiatrists' own diagnoses—not based on standard definitions—and thus are only an approximate indication of the content of practice. Most commonly, the office-based psychiatrists engaged in psychotherapy with the patient (86 percent of all visits). The average visit was for 47 minutes in contrast to the average of 15 minutes for all physician visits.

Between 1955 and 1983, the number of episodes treated in organized mental health facilities increased from 1.7 million to 7 million. Prior to 1955 the severely ill were treated predominantly in mental hospitals, while those with less incapacitating conditions and adequate economic resources received care from private office-based psychiatrists or in private clinics. The number of resident patients in state and county mental hospitals in the United States climbed during the early 1950s to a total of almost 560,000 in 1955. With the introduction of new psychoactive drugs, changes in social ideology and administrative viewpoints, and growing concerns about the costs of maintaining large numbers of long-stay patients in public hospitals, a downward trend began (U.S. President's Commission on Mental Health, 1978, Vol. II, p. 94). The number of resident patients in public mental hospitals declined to less than 200,000 in 1975 despite a substantial increase in admissions (Clausen 1979, p. 101). In 1955 there were only

178,000 admissions to public mental hospitals; by 1975 admissions exceeded 435,000. Contrary to the earlier pattern, patients now stay in such hospitals for only a brief period of time before they return to the community. Many chronic patients, however, follow a "revolving-door" pattern with a large number of admissions.

The history of mental health service delivery reflects the inequalities of American medicine generally but in an exaggerated form. Traditionally, persons with means were served by private practitioners, while those who were poor were either ignored, incarcerated, or maintained in large custodial hospitals. Although there were instances in early American history of mental institutions practicing a high level of "moral treatment" (Bockoven 1972), changing social conditions in the nineteenth and twentieth centuries, including decreased community tolerance for the mentally ill and the accumulation of chronic patients in hospitals, led to the era of the large custodial mental hospital (Grob 1973). While the development of such hospitals was stimulated by reform movements intended to separate the mentally ill from criminals and to provide a more sympathetic environment, a variety of conditions resulted in large, crowded, understaffed, and underfinanced custodial institutions.

After the progress made from 1960 to 1980, many of the traditional inequalities in mental health care are again increasing. The most severely mentally ill are commonly uninsured, frequently do not receive the welfare benefits for which they are technically eligible, and constitute a significant proportion of the homeless in most of our nation's large cities. The present situation to which much of this book is directed reflects a shameful instance of social and medical neglect of a needy and dependent population.

American psychiatry as we know it today, unlike much of European psychiatry, did not take root in the hospital context, and most public mental hospitals in the post–World War II period had few psychiatric, medical, or mental health professional staff (Deutsch 1949, Belknap 1956). The most prevalent group of employees were untrained orderlies whose major function was to maintain order and not to provide treatment. Although many were undoubtedly kind and dedicated, the need to control large numbers of disturbed patients with minimal staff created a situation in which a rigid form of authority and bureaucratic response was functional. Goffman (1961), in his essays on *Asylums*, vividly described such total institutions, the way they were managed, and their impact on patients.

In 1947 there were only 4,700 psychiatrists in the United States, and only 23,000 mental health professionals in the core areas of psychiatry, clinical psychology, psychiatric social work, and psychiatric nursing in contrast to the large numbers available today. A large influence on this increase in personnel was the training and manpower programs of the National Institute of Mental Health. The majority of the new psychiatrists trained in the 1950s and early 1960s had a psychodynamic orientation and were mainly attracted to fee-for-service private practice with middle-class patients. In *Social Class and Mental Illness*, two eminent writers, one a sociologist and the other a psychiatrist, studied the prevalence of mental illness among New Haven residents in 1950 and the treatment they received. It was clear that while the lowest social classes carried the largest burden of mental illness, they received the least care (Hollingshead and Redlich 1958). Most care provided by psychiatrists was for higher-status patients with less severe disorders. Psychiatry was finally discovering the hard facts of social stratification.

In the 1950s and 1960s psychoanalytically oriented psychiatrists dominated the major psychiatric teaching centers, and America's romance with Freud and psychoanalytic theory had a pervasive (some say perverse) effect not only on psychiatry but also on social work, psychiatric nursing, and clinical psychology. This not only affected the types of practice mental health professionals engaged in but also provided an inhospitable climate for developing a rigorous scientific approach to the problems of mental illness. Such power bases erode slowly, and such intellectual trends take a long time to reverse. There is evidence that the psychiatric professions are changing substantially, but the traces of an office-based psychotherapeutic bias will remain for a long time to come. Psychoanalysis now accounts for only about 6 percent of clinical time, but psychoanalytic thinking still has significant influence.

While psychiatry in most European countries developed within the field of medicine during the 1950s and 1960s and was part of an integrated medical care system, psychiatry in the United States during this period operated alongside the medical care system but was not really a part of it. In the National Health Service in England, most psychiatric specialists were part of the health care system, were employed primarily in hospitals, and worked more closely with general practitioners and other medical specialists than psychiatrists in the United States. They also contributed to developing a better balance among varying types of services and greater reform of mental hospitals than was evident in the United States during the same time.

The psychodynamic orientation of American psychiatrists during the post–World War II period made it difficult to integrate psychiatry as a consulting specialty into the general medical system. The cardinal principle of the dominant psychoanalytic perspective was that behavior was dominated by unconscious processes that could contribute to inappropriate social functioning and psychological distress. These processes could be discovered and treated only through the use of the psychoanalytic method in which the therapist and patient repeatedly and intensively explored the patient's psyche. Thus, the form of treatment advocated was expensive in terms of the therapist's time and the small number of patients he or she could treat. In short, psychoanalytic therapy required private practice and rich patients.

Psychoanalytic therapy is more "religion" than "science," and its nurturance required enough people intellectually attracted to it and willing to pay for it. The large cosmopolitan urban areas provided such a clientele, and it was in such cities as Washington, D.C., New York, Chicago, Los Angeles, and Philadelphia that such therapists concentrated. Because the therapy was viewed as requiring verbal and other middle-class abilities, the requirements for therapy justified its focus on an "elite clientele." Until the development of psychiatric outpatient services in hospitals and mental health centers, the poor and those with the most serious and incapacitating conditions had no significant source of help other than mental hospitaliza-tion or the services of primary care physicians. Although general physi-cians who were poorly trained in psychiatry could have benefited signifi-cantly from an effective consulting psychiatric specialty, the average doctor had difficulty understanding or sympathizing with the strange theoretical conceptions of mental illness held by the psychodynamically oriented prac-titioners. The psychiatrist was typically viewed as esoteric, impractical, and not particularly helpful.

Psychiatric training in the 1980s has been more eclectic, with growing concern for scientific rigor, more precise classification, and the investiga-tion of biological hypotheses. After a long period of dormancy in scientific work, departments of psychiatry are engaging in more clinical, epi-demiological, biological, and social research. Advances in the neurosciences and in genetics and the technological tools made possible by the new biolo-gy and advances in brain imaging have redirected psychiatry to its medical origins and to intense investigation of biological hypotheses. Clinical psy-chology has become more behaviorally oriented, developing therapeutic approaches based on learning theory and developments in psycho-physiology and social psychology. Social work is less concerned with the psychodynamics of the patient and more concerned with coping, social networks, and social supports. Mental health workers of all types are more commonly found in organizational settings, such as mental hospitals, gen-eral voluntary hospitals, mental health centers, and community facilities, such as day hospitals, halfway houses, and sheltered workshops. The dec-ade of the 1960s was a period of expansion and chaos in psychiatric ser-vices; the 1970s was a period of consolidation, sorting the worthwhile from the worthless, and beginning the building of necessary links between men-tal health and physical health. The 1980s have brought a new emphasis, more pragmatic and closer to general medical care.

In the period beginning in approximately 1966 and extending until the late 1970s, there were not only large extensions of psychiatric outpa-tient care but also impressive improvements in mental hospitals. The typ-ical mental hospital is smaller, better staffed, and more treatment-oriented than in the past. While the numbers of such hospitals have not changed dramatically, they are substantially different institutions. By 1982, the typ-ical state mental hospital had 529 inpatients and 807 employees, with average expenses per patient of more than $31,000 per year. Between 1970 and 1982, the average ratio of patients to employees was reduced from 1.7 to .7 and average expenditures for patients increased from $4,359 to $31,000 per year ($12,500 after controlling for inflation). These hospi-tals now deal with the sickest, most disabled, and most difficult patients. In contrast, most acute care for serious mental illness is provided in short-stay general hospitals. In 1984, there were 1.7 million discharges from such hospitals of patients with a primary mental illness diagnosis and an average length of stay of approximately 12 days (Dennison 1985). The elderly demented as well as many elderly mentally ill are now in nursing homes; estimates made on the basis of the 1977 Nursing Home Survey total some 668,000 patients with mental illness or dementia (Goldman, Feder, and Scanlon 1986). In short, there was a dramatic reorganization of inpatient psychiatric care, a major change in the distribution of patients among sites of care, and a transformation of the pattern of hospitalization for acute psychiatric illness.

As a consequence of reductions in the populations of public mental hospitals and the transfer of many hopeless chronic patients to nursing homes, the public mental hospital was in many instances transformed from a custodial institution to an active treatment unit. The professional:patient and staff:patient ratios improved enormously, and active treatment and rehabilitation programs were developed to a point where in many instances there was little resemblance between the hospital as it had once been and what it now was. Although many hospitals and programs still depend substantially on psychiatric aides with limited education and training, these staff members are more carefully selected and supervised than in the past. Government programs such as Medicare and Medicaid provide entitlement to psychiatric services, and psychiatric insurance coverage has improved. Perhaps most important, treatment techniques have been developed that provide significant assistance to many psychiatric patients, helping them to return to their usual roles and responsibilities. The mentally ill are less stigmatized than in the past, and there seems to be more public understanding of the problems of the mentally ill.

To note advances is not to neglect the profound problems that lie ahead, not only for the mentally ill and their families, but also for public policy. Large numbers of chronic psychiatric patients have been retained in or returned to the community without the development of appropriate services necessary to assist them to maintain a reasonable level of functioning and life satisfaction. With the assistance of Medicare and Medicaid, many mental patients are now in nursing homes, some receiving care no better and perhaps worse than in poor mental hospitals. There has been a large growth of community sheltered care, which is highly variable in quality. Psychiatric insurance benefits tend to benefit mainly the affluent and reinforce by their definition of reimbursable providers a medical and hospital-based approach to mental health care. Knowledge of psychiatric disorder is still very limited, and the infrastructure of basic and clinical research in psychiatry remains weak. Although the civil liberties movement in the mental health area has brought some real gains in protecting patients' constitutional rights, it has also brought some new dilemmas. Concepts of mental disorder remain vague and confusing, and treatment of patients still proceeds as if anything goes. The field is handicapped by loose thinking, loose practice, and a reasonable amount of fraudulent activity. Funding for services, research, and professional development remains very tight. The relationships between psychiatry and medicine and between psychiatrists and other mental health professionals remain uncertain, and the public financing of care for the most impoverished and disabled of this population is inadequate and uncertain for the future. With changes in employment patterns, redevelopment of cities, gentrification, and reductions in federal housing programs, the housing available to low-income persons in many cities has diminished, and many of the mentally ill have joined the ranks of the homeless. Financing of mental health care is fragmented, and the organization of necessary services in most localities is in chaos. Public mental health systems are in a shambles and in desperate need of reform and consolidation.

The policy agenda, thus, is large and difficult. How should mental health care be financed, and how could funds now available be used more effectively? What incentives could be provided to manage care better and to achieve more rational organization? How can we direct more mental health services to the most disabled and needy clients? How can we best resolve the conflicts between civil liberties and the need for treatment? Exploration of these and many other issues of public policy are the task of the chapters that follow. But, first, we must be clear about what we mean by the concepts of mental health and mental illness.

Chapter Two

What Are Mental Health and Mental Illness?

If we are to discuss mental health policy, we must be aware of the scope and limits of our topic. If our goal is to develop policies to deal with the prevention and treatment of mental illness and the facilitation of mental health, then we must clearly outline the dimensions of each of these concepts. Are mental health programs to be limited to persons who come under the care of mental health workers, or are they to extend to those who see no need for psychiatric services and who have not been defined as problems by their communities? Are such programs to be restricted to persons suffering from clear psychiatric syndromes, or should they include those with ordinary problems, such as nervousness, unhappiness, and social and family conflict? Are deviations such as delinquency and criminal behavior part of the mental health problem, or are they more fruitfully dealt with outside the sphere of psychiatry? Are such situations as poverty, discrimination, and unemployment central aspects of the mental health problem, or do they relate more significantly to other fields? Is failure in performance resulting from a low level of education a mental health problem, or is it primarily a problem of education? Each of these questions and many others must be answered before it is possible to consider alternative mental health policies.

Psychiatrists, mental health workers, and the public in general disagree about the appropriate criteria for ascertaining the presence of mental illness. Much of this disagreement stems from a lack of consensus as to how broad or narrow the conception of mental illness should be. While some psychiatrists restrict the definition of mental illness to a limited set of disorders, others include a great variety of problem situations within the psychiatric sphere.

PSYCHIATRIC DIAGNOSTIC MODELS

As in medicine in general, psychiatrists have developed descriptive diagnostic labels that they use in categorizing and dealing with patients. Although most psychiatrists use these designations, they do not agree on their nature, significance, or utility. Increasing numbers of psychiatrists maintain that the labels denote different disease conditions; others maintain that they apply to reaction patterns having manifest similarities but do not describe specific disease conditions. The opinions of most psychiatrists probably fall somewhere between these two; they accept some of the diagnostic categories as disease categories, and they view others as convenient ways of grouping reaction patterns.

The American Psychiatric Association has traditionally divided psychiatric conditions into three major groups: (1) those conditions caused by or associated with impairment of brain tissue (for example, disorders caused by infection, intoxication, trauma, and metabolic disturbances); (2) mental deficiency; and (3) disorders without clearly defined clinical cause, those not caused by structural change in the brain and those attributed to psychogenic causes. We will focus our discussion on this third category.

The American Psychiatric Association further divided this category into five subcategories: (1) psychotic disorders; (2) psychophysiologic, autonomic, and visceral disorders; (3) psychoneurotic disorders; (4) personality disorders; and (5) transient situational personality disorders. These subcategories descriptively depict the gross reaction patterns recognizable among patients.

The *Third Edition of the American Psychiatric Association's Diagnostic and Statistical Manual*—a statement of criteria for diagnostic classification—breaks away from traditional usage of diagnostic terms and attempts to develop a more logical set of diagnostic criteria (Spitzer and Endicott 1978). Major categories in the DSM-III include the organic mental disorders such as senile and presenile dementias, substance abuses such as alcoholism, schizophrenic disorders, paranoid disorders, affective disorders such as depression or manic-depressive states, anxiety disorders including phobias and generalized anxiety, and personality disorders. The traditional distinction between organic disorders and functional disorders (those without a demonstrable organic basis or structural abnormality) is discarded because the distinction is now viewed as simplistic, and the concept of neurosis is eliminated because it is too vague. These new definitions, however, do not provide adequate differentiation between *disease states* and social behavior, nor is it clear that such distinctions are always possible, as this chapter will make clear.

DSM-III has had a major influence on psychiatric thinking and diagnosis, but the system is largely based on pragmatic description rather than any underlying theoretical basis. It constitutes a committee effort to achieve uniformity among psychiatrists with radically varying theoretical orientations ranging from the biological to the psychodynamic. The controversy was often more political than scientific in its character, and political compromises were necessary to achieve consensus. One of the most bitter disputes involved the classification of neurotic disorders, and in all likelihood these disputes will continue through subsequent revisions of the DSM. As Bayer and Spitzer (1985) note in their discussion of the controversy over neurosis and psychodynamics, "the entire process of achieving a settlement seemed more appropriate to the encounter of political rivals than to the orderly pursuit of scientific knowledge" (p. 195).

Despite the limitations of the DSM, the process of codification and the efforts to be as specific as possible about diagnostic criteria have encouraged greater care in diagnosis and more uniformity in the use of psychiatric designations. Most psychiatrists regard DSM-III in a serious way, and greater precision in the use of psychiatric labels have facilitated clearer communication among professionals. The DSM-III has also been extremely important for research because research criteria based on these definitions facilitate defining samples of patients more precisely and help communicate better to which groups of patients the findings apply. On the negative side, the codification process takes on a life of its own, and insurance companies, courts, and other social agencies attribute to DSM-III definitions more validity than they truly have.

In examining psychiatric practice, it is necessary to use the available diagnostic statistics, in which the diagnostic criteria may not be as carefully applied or standardized across settings as they might be in a research study. Data on admissions to major mental health facilities are reported for the United States in respect to inpatient, outpatient, and partial care as part of a continuing effort of the Survey and Reports Branch of the NIMH to monitor changes in mental health services. The most chronic and disabled patients are usually found in state and county hospitals, with almost two-fifths of the admissions diagnosed as schizophrenic and more than a quarter with alcohol and drug diagnoses. For example, in 1980 65 percent of admissions to state and county hospitals had such diagnoses in contrast to 33 percent in private psychiatric hospitals and 36 percent in nonfederal general hospitals. In contrast, while affective disorders accounted for only 13 percent of admissions in public hospitals, they accounted for 43 percent of admissions in private hospitals and 31 percent in general hospitals (Rosenstein et al. 1986). In outpatient and community mental health settings, the diagnoses are more diverse, but affective disorders (primarily depression) are the most common problems. Other frequent diagnoses include schizophrenia, childhood disorders, social maladjustments, and alcoholism.

There are a large variety of psychiatric conditions, and this is not the context to review the range or variety that the mental health professions deal with. For the purposes of discussing mental health policy, the disorders we will focus on are the affective, the paranoid, and the schizophrenic reactions. Less descriptive attention is given to alcohol and drug problems, developmental problems, and those associated with personality, but they are clearly important as are many others not even mentioned.

Affective disorders, involving disturbances of mood, are highly prevalent and the depression and/or elation can be extraordinarily painful, disabling, and disruptive to everyone around the patient. Depression, the more obvious of the two types of mood disturbance, can vary from painful but not disabling mood to feelings and behavior that are truly devastating. Distinctions are typically made between major depression and bipolar disorder (manic-depressive disorder), in which manic episodes are evident. Bipolar disorder is less prevalent than major depression and has a different epidemiology suggesting that it is a fundamentally separate condition or set of conditions. Persons with both major depression and bipolar disorder appear to have an important genetic vulnerability, and important progress has been made in locating a genetic marker for at least one, and possibly two, of the manic-depression genes. Studies of the Amish, a group living in isolation from the mainstream culture and who have large families and good genealogies, have contributed to identifying a dominant gene on the chromosome that significantly increases vulnerability to the condition. Not all who have the gene, however, develop the illness, suggesting a complex etiology (Kolata 1987). Patients with a bipolar disturbance respond to the drug lithium, while most depressed patients do not, also suggesting that bipolar disorders are separate conditions.

Paranoid reactions are typically characterized by persecutory or grandiose delusions or delusional jealousy. The suspiciousness characteristic of the paranoid is commonly seen in the general population, and its more extreme forms frequently accompany schizophrenia. When extreme symptoms occur without hallucinations and cannot be attributed to schizophrenia, they are separately diagnosed, but the differentiation of these diagnoses is unclear. While extreme paranoid disorders are not extremely prevalent, the resentment and anger associated with these states are believed to be associated with potential violence and thus require careful management. Such patients who become violent are also often schizophrenic or are substance abusers, and thus the relationship between paranoia and dangerousness remains unclear.

Schizophrenic reactions, although a relatively small component of all mental illness, involve for many long-term disability, continuing need for care, and the consumption of vast public resources. Thus, it represents the prototype of the challenge that public policy must intelligently address. Although psychiatrists generally agree that schizophrenic reactions encompass different conditions with surface similarities, there is little evidence that subtypes can be reliably differentiated, and, under ordinary conditions of practice, even the gross diagnosis is less than fully adequate in its reliability. Because schizophrenia is one of the most important psychiatric conditions—and the one most studied and written about—I shall illustrate some of the general problems of psychiatric conceptualization using schizophrenia as an example.

SCHIZOPHRENIA: AN EXAMPLE
IN PSYCHIATRIC CONCEPTUALIZATION

Psychiatrists usually diagnose schizophrenia on the basis of bizarre behavior characterized by inappropriate verbalizations and distortions of interpersonal perception as evidenced by the presence of delusions and hallucinations. Schizophrenics often withdraw from interpersonal contacts and engage in a rich and unusual fantasy life. In its more extreme manifestations, schizophrenia is associated with disregard for conventional expectations and with habit deterioration. One definition describes schizophrenia as a set of reactions involving disturbances in reality relationships and concept formation, accompanied by a variety of intellectual, affective, and behavioral disturbances varying in kind and degree. McGhie and Chapman (1961) note that early schizophrenia often involves disturbances in the processes of attention and perception (including changes in sensory quality and in the perception of speech and movement), changes in motility and bodily awareness, and changes in thinking and affective processes. Patients classified as schizophrenic often give the impression that they are retreating from reality and are suffering from unpredictable disturbances in their streams of thought. Depending on the stage of the condition and the level of personal deterioration, schizophrenia may be easy or difficult to identify.

> The diagnosis of schizophrenia is either very easy or very difficult. The typical cases, and there are very many such, can be recognized by the layman and the beginner; but some cases offer such difficulties that the most qualified experts in the field cannot come to any agreement. Such difficulties hardly can be surprising; there is no clear, fundamental definition of schizophrenia and there are marked differences in international psychiatry as to what is meant by the term. In the United States, the concept of schizophrenia is broader than in the rest of the world and includes marginal types. In general, the diagnosis of schizophrenia is made too frequently; we are inclined to believe that the less skilled the psychiatrist, the more often the diagnosis of schizophrenia. As the diagnosis still has a connotation of malignancy and grave implications for patients and their families, it encourages drastic therapies and should be made with great circumspection. It is based entirely upon psychological and rather subjective criteria. All too often the diagnosis is made without specification of stage and severity. (Redlich and Freedman 1966, pp. 507–8)

In recent years considerable effort has been made to improve the diagnostic classification of schizophrenia and to achieve greater reliability in diagnostic assessment from one context to another. DSM-III has contributed to clearer diagnostic specification, and growing interest in biological models results in more attention to careful diagnosis. A number of models have been developed for more systematic diagnosis. John Wing, for example, has developed a technique of interviewing patients—called the "Present State Examination"—which has been used in a variety of diagnostic studies (Wing 1978). The procedure involves a set of rules based on clinical experience that allows allocation of patients to diagnostic categories. This system has been computerized (known as CATEGO) (Wing, Cooper, and Sartorius 1974) and has been established to have high reliability for the classification of schizophrenia in different cultures (John Wing et al. 1967, World Health Organization 1973). Its usefulness to predict prognosis, however, is unclear (Kendell, Brockington, and Leff 1979).

Symptoms used in the diagnosis are divided into various classes. In the case of an acute problem, the central symptoms that account for two-thirds of all clinical diagnoses of schizophrenia include thought insertion, thought broadcast, thought withdrawal, auditory hallucinations of a specific type, and delusions of control. Thought insertion is the experience that thoughts other than one's own are being inserted into the mind. The patient believes that alien thoughts are inserted in his or her mind through radar, telepathy, or some other means. Careful questioning is required to establish that the patient truly understands and that he or she is not exaggerating a commonly occurring experience. In fact, the symptom is rare. Other groups of symptoms may also be used to establish a diagnosis of schizophrenia, such as other types of delusions or hallucinations or persistent talking to oneself. Still other symptoms are more ambiguous, and it becomes difficult to make a clear differential diagnosis between schizophrenia and other clinical conditions. In the case of more marginal symptoms, agreement among psychiatrists decreases.

The chronic schizophrenic is often highly disabled socially. Two main types of symptoms tend to be present: (1) "a syndrome of 'negative' traits, such as emotional apathy, slowness of thought and movement, underactivity, lack of drive, poverty of speech, and social withdrawal"; and (2) "incoherence of speech, unpredictability of associations, long-standing delusions and hallucinations, and accompanying manifestations in behavior" (Wing 1978, p. 110). The consequences of these types of symptoms and their effects on work, interpersonal relations, and family life make the chronic schizophrenic a major challenge for any program seeking to achieve reasonable community adjustment (Estroff 1981). It is difficult to rehabilitate the schizophrenic patient, and limiting the chronicity of the condition is itself a formidable challenge. Recent studies, however, demonstrate that the prognosis of schizophrenia is less discouraging than clinicians have typically believed and that well-conceived and appropriately managed programs of care can significantly limit the disabilities associated with schizophrenia and improve patients' level of function and quality of life. These points are of great importance and require brief summary here.

Clinicians have expressed pessimism about the inevitable deterioration associated with schizophrenia and the intractability of the disease to intervention. In contrast, long-term studies show extraordinary variability in adaptation and function over time suggesting that these patients have much greater potential than many clinicians believe. Each of five long-term studies reported since 1972 shows varied outcomes with significant numbers of long-term remissions (Harding, Zubin, and Strauss 1987). For example, in a remarkable clinical study carried out over 27 years, Manfred Bleuler (1978) studied the course of disorder among 208 patients in Zurich in various cohorts over two decades. He described the continuing adaptations among these patients who fluctuated between varying outcomes.

One-half to three-quarters of the schizophrenic patients achieved long-term recoveries, and only 10–20 percent became severe chronic schizophrenics. The estimate of recovery is conservative, since it only includes patients reaching an end-state, and, as Bleuler notes, prognosis of all schizophrenia combined is better. Moreover, in some patients, even after 40 years of psychosis, marked changes still occur. Long-term studies carried out by Ciompi (1980) in Lausanne and by Huber, Gross and Scheuttler (1979) in Bonn confirm Bleuler's conclusion on the variable and often favorable course of schizophrenia.

In the American context, follow-up after an average of 32 years of a group of 269 chronic patients released from Vermont State Hospital revealed that one-half to two-thirds had significantly improved or recovered, confirming European results (Harding et al. 1987a,b). The patients studied had, on average, been totally disabled for ten years and had been continuously hospitalized for six years. Most were functioning adequately in the community in later life, although ten years after release many of these patients had uncertain adjustments and were socially isolated. Using records, the investigators rediagnosed patients, selecting those 118 patients who met DSM-III criteria for schizophrenia at hospital admission in the mid-1950s (Harding et al. 1987b). At follow-up most were living in the community and needed little or no help in meeting basic needs. Two-fifths of patients of working age were employed in the prior year, a majority had few significant symptoms, and about three-quarters were assessed as leading "moderate to very full lives." The picture that emerges is one highly divergent with clinical assumptions and suggests that the image of inevitable deterioration that dominates the psychiatric literature may have been a self-fulfilling prophecy. Similar findings have been reported by Clausen, Pfeffer, and Huffine (1982), and while Tsuang, Woolson, and Fleming (1979) found in a 30- to 40-year follow-up that schizophrenics had a less favorable course than patients with affective disorders, a significant number of schizophrenics had "good" outcomes.

It is not too difficult to reconcile the lack of congruency between these studies and the level of pessimism found among many clinicians. Clinicians are often unaware of the epidemiological picture because they see their patients primarily in a short-term, cross-sectional perspective (Harding, Zubin and, Strauss 1987). Moreover, many patients who function well may no longer seek care or require intensive treatment, giving more salience to those patients who do not get well and repeatedly return for inpatient care. The difficult and intractable cases come to dominate the clinician's time and perceptions. A longitudinal perspective, in contrast, would not only provide a more hopeful picture but provides the perspective necessary for the types of care essential for this needy population. A large number of studies, which we will review later, show persuasively that effectively organized community alternatives to hospital care consistently achieve superior results whether measured by clinical outcomes, psychosocial participation, levels of function, or patient and family satisfaction.

The causes of schizophrenia remain unknown, and there is still much disagreement about its classification. Theories of its origins range from biologically oriented models (Kety 1986) to those that posit the roots of schizophrenia in social interaction and family life (Mischler and Waxler 1965). Debate continues as to whether it is more valuable to view schizophrenia as a variety of diseases with common manifestations or as reaction patterns. In recent years, the dominant view has moved closer to biological and biomedical models, but almost everyone accepts the idea that both biology and environment play some role. As John Strauss (1979) notes: "No single variable, biological or psychosocial, appears to be necessary or sufficient to make someone schizophrenic" (p. 291).

With the growing dominance of the biomedical orientation, there is much more attention devoted to specifying precise diagnostic criteria, as was noted in our discussion of DSM-III, and more interest in diagnostic reliability. In contrast, those who view schizophrenia as a convenient term for a particular reaction pattern that has no underlying disorder use the label more loosely and are less concerned with the reliability of the concept because the diagnosis is not seen as the primary factor in decisions concerning the care and treatment of the patient. But even these new efforts at diagnostic clarity, such as DSM-III, are empirically derived and have no clear theoretical basis. There are now many operational definitions using different criteria and combinational rules and giving varying importance to longitudinal considerations. McGuffin, Farmer, and Gottesman (1987) note that "disappointingly, a straightforward 'Chinese menu' set of criteria such as DSM-III appears to be more serviceable. . . . However, we consider that the work of constructing appropriate criteria is not yet done and that there must still be a continuing process of revision and reassessment" (p. 154).

As research proceeds, most scientists have developed a complex multifaceted view of schizophrenia, but the following statements reflect the wide range of approaches and theoretical conceptions that have guided efforts in this field as well as the extent of disagreement.

Constitutional resistance to the main genotype of schizophrenia is determined by a genetic mechanism which is probably non-specific and certainly multifactorial. . . . For various reasons it does not seem likely, however, that the genetic mechanisms controlling susceptibility and lack of resistance to schizophrenia—that is, the ability to develop a schizophrenic psychosis and the inability to counteract the progression of the disease—are entirely identical with each other. (Kallman 1953, pp. 96–97)

. . . Virtually all the participants in the Conference subscribed in some form to a diathesis-stressor framework (DSF) for explaining the appearance of schizophrenia. With the exception of Kringlen, the contributors . . . emphasize a large and rather specific genetic 'something' interacting with non-specific, perhaps universal environmental factors. (Gottesman 1978, p. 60)

. . . Environmental factors play a considerable role in schizophrenia development. The results give no support to any simple dominant or recessive transmission. If one accepts a polygenic transmission, one has to admit that based on these data the polygenic predisposition is of a rather modest degree. More than 70% of children of two schizophrenic parents do not develop schizophrenia despite a double risk genetically and environmentally. (Kringlen 1978, p. 23)

It is now clear that several chemically different types of drugs attenuate the manifest schizophrenic symptoms in many patients, and that a blockade of dopamine synapses is their common pharmacologic action. One would hesitate to conclude that the dopamine system therefore plays a primary role in the etiology of schizophrenia. Since the dopamine system interacts with many other transmitter systems, including serotonin, GABA, norepinephrine and certain polypeptides, any of these or others still undiscovered could be the site of the biochemical alteration, the existence of which is implied by the genetic evidence. (Kety 1978, pp. 156–57)

A great many observers have attempted to explain the manifestations of schizophrenia as being the result of disturbed interactions between the parents and the child who later develops a schizophrenic illness. These investigators have focussed on the *psychological disturbances* of the ego functions that result from deviations in normal development, maturation, and ego integration. (Rubinstein and Simons 1981, p. 613)

We suggest that the double bind nature of the family situation of a schizophrenic results in placing the child in a position where if he responds to his mother's simulated affection, her anxiety will be aroused and she will punish him . . . to defend herself from closeness with him. Thus, the child is blocked off from intimate and secure associations with his mother. However, if he does not make overtures of affection, she will feel that this means that she is not a loving mother and her anxiety will be aroused. Therefore, she will either punish him for withdrawing or make overtures to the child to insist that he demonstrate that he loves her. . . . In either case in a relationship, the most important in his life and the model for all others, he is punished if he indicates love and affection and punished if he does not. . . . This is the basic nature of the double bind relationship between mother and child. (Bateson et al. 1956, p. 258)

Social withdrawal, for example, is a characteristic of most forms of chronic schizophrenia, irrespective of social setting, and a biological component (seen at its most extreme in catatonic stupor) must be accepted. (Wing 1963, p. 635)

Confusion may arise if one does not keep in mind the nature of the concept of schizophrenia. It is not, and should not be treated as, a disease entity of a biochemical or genetic nature, but merely a reaction type which has been selected more or less arbitrarily because of its operational usefulness. (Ødegaard 1965, p. 296)

In psychoanalytic terms, the schizophrenics represent those who have failed to evolve the ego interactive processes or strengths necessary to resolve flexibly conflicts between their (id) drives and over-demanding superego attitudes and the aspirations of the ego ideal. They are thus defective in the capacity to adapt to the social demands confronting them and to their own drives. They thereby lack a harmonious self-concept and ego ideal with clear goals and motivations. Much of their adaptation is made, instead, through partially satisfying regressive or fixated infantile behavior. (Kolb 1977, p. 375)

When gross rule-breaking is publicly recognized and made an issue, the rule-breaker may be profoundly confused, anxious, and ashamed. In this crisis, it seems reasonable to assume that the rule-breaker will be suggestible to the cues that he gets from the reactions of others toward him. . . . The rule-breaker is sensitive to the cues provided by these others and begins to think of himself in terms of the stereotyped role of insanity, which is part of his own role vocabulary also, since he, like those reacting to him, learned it early in childhood. In this situation, his behavior may begin to follow the pattern suggested by his own stereotypes and the reactions of others. That is, when a residual rule-breaker organizes his behavior within the framework of mental disorder, and when his organization is validated by others, particularly prestigeful others such as physicians, he is "hooked" and will proceed on a career of chronic deviance. (Scheff 1984, p. 67)

VARYING CONCEPTIONS OF MENTAL ILLNESS

The above descriptions indicate the diverse conceptions of the character and cause of schizophrenia; similar controversy surrounds many other mental disorders including the affective disorders, personality disorders, and substance abuse. It is not surprising that in the absence of causal understanding many different conceptions prevail and compete. Uncertainty also allows ideological beliefs to play a major role since how mental illness is viewed has implications for social reform efforts and for concepts of personal change and autonomy.

The ideological debate reached its perhaps most divisive form during the decades of the 1960s and 1970s, a period characterized by optimism about the potential of social reform and strong advocacy for civil rights and civil liberties. Those who believed strongly in human betterment through environmental manipulation resisted biological and genetic explanations because they feared that if mental illness was seen as biologically caused there would be less sympathy for social efforts to improve people's lives. In contrast, if mental illness was a product of social environments, there would be an additional strong incentive for social programming. There is, of course, no clear or simple relationship between conceptions of etiology and society's willingness to attack social problems, but, in general, those who endorse strong biological positions tend to be more skeptical about the potentials of social reform and more conservative in their political views.

A second ideological dimension concerns liberty interests in contrast to therapeutic ones. Following a long history of philosophical debate, there are those who strongly believe in maintaining and protecting the rights of individuals to live as they wish without interference from the state for whatever reason. In their view, people must retain the right to personal autonomy even if in the view of others they behave in ways highly damaging to themselves. In contrast, those with a therapeutic ethic believe that intervention should override individual liberties if the person is mentally ill and in need of treatment. Those endorsing liberty interests argue that interventions should be minimized and are only justifiable in instances of imminent danger to others. The laws shift from time to time with changing public opinion, but the issue itself is irresolvable because it reflects deeply felt opposing positions about the nature of people and their relationships with society.

In the 1960s the liberty interests were championed by public interest

134855

lawyers who came out of the civil rights movement, many social scientists, and some psychiatrists. As a spokesperson for the extreme libertarian position, Thomas Szasz (1960, 1974), a professor of psychiatry and a psychoanalyst, vigorously maintained that mental illness was a myth and that the standards by which patients are defined as sick are psychosocial, ethical, and legal but not medical. Although Szasz's use of the myth metaphor did little to stimulate reasonable and rational debate, he presented a point of view that requires serious scrutiny.

Szasz argued, and continues to argue today, that the concept of mental illness results from conditions such as syphilis of the brain, in which it is demonstrable that peculiarities in behavior and thought are linked with a physiological condition. He argued that, in contrast, most symptoms designated as mental illness are not the result of brain lesions or biological dysfunctions but rather are deviations in behavior or thinking. Thus Szasz contends that the metaphor of illness is used to characterize problems having no underlying biological basis and that judgments of mental illness are based primarily on ethical or psychosocial criteria. He concedes that specific disorders in thinking and behavior result from brain dysfunctions, but he argues that it is better to say that some people labeled as mentally ill suffer from a disease of the brain than to assert that all of those called mentally ill are sick in a medical sense. In Szasz's opinion, the use of the concept of mental illness to characterize both disorders of the brain and deviations in behavior, thinking, and affect due to other causes results in confusion, abuses of psychiatry. and the use of medical terminology to deprive patients of their civil liberties through involuntary hospitalization and other forms of coercion.

The issues in the debate between those advocating a disease model of schizophrenia and those maintaining that it is primarily a deviant response pattern have been posed sharply by a demonstration in which eight "normal" pseudopatients complaining of a bogus symptom presented themselves at twelve hospitals.

> After calling the hospital for an appointment, the pseudopatient arrived at the admissions office complaining that he had been hearing voices. Asked what the voices said, he replied that they were often unclear, but as far as he could tell they said "empty," "hollow," and "thud." The voices were unfamiliar and were of the same sex as the pseudopatient. The choice of these symptoms was occasioned by their apparent similarity to existential symptoms. . . . Beyond alleging the symptoms and falsifying name, vocation, and employment, no further alterations of person, history, or circumstances were made. The significant events of the pseudopatient's life history were presented as they actually occurred. . . . Immediately upon admission to the psychiatric ward, the pseudopatient ceased simulating any symptoms of abnormality. (Rosenhan 1973, p. 251)

All of the patients were admitted to the psychiatric hospitals. In every case but one, the pseudopatients were discharged with the diagnosis of schizophrenia "in remission." The remaining diagnosis was simply schizophrenia. Length of hospitalization averaged 19 days with a range of seven to 52. The pseudopatients were given 2,100 pills, including antipsychotic agents such as Stelazine, Compazine, and Thorazine. Rosenhan describes the powerlessness and depersonalization characteristic of psychiatric hospitalization and the extent to which the assumption that these patients were ill influenced interpretations of what they said and did. Rosenhan concludes that "we have known for a long time that diagnoses are often not useful or reliable, but we have nevertheless continued to use them. We now know that we cannot distinguish insanity from sanity" (Rosenhan 1973, p. 257).

There have been many critiques of Rosenhan's demonstration, but the most careful review has been provided by Robert Spitzer (1976), a research psychiatrist. Spitzer argues that all Rosenhan has actually demonstrated is that patients reporting unusual symptoms frequently associated with a serious psychiatric ailment are suspected of having that ailment and can be admitted to a hospital. From the perspective of differential diagnosis, the absence of symptoms other than auditory hallucinations excludes most alternative diagnoses. One alternative would be that the patient is trying to deceive the physician by malingering—a situation that sometimes occurs—but it is a relatively unlikely alternative because few patients feign schizophrenia, and there are likely to be few benefits to such deception. Quoting Kety, Spitzer makes the point that if a patient drank a quart of blood and came to a hospital emergency room vomiting blood, the hospital staff would assume that the patient had internal bleeding. Kety then asks whether such a demonstration would argue convincingly that medicine does not know how to diagnose peptic ulcers. Furthermore, Spitzer maintains that the discharge diagnosis of all but one of the pseudopatients as having schizophrenia in remission is highly atypical, suggesting that these pseudopatients were puzzling to the psychiatrists who evaluated them.

There is nothing in the Rosenhan demonstration that addresses in any definitive way the usefulness or validity of psychiatric diagnosis. What Rosenhan has shown is that hospital staff can be fooled by a patient who reports a serious symptom that cannot be independently validated, a situation characteristic of many areas of medical practice. In much of medical practice, problems are identified by the fact that patients experience pain and discomfort and come seeking help; the patient's history and reports of symptoms are important aspects of the assessment. Rosenhan, however, like many others before him, does raise important issues concerning typical psychiatric practice. His study suggests the bias of physicians toward active treatment in situations of uncertainty, when the treatment may potentially do more harm than the symptoms disturbing the patient. He showed how readily psychiatric hospitalization was achieved, particularly if the patient was receptive to hospital admission. Such practices have implications not only for the patient and his or her self-concept but also for the medical care system, because hospitalization is an expensive endeavor. Rosenhan, like Szasz, raised more issues about the manner in which psychiatrists perform than about the usefulness of a medical disease model for psychiatry.

The position stated by Szasz and others that the concept of mental illness is largely a social judgment of deviant and disturbing behavior is contested strongly by most psychiatrists. They contend that mental illness does not simply connote nonconformity but also disturbance of psychological functioning as evidenced by delusions, hallucinations, disorganized thinking, and disturbed emotional states, such as extreme anxiety or depression. (For a classic statement of this view, see Lewis 1953.) Although there are no valid laboratory tests or diagnostic procedures to assist judgments of psychological dysfunction, they believe that these psychopathological criteria are as relevant as the criteria used in the diagnosis of physical illness. The problem that leads to such great controversy is that psychiatric assessments of pathology depend almost exclusively on the clinician's judgment, while in physical medicine more objective investigatory procedures are frequently available in making such assessments.

One of the typical problems in such debates is that the adversaries are not really addressing themselves to the same point. Szasz bases his argument on the observations that psychiatrists frequently define mental illness solely on the basis of social and psychosocial criteria, that psychiatrists often become involved in questions of ethics and in conflicts of interest rather than being concerned with illness per se, and that the psychiatric role is used to deal with social problems and to achieve social goals that are only remotely related to clinical assessments of pathology; he is correct in all these observations. However, he never really adequately addresses the possibility of assessing mental illness on the basis of disturbances in psychological processes, and it is to this question that his critics usually respond.

The difficulty with the notion that mental disease is a myth is a logical one. The diagnostic disease approach is a tool used for identifying, studying, and treating persons with particular types of problems. By refining the definition of a particular problem, we can then study it, try to ascertain causes, and observe what happens to the problem over time and the way it responds to different types of influences. Most typically, patients come to doctors in distress; they are suffering and want some relief. Differential diagnosis is a technique the doctor uses to identify the specific nature of the problem and what medical knowledge may have to offer. In any given instance, one can ask how useful it is to approach certain types of problems with a disease model as compared with some other intervention. To ask whether the disease model is true makes no more sense than asking whether a shovel is true. Both the disease model and shovels are tools— they are useful for dealing with some problems and not with others. Both can be inappropriately used in situations in which they cause more damage than good as when a shovel is used to try to jack up a car with a flat tire or the disease model is used to try to help a student who has difficulty understanding this book.

The conditions we call disease are totally arbitrary. A disease is a social judgment based on cultural concepts of what is disturbing. We typically view conditions as diseases if they shorten life, disrupt functioning, or cause pain and distress. But whether we feel pain or not depends not only on our physical being but also on cultural conditioning and social expectations. What may be painful and limiting in one social context may be viewed differently in another. Behavior occurs in a social context, and our goals and definitions of self are culturally shaped. Science and medicine are part of the larger culture and help define the meanings we attribute to various events. Every outcome has causes; the challenge is to identify these determinants correctly. The disease model is one approach to studying causes of the human response patterns that we regard as significant and needing some form of remedy.

Studying a problem requires us to identify it and differentiate it from other problems. By doing so, we can better locate its determinants, the way it evolves over time, and the way it can be successfully modified. In the study of disease, efforts are made to identify clusters of symptoms on the assumption that they stem from some underlying dysfunction. By accurately describing and studying these symptoms, we are better able to advance our knowledge of them and identify causes and treatments. Over the years we have learned a great deal about many diseases—patterns of typical and atypical symptom occurrence, symptom development over time, causes, and effective treatments. In other instances we have incomplete knowledge or very little knowledge. At any given point in time, the physician must work with disease models, some of which are well developed and highly useful, others that are incomplete and of more dubious value.

Confirmed disease theories provide all the necessary information concerning the cause of the condition, what is likely to occur if it is untreated, and what regimen is available to retard it. A correct diagnostic assessment thus leads to correct action. It should be obvious why diagnostic reliability is so important; if the patient has pernicious anemia and the physician diagnoses the condition as tuberculosis, he will be proceeding on incorrect inferences concerning the cause of the problem and the appropriate actions that will remedy it. (For a more complete discussion of this issue, see Mechanic 1978, pp. 95–105.)

Although the debate as to whether a particular problem is a disease or not most commonly occurs in the psychiatric area, there is no difference in the application of disease models in medicine or psychiatry. The debate rages in psychiatry because the disease theories used by psychiatrists have a lower degree of scientific confirmation than many such theories in general medicine, although both areas have many unconfirmed theories. We are talking about a matter of degree. When a physician assigns the label of pernicious anemia to a patient's problem, the doctor's understanding of the problem and its treatment derive directly from the diagnosis. In contrast, if, as Ødegaard (1965) maintains, assignment of the label of schizophrenia to a patient's condition does not affect the choice of therapy or chance of recovery, the advantage of using a disease model can be questioned because it might detract attention from more effective approaches. Psychiatric disease models, however, are not as poor or unspecific as the critics suggest. Differentiation of bipolar and other types of depression usually results in different specific treatments, and depression is typically treated differently from schizophrenia. In everyday ambulatory medical care, it is estimated that one-quarter to one-half of all patients do not fit existing models of disease (White 1970), and primary care physicians are increasingly adopting a problem-assessment approach in managing such patients in contrast to imposing disease labels on them.

The defining characteristics of disease models are constantly changing. What we can or cannot do depends on the state of our knowledge and understanding at the moment. The fact that a confirmed disease theory does not exist for a particular cluster of symptoms, signs, or problems tells us little about the future state of our understanding. Knowledge about mental disorders and human behavior is increasing. Although psychiatrists with a psychodynamic perspective tend to apply a similar approach to most conditions that they regard as treatable, there is a growing tendency to use specific treatments for particular disorders. Obviously, the overlap in treatment techniques for differing conditions reflects the ambiguous and uncertain state of the field, but the overall level of ignorance is not so large as some would imply.

In deciding whether a disease orientation is useful, it is necessary to balance the gains achieved from using such a perspective against its various disadvantages. The adoption of a disease perspective involves certain risks. Characterizing a particular problem as a mental disease may lead to greater stigmatization than alternative definitions. The implications that the condition is within the individual rather than in the social situation and that it is not subject to his or her control or that of others may, under some circumstances, lead to attitudes that are serious deterrents to rehabilitation. The most serious result of using disease models when they yield little information is the possible encouragement such a model may provide for failing to explore alternatives for rehabilitation outside the disease perspective. Gerald Grob (1966), an intellectual historian who has studied the history of mental hospital care, notes the following problems.

> The continued insistence by psychiatrists that their profession was truly scientific, however, exerted a profound, though negative influence over the character of the mental hospital. As we have seen, the assumption that mental disease was somatic in nature invariably led to therapeutic nihilism. Moreover, somaticism often precluded alternative approaches, particularly along psychological and other nonsomatic lines. Lacking any visible means of therapy, psychiatrists tended to engage in a vast holding operation by confining mentally ill patients until that distant day when specific cures for specific disease entities would become available. (Grob 1966, pp. 356–57)

DEVELOPMENTAL MODELS

The major competing view to the disease perspective is one that conceptualizes problems in terms of their psychodynamics. Instead of concerning themselves with establishing a disease diagnosis, psychodynamic psychiatrists and other mental health professionals attempt to reconstruct a developmental picture of the patient's personality; they believe that such an exploration will provide an understanding of the way the disturbed state of the patient has developed and the functions that the disturbed behavior has in the patient's adaptation to the environment. Kolb (1977), in instructing the psychiatrist on the examination of the patient, made the following observation.

> The purpose of the psychiatric examination is to discover the origin and evolution of such personality disorders as may be interfering with the happiness, satisfactions, efficiency, or social adjustment of the patient. One seeks,

therefore, to secure a biographical-historical perspective of the personality, a clear psychological picture of the living person as a specific human being with his individual problems. It will be found that there is a logical continuity in any personality manifestations, whether the manifestations be those that are called normal or those that are called abnormal. The fundamental dynamic laws of behavior and of personality development are the same for both. (Kolb 1977, p. 197)

A basic assumption of the psychodynamic therapist is that disturbed behavior is part of the same continuum as normal behavior and is explained by the same theories that govern our understanding of normal personality development and social functioning. If disturbed behavior is a form of adaptation of the personality in response to particular situations and social stresses, then it is logical to study such behavior from the same perspectives and orientations as those from which we study any other kinds of behavior.

Psychodynamic therapists do not make serious attempts to ascertain whether or not the patient is mentally ill for this is not a meaningful perspective within their frame of reference. They assume the existence of mental illness or personality disturbance by the fact that the patient is suffering and has come for help or by the fact that the patient's social behavior is sufficiently inappropriate to lead others to bring him or her to the attention of care providers. Using a developmental approach, the therapist attempts to ascertain what aspects of the person's past experience have led to the development of patterns of functioning that have created the present difficulty. Strong inferences in this approach are that the source of the difficulty is within the patient's personality development and that the problem can be alleviated or remedied by changing some aspect of functioning.

Because the psychodynamic perspective does not differentiate mental illness from ordinary problems of mental discomfort or social adjustment, professionals of this persuasion tend to accept for treatment people with a wide variety of problems, such as marital dissatisfaction, poor adjustment to school, alcoholism, neurosis, and feelings of lack of fulfillment. Although such professionals may be attuned to some extent to the social aspects of some of these problems, they basically proceed as if these problems stem from the personality of the patient rather than the social situation, deprivation and injustice, or other environmental contingencies.

In recent years psychotherapeutic perspectives have diversified, and there are many competing concepts of appropriate therapy. Varying therapies focus on early development, communication, family role conflict, behavior modification, and other areas. Explanations for psychological distress vary from conflicts in early family development to faulty learning and increasingly give emphasis to such factors as self-confidence and assertiveness, social stress, social support systems, conflicting expectations, and emotional repression. Therapies range from individual encounters with professionals to interactions in families, groups, and larger social networks. Competing with more formal therapies are encounter groups, self-help organizations, and recreational sensitivity group experiences (Back 1972). The term *therapy* has come to encompass the most diverse ideas varying

from a range of reasonable theoretical approaches as in interpersonal theory and behavior modification to the inane and "insane." In this arena it
seems as if anything goes, and whatever else can be said about it, it is
evidently a "growth industry."

Discounting the abuses and obvious charlatanism characteristic of the
"therapy movement," it is evident that it reflects a change in focus from
early development to situational problems and discomforts. There is increasing emphasis on the idea that personal distress flows from a discor-
dance of individual personality and individual needs and the nature of the
person's social environment. It is commonly noted that persons with similar
personality strengths and weaknesses may make better or poorer adjustments depending on social circumstances. Persons with strong aggressive
needs, for example, may or may not have problems depending on whether
they are in positions of authority or in subordinate jobs. In addition to the
question of fit between person and environment, much attention is given to
the way people relate, express intimacy, and become entangled in confused
role structures. The growing emphasis on behavioral therapies, in part a
result of demonstrated effectiveness of behavior modification in a variety
of situations, has focused more attention on the idea that many maladaptive responses are learned and can be extinguished under appropriate
conditions.

Among the many different therapeutic approaches to psychological
disorder, a few have been consistently useful and have gained wide acceptance. The application of learning principles through behavior therapy is
widely accepted, and these learning approaches are used in a great variety
of therapies seeking to modify behavior and dysfunctional thinking processes. Two approaches in the treatment of depression—cognitive therapy
and interpersonal therapy—are widely used, and their efficacy is being
studied by the NIMH in a large-scale collaborative study. In this study,
these two therapies are being compared in a randomized controlled trial
with patients receiving a tricyclic antidepressant drug (imipramine) and
placebos. Cognitive therapy, developed by Aaron Beck (1976), seeks to
change the meanings individuals attach to their life situations which he
believes lead to different types of emotions. Interpersonal therapy focuses
more on interpersonal relations and on conflicts in roles and relationships
(Klerman et al. 1984). Long-term results are not yet available from this
controlled study, but in the short term all three approaches performed
better than placebo. Imipramine brought improvement more quickly than
the psychotherapies, but after three months the drug and therapy groups
were comparable. Interpersonal therapy appears to outperform cognitive
therapy, particularly for the more severely depressed patients. Studies
most generally show that combining drug and psychotherapy approaches
outperforms any single approach (Conte et al. 1986). The extent to which
short-term therapy of any kind produces lasting results remains an issue to
be carefully explored.

While some patients with mild and moderate disorder may benefit
from short-term therapy and retain such benefits well into the future, this
acute treatment model may not be appropriate for other patients. Many
schizophrenic patients, for example, require long-term and continuing

care and quickly relapse when they discontinue their medication. An acute care model serves these patients badly, and proper care should be seen as more like the appropriate care of a diabetic patient who requires insulin and continuing monitoring than like the care of a person with an acute infectious disorder who returns to a normal situation after the infection is successfully treated. The issue of the appropriate treatment perspective is a crucial one for public policy, since the application of the wrong model not only contributes to great personal suffering but also to poor public under- standing and disillusionment with the mental health system of care.

CHANGING CONCEPTIONS OF MENTAL ILLNESS

Conceptions of both the causes of psychological disorder and modes of dealing with it are shaped by their cultural context and reflect not only the state of scientific knowledge and belief but also larger social forces. In the 1950s, the dominant view of such disorders, influenced by psychoanalytic thinking and the larger cultural milieu, was that they were intrinsic to the personality and its development. Although the impact of social conditions was not discounted, it was felt that a well-integrated and "healthy" person- ality could cope with all but the most extreme circumstances and that persons who do get into difficulty usually have significant weaknesses of personality. Thus, dissatisfaction and distress among women was seen as a personal problem and not a consequence of blocked opportunities and unequal roles. Illegitimacy among blacks was viewed as a problem of per- sonality in contrast to being a consequence of cultural norms, poverty, discrimination, and a welfare system that penalized members of intact families.

The decade of the 1960s brought rapid social changes, increased opportunities, and much social disruption. There was a growing rejection of the idea that biology and personality limit social potential and an empha- sis on explanations that viewed social problems and personal disorganiza- tion as consequences of a social structure with inequalities, blocked oppor- tunities, and exploitation. The focus was on social environment and social reform, based on the assumption that personality was completely malleable if only we could diminish inequities and injustice. Psychiatry discovered the concepts of social class, community, and political structures. Psychiatrists were encouraged to play doctor for communities as well as for individual patients. The strict environmental bias of the 1960s, like the earlier person- ality bias of the 1950s, failed to explain why in the same circumstances most persons manage to adapt while others have great difficulty. If dissatisfac- tion, illegitimacy, and failure were simply a consequence of social structure, why, indeed, did so many deprived persons cope so well?

The decade of the 1970s was a period of theoretical consolidation, characterized by a growing appreciation of biological limits, developmental influences, and structural pressures. The excessive psychobiological deter- minism of the 1950s and exaggerated social determinism of the 1960s have yielded to a more balanced, complex, and sophisticated picture of social behavior. There has been a resurgence of biological interest within psychiatry, a growing appreciation of genetic studies, and much greater concern with the interaction of individual predispositions with environmental pressures and the way such pressures are modified by varying types of social supports or exacerbated by vulnerabilities.

At present, much of the interest in psychiatry has shifted toward biology and the neurosciences, hoping to capitalize on the advances in biotechnology and imaging techniques. Such new technologies as Positron Emission Technology (PET) and Nuclear Magnetic Resonance (NMR) allow us to image the brain in a way difficult to imagine just a short time ago. Advances in molecular biology make it possible to develop molecular probes to identify markers for genes that increase susceptibility to specific mental illnesses, a technique used successfully in the search for genes related to manic-depressive psychosis. Such developments are exciting and deserve encouragement and support, but with some cautions.

The present excitement in biology is no justification to neglect research and understanding in the behavioral and social sciences. Most mental illness is a product of biological factors interacting with varying vulnerability factors, and these conditions are shaped by the social environment as well as by biology. Improved understanding of the social environment and behavior may contribute as much to prevention and intervention as advances on the genetic and molecular levels. It would be wise not to neglect the lessons of history concerning excessive enthusiasm for biological solutions. In undermining support for social factors and good social care, under the assumption that illness was biological, great harm resulted for patients and their families.

The evidence now available suggests that biology, development, and the shape of the environment all contribute importantly to serious mental illness. In many instances, the application of a disease model remains uncertain and its ultimate value unclear. In other instances, the disease model has done much to encourage careful thinking, to stimulate research, and to improve care. However we proceed, we must also make sure that the assumption that mental disorders are diseases does not undermine the use of other approaches in helping afflicted persons. Whatever the dominant view of mental disorder, such conditions tend to involve unique problems in their recognition and care. We now turn to a discussion of some of these problems.

SOCIAL CONCEPTIONS OF MENTAL ILLNESS

We usually recognize and define psychiatric problems through the appearance of particular patterns of deviant behavior or deviant feeling states. Sometimes individuals come to view themselves as having psychiatric problems on the basis of their conceptions of normal functioning and their own knowledge and experience. On other occasions people become aware of their problems as psychiatric ones only after others in their milieu point them out as such. Kadushin (1958) cites an example of the way such a definition may be formed.

I think I have had an emotional disturbance for some time, and I finally decided to do something about it. . . . Before my marriage I had a lot of conflict between my mother and myself. . . . My mother visited us . . . about two weeks ago, and she is always complaining that I never confided in her, and why I wasn't happy at home with my husband . . . and I sort of put the blame on her. She would patch things up after each conflict, and a couple of days after her visit I got an eight-page letter which told me off. She said she noted my unnatural feelings toward my son. That I give more affection to the cat. . . . Several years ago she said that she would take me to a psychiatrist, without my knowing it. . . . Because, she said, that I didn't love my husband. Now, I didn't see it that way. But now I think I need it. I get upset very easily. . . . I'm very emotional. (Kadushin 1958, p. 395)

On other occasions, individuals or those closest to them resist a definition of mental illness; they are eventually defined as being mentally ill when a crisis develops because of their bizarre and difficult behavior or when they come into difficulty with community social agencies. The following example illustrates the process.

Mr. B's wife had become violently distrustful of him, especially in the past 18 months, but the first indication had come nearly five years ago. He recalled: "It was when Sue [the daughter] was about three months old. My wife was jealous if I played with the baby. She resented it." From this time, Mr. B thought of his wife as having "a nasty streak in her that made her act jealous." She was frequently accusatory and he was frequently angry with her, especially when she falsely accused him of running around with other women. Still, she was a good mother to the children and when she flew off the handle, he would go out for a walk to avoid further conflict. He first thought that the problem might be serious when she said that someone had "done something" to the alarm clock to change its shape. She began to restrict the children's play. When a neighbor came to see how Mrs. B was, she ordered her former friend out of the house, waving a butcher knife. Lorraine B. moved out of her husband's bed, but frequently kept him awake much of the night while she prowled the house to "protect her papers and books." These events led eventually to medical intervention. (Adapted from Clausen 1961, pp. 128–29)

The recognition of mental illness generally takes place in community contexts; therefore, we should understand the way the public forms its conceptions of mental illness.

From the point of view of lay definitions, the two most pervasive and influential perspectives on deviation are those based on the health-illness and the goodness-badness dimensions. Each of these perspectives represents one aspect of our conflicting philosophical conceptions concerning deviant behavior. While we predicate our legal system and much of our social life on the assumptions that individuals are able to control their actions and must be held accountable for their responses (or, in other words, their actions are consciously motivated and willful), the sciences and scientific perspectives have encouraged a contrasting view based on the assumption that deviant behavior is the product of a particular developmental history and cannot seriously be viewed as being within the control of the individual. Because both views are important in social life, we tend to pave a middle path between them, often accepting the assumption of accountability for behavior but at the same time arbitrarily recognizing certain exceptions to this assumption.

The view taken of the deviant largely depends on the frame of reference of the observer and the extent to which the deviant appears to be willing or able to control his or her responses (Mechanic 1962a). The evaluator usually judges an act within the context of what is believed to be the actor's motivation. If the actor's behavior appears reasonable and if it appears to enhance self-interest in some way, then the evaluator is likely to define the deviant response in terms of the goodness-badness dimension. If the behavior appears to be peculiar and at odds with the actor's self-interest or with expectations of the way a reasonable person is motivated, the evaluator is more likely to characterize such behavior in terms of the sickness dimension. Most people, for example, find it difficult to understand why a rich person would steal small items from the five-and-ten-cent store; they are likely to view such a person as being sick rather than as being bad because it is not clear how such acts serve self-interest. More people would label the same act committed by a working-class person as being bad. The difference in definition lies not only in the act but also in the motivation imputed to the actor.

Most physical illnesses fall within the usual conception of sickness rather than badness. We rarely hold people responsible or accountable for their physical ills, and, although persons may not always take the necessary precautions to avoid illness, we assume that illness happens to people, that it is not in their interest, and that it is, therefore, not motivated. For the community, difficulties in defining an act as sick or bad arise most frequently in the area of psychiatric disorders. Many psychiatrists take the position that many delinquents and criminals are sick rather than bad. But, although emotional difficulties can certainly be observed among such violators, we have difficulty establishing that the disturbing behavior is a result of the emotional makeup of the person rather than of some aspect of his social character. Because such attributions of cause can never be proven and because views in the community conflict as to the most appropriate perspective for determining deviance, the differences between violators sent to psychiatric institutions and those who find themselves in prisons are not as large as generally assumed. As the behavior and motivations of the individual become more bizarre and difficult to understand, we more readily apply the definition of sickness, but psychiatric conceptions of behavior include large residual categories, such as the disordered personality and character disorders, that clearly overlap with public and community conceptions of badness.

The tendency for many mental patients to be viewed as being responsible for their condition, in contrast to the usual absence of such motives being attributed to the physically ill, explains in part the stigma associated with psychiatric disturbances. This stigma is also attributable to the fact that mental illness is frequently socially disruptive; it may threaten and frighten others, and it may involve a large element of social unpredictability. Although some physical conditions can lead to similar social problems, most persons who are physically ill do not threaten the community in the same way that many psychiatric patients do. Most people have at one time or another suffered from physical morbidity, and they recognize that becoming ill is a common occurrence, but they do not recognize themselves as having suffered from psychiatric conditions, and they do not necessarily accept the idea that people like themselves become mentally ill.

The lack of correspondence in the public's attitudes toward physical and mental illness also stems from the common tendency to equate all mental illness with acute psychoses. A large proportion of the population conceives of the mental patient as being crazy, but the depressed, or highly anxious, or withdrawn person is not thought of as suffering from a psychiatric condition. Even many people who have been patients in mental hospitals, including those who have been admitted several times, fail to conceive of themselves as being mentally ill; they frequently characterize their difficulties in physical terms (Linn 1968). In addition, unlike physical illness, mental illness is usually thought of by the public as characterizing the whole person rather than just one aspect of his functioning. The implication is that because mental illness marks the entire person, he or she cannot be trusted to understand the situation or to make decisions concerning his or her welfare. This assumption is often untrue, and it is not difficult to understand why patients wish to resist being viewed in this way.

In many ways the terms *psychiatric condition* and *mental illness* have become dysfunctional, especially when they are used to refer to a wide constellation of difficulties. These terms associate in the public mind any psychiatric difficulty with the stereotype of the severe psychoses and build an image of people totally incapable of caring for themselves. This image, shared by many patients as well, leads to resistance in accepting psychological problems and difficulties as being appropriate for psychiatric or psychological assistance. Given this barrier to receiving care, we might more reasonably view many people with psychiatric problems as having difficulties in interpersonal relations, as being inadequately trained, as being deficient in social skills, or as having organic imbalances. To think of oneself as a person lacking particular skills is hardly as threatening to one's self-esteem as is thinking of oneself as a disordered personality. Similarly, the definition of a mental patient as a person having particular difficulty in getting along with others or as one who is particularly anxious when faced with certain situations is a familiar and acceptable view to the layman. Such explanations are probably more comprehensible than are those implied by such labels as "mental illness," "insanity," or "psychosis."

VIEWS OF MENTAL ILLNESS IN RELATION TO SOCIAL POLICY

It is appropriate to inquire how varying mental health conceptions affect the formulation of public policy. It is reasonable to maintain that if people need help, it is the public's responsibility to provide it, whether or not it falls within the confines of mental illness, but limitations always exist on the resources available. Decisions concerning the way such resources are to be allocated among those who need help depend, therefore, on our conceptions of the problems that constitute greater and lesser need.

Since optimal mental health is a utopian ideal, therapeutic programs always encounter never-ending layers of problems. Because the provision of services is one of the conditions affecting the demand for services, if the field is defined too broadly, infinite amounts of money, personnel, and time could theoretically be absorbed in providing mental health care. Resources, however, are never unlimited; we must weigh investments in mental health care against investments in education, transportation, recreation, housing, and the like; we must base such decisions on some concept of priorities and some notion of the criteria by which these priorities are to be established.

Priorities always depend on values; two paramount values are ordinarily applied in thinking about mental health needs. The first is a humanitarian value—the concept of *need;* it is based on the idea that services should be made available to those who need them despite the cost, the difficulty in obtaining them, or the pressure on resources. The second concept—the notion of *gain*—is based on the idea that services should be made available when the result achieved is equal to the investment or greater than alternative investments. The widespread use of cost-benefit and cost-effectiveness analysis has focused increasing attention on the concept of gain. This concept, however, clearly comes into conflict with humanitarian needs and values at some point, and, therefore, public policy usually involves some marriage, however uncomfortable, between the notions of need and of gain.

We can define the concept of need in terms of sickness and disability, and we can also view it from an economic perspective. Need depends on the severity of the condition in question and the severity of the handicap it causes. The economic costs of reasonably dealing with severe and disabling psychiatric conditions are usually outside the income range of most of the mentally ill making the ability-to-pay criterion irrelevant to the question of public responsibility.

From the perspective of cost-effectiveness (gain), several very different issues require resolution before an intelligent public policy can be formulated. The provision of services to the mentally ill and decisions regarding allocation of available resources should, in part, depend on the efficacy of alternative services, but such decisions are difficult to make. Vast investment in unproven and ineffective services may result in little gain beyond the humanitarian gesture of offering help to a person in need. Indeed, just as in the case of the use of drugs, X-rays, or other diagnostic and treatment procedures, some psychiatric services may harm the patient by adversely affecting concepts of self, the reactions of others, or opportunities or by noxious drug effects. One long-term study of predelinquent boys randomly assigned to treatment and control groups in Massachusetts found that the treated boys had more repeated arrests, more job dissatisfaction, and earlier deaths than those in the control group (McCord 1976). In another study involving the California Youth Authority, delinquent boys were treated through a confrontation technique in a "therapeutic community." Those receiving the treatment did considerably worse than matched delinquent controls (Robins 1979a,b). We cannot assume that treatment is benign and that people do not suffer from many of the approaches that are now prevalent. It would be foolish to invest large amounts of public money to subsidize therapies that have no demonstrated effectiveness. We obviously need sufficient data to make informed assessments for the most reasonable directions for publicly subsidized programs.

Efficiency is also gained if the therapy provided not only cares for the illness when it occurs but also retards possibilities of recurrence or more extensive illness later on. With all other factors constant (which they never are), we would expect curing the condition of a child or a young adult to result in continuing gains throughout the person's life. The same cure in the case of an older person would not produce an equal yield. Social values and humanitarian concerns often take precedence over the concept of gain, and services are provided in many situations on the basis of need, irrespective of cost-effectiveness. Extensive use of the concept of gain obviously conflicts with a sense of compassion.

It has been argued that major emphasis should be placed on preventive psychiatric services and early treatment on the assumption that such programs locate morbidity conditions early, retard continuing morbidity and disability, often prevent disability entirely, and stimulate positive mental health (Felix 1967). We still cannot be confident, however, that we have the appropriate knowledge and skills to do these things effectively. Some preventive programs involve risks of iatrogenic illness—morbidity that results from the services rendered rather than from the condition itself. Because many neurotic symptoms and fears are widely distributed and transitory in nature, treating them as though they were aspects of emotional illness may encourage a feeling of helplessness in the patient. Such treatment may structure the symptom and the condition as part of one's self-identify and discourage persons from realistically coping with and overcoming their problems.

The conception of mental illness underlying public policy is important because different views suggest varying approaches to classifying psychiatric conditions and to caring for the patient. If we assume that psychological difficulties and problems are pervasive throughout the society and have always been so and that those who suffer from psychiatric disease are fundamentally different from the mass of people who have common psychological problems, we are in a very different position than if we believe that mental illness is a continuum on which all these problems fall depending on their degree of seriousness.

Differing assumptions may lead to conflicting implications. The traditional Freudian tends to believe that personality is formed in early life and is not highly susceptible to change from external environmental influences later on. However, a clinician working from the symbolic-interaction perspective, who believes that personality may constantly be modified by the environment and by the nature of an individual's associations, is more inclined than the Freudian to seek ways of changing the patient's current environment to achieve changes in response patterns. On some occasions in the past, as noted earlier, a biological view of mental illness minimized the importance of providing a healthy environment for the patient. The kinds of interventions attempted depend on the kinds of assumptions made about the nature of mental illness itself. We must carefully consider the full implications of each of the relevant alternatives if we wish to understand the nature of the commitments we are making.

Limited resources and the need for priorities necessitate some limits to the concept of psychiatric need. If mental illnesses are fundamentally different from ordinary problems in living and are defined not by social standards but by medical diagnoses of disease, public health policy should give highest priority to those patients who are clearly sick in a traditional psychiatric sense. Here we might assume on the basis of considerable evidence that many ordinary problems are transitory, while psychiatric disease states tend not to disappear so readily. Thus, public policy must give greatest emphasis to limiting and alleviating the disability of the chronically ill patient.

In contrast, if chronic mental illness and the psychoses are part of the same continuum as are other problems, we can treat all such conditions in fundamentally the same way—chronic disability is simply a manifestation of untreated and neglected illness. Indeed, early intervention may prevent chronic and severe mental illness. If one accepts these assumptions—and they are assumptions rather than proven facts—it is reasonable to devote considerable resources to preventive work and to treating mild and moderate psychological disabilities.

One can understand the significance of these diverse approaches by looking at a difference of opinion that developed at a government-sponsored mental health conference. Alexander Leighton (1967) took the position that mental disorders should be seen as part of a continuum.

> Typologies of this sort are able to handle the complex continuity that appears to exist between patterns of health and patterns of illness. One can picture this, diagrammatically, as comprising two extremes in a field: one side, health behaviours, is a dense population of white dots, and the other, psychiatric behaviours (symptoms) is a dense population of black dots. As one looks across the field from light to dark, the whites grow less and less and the blacks become thicker and thicker. (Leighton 1967, p. 339)

Paul Lemkau took strong exception to Leighton's formulation.

> We cannot properly look at our problem in this way, at least not all of our problems in this way; when we do so, we make the assumption almost automatically that the same kind of program will apply all the way across the board, all the way across these various shades of gray. All we need to do is intensify or de-intensify a panacea-like program. I think this is false. I think it covers up the complexity of the task we have to do in therapeutic and preventive psychiatry. You don't cure phenylketonuric oligophrenia with psychotherapy, you prevent it by adjusting diet.
> Now, I don't think that that fits in this scale of grayness. One can go on and on with these kinds of things and point out that the preventive and therapeutic programs are very large in number if we are going to fit the particular cases that, in reality, exist. I think Dr. Leighton does us a disservice

when he tries to tell us that the matter is just gradations of the same thing. It isn't, and I don't think the *abandonment* of proper classification of illnesses is the answer to this kind of problem. (Kramer et al. 1967, p. 363)

By drawing these positions sharply, we can exaggerate the extent to which two separate camps exist. Most mental health professionals are probably not clear about their views of mental illness or the assumptions that underlie them. They usually hold both opinions simultaneously, although the opinions themselves may be formally contradictory. Other complications bring the two views together. Moderate problems (even if they are not regarded as psychiatric illnesses) may become severe problems that incapacitate the individual in carrying out social roles. These serious problems are worthy of help regardless of whether they are part of the same order of phenomena as schizophrenia or other traditionally recognized psychiatric conditions.

The development of a coherent and intelligent public policy depends partially on the perspectives taken but mostly on the resolution of specific empirical questions. Which untreated conditions and problems become chronic, and which ones are transitory? Obviously, no rational person would suggest that a large bulk of our medical resources be given to the treatment of the common cold because the condition is self-limited in any case. Similarly, we must be able to identify psychiatric conditions analogous to the common cold. We must be able to specify the effects of varying systems of intervention in psychiatric disturbances. Which social services and policies limit disability and handicap, and which ones exacerbate such problems? Do preventive psychiatric services increase the number of iatrogenic disturbances or encourage psychological hypochondriasis? How successful are preventive psychiatric services in insulating persons from future serious morbidity and disability? Although the answers to many of these questions are unknown, we must continue to ask them in a way amenable to empirical investigation. Finally, although public policy must continue to develop despite the uncertainty of knowledge, the importance of such information should lead those government agencies financing care to insist that serious attempts be made to evaluate program effectiveness.

THE PATIENT AND THE SOCIETY: AN INSOLUBLE DILEMMA

Because there are varying ways of looking at mental illness, the views of different evaluators may come into conflict. Most typically, psychiatric difficulties are defined in terms of the distress a person is experiencing or in terms of the performance of social roles. Although psychological comfort may contribute to adequate social functioning, the factors influencing these two aspects of adaptation may vary. Individuals and communities have long-range as well as short-range goals, and they must frequently incur immediate psychological costs to achieve more important but more distant goals. In addition, successful adaptation as the long-range goal requires learning to cope successfully with adversity and acquiring a sense of efficacy, control, and self-esteem. There are both theoretical (Seligman 1975) and empirical reasons (Elder 1974) to believe that exposure to adversities that persons can overcome contributes to the development of adult well-being.

No society in history has been completely devoted to eliminating personal discomfort and pain. We usually work to alleviate forms of distress that have no social function. Our most valued social institutions, however, do much to produce psychological stress, and we need to go no further than the educational system to illustrate this point. University education frequently undermines students' most cherished beliefs; students are not infrequently failed in courses and dismissed from universities. The educational system is always setting goals that some students cannot meet, resulting in a sense of failure and a loss of self-esteem. Implicit in the value structure of universities, however, is the idea that the incentives for performance or the need for acquisition of information and skills requires inducing some stress and personal pain into the student's life. Most societies operate on the premise that stress provides incentives and facilitates the development of important instrumental goals. Therefore, although it is often possible to relieve personal distress by reducing obligations and responsibilities, we frequently choose not to do so.

A major dilemma in psychiatry involves the emphasis to be placed on performance in contrast to that placed on the control of personal distress. Psychiatrists employed by particular institutions, such as the military, seek to minimize the number of psychiatric casualties from the perspective of social performance, but, no doubt, the performance is achieved at some cost to the psychological comfort of the people involved. When a time dimension is built into perspectives on mental health problems, such problems become even more complicated. The value of one alternative in relation to others obviously depends on the long-range goals of individuals and groups and on the extent to which societal pressures are necessary to achieve such goals. If we minimize psychological distress at one stage in a person's life, at some cost to performance and the extent to which new skills are developed, we may find at some later point that this lack of skills is an important cause of the current distress. On the other hand, if we neglect the issue of personal distress and place value only on the development of performance skills, we may "stress" a person to the extent that he or she is continuously uncomfortable and may refuse to function at all. We must achieve some balance between mastery of the environment and individual comfort, not only for humanitarian reasons but also to facilitate continuing performance and mastery.

SOCIAL PROBLEM OR MENTAL ILLNESS?

We have already discussed the consequences of viewing disturbances in psychological functioning from the perspective of personality development as contrasted with a biological or social perspective. Although mental illness is clearly a social problem, it is not obvious which social problems fall within the domain of mental illness. Many women are distressed and lack self-confidence, but to define such problems mainly from the psychiatric perspective neglects the social and environmental problems that lead to such distress. Although women are more likely to suffer from depression than men (Weissman and Klerman 1977), simply defining this as a clinical problem is a disservice to both women and society. Similarly, delinquency thrives in impoverished areas and among certain minority groups. To define delinquents as children in need of psychiatric care, although many may have such needs, may divert us from considering the social forces and conditions that lead to behavior defined by the larger society as unlawful. The concepts of mental health and mental disorder are frequently used in an imprecise and ambiguous way and come to encompass a wide range of social problems. These psychiatric definitions implicitly suggest that these problems reside more in individuals than in the organization and patterning of the community itself. Another implication is that the proper means of changing these conditions is through changing the personalities and inclinations of individuals rather than through changing the structure of the society itself. Some mental health professionals believe that persons who illegally use drugs must be emotionally disturbed; it is equally plausible to consider whether certain laws pertaining to the use of specific drugs are truly consistent with scientific knowledge and, indeed, whether the inclination of many people to experiment with drugs is a reasonably normal response.

I do not mean to suggest that psychiatrists are unaware of the societal difficulties faced by women or the social influences affecting delinquent behavior or the use of drugs among college students. As long as the craft of psychiatry is practiced, however, the problem of mental illness will inevitably be approached from the viewpoint of changing the patient rather than changing the society. This contradiction has led some psychiatrists to reject traditional psychiatric roles and to direct themselves instead toward changing society itself. Some of these efforts are characterized as preventive psychiatry. Many psychiatrists, however, have overreacted to their professional dilemma. In conceptually moving from the individual to the society, they have argued that mental illness in general is a product of social forces and social structure and that the psychiatrist must be concerned with the community. This position widely expands the horizons of psychiatric work and the scope of psychiatric activity and places the psychiatrist in the political arena.

Another alternative to the psychiatric dilemma exists, however. By noting that the problems of various groups in society are rooted as much in the influences and definitions of the society as in the conditions of individuals, we might appropriately conclude that such problems realistically are not the province of psychiatry at all, unless the person is also mentally ill in the more narrow sense. These problems are frequently associated with general conditions in the society rather than with specific conditions characterizing the person's inability to make an adequate adjustment without profound suffering. The mental health professional, in order to perform a specific function in society, cannot hope to be all things to all people. He or she must be trained to take on tasks that make a specific contribution. My view is that psychiatrists should have a limited function—

to provide help to individuals who are disabled because they suffer from the specific kinds of problems that psychiatrists are uniquely trained to handle. There are many more such patients than psychiatrists can easily provide care for, and while psychiatrists have increased the scope of the problems they deal with in society, they have neglected the patients suffering from more traditional psychiatric syndromes.

Psychiatric problems, of course, may contribute to larger social problems, and social problems may cause profound psychological distress. The issues that require clarification are whether it is reasonable or fruitful to treat most social problems as problems of mental health and whether the same professionals who are trained as experts in treating schizophrenia, depressive disorders, and other more typical psychiatric conditions are those who can most appropriately deal with problems resulting from environmental impoverishment, cultural deprivation, social change, economic and social discrimination, and other societal conditions. Because the availability of mental health professionals is limited, their involvement in social problems leads to the neglect of the victims of hard-core mental illness.

In raising such issues, I do not wish to imply that the society should not devote large resources to alleviating social problems and the many forms of inequality that exist. We must, however, entertain the hypothesis that in allowing the psychiatric perspective to muddy the social waters, we may be diverting attention from more important questions involving both social problems and mental illness. Many of the major social problems we face require a large effort to develop an adequate system of social, economic, and educational services and opportunities available to all. The major problem of mental illness is to treat and, if possible, to prevent the psychological suffering and social handicaps evident among those so afflicted. Whether such problems are better attacked as separate questions or together is an important social-policy issue.

In suggesting that psychiatry, as a profession, might give greatest emphasis to the development of its specialized and traditional skills, I do not mean to indicate that the contexts for treating the mentally ill need to be separated from contexts in which other medical and social difficulties are handled. The same patients may frequently have a variety of difficulties and problems—some requiring psychiatric assistance, some requiring help from other professionals. It is desirable to coordinate and integrate the care such persons receive, both to facilitate their understanding of their needs and to allow professionals to provide the best overall program for their care and rehabilitation.

It is difficult to find agreement on policy questions pertaining to mental illness because different persons have varying conceptions of these disorders, and such conceptions determine in which direction it is most appropriate to move. We should therefore inquire more fully into the way patients come into contact with the mental health system, the varying conceptions of the causes of mental illness, and the measures that might prevent their development. The next two chapters deal with these issues.

Chapter Three

Psychological Disorder and the Flow of Patients into Treatment: The Study of Psychiatric Epidemiology

The study of mental illness requires the identification of specific disorders and the way persons who are treated for these disorders differ from those who are not. Cases of psychiatric illness are most easily identified in treatment institutions, but in studying such cases it is difficult to separate the factors related to the occurrence of these conditions from those that affect the processes of seeking and receiving help. Although the study of treated cases of severe mental illness may approximate all such cases, many who are afflicted, even with schizophrenia, do not make contact with conventional psychiatric facilities.

We have learned a great deal from the study of treated cases and have depended on such studies because of the difficulties of carrying out community investigations. It has become evident that in many areas of concern treated cases only poorly approximate the sick population in general, and persons with similar conditions may not receive treatment at all or be treated by general practitioners, social workers, or religious counselors. We must either increase our scope of identifying cases in other than psychiatric facilities or initiate community epidemiological surveys in which case-finding assessments are made within community populations.

Psychiatric epidemiology faces two major problems. The first is to differentiate as carefully as possible new cases from cases that have continued over some long period of time. The epidemiologist distinguishes *incidence* (the number of new cases that occur during a particular interval) from *prevalence* (all cases existing during a particular period of time). The prevalence rate includes all new cases that develop in the interval as well as those that began at some earlier time but continued. While prevalence gives some indication of the total magnitude of the problem and the need for services, incidence is a more useful statistic for the study of causation. The second problem is having clear criteria for identifying cases of a particular disorder and differentiating it as precisely as possible from other disorders. Rigorous case identification is also an essential prerequisite for study of causation.

In order to understand the causes of a disorder, it is helpful to differentiate factors that contribute to its initial occurrence from those that affect its course—whether it persists, disappears, or fluctuates. For example, the treatment of a streptococcal infection with antibiotics will eliminate the infection, but the lack of such treatment, allowing the illness to persist, is not a cause of the infection. Although the incidence rate will tell us the number of new infections that occur during a specified period, the prevalence rate combines these with older infections that have persisted. The study of prevalence will not allow us to separate clearly the factors *causing* a condition from those that affect its *course*.

Similarly, as we noted in our discussion of disease models, it is essential to be as precise as possible about the entity being studied. Disorders are extraordinarily varied and complicated and have different causes, natural histories, and biological and social consequences. If the condition being studied is poorly defined and combines different disorders, the knowledge generated will also be confused. Precise definition makes it more likely that we will learn something new in psychiatric epidemiology. Although this field is in part handicapped by the inadequacies of our current systems of classification, we should not make matters worse by being careless about case definition.

Epidemiologists of mental disorder often face difficult practical problems. Schizophrenia, for example, is a relatively infrequent condition in populations. If it is to be studied in community samples, large samples would have to be examined to identify a sufficient number of new cases for causal studies. Obtaining such samples is both expensive and strategically difficult. In contrast, treated samples have the difficulties associated with selective help seeking we have already noted, especially when they come from only one or a limited number of treatment institutions. One compromise is to select samples of treated cases from community case registers gathered from a wide range of institutions. Such registers, which maintain records of patients contacting many different facilities, allow for a broader sample of cases in the study of any particular disorder (Wing and Hailey 1972). However, they cannot provide information on persons who do not seek care or those who contact practitioners not covered by such registers, such as primary care physicians. Also, when data are reported from a variety of facilities and institutions, reliability of diagnosis and other information becomes problematic. Such registers are very expensive to maintain and involve serious legal and ethical issues, and it is usually difficult to maintain long-term cooperation from reporting institutions. Although some registers have been useful for sampling and other research purposes, they have not achieved the high expectations associated with their development.

IDENTIFYING PSYCHOLOGICAL PROBLEMS
IN COMMUNITY POPULATIONS

As the extent of social selection in seeking treatment became evident to researchers, they sought to study the prevalence of psychiatric disorder in community populations. In some classic studies, psychiatrists personally interviewed the populations of entire communities for the purpose of identifying all persons with psychiatric illnesses (Essen-Möeller 1956, Hagnell 1966). Although such studies provided valuable information, they were dependent on the psychiatric conceptions of the interviewers and had uncertain reliability and validity. It was also exceedingly expensive for psychiatrists to interview personally large numbers of people in community populations; consequently, such epidemiological studies were very limited.

During World War II the practical needs of the military required screening instruments to identify prospective soldiers likely to suffer psychiatric breakdowns. Researchers developed an instrument—the Army Neuro-Psychiatric Screening Adjunct—that could differentiate to some extent between psychiatric and normal populations. Following the war, when epidemiologists turned to the problem of studying psychological disorder in community populations, they used this instrument as a basis for developing measures of impairment. The Midtown Manhattan Study (Srole et al. 1962) stimulated the development of a variety of interview measures for screening persons in community populations. These techniques all tend to include items measuring depression, anxiety, and psychophysiological discomforts but not psychotic symptoms or antisocial behavior. They focus more on *neurotic* distress than disturbed thinking. One of the most commonly used measures of this kind—the Langner 22-item scale (Langner 1962)—can differentiate between normal and treated psychiatric populations and is correlated with such variables as sex, social class, and stressful life events (Langner and Michael 1963, Dohrenwend and Dohrenwend 1969). Examples of the 22 items in the scale are:

> I feel weak all over much of the time.
> I have had periods of days, weeks, or months when I couldn't take care of things because I couldn't "get going."
> Have you ever been bothered by your heart beating hard?
> Are you ever bothered by nervousness?
> You sometimes can't help wondering if anything is worthwhile any more.
> Do you ever have trouble in getting to sleep or staying asleep?

Many of the items are scored by the frequency of symptom reports and not by simply reporting the symptom.

The value of such global measures of psychiatric impairment and their appropriate use have generated much critical debate. At the methodological level, it has been suggested that these scales suffer from various response biases, such as yea saying/nay saying among certain respondents, distorting effects because of different perceptions of the social undesirability of items, and confusion of symptoms of physical and psychological illness (Manis et al. 1963, Crandell and Dohrenwend 1967, Phillips and

Clancey 1970, Seiler 1973, Tousignant et al. 1974). It was noted that such biases resulted in persons with physical illness reporting more symptoms than their psychological state warranted because of confusion in the items and that persons of varying ethnic groups saw the symptoms as more or less stigmatizing, thus affecting the way they would respond. At the substantive level, concern was raised by the finding that psychiatric outpatients score higher on such items than more severely disabled inpatients (Dohrenwend 1973), and that competent youth—such as college students—may score extremely high (Mechanic and Greenley 1976). Also, correlations among psychiatric patients who were retested a year later were higher than were correlations between test and retest results in community samples (Dohrenwend 1973, pp. 485–86), suggesting that among patients the scales measure some stable problem while among a community sample they may reflect transient stress to a larger extent.

Despite the criticisms, further study suggests that these scales measure disabling distress and, although not comparable to psychiatric diagnoses, persons with these symptoms suffer and use many types of medical and psychological assistance (Greenley and Mechanic 1976, Wheaton 1978, Dohrenwend et al. 1979). The question then is what do these scales actually measure? Dohrenwend and his colleagues, who have studied these scales in some detail, observe that they particularly seem to tap anxiety, sadness, psychophysiological symptoms, lack of enervation, and a perception of poor health, and that this tends to constitute a single dimension of response. In my own work on the Langner scale, I found results comparable to those reported by Dohrenwend (Mechanic 1979b).

Dohrenwend and his associates (1979) explored various explanations of high scores on such scales: that they measure neurosis; that they reflect a particular mode of expression in which the individual reports dissatisfactions mainly within him- or herself; that the scales measure something akin to fever in physical illness; or that they measure a *quasi neurosis* reflecting psychological discomfort and maladjustment. Dohrenwend favors as an explanation Jerome Frank's concept of demoralization—a situation in which a person cannot meet expectations, but also cannot get out of (Frank 1974). Demoralization is believed to be associated with constitutional defects, environmental stress, learned incapacities, existential despair, psychiatric symptoms, and physical illness. In my own work on the development of such distress syndromes (Mechanic 1979b), I have developed the hypothesis that they partially reflect a learned pattern of illness behavior involving a focus on internal feeling states, careful monitoring of bodily sensations, and a high level of self-awareness and introspection. This pattern of illness behavior is associated with and contributes to disabling psychological pain. This response pattern is learned in part, I believe, and is reinforced through childhood illness, parental behavior toward the child (particularly negative behavior), socially acquired attitudes, and social stress. A great deal still needs to be learned about what these scales measure and their implications for social policy. The meaning of a high distress pattern still requires further research, but we have some useful information about the implications of distress for perceptions of illness and the utilization of care.

ESTIMATES OF PREVALENCE OF DISORDER
IN COMMUNITY POPULATIONS

It is difficult to estimate prevalence of psychiatric illness using global measures of psychological distress. Although many community studies have been carried out, estimates of mental illness vary a great deal depending on the broad or restrictive nature of the concepts of disorder (from 1 percent to more than 50 percent of the population). Dohrenwend and Dohrenwend (1969), considering only more thorough studies involving direct interviews with subjects, note a tremendous increase in rates for functional psychiatric disorders in studies published after 1950 as compared with those before 1950. The only plausible interpretation of these findings is that there has been a broadening of definitions of psychiatric disorder, and what one finds depends on the assumptions of the researcher as to what constitutes disorder. The Dohrenwends (1969, 1974a,b) have worked these studies over laboriously, but it is impossible to make the results of studies based on such varying definitions of disorder compatible, especially in respect to less disabling nonpsychotic disorders. Although estimates for schizophrenia might vary from 0.5 to 3.0 percent of the population, and there is agreement that manic-depressive psychosis is relatively uncommon (less than 0.5 percent), reported rates of neurosis, depressive disorders, and personality problems vary substantially from one study to another. The estimates available to the President's Commission on Mental Health (1978, Vol. II, p. 16) of neurosis (including nonpsychotic depressive disorders) was 8 to 13 percent. Estimates have now been improved through the Epidemiological Catchment Area Program (ECA).

THE EPIDEMIOLOGICAL CATCHMENT AREA PROGRAM

As the foregoing suggests, the availability of measures that could be administered at a community level stimulated epidemiological work, but there was much uncertainty as to the meaning and clinical significance of the distress measures used. The development of DSM-III and the more refined specification of diagnostic criteria contributed to a revitalization of epidemiological measurement and led to the establishment of the Epidemiological Catchment Area Program (ECA) involving a collaborative epidemiological study of about 20,000 individuals in five sites: New Haven, Baltimore, Saint Louis, Los Angeles, and Durham, North Carolina (Eaton and Kessler 1985). All sites used the Diagnostic Interview Schedule (DIS), developed by Lee Robins at Washington University, Saint Louis, which allowed diagnoses to be made by diagnostic algorithms according to DSM-III and was adaptable to other diagnostic systems as well (Robins et al. 1984, 1985). The purpose of the ECA project was to obtain prevalence rates of specific mental disorders and to examine their relationship to demographic factors, family history, life events, and neurobiological variables. The ultimate purpose is to gain a better understanding of etiology, clinical course, and treatment response in relation to specific disorders (Regier et al. 1984, National Institute of Mental Health 1985).

The ECA project still continues, following those interviewed in the first wave, but extensive analyses are available from the initial interviews in three of the sites: New Haven, Baltimore, and Saint Louis. While the survey reports both lifetime and six-month prevalence, the latter is emphasized here since these data are less likely to be distorted by memory, respondent reconstructions of past events, and other method biases. Validity continues to be a critical and debated issue (Anthony et al. 1985, Robins 1985).

Total six-month prevalence of disorders as assessed by questions based on DSM-III criteria ranged from 15 to 23 percent depending on study site and sex (Myers et al. 1984). Phobias and major depression were the most common diagnoses for women and alcohol abuse and/or dependence for men. The above prevalence data exclude dysthymia (a persistent feeling of loss of interest and pleasure in most activities), which if included might contribute another 1–4 percent to total prevalence. Rates of disorder were lower in the group over age 45, with the exception of cognitive impairment, which is substantially higher in the elderly group. Six-month prevalence for schizophrenia varied in the three sites from 0.6 to 1.2 percent, major depressive disorder from 2.2 to 3.5 percent, alcohol abuse/dependence from 4.5 to 5.7 percent, manic episodes from 0.4 to 0.8 percent, and drug abuse and dependence from 1.8 to 2.2 percent. While these constitute only a modest proportion of all disorders, they constitute some of the most difficult and persistent challenges to the mental health services system. Tables 1 and 2 show the most frequent DIS/DSM-III disorders by age and sex, and provide estimates of the number of Americans likely to be affected by each disorder.

These prevalence estimates must be viewed as relatively crude given the method artifacts and biases inevitable in such studies and the difficulty of establishing validity of diagnosis, but even if we assume relatively wide confidence levels, the ECA studies quite convincingly substantiate many other community studies documenting high levels of psychiatric disorder in general populations and associated limitations of function (Dohrenwend et al. 1980). This observation is not qualitatively different from epidemiological evidence documenting a high prevalence of various untreated medical disorders and symptoms. Contact with the medical care system is influenced by severity of symptoms and disability, illness behavior orientations, and factors characterizing the financing and organization of services (Mechanic 1978), an issue to which we now turn.

PSYCHOLOGICAL DISORDER AND UTILIZATION OF CARE

The distress syndromes and DIS/DSM-III disorders measured by the instruments described involve components suggesting poorer perception of physical health. Studies show that people react to their health in a global or holistic way, and psychological difficulties or psychosocial problems influence the extent to which they view their health as poor even if differences in physical health status are controlled (Tessler and Mechanic 1978). Persons who are distressed are not only more likely to visit psychiatrists, counselors, and social agencies of various kinds (Greenley and Mechanic 1976,

TABLE 1   Four Most Frequent DIS/DSM-III Psychiatric Disorders[1] by Rank, Sex, and Age, Based on 6-Month Prevalence Rates

Rank	18–24	25–44	45–64	65+	TOTAL
			AGE GROUP		
Male					
1	Alcohol abuse/ dependence	Alcohol abuse/ dependence	Alcohol abuse/ dependence	Severe cognitive impairment	Alcohol abuse/ dependence
2	Drug abuse/ dependence	Phobia	Phobia	Phobia	Phobia
3	Phobia	Drug abuse/ dependence	Dysthymia	Alcohol abuse/ dependence	Drug abuse/ dependence
4	Antisocial personality	Antisocial personality	Major depressive episode without grief	Dysthymia	Dysthymia
Female					
1	Phobia	Phobia	Phobia	Phobia	Phobia
2	Drug abuse/ dependence	Major depressive episode without grief	Dysthymia	Severe cognitive impairment	Major depressive episode without grief
3	Major depressive episode without grief	Dysthymia	Major depressive episode without grief	Dysthymia	Dysthymia
4	Alcohol abuse/ dependence	Obsessive compulsive disorder	Obsessive compulsive disorder	Major depressive episode without grief	Obsessive compulsive disorder

[1]Dysthymia included. The basis for ranking was the mean six-month prevalence rates for New Haven, Baltimore, and St. Louis combined. DIS indicates Diagnostic Interview Schedule.
Source: National Institute of Mental Health, *Mental Health, United States 1985*. DHHS Publ. (ADM) 85-1378, 1985, p. 5.

Greenley, Mechanic, and Cleary 1987), but they are also more likely to visit nonpsychiatric physicians (Tessler, Mechanic, and Dimond 1976). Such patients may or may not have an identifiable psychiatric diagnosis, but they constitute a major component of demand for medical and psychiatric services.

TABLE 2   Six-month Prevalence of DIS/DSM-III Disorders for Estimated Number and Percent of U.S. Civilian Population, Based on 1980 U.S. Census and Three ECA Sites[1]

DISORDER	ESTIMATED U.S. POPULATION AGED 18 OR OLDER	
	NUMBER (IN MILLIONS)	PERCENT
Any DIS disorder	29.4	18.7
Any DIS disorder except phobia	22.6	14.4
Any DIS disorder except substance abuse	22.1	14.0
Substance abuse disorders	10.0	6.4
Alcohol abuse/dependence	7.9	5.0
Alcohol abuse	7.2	4.6
Alcohol dependence	4.6	2.9
Drug abuse/dependence	3.1	2.0
Drug abuse	2.1	1.3
Drug dependence	1.7	1.1
Schizophrenic/schizophreniform	1.5	1.0
Schizophrenia	1.4	0.9
Schizophreniform	0.1	0.1
Affective disorders	9.4	6.0
Manic episode	1.0	0.7
Major depressive episode	4.9	3.1
Dysthymia	5.1	3.2
Anxiety/somatoform disorders	13.1	8.3
Phobia	11.1	7.0
Panic	1.2	0.8
Obsessive compulsive	2.4	1.5
Somatization	0.1	0.1
Antisocial personality	1.4	0.9
Cognitive impairment (severe)	1.6	1.0

[1]The three ECA sites were not chosen to be a representative sample of the United States, so the study results cannot be used to estimate precisely the number of Americans afflicted. However, by projecting the data and standardizing the rates to the 1980 Census on the basis of age, sex, and race, an approach is provided for those who wish to make projections to the total population.

Source: National Institute of Mental Health, *Mental Health, United States 1985.* DHHS Publ. (ADM) 85-1378, 1985, p. 4.

Data from the ECA program indicate that while most of those with a DIS/DSM-III disorder had no care for this problem during the prior six months, about one-third of those who sought care for an emotional problem had no DIS/DSM-III disorder. The relationship between having a disorder as measured by DIS/DSM-III and having a "need" for care remains uncertain, and the fact that a person does not have a specific disorder does not exclude the possibility that they are in great distress. Also, many factors other than diagnosis affect the help-seeking process.

For example, Brown, Craig, and Harris (1985), in a study of depressed women in Islington, a section of London, England, rigorously studied a population sample of women with levels of depression comparable in severity to depressed patients typically treated by psychiatrists. Those who were actually referred to psychiatrists did not differ in number of core symptoms of depression compared with those who only received care from general practitioners. However, psychiatric referral occurred when the depression was expressed in certain disturbing ways such as threats or plans of suicide, exhibition of socially disruptive behavior such as violent outbursts, and abuse of drugs. This suggests that referral depends not only on the severity of the illness but also the social consequences of its expression as in high risk behavior. General practitioners may be more likely to refer such patients because they believe them to be more disturbed or feel unable to cope with the behaviors involved.

Such studies help explain why diagnosis is inadequate by itself to explain either need for care or referral processes. Consider, for example, the DSM-III definition of major depression. Criteria for such a diagnosis include five symptoms that are present during the same two week period and represent a change from previous functioning (American Psychiatric Association 1987, pp. 222–223). At least one of the symptoms must be either depressed mood or loss of interest or pleasure, but the other four can be any from a list of 8 possible types of symptoms. Thus, from the diagnostic point of view, the other symptoms are comparable in importance. They vary, however, from such symptoms as insomnia nearly every day, significant weight loss or gain when not dieting, and fatigue or loss of energy nearly every day to a suicide attempt or specific plan for committing suicide or psychomotor agitation or retardation nearly every day observable to others. Clearly, the social risks associated with some of these symptoms is much greater than others and doctors respond to risk as well as to diagnosis. Contingencies associated with symptoms of depression such as risk and social disruption contribute to definitions of "need" and to referral processes. The ECA project, which I now briefly review, reflects the criteria of DSM-III diagnosis and incorporates both its strengths and limitations.

Approximately two-thirds of individuals in each ECA site who were assessed as having a recent DSM-III disorder, as measured by the Diagnostic Interview Schedule, made an ambulatory visit for health services of some kind during the previous six months (not necessarily for a psychological disorder) (Shapiro et al. 1984). Depending on site, this was only about 8–10 percent more than in the population as a whole. In contrast, the average number of medical visits was considerably higher among those with a psychiatric diagnosis, as were inpatient admissions. Inpatient admissions for mental health reasons, however, explain most of the excess, and in one site (Saint Louis), excluding mental health admissions results in a lower proportion of respondents with DSM-III diagnoses having hospital admissions than among those with no diagnosis. A majority of visits and admissions occur in the general medical sector, in contrast to psychiatric settings, with considerable variation among study sites.

Most important is that a majority of patients in almost all disorder categories received no care for a mental health problem during the six-month period under consideration. Such care seeking is particularly low among persons with cognitive disorders and substance abuse and/or dependence. More detailed data have been reported on help-seeking patterns for Baltimore (Shapiro et al. 1985) and New Haven (Leaf et al. 1985). In Baltimore, 62 percent of persons judged to have a DSM-III disorder in the prior six months did not receive any mental health services during that period from either physicians in general or the specialized mental health sector. Those diagnosed as schizophrenic were most likely to receive some care (55 percent), while the group least treated were those with severe cognitive impairment (25 percent). Receipt of care for a mental health problem was particularly low among the elderly and nonwhites.

In the New Haven sample, efforts were made to assess use of mental health services provided by a wider range of health professionals and clinics. Sixteen percent of the sample met criteria for a DSM-III disorder during the six months prior to interview, but most received no mental health services. In the sample overall, 6.7 percent had a mental health service in the six-month period: 2.6 percent only from general physicians; 3.2 percent from the specialized psychiatric sector; and 0.9 percent from both (Leaf et al. 1985). Utilization was highest for schizophrenia, panic, antisocial behavior, and somatization, and lowest for alcohol or drug abuse or dependence.

Leaf and his colleagues used regression analysis to examine a variety of factors associated with having a mental health visit during the previous six months and number of such visits, controlling for DSM-III disorder. Among the factors limiting the likelihood of such visits were being male, being under age 24 or over age 65, non-white and lower educational status, and not being married. Persons who lacked a regular source of care, who had less receptive attitudes to mental health professions, and who faced barriers to access also were less likely to receive such care. If patients entered the specialized mental health system, they had many more mental health visits than those treated solely by generalists (a mean of 15.6 for those exclusively treated by the specialty sector as compared with 2.1 for those treated by generalists).

It is difficult to correctly estimate help seeking for emotional problems from the general medical sector. Survey questions related to such ambulatory visits will typically not identify patients who emphasize somatic aspects of psychiatric disorder in their presentations and patients who believe it is inappropriate to present emotional symptoms as a basis for a medical visit. Cross-cultural studies indicate that patients select presenting symptoms they believe to be consistent with the help-seeking context (Cheung and Lau 1982). Patients visiting general physicians are likely to focus on the physical concomitants of distress and may be unwilling to discuss emotional problems or only do so when physicians give indications of interest in such symptoms (Ginsberg and Brown 1982).

The relationship between the presence of a DSM-III disorder and need requires careful examination. Assuming that the DIS provides reasonable approximations of true disorder, the fact that as many as 45–63 percent of schizophrenics, 55–75 percent of depressed patients, and the vast majority of phobic patients are out of contact with any mental health services for as much as six months prior to being assessed as having these disorders suggests major unfilled needs. It is reasonable to expect that many of these patients could benefit from professional care. In some instances of substance abuse, antisocial personality, and severe cognitive impairment among the elderly it remains unclear what benefits would derive from increased mental health intervention. Often, there is little that mental health professionals can do, and some patients have learned through experience with the mental health system that they get limited help. We need better data to define clearly which of these patients should be induced into care through public policy initiatives and what types of services they should receive. Even in the case of cognitive impairment among the elderly it is important to assess to what degree such impairment may be a function of depression and whether patients could be assisted in learning skills that help maintain functioning despite memory loss.

Assessing the issue of need and appropriate care requires information on the long-term course of treated and untreated DSM-III disorders as measured both clinically and by survey, particularly among subpopulations who choose not to seek care from the medical care system or who do so but in the more narrow context of physical complaints. It is essential to distinguish patients who present their complaints somatically because they perceive such presentations as appropriate to the context, but are receptive to explicit mental health interventions, and those who are not. In the case of the former, there is some evidence suggesting that attention to mental health issues reduces the use of nonpsychiatric medical services (Jones and Vischi 1979, Smith, Monson, and Ray 1986). Patients with psychiatric morbidity and distress use more outpatient and inpatient care than others in the population (Mechanic, Cleary, and Greenley 1982). It remains uncertain whether savings in total expenditures are achieved when use of both general medical care and mental health services are taken into account (Borus et al. 1985). Among those resistant to mental health treatment, physicians have little alternative but to treat patients with a more narrow medical definition and provide whatever support and encouragement feasible.

Despite the inadequacy of definitions of need, the data identify a variety of barriers to care. These include: (1) the unwillingness of many patients to define themselves as having a mental or emotional disorder, or to seek care for such a problem from a mental health professional; (2) perceived stigma associated with mental health services and the lack of support from significant others in using such services; (3) barriers to access to appropriate care including the lack of a regular source of medical care, inadequate insurance coverage for mental health services, and high levels of co-payment in using such services; and (4) lack of knowledge or sophistication among physicians in recognizing mental health problems and making appropriate referrals, or attitudes among physicians that inhibit appropriate care and referral. Primary care studies suggest that how physicians manage patients with mental health needs depends substantially on their attitudes, interests, workload, and on financing mechanisms (Shepherd et al. 1966, Mechanic 1974, 1976, Goldberg and Huxley 1980). Referral to specialized mental health settings, in turn, depends on the doctors' confidence and interest in managing the patient, attitudes toward mental health professionals, the patients' wishes and inclinations, and the overall structure of reimbursement as it affects both the doctor and patient.

SOCIAL FACTORS ASSOCIATED WITH PSYCHIATRIC CONDITIONS IN THE COMMUNITY

We now have a large number of community studies using broad measures of psychological distress and impairment as well as the more specific diagnoses derived from such instruments as the DIS. Generalized distress and impairment are greater among persons of low socioeconomic status, among women, among the divorced and separated, and among blacks (Dohrenwend and Dohrenwend 1969, 1974, Pearlin and Johnson 1977, Kessler 1982, Kessler and Neighbors 1986). As one examines specific diagnoses, however, the associations with social and demographic factors vary. This should be no surprise since mental illnesses are varied, have many different causes, and, therefore, should have different correlates. The only acceptable generalization is that the burden of illness and disability is much greater among the poor than the affluent. More detailed statements require examination of the epidemiology of each condition. Some examples illustrate the issues.

The single most consistent finding in the epidemiological literature is the relationship between socioeconomic status and the prevalence of schizophrenia (Dohrenwend and Dohrenwend 1969). The onset of schizophrenia is usually in young adulthood, but it does not markedly vary by sex, region, or cultural area. There is some indication, however, that schizophrenia may be more prevalent in urban than in rural areas, but these differences are not large (Dohrenwend 1975, p. 370). For the past 50 years, there has been much speculation concerning the link between social class and schizophrenia.

Despite many studies on class and schizophrenia, there are few studies with sufficient numbers of new cases of schizophrenia. The limited and flawed incidence data—such as in the Hollingshead and Redlich (1958) study—suggest that an incidence difference in relation to social status may exist, but the large number of lower-class schizophrenics is particularly apparent in prevalence data. These and similar findings have generated a long debate between advocates of a social causation as compared with a social selection interpretation. Those favoring a social causation view argue that there is something about the environment of lower-class living that increases vulnerability to schizophrenia. Melvin Kohn (1973, 1977) maintains that a genetic vulnerability, social stress, and an inflexible and rigid value system that hampers coping interact to produce an excess of schizophrenics in the lower class. The more common view, and one I believe to be better supported by the existing evidence (Mechanic 1972a), is that the lower-class status of schizophrenics is largely a result of the debilitating effects of the condition itself. Persons with the condition are hampered in their work and either suffer downward mobility or fail to rise with increased opportunity, as their peers do (Turner and Wagenfeld 1967). Although there is persuasive evidence that stress contributes to the occurrence of schizophrenic episodes (Brown and Birley 1968), differences in stress cannot explain the link between schizophrenia and social class. The evidence on these issues is not all in, but the etiologic role of social class in schizophrenia is yet to be demonstrated.

In recent years, depressive illness has been receiving more attention, and measurement of cases for epidemiological study has improved. There is strong and consistent evidence that depressive illness occurs more commonly in women than in men (Weissman and Klerman 1977). The excess of women is not as marked in the manic-depressive syndrome as it is in neurotic depression. It has been hypothesized that women express distress inwardly while men are more likely to act out through alcoholism, drug addiction, violence, and other antisocial activities. These differences are not clearly understood, but the fact is that there are more depressed women than men in both the population at large and among treated populations.

Community sample studies provide more representative cases for epidemiological investigation. The most ambitious study of depression carried out in a community setting was done by Brown and Harris (1978). They compared a population of women in the Camberwell district of London with depressed women receiving outpatient care. This study allowed comparison between women within the community sample who became depressed and those who did not, as well as between depressed women in the sample who were untreated and those receiving outpatient care. Brown and Harris found that stressful life events, such as losses of relationships, status, or love, occurred more commonly to the women who became depressed than to those who did not. Women who had no intimate relationship, who had three or more young children in the home, who did not have an outside job, and who lost their mothers early in life were more vulnerable to depression. These circumstances existed more frequently among lower-class women, explaining the higher rate of depressive conditions in this social stratum. The same conditions were found in the psychiatric outpatient sample. Within the model presented by Brown and Harris, stressful life events are provoking agents. The way women deal with these agents depends on their vulnerability, on the presence or absence of social support available to them through intimacy, and on the extent to which there is reinforcement outside the home, such as a job. Depression results from a lack of resources to deal with life provocations, leaving the person feeling helpless.

The various predictors such as an outside job or the number of children at home are simply proxies and may vary depending on the population being studied and the social context. The meaning of these predictors in particular social contexts is most important, and these are still being explored. For example, we found that having children in the household was especially stressful for working women, but particularly among those with low family incomes (Cleary and Mechanic 1983). These data suggest that among working women the relationship between having children at home and depression depends on the time and work demands from this dual role and the help available, which more affluent mothers can afford.

Loss of mother in childhood as a vulnerability factor is more difficult to explain in its relation to depression, but Harris, Brown, and Bifulco (1987) have begun to explicate how this major life event affects subsequent life transitions. Their tentative explanation is based on the fact that early loss of mother is associated with lack of adequate care, which in turn is associated with premarital pregnancy, less effective coping, and early and often unsuitable marriages. While these patterns are linked with lower social class, the process is seen as having importance beyond the effects of social class itself. This perspective of the development of the life course assumes that experience at any point is dependent on earlier influences and choices that affect the range of options at subsequent points. Choices about schooling, job, marriage, childbearing, and their timing establish the conditions for future transitions (Brown 1986).

The Brown and Harris study reflects the recent shift of the focus of psychiatric epidemiology from description to investigation of stressful events, vulnerability factors, social supports, and coping. Although it is widely accepted that adverse life events are associated with all types of pathology, the crucial issue involves why persons react so differently to such disturbing events. It is not remarkable that people succumb to major stressful events, but rather that so many remain resilient despite enormous difficulties and exposure to adverse environments. Social epidemiologists have turned to identifying people's capacities and resources, their social networks and sources of social support, and the developmental experiences that facilitate their resistance to provoking agents. Interest is increasingly focused on the reasons why many children of two psychotic parents adapt adequately while others have major difficulties. Major measurement problems remain to be solved because coping capacities and social support are relatively new concerns, but they raise exciting questions. Elder (1974) studied a cohort of children born in 1920–1921 who were part of the Oakland Growth Study and who grew up during the Great Depression. Data were available concerning adult adaptation as reflected in anxiety and tension, psychosomatic illness, behavior disorders, serious somatic illness, and psychotic reactions. Children from the working class faced greater adversities during the depression and had more problems of adaptation later. More interesting, however, was the fact that middle-class children who faced deprivation during the Great Depression were more symptom-free in adult life than those who were sheltered from deprivation. Twenty-six percent of the nondeprived middle class had behavior disorder problems as compared with 7 percent of the deprived group. Heavy drinking in adulthood was much more common in the nondeprived middle class than in the deprived middle class (43 percent versus 24 percent).

These findings, as well as similar findings from other studies, suggest some provocative hypotheses. Are persons who are insulated from difficulties that allow for the development of competence and mastery handicapped as a result of a life experience that is too protective? What are the positive social functions of stress, particularly when it is not overwhelming and when persons learn to deal with it effectively? How much stress is necessary in early life to prepare persons for later adversity? The results of such studies as Elder's are consistent with the experimental work in the area of helplessness (Seligman 1975) that suggests that individuals' beliefs in their ability to affect what happens to them is important for well-being. Dealing effectively with adversity reinforces a sense of competence and confidence. These ideas will be explored in greater detail in Chapter 7 when we examine coping theory.

THE EPIDEMIOLOGY OF ANTISOCIAL BEHAVIOR AND BEHAVIOR DISORDERS

There is impressive evidence from epidemiological longitudinal studies that antisocial behavior during childhood often results in many adult difficulties (Robins 1966, 1979a,b). Resistance to authority during childhood, as reflected by delinquency, drinking, and sexual behavior, seems to be correlated with the development of serious problems in adulthood, such as employment difficulties, problems with the law, alcoholism, drug abuse, and early death. Children in this group are often identifiable early in their school experience by low IQ, poor reading and poor school performance in general, and truancy. The causal factors relating to such behavioral development are complex and poorly understood. What emerges from many studies is the sad trajectory that so many of these children follow, the compounding of problems as they grow older, and the disastrous outcomes for both them and society. In marked contrast, children with neurotic symptoms often tend to have transitory problems and are much more likely to develop satisfactory adjustments in adult life.

As Robins (1979b) notes in her extensive reviews of the developmental literature, there is a great deal of consistent data suggesting that achievement patterns, social skills, and aggressiveness develop well before adolescence and set the stage for future life adaptations. This does not imply that many children with conduct problems, school difficulties, and poorly developed skills do not successfully overcome these problems in adult life, but the risk of adult difficulties for such children is considerable. A major challenge for mental health workers—and for policy makers—is to identify interventions that effectively block the realization of such poor prognoses and improve the life chances of these children.

Although violent and aggressive behavior in childhood does not necessarily ensure such patterns in adulthood, such behavior is unlikely to develop in adulthood if it was absent in childhood. The effects of social deprivation, low social status, and certain cultural environments can be overcome. Children living in well-functioning homes under such conditions do well in adult life. Poor social and economic conditions, however, are more conducive to family pathology, child abuse, alienation, and lack of encouragement for achievement and increase the probability that children growing up under such conditions will have difficulties. Many of the negative factors, such as social deprivation, broken homes, illegitimacy, parental deviance, and little parental supervision or interest in the child are correlated, making it difficult to isolate the central causal factors contributing to behavior maladjustment.

Epidemiological study suggests many leads and poses many questions.

This discussion gives only a brief and limited view of the scope and richness of epidemiological inquiry and focuses primarily on those findings linking social class and schizophrenia and linking sex and depression. In the next chapter, we turn to a more detailed examination of conceptions of the causes of mental disorder and their implications for social policy.

Chapter Four

Conceptions of the Causes of and Means of Controlling Mental Illness

Psychiatry today has no dominant perspective. Present concerns focus on genetic factors, brain and behavior relationships, psychopharmacology, psychodynamics, social learning, communication patterns, stress and coping, and larger structural forces. This chapter briefly reviews these major perspectives, particularly as they pertain to larger social policy issues. Although the use of drug therapy is very important, we discuss such therapy only as it is relevant to policy issues.

THE IMPACT OF ENVIRONMENT ON MENTAL ILLNESS

Mental health professionals agree that environmental influences have an important impact on the development and course of mental illness as well as on the processes of help seeking. They differ on such questions as whether or not environmental factors have the major impact on the causes or course of mental illness, and how environmental forces influence and interact with biological and personality influences. At one extreme are those investigators who believe that a biological or a physiological defect is a *necessary condition* for a serious mental illness and that such conditions as schizophrenia or bipolar affective disorder occur only when persons with such inherited defects are faced with adverse circumstances that bring out their latent biological vulnerabilities. At the other extreme are those who see psychiatric morbidity as simply the result of compounded stresses and adverse environmental events.

In discussing the impact of the environment on psychiatric conditions, it is necessary to separate the effects of environment on the causes of specific psychiatric conditions, its effects on the development of secondary disabilities (the course of the disorders) (Lemert 1951, Wing 1962), and patterns of illness behavior and responses to care (Mechanic 1978). Most mental health professionals are aware that persons with the same primary condition—such as depression or schizophrenia—may fare better or worse depending on the social and environmental circumstances they face and the kind of treatment and support they receive. Although in some instances social forces may affect both the occurrence of the condition and the subsequent disability, in other instances the environment is most important in determining the extent of handicap. It is important to be as precise as possible as to the way environmental factors may affect a condition.

Because it is impossible, given the state of our knowledge, to come to any definitive view on such issues, all I can do here is to present some of the contrasting positions concerning the etiology of mental disorders and develop some of the implications of each. I shall discuss the following perspectives: heredity, psychosocial development, learning, social stress, and societal reaction. Although I shall attempt to polarize these views to illustrate their distinctive aspects, it is important to recognize that most investigators adopt an eclectic view that synthesizes elements of each of these perspectives.

THE QUESTION OF INHERITANCE AND ENVIRONMENT

The evidence is strong that genetics play an important role in major mental illness such as schizophrenia and manic-depressive illness, and there is further evidence supporting its relevance in severe alcoholism, sociopathy, and suicide (Kety 1986). But genetic factors in these conditions do not follow conventional patterns, and there is no clear understanding of the mode of genetic transmission. Schizophrenia has been studied more intensively than other conditions, and various studies show a higher concordance of schizophrenia among identical as compared to fraternal twins. While these studies are not above criticism, they provide as much basis for a heredity theory as any other (Rosenthal 1970, Gottesman and Shields 1982, Cloninger et al. 1985).

Evidence for a genetic etiology of schizophrenia also comes from studies comparing the offspring of schizophrenic parents with those of parents who were not mentally ill. Heston (1966), for example, compared the adjustment of 47 adults born to schizophrenic mothers with a matched control group of adults born to mothers who were not mentally ill. Those in both the subject and the control group were separated from their natural mothers during the first few days of life and were reared during their early years in foster homes. The investigator found that the occurrence of schizophrenia and other pathologies was higher among the offspring of schizophrenic mothers than among the matched controls. Because the subjects of the study were removed from their schizophrenic mothers shortly after birth, we cannot conclude that the higher rate of pathology was a result of interaction with a schizophrenic mother.

This theory, however, does depend mostly upon studies of twins, and further consideration of the implications of such studies is necessary. Perhaps most influential among early studies were the investigations carried out by Franz Kallman (1953). He found that although schizophrenic concordance varied from 10 to 18 percent among fraternal twins, it was 78 to 92 percent among identical twins. If we assume Kallman's findings to be correct, even though there were considerable inconsistencies among the findings of other studies of twins, they still leave room for positing factors other than genetic ones. If genetic factors were the only ones operating, the identical heredity of monozygotic twins would produce a perfect concordance rate.

In the last 15 to 20 years, interest has persisted in the investigation of the heredity hypothesis, and studies have been relatively consistent in demonstrating a higher concordance for schizophrenia in identical as compared with fraternal twins or siblings. Studies of adopted children of schizophrenic mothers and adopted monozygotic twins reared separately also provide confirmation of a hereditary link (Rosenthal 1970). However, in more recent years, the levels of concordance in schizophrenia found among identical twins have been lower than in prior investigations—more in the range of 15 to 20 percent. These lower levels of concordance reflect tighter methodologies and minimization of investigator bias as well as sampling differences and the use of schizophrenic patients who are less severely affected by the illness. If schizophrenia is a group of conditions influenced by a variety of genes and if such genes vary in their penetrance, selecting less severe cases might lessen the probability of finding concordance.

What should be noted, however, is that even in those studies finding high concordance—as in Kallman's studies—concordance rates are much lower than the 100 percent one would expect on the basis of a pure heredity hypothesis. Kallman's position was that "a true schizophrenic psychosis is not developed under usual human life conditions unless a particular predisposition has been inherited by a person from both parents" (p. 98), but that the disease resulted from the intricate interactions of genetic and environmental factors. He maintained that schizophrenia could be prevented or cured. Because environmental and psychosocial elements could predispose a person to, precipitate, or perpetuate psychoses, understanding of and control over such elements could retard the disease process. Even in instances where both parents are schizophrenic, less than half of their offspring develop this illness during their lifetime (Gottesman and Shields 1982). The functional psychoses do not follow simple Mendelian patterns of inheritance (Cloninger et al. 1985).

Theorists have analyzed the situation extensively, but they have not clearly defined the precise environmental factors contributing to a schizophrenic breakdown. Various evidence, however, shows that a psychotic breakdown is frequently preceded by a stressful event of some magnitude.

Brown and Birley (1968) studied 50 patients suffering from an acute onset or relapse of schizophrenia and a group of 377 normal controls. These groups differed in the proportion experiencing at least one major change in their lives in the three-week period preceding investigation. Although 60 percent of the patient group had such an experience, only 19 percent of the control group were so affected. Possibly, environmental stress leads to the initiation of treatment rather than to the illness itself, and persons similarly ill who do not suffer severe environmental stress are less likely to define themselves as requiring treatment. Because the condition studied, however, was a severe one, this interpretation probably does not explain the result obtained. This study is impressive in that the investigators separated the social changes into categories according to the extent to which the patient may have had control over them. The fact that the relationship held for events over which the patient had no control as well as for those he or she could affect supports the idea that this finding could not be explained by the argument that schizophrenic patients tend to get themselves into social difficulties because of their illness. The study suggests, in contrast, that significant changes in the patient's life adversely affected his or her psychological and social functioning. Other studies also suggest a relationship between the cumulation of stresses in a person's life and the occurrence of psychiatric morbidity, but the causal links in such relationships are not clearly understood (Langner and Michael 1963).

Various theories have been formulated to explain the link between the occurrence of changes in a person's life and schizophrenic breakdown. Studies have found that schizophrenic patients living in family situations of high emotional involvement (mainly negative involvement) are more likely to have a recurrence of their symptoms (Brown et al. 1962, Vaughn and Leff 1976, Leff and Vaughn 1985). One conception of the process is that those genetically predisposed to schizophrenia are particularly vulnerable to the intense brain stimulation that might occur during stressful life events or intense emotional involvement. The schizophrenic might be seen as a potentially vulnerable person whose illness is triggered by a highly stimulating life situation. Consistent with this is that social distance from relatives and maintenance phenothiazine medication seem to protect against relapse. Study of patients' psychophysiological responses in the home confirm the fact of biological arousal in the presence of relatives with whom the patient has high emotional involvement (Tarrier et al. 1979). An alternative explanation for the vulnerability of schizophrenics to major changes and intense emotions involves the assumption that such events or situations are threatening to persons who lack the ability to handle problems. Because of biological incapacities or inadequate social training, schizophrenics may lack the coping skills that assist in facing and dealing with challenging situations, and the combination of biological vulnerability and personal inadequacy increases the probability of breakdown. There are many other formulations of the process of schizophrenic breakdown, but the fact is that we just do not really understand this condition. At best we have some leads and many hypotheses that have not achieved confirmation; we are still a long way from understanding the causes of this illness.

Despite the limitations of our knowledge, direction over environmental forces acting on the patient or on the patient's capacity to tolerate or cope with particular changes may allow us to contain and to control illness and disability. The difficulty, however, is in specifying the particular environmental supports that are most conducive to an optimal outcome. In the past, hospitals were much more willing to release schizophrenic patients who returned to family surroundings than they were to release those who had to make other living arrangements, but research findings suggested that particular family environments may not provide the best context for an optimal outcome (Carstairs 1959, Freeman and Simmons 1963). Whatever the final determination of such matters, mental health workers believe that schizophrenics and other mentally ill persons in the community require the kind of supportive care that helps them deal more effectively with inevitable crises and helps correct situations that are detrimental to their future comfort and welfare.

Studies of the affective disorders are more recent, but considerable progress has been made in a relatively short time span. It is clear that these disorders aggregate in families, and both twin and adoption studies support a genetic basis for both bipolar (manic-depressive) and unipolar affective disorder. The extent of these effects are difficult to estimate because they vary a great deal among studies and no specific process of transmission has been established (Reich et al. 1985). Manic-depressive disorder appears to be different from unipolar affective illness and has a distinct epidemiology, but the siblings and offspring of those with bipolar disorder have an elevated lifetime risk of both bipolar and unipolar disorder. The risk of disorder is higher in families with bipolar illness suggesting a stronger genetic effect than is characteristic of unipolar disease, which appears to be more closely linked to the social environment.

In sum, work in genetics and the neurosciences has demonstrated a very considerable role for biological substrates of mental illness. In addition to genetic factors, just briefly reviewed, is the growing understanding of biological mechanisms in the brain. It is now established that chemical neurotransmitters operate at most brain synapses, and they are now described as multidimensional nodes that are "genetically endowed but variously modified by a host of environmental influences" (Kety 1986, p. 23). Moreover, particular types of drugs act specifically on various symptoms of major mental disorders. As we better understand the activity of the chemical transmitters, we are likely to develop more effective and less adversive drugs. The challenge is also to identify how psychosocial events trigger brain processes, a topic to which we now turn.

THE PSYCHOSOCIAL-DEVELOPMENT PERSPECTIVE

Much research in the mental health field has been based on the premise that early psychosocial environment and family interaction are influential in the development of personality and of mental disorders in later life. In the United States the importance of psychoanalytic and neopsychoanalytic theories of psychological and social development had a pervasive influence on the hypotheses developed and the research undertaken.

Intrinsic to the psychosocial approach is concern with how children are socialized, how parents react to their behavior and train them, and, most importantly, the emotional tone of family interaction and of the relationships among the child, siblings, and peers. Among the variables frequently studied are the use of punishment by the parents, the degree of parental warmth, the dependency patterns in the family, the means of handling aggression, the forms of parental social control, and the family role structure (Maccoby 1961).

In the study of schizophrenia, several research groups attempted to specify aspects of family functioning and relationships that predispose members to a schizophrenic reaction pattern. Bateson and his colleagues (1956) emphasized the idea of the double bind, a situation in which a person is subjected to incongruent or conflicting messages; the appropriate response is unclear, and the danger of being rebuked exists regardless of which message the person responds to. Other investigators with a psychosocial perspective see schizophrenia as the confusion in identity resulting from distorted family role structures. Lidz (1963) described two kinds of schizogenic families—one built around a sick, dominating parent, usually the mother, and the other characterized by chronic hostility and mutual withdrawal of family members. Other approaches gave primary emphasis to family interaction and communication, the organization of family role patterns and identities, and the peculiar use of sanctions (Mishler and Waxler 1965).

Various investigators point to early peer relationships and adolescent problems to explain schizophrenic conditions. Harry Stack Sullivan (1953) emphasized the importance of preadolescence—the period when, he believed, the capacity to love matured. Sullivan theorized that this capacity is first developed through association with a chum of one's own sex. Such a relationship allowed preadolescents to see themselves through others' eyes and provided them with consensual validation of their personal worth. During the adolescent period, the maturation of competence was particularly important; if individuals successfully negotiated this period, they developed self-respect adequate to almost any situation. Such theories have encouraged various investigators to explore peer contacts and social isolation during adolescence in attempts to account for schizophrenic illness, but findings in this area have not confirmed these views (Kohn and Clausen 1955).

The importance of psychosocial development and the role of the family in psychiatric disorder have been accepted and extensively studied, but it has been incredibly difficult to identify any consistent psychosocial predictors of schizophrenia, depression, the neuroses, behavior disorders, or generalized psychological distress (Frank 1965, Marks 1973, Robins 1979b). The literature is characterized by dogmatism, conjecture, and wild and irresponsible statements. Careful evaluation of the literature and systematic studies fail to show the importance of such frequently cited influences as child-rearing practices, family communication and role constellations, and maternal and other parental qualities. It has become increasingly clear how little we really know about the development of these disorders, how inadequate our research models are, and how important it is to differentiate varying types of disorders in pursuing predictive studies.

Some firm findings, however, are beginning to emerge from careful longitudinal studies, as noted in the previous chapter. Aggressiveness, achievement patterns, and social skill development in children are generally established before adolescence, and childhood problems in these areas frequently persist into adulthood (Robins 1979b). Antisocial behavior in childhood increases vulnerability to a variety of mental disorders, alcoholism, and other problems in adult life. In contrast, children with neurotic problems often do quite well in adulthood, suffering much less illness, disability, and maladjustment than the antisocial child (Robins 1966, Rutter 1972). Children having difficulties with authority figures often end up having problems with alcohol, sex, and the law. Seriously disturbed children, such as those with childhood psychoses, have serious and disabling adult disorders. Fortunately, such disorders are relatively infrequent. (For outstanding reviews of the longitudinal studies, see Robins 1979a,b, 1983.)

Although theorists are very interested in the psychosocial aspects of schizophrenia and other mental illnesses, they have little conclusive evidence on which to base preventive work. The usual variances in child-rearing patterns appear to play a relatively small part in producing the profound difficulties that we are concerned with here, and, indeed, the relevance of different child-rearing practices in personality development in general has not been established (Sewell 1952). Any relatively warm, accepting family climate that nurtures a sense of self-esteem in the child and provides training experiences somewhat consistent with social realities will probably produce a "normal" child. Despite the earlier theoretical assumptions that perpetuated the myth of the fragile child, children are exceedingly flexible and adaptive and relatively strong and invulnerable to modifications in their environments. Indeed, adversity in childhood that is manageable may lead to the development of mastery and strength (Elder 1974). The contexts that appear to breed pathology are those that are emotionally bizarre or highly deprived and in which the child experiences profound rejection, hostility, and other forms of physical and emotional abuse and is exposed to inadequate, ineffective, and incongruous models of behavior.

Family factors most frequently predicting adult functioning "include family size, broken homes, illegitimacy, adoption or foster placement, socioeconomic status, supervision by parents, attitudes of parents toward the child, parental expectations for his achievement, behavior problems in the parents and siblings, and psychiatric disorder in the parents" (Robins 1979). These factors all tend to be intercorrelated and reflect many other aspects of family life and position in the society in addition to genetic transmission, and it is difficult to identify causal mechanisms.

It is not fully clear why such extensive effort to identify precursors has yielded so little understanding of the major mental disorders. The problem may be that there are just too many contingencies in the life course, and outcomes may depend on complex pathways that are in no sense inevitable. As George Brown (1986) notes, "the study of various life stages in a series of separate studies is of limited use. For many problems it is necessary to follow an individual from childhood through adult life to determine how various experiences interrelate" (p. 191).

The longitudinal study by Quinton and Rutter (1984a,b) of girls in local authority care (the British equivalent of a foster institution) and an appropriate comparison group found that those who received institutional care were more likely to have pregnancies early in adult life, to enter unstable cohabiting relationships, to have serious problems in relating to and caring for their children, and to have psychiatric disorders. They were less likely to plan their relationships with men and more likely to cohabit with a person who had significant personal problems and who provided little support. When such women had a supportive spouse, many of the parenting difficulties were alleviated. Retrospective study of these women, who were in institutional care as children, suggested that they more commonly had adverse childhoods than comparison mothers, comparable to those now being experienced by their own children. These experiences included teen-age difficulties, leaving home early because of rejection or conflict, and early pregnancy. Thus, many of the noxious patterns of child care and ineffective coping seemed to replicate themselves across generations.

The research literature suggests complex causal mechanisms, and much attention has shifted to the study of stressful life events, coping, sense of control, and social supports. It seems clear, however, that while it is difficult to isolate any single factor particularly promotive of mental illness, social and family environments characterized by abuse and neglect are major contributors, and these conditions are more prevalent in impoverished environments. Healthy parents who create a warm and constructive environment for their children, make them feel valued, and encourage their acquisition of skills can do much to protect against psychological disorder, although biological vulnerabilities can be manifest in the best and most loving environments. In recognizing the importance of a high quality of parental caring, we must not make the mistake of blaming parents whose children develop disorder.

Many conditions contribute to poor parenting including premature parental roles and a lack of child-care skills. Parents who are themselves mentally ill or who face difficult life stresses with which they cannot cope have more difficulty attending to the needs of their children (Feldman et al. 1987). These problems are exacerbated by poverty, poor housing conditions, inadequate schooling, and discrimination. Poverty increases risk, but most poor children develop reasonably and acquire the necessary psychological and coping skills. The relative role of biological predisposition and environment depends of course on the specific disorder being considered. Such issues as altering living patterns, improving housing conditions, eliminating social discrimination, and providing good schools are very much intertwined with political and social processes, and society will probably not alter its priorities and decisions merely because mental health workers feel that current conditions may lead to poor mental health. These and similar battles, if they are to be fought at all, must be fought in the political realm—a realm in which mental health workers have demonstrated no special ability.

The usual approach taken by workers with a psychosocial perspective is to alter individual family conditions and understandings that they believe are not conducive to the mental health of its members. They contend that encouraging people to seek supportive help and counseling when difficulties and crises first occur alleviates problems and avoids future complications conducive to morbidity. Family problems and patterns of interaction, however, are frequently hard to solve or alter. Mental health workers are not at all sure just what aspects of family functioning are central to the morbidity condition. Also, the therapeutic relationship, even if properly directed and effectively organized, constitutes such a small part of family interaction that it may not be able to overcome the more common experiences family members have with one another and with their community. Finally, we cannot always separate those aspects of family interaction that were conducive to family pathology in the first place and those that constitute adaptive responses to the presence of pathology. The frequent occurrence of a dominant mother and a weak, withdrawing father in families with a great variety of social and psychiatric problems suggests that family structures may be a reaction to sickness in one of the members rather than an important cause.

The literature evaluating psychosocial interventions to either prevent or alleviate mental disorders or behavior pathologies provides little cause for a high level of optimism. There have been very few studies demonstrating important long-term outcomes resulting from treatment (Robins 1973), and, as previously noted, even seemingly helpful approaches have not only failed to produce positive effects, but have been linked to adverse outcomes. Even the best motives and personal dedication can be harmful if therapists do not know what they are doing. Behavior modification approaches seem more promising at least in specific instances, such as the treatment of childhood fears and phobias, but many of these symptoms have a high rate of spontaneous remission in any case (Marks 1969).

In a study involving the use of child guidance facilities at a well-known mental hospital, Shepherd, Oppenheim, and Mitchell (1966) matched treated children with other children having similar problems who were not receiving treatment. Varying parental needs and patterns of illness behavior accounted for the fact that some children were treated but others with identical problems were not. When the researchers reevaluated the treated and untreated groups of children two years later, they found little difference in rates of improvement. Even within the treated group, the amount of improvement was unrelated to the amount of treatment provided. Approximately two-thirds of both groups of children—treated and untreated—had improved in the two-year period. How are we to interpret these findings?

The investigators concluded that many of the treated symptoms were no more than temporary exaggerations of reaction patterns occurring normally in human development. They believe that clinicians who have concentrated on morbidity have an incomplete appreciation of the normal range of reaction patterns and give exaggerated significance to symptoms and problems that are not really pathological and do not ordinarily require treatment (Robins 1966, pp. 300–303). Those more skeptical about such studies point out an important differentiating factor between the treated and untreated groups. The fact that some children were brought into treatment suggests that their parents were either unable or unwilling to cope with their problems, and the findings suggest that such parents also had fewer resources for dealing with the difficulties of their children. Because these children did no worse than those whose parents had more effective coping resources, therapy may have been helpful and effective. The data on hand do not really allow us to evaluate the opposing arguments conclusively. However, even if we accept the argument of the proponents of child therapeutic services, the outcomes achieved by such services are at best very modest. We must be willing to consider the possibility of using equivalent resources in a manner encouraging a larger and more effective return.

In discussing the application of psychosocial approaches to mental disorder in such general terms, I do not wish to suggest that researchers and therapists assuming this perspective are of one mind. In this section I have directed attention primarily to those approaches based on the assumption that it is important for patients to appreciate the nature of their social relationships and psychological and social inclinations. In the following section we shall consider orientations that have psychosocial aspects but do not necessarily require that the patients achieve insight.

THE LEARNING PERSPECTIVE

Over the years psychologists have achieved substantial understanding of the learning process. Although some early attempts were made to translate these findings into a therapeutic approach, such attempts have now become a major investment and an enterprise of some importance in therapeutic research.

One of the first systematic attempts to link learning theory and psychoanalytic practice was presented in *Personality and Psychotherapy* written by John Dollard and Neal E. Miller in 1950. They brought together the formulations of Hullian learning theory and various psychoanalytic concepts and tried to specify the conditions under which habits are formed and changed. They reformulated various psychoanalytic concepts such as the unconscious, conflict, and repression into stimulus-response terms using the concepts of drive, cue, response, and reward. They pointed out that repression is the learned avoidance of certain thoughts. Because some thoughts arouse fear (a secondary drive stimulus), ignoring them leads to drive reduction and to reinforcement; in this way the response becomes a learned part of a person's repertoire.

Although various efforts to analyze psychotherapeutic processes within a learning frame of reference continued, *Psychotherapy by Reciprocal Inhibition* by Joseph Wolpe (1958) gave considerable impetus to the use of

learning theory in psychotherapy. Wolpe maintained that psychotherapeutic effects were produced mainly by complete or partial suppres-
sion of anxiety responses by the simultaneous evocation of other responses
physiologically antagonistic to anxiety. Wolpe maintained that neurotic behavior is a persistent but learned and unadaptive anxiety response acquired in anxiety-generating situations. Such anxiety responses are unadaptive because they are manifest in situations that contain no objective
threat. Given these assumptions, Wolpe and others have developed
therapeutic approaches, such as desensitization, relaxation, and operant
conditioning, techniques now commonly practiced in psychotherapy.

The learning approaches to psychotherapy, or what is more commonly called behavior therapy, are based on the idea that it is possible to
develop reinforcement schedules that weaken unadaptive responses and
reinforce more adaptive behavior. This approach is specifically directed
toward changing particular aspects of the person rather than toward such
ambitious but unrealistic results as psychic reintegration.

Critics of behavior therapy have charged that such procedures may
change symptoms but are not directed toward basic causes, an argument
that has weakened over time. They also have maintained that except for
specific conditions that are dominated by a single symptom, such as phobias and sexual impotence, mental conditions are characterized by complicated syndromes for which it is difficult to discern and develop specific
reinforcement schedules or other remedial procedures. They argue that
one must understand the relevant, important cues and stimuli in the patient's illness before proceeding but, more frequently than not, learning
these requires a long period of therapeutic work.

The contention that behavior therapy just reduced particular symptoms or substituted one for another has proved to be an invalid criticism.
Implicit in it is the assumption that a more basic cure is possible, but little
evidence supports such a claim. Changing destructive, specific patterns of
behavior, such as self-mutilation or fear of leaving one's house, is anything
but trivial. The second argument, concerning the difficulty of locating
specific cues and the patterns of behavior and thinking to which they are
associated, points to a more serious problem. But over time, the techniques
of behavior change have been incorporated into a wide variety of
therapeutic approaches. If we are to evaluate behavior therapy, we must
consider the success of its techniques in treating what it purports to treat.
Because it is probably more useful in some cases than in others, we must
consider the way it compares in each specific instance with the other forms
of therapy available.

A major problem with many psychotherapeutic approaches is that
they are diffuse and vary little from one patient to another regardless of
the problem, the patient's situation, or the needs for practical action. The
psychoanalyst, for example, approaches many different types of patients in
the same way, taking a global approach in contrast to clearly specifying the
patient's problem and defining a series of specific goals toward which both
therapist and patient can work. A major contribution of the behavioral
approach is its emphasis on specifying precisely what is to be accomplished

in terms of observable behavior by designating intermediate objectives and working toward modifying more complex patterns of response (Bandura 1969).

Behavior therapy is no panacea, but there is much evidence that it is a constructive and relatively effective approach to modifying behaviors that are painful to people and that cause them difficulty in relationships with others. Although this approach has limited value as a cure for persons with serious mental disorder, as in the case of the schizophrenic patient, it facilitates modification of certain behaviors that help the rehabilitation and community adjustment of the patient. Such behavior modification may not only be valuable on its own terms but may also contribute to the patient's sense of psychological comfort, psychological control, and self-confidence.

Behavior therapy consists of a series of techniques including systematic desensitization, flooding, modeling, and stress inoculation (Sutherland 1977). In systematic desensitization, the patient is introduced to the disturbing stimulus in increasing intensity so as to develop tolerance of it. As the patient masters fear in response to one of the graded exposures, rewards may be given, such as encouragement and compliments. In flooding, the patient is asked to imagine the most frightening examples of feared objects until the fear diminishes. Although this technique may make the fears worse if the patient cannot tolerate the imagined scenes, the method is often combined with the use of tranquilizing drugs that reduce anxiety. In modeling, the patient is encouraged and rewarded in repeating the behavior of the therapist in dealing with some troubling situation. Rewards and punishments are increasingly used on hospital wards in an explicit way to induce constructive behavior. Token economies have been used in mental hospitals to encourage patients to take responsibility and to cooperate in ward endeavors. In stress inoculation, patients learn slow breathing and muscular relaxation (which inhibit anxiety) while being exposed to electric shock. They also learn to reassure themselves and engage in thinking conducive to coping. These learned techniques are then used in real-life situations that are threatening to the person.

An extension of behavior therapy involves self-control, in which the person learns to induce self-selected behaviors without external reinforcement or contingency schedules controlled by outsiders (Halleck 1978). Techniques that are taught include control over the stimuli to which people expose themselves, self-observation, self (positive and negative)-reinforcement, self-instruction, and developing alternative response sequences. One application of this technique is to teach patients to recognize when they are having symptom exacerbations, to teach them to reduce exposure to events upsetting to them, and to shape their expressions in a less stigmatizing way so that they are less frightening to others. These techniques have been used with psychotic patients by inducing self-monitoring and self-evaluation, which presumably leads to self-control through changes such as reducing or increasing particular types of activities. It has even been suggested that it may "be possible to teach schizophrenic patients a behavioral approach for talking themselves out of their symptoms" (Breier and Strauss 1983, p.

1141). While these techniques are no panacea, they can be a useful adjunct to the care process.

Behavior therapy, in short, is a practical response to many types of behavior problems. It is not only used by therapists and counselors, but is increasingly taught to patients, clients, and their families to assist them in modifying their own behaviors. The underlying conception, perhaps most forcefully and extremely stated by Skinner (1971), is that maladaptive behavior and symptoms are largely learned, and by appropriately modifying reinforcement schedules implicit in the social structures of communities, families, schools, and hospitals, we can shape the future behavior of man.

THE SOCIAL-STRESS PERSPECTIVE

The study of stress has been one of the most active areas of social research in psychiatry. As we have already noted, stressful life events have been associated with the occurrence of schizophrenic episodes and are believed to play a major role in depression. Although concern with stress goes back a long way in psychiatric discussions, there has been an enormous growth of research in the last decade or two on the relationship of stressful life events to a wide range of physical and psychiatric conditions (Dohrenwend, B. S. and Dohrenwend, B. P. 1974, 1981). The research itself is increasingly specific and sophisticated, and methodological refinements are evident.

In its simplest form, stress conceptions suggest that all people have a breaking point and that mental illness and psychiatric disability are the products of the cumulation of misfortune that overwhelm their constitutional makeup, their personal resources, and their coping abilities. Stated in this way, the perspective is not very useful for it cannot successfully predict who will break down but in retrospect can explain everything. There is considerable evidence that many persons can withstand pronounced stress without psychiatric difficulty and that psychoses do not increase substantially during major catastrophes, such as war, disasters, and other calamities (Murphy 1961, Reid 1961, Fried 1964). Pronounced exposure to extreme stress and deprivation, such as occurred in concentration camps, resulted in a high prevalence of long-term psychiatric disability, however, and there is considerable evidence that increased stress is associated with nervousness, anxiety, and other physiological symptoms (Dohrenwend and Dohrenwend 1969).

Workers in the stress area are differentiating among types of events, types of personal vulnerabilities and assets, and types of disorder. In the case of events, one issue is whether all life changes—favorable as well as adverse ones—produce disruptions in feelings and functioning. Are there different types of adverse events—for example, events involving loss of a loved one or an important relationship—that have a greater influence than other types of adverse events—loss of money or a job—on such conditions as depressions? Although the occurrence of some conditions such as depression seems to follow primarily adverse events and particularly loss, other conditions such as schizophrenia may be precipitated by an intense positive experience. This suggests that we need clearer specification of the way different types of life changes affect certain conditions. Stress theory, as stated in a global and general sense, encompasses different and even competing conceptions.

Life change events may be hypothesized to play a role in the formation of a disease process, to trigger a disease process to which a person is constitutionally vulnerable, to stimulate help seeking, or to shape the mode of expression of distress. Brown and Harris (1978), in their research on depression, maintain that life events play a significant causal role in the occurrence of depression; however, they argue it is not any type of event that is important, even if very unpleasant, but rather only certain severe events involving long-term threat.

> The distinctive feature of the great majority of the provoking events is the experience of loss or disappointment, if this is defined broadly to include threat of or actual separation from a key figure, an unpleasant revelation about someone close, a life-threatening illness to a close relative, a major material loss or general disappointment or threat of them, and miscellaneous crises such as being made redundant after a long period of steady employment. In more general terms the loss or disappointment could concern a person or object, a role, or an idea. (Brown and Harris 1978, pp. 274–75)

Such events are by their very nature adverse, and positive life events do not cause depression.

A contrasting view of the way life events may affect disorder is suggested by the previously reviewed research studies of schizophrenia (Brown et al. 1962, Brown and Birley 1968, Vaughn and Leff 1976). These studies suggest that events in general—not only adverse ones—contribute to schizophrenic breakdown. The hypothesis here is that schizophrenics, because of biological constitution or genetic makeup, are particularly vulnerable to high levels of arousal, and events that excite the patient trigger symptoms. Unlike the depression analysis, events within this conception are more a trigger than a basic aspect of the illness.

Still a third conception is that events may not affect the illness itself, but may induce greater concern with symptoms and result more readily in the acquisition of help. Studies indicate that a stressful event and the distress associated with it increase the probability that assistance will be sought. A final conception is that certain events may influence the way the illness is expressed. Being fired from one's job will not cause paranoid schizophrenia, but this event might provide substance for the patient's paranoid ideation. In sum, although it is very difficult to do in practice, it is important in discussing stress and mental disorder to specify clearly the types of stresses involved, the particular disorders referred to, and the specific influences relating the stress events and the varying aspects of the illness process.

As research on stressful life events has progressed, it has become clear that such events by themselves predict outcome measures to only a modest degree. Stress is common in peoples' lives, but some manage it much better than others. Attention has thus shifted to intervening variables that either increase vulnerability or contribute to resilience. Such factors include personality, coping strategies, and social support. Personality factors include such concepts as type A (Friedman and Rosenman 1974), sense of control (Rodin 1986), and hardiness (Korbasa 1979). Coping includes problem-solving approaches, modes of information acquisition, anticipation and planning (Leventhal 1970); focus is often on whether persons emphasize problem-oriented or emotion-oriented approaches. Social support has been approached in many ways including both subjective and objective measures of social networks available and the help given and received.

Each of the relevant component areas of the stress-coping paradigm (the measurement of stress, the description of social networks, and depiction of the coping process) is characterized by vigorous debates about assumptions, conceptualization, and methodology, but these debates have significantly sharpened thinking. In the measurement of stress, divergent views abound on the emphasis to be given respectively to positive and negative life events, subjective and objective measures, and major life events as compared with daily irritations. There also has been controversy as to the methodology of measuring events (whether by respondent report or independent evaluations), the significance of precisely timing the event, and the need to distinguish carefully between events totally outside the individual's control, as compared with those to which the person could have contributed such as divorce, loss of job, or economic difficulties (Brown and Harris 1978, Dohrenwend and Dohrenwend 1981, Lazarus and Folkman 1984). The value of focusing on independent events is clear, but relatively few stressors are completely independent of a person's past history or behavior.

The concept of social support has been subjected to similar types of debates. While the evidence linking measures of social support to health outcomes has been substantial, neither the measurement of the concept nor the results have been fully consistent. The concept may refer to the extent and structure of social networks, the availability of intimate others, social contacts, voluntary community participation, and similar phenomena. Theories underlying alternative approaches to measurement have not always been clear, and the specific causal mechanisms intervening between support and outcomes are not well developed, although specification of alternative statistical models has advanced (Wheaton 1985). Studies of support have been relatively one-sided, with little attention having been paid to the constraints, responsibilities, and stresses often associated with kinship ties and other close interpersonal relations.

Decisions about measurement often involve assumptions that close the opportunities to examine particular theoretical ideas. Life event scales that failed to differentiate clearly between positive and negative life changes made it impossible in many studies to test the assumption that life changes, independent of positive or negative features, contributed to morbidity. Existing evidence suggests that loss events relate to depressive illness, but that a wider range of events may be relevant to triggering schizophrenic episodes. Measurement approaches must allow testing of the underlying assumptions that motivate investigation in the first place. Similarly, the counting or scoring of life change events, in examining direct relationships between life change and health outcomes, ignores much developmental research, which suggests that growth and competence are attained through mastering challenging life events. Within this context, stress describes a relationship between a situation and an individual's resources to deal with it and not a specific event (Mechanic 1962b, Lazarus and Folkman 1984). The most typical measurement models are not always well constructed to capture the richness of our ideas.

The examination of people's sense of personal control and the exercise of "mastery" is a large and promising research area; this has immediate practical implications because it is possible to intervene in many social contexts to enhance people's control over their immediate environments (Rodin 1986). It is also consistent with developments in clinical psychology and cognitive therapy that relate to helplessness and depression. In some contexts studied, such as nursing homes, small changes in personal control have an impressive effect on psychological response, health, and even mortality (Rodin and Langner 1977), but questions about this remain unanswered. It is not apparent to what degree these effects operate within the normal range of human control, compared with situations of deprivation. Nor is it evident how enhanced control interacts with personality, attribution styles, cultural values, age, and other variables. The area remains an important one for continuing research and development.

Our understanding of the interaction of life events with other factors in affecting psychiatric morbidity, though still primitive, is used as an important rationale for preventive and community mental health efforts. Building on the idea that outcome depends on the ability of individuals to withstand adverse life events through coping skills and social supports, efforts are made to provide increased assistance during transition crises, such as divorce, and to assist people in actively coping with the problems associated with their life situation. While some self-help groups make assistance available to anyone going through the experience, such as Parents Without Partners (Weiss 1975), other groups, such as Alcoholics Anonymous, are provided for individuals suffering from a specific disorder. There are no examples of effective programs in preventing the occurrence of mental illness, but successful programs based on a model of teaching coping techniques and providing social support have been developed that have minimized secondary disabilities associated with mental illness and prevented the hospitalization of the patient. Such programs are discussed in detail in the chapter on coping theory.

THE LABELING PERSPECTIVE

In the 1960s and 1970s, labeling theory played a major role in the ideological debate that helped shape the deinstitutionalization movement. Conceptions of labeling and its effects varied greatly from those who presented labeling theory as a causal model to explain mental illness to others who viewed labeling primarily as a process contributing to chronicity and disabilities that extended beyond those that were direct results of mental disorder. Labeling theory was derived from a theoretical approach in the study of deviant behavior and societal reactions that focused less on the origins of deviant response and more on those social forces that help structure, organize, and perpetuate such reactions. Advocates of this perspective argue that deviant response is reinforced and perpetuated by social reactions to it, by the manner in which it is labeled, and by the resultant exclusion and discrimination against the deviant. The basic assumptions underlying this approach are that each society produces its own deviants by its definitions and rules and that such processes of definition help maintain the boundaries of the society (Lemert 1951, Erikson 1966).

The model most usually presented is a sequential one in which, over time, a pattern of deviant response is labeled in a fashion that increases the probability that further similar responses will occur (Becker 1963). As the definition of the deviant response persists and as normal roles become more difficult for the deviant to assume because of limited opportunities and growing exclusion, deviant acts become organized as part of one's social identity and as an ongoing deviant role. Thus the labeling process itself helps convert transitory, common deviant behavior into a more stable pattern of persistent deviant response.

In the case of mental illness, Scheff (1984) argued that such disorders are residual forms of deviant behavior for which we have no other appropriate labels and that such behaviors arise from fundamentally diverse sources. He maintained that the occurrence of such symptoms or deviant responses is frequent and is usually neither labeled nor defined. Because such behavior occurs within normal and conventional response repertoires, it is usually temporary and nonpersistent. However, when such behavior is explicitly identified and labeled, the forces produced help organize the behavior into a social role. Scheff hypothesized that, although deviants do not explicitly learn the role of the mentally ill, they are able to assume it because they have learned stereotyped imagery of what mental illness is from early childhood; the movies, television, radio, newspapers, and magazines inadvertently but continuously support and supplement this imagery. Scheff believes that deviants labeled as mentally ill may receive a variety of advantages by assuming the role and enacting it, although their assumption of the role need not be a conscious process. He argued that when such persons attempt to return to normal, conventional roles, their opportunities are restricted, and they may be punished as a result of the stigma associated with their past difficulties. They often have problems in obtaining adequate employment and have difficulties in relations with others because they have been classified as mentally ill. As Scheff sees it, the transition from mental symptoms as an incidental aspect of social performance to mental illness as a social role occurs when the individual is under considerable personal and social stress. In such circumstances, the persons may themselves accept the societal definition of their status and develop deviant concepts of their identities.

Although the societal-reaction approach is provocative and obviously identifies processes that occur to some extent in the definition and care of mental patients, the relative importance of such processes were very much exaggerated. No one would deny that social labels can have powerful effects on individuals, but little evidence supports the idea that such labeling processes are sufficiently powerful to be major influences in producing chronic mental illness. The labeling process is not sufficient in itself to produce mental illness, but existing theories of the societal reaction are extremely vague in defining clearly the conditions under which labeling will or will not produce deviant behavior. Some patients get well rather quickly and stay well, while others, such as schizophrenics, commonly develop chronic disabilities. The theory of labeling does not explain why such differences occur.

Robins (1975) has presented a useful critique of labeling theory, specifically examining the theory in relationship to existing knowledge about alcoholism. She notes numerous inconsistencies between what labeling theory suggests and the facts. First, she observes that predictors of deviance are similar for both labeled and unlabeled alcoholics if the severity of the problem is taken into account. Second, while all common forms of deviant behavior decrease with age, cumulation of labeling associated with deviance must obviously increase over the life span. Thus, from this perspective, deviance should increase with age. Third, labeling theory would suggest that persons labeled in a certain way—say as a prostitute or thief— would increasingly display such behavior. In contrast, however, specific types of deviance in younger life are associated with later deviance, but often the content of the deviant behavior changes. Young girls caught stealing are more likely in later life to attempt suicide or to be sexually promiscuous or alcoholic than they are to be adult thieves. Fourth, several studies show that parents' deviance is associated with the probability that their children will be schizophrenics or alcoholics even when the children are separated from their parents and do not know the parents' identification, as in the case of infant adoptees. Moreover, Robins argues, the process of labeling itself is quite different from theoretical conceptions. The alcoholic, for example, is usually labeled only after many years of excessive drinking, and it is typically the family and not public authorities who become concerned about the problem. Although labels of "alcoholism" are withheld from many heavy drinkers for many years, the behavior is often self-sustaining and may lead to physical dependence. The most successful group approach to containing excessive drinking—membership in Alcoholics Anonymous—requires the persons to label themselves as alcoholics in order for behavior change to proceed.

There is considerable stigma associated with mental illness, and many people associate the term with psychotic behavior in contrast to the variety of emotional problems that occur in populations. For those who have contact with the mentally ill, concepts of illness, perceptions of danger, and degree of stigma are associated with the nature of the experience one has (Huffine and Clausen 1979, Clausen 1981, Link and Cullen 1986). Individuals test their general impressions against actual experience and often revise their expectations in a favorable direction. While labeling and its consequences may be important, the form and content of such labeling is highly interdependent with the behavior of the mentally ill. Some mental patients behave in a stereotypical fashion, but most do not and their families and the community differentiate among different patterns of behavior.

As Robins's critique suggests, labeling theory is vague in its formulations, in its specification of the ways labeling affects illness, and in the specific types of disorders that may be affected more than others. Robins suggests that labeling conceptions may be more predictive in situations in which the behavior is highly inconsistent in content with social norms, such as in homosexual behavior, as compared with exaggerated forms of usual behavior, such as heavy drinking. Addressing specific forms of behavior rather than general categories may contribute to the usefulness of labeling theory. Even more important is that labeling theorists be specific as to whether they are discussing the causes of disorder, or whether they are primarily concerned with the establishment of disabilities associated with a primary disorder as in the adoption of a chronic sick role.

Although labeling theory has not been very useful in clarifying etiologic questions, it is a powerful perspective for examining how the definitions of a problem and its management affect its course or social outcome. It suggests that the manner in which the community defines and deals with sick and vulnerable people may either encourage disability, sick role behavior, and dependency or prevent it. The expectations we communicate to the mentally ill are important indeed, and the range of potential functioning of the mentally ill is fairly large depending on social definitions and social arrangements in the community. The political aspects of this problem can be considered under the designation of *collective mobilization*.

COLLECTIVE MOBILIZATION

Mental illness or any other type of deviant behavior may be viewed as a central or tangential aspect of a person's social identity. It can be considered an incidental aspect of persons' social roles and community participation or as the major fact of their social existence. While severe chronic mental illness, by its very nature, affects the person's family life, work, and social networks, the way the community views problems and the identity of those who have them may allow for varying degrees of normal social participation and, therefore, different levels of social disability.

In recent years there has been growing recognition that many of the disabilities experienced by the moderately retarded, the mental patient, the elderly, and other handicapped groups are as much the product of social expectations, social stigma, and exclusion from opportunities as they are a direct function of the mental or physical handicap the patient has. Organizations representing these groups are becoming politically active and more militant, demanding that the handicapped not be excluded from educational opportunities, jobs, and access to social participation simply because they are impaired or different. These efforts are increasingly supported by legislation that affirms the rights of the handicapped to equal opportunity and provides a context in which they can participate more fully in community activities. Such collective mobilization efforts to change social definitions and to alter opportunities for the impaired have important effects on the degree of social disability and dependence they suffer. Modification of community expectations and social arrangements has enormous potential for preventing the elaboration of disability and suffering. It constitutes an essential preventive strategy for those concerned with the welfare of handicapped people as well as the handicapped themselves as a social group.

In sum, many of the social problems associated with chronic mental illness as well as other types of handicaps stem from physical and social arrangements in the community as well as from individual incapacities. As patient groups and their representatives have come to recognize this, they have initiated political campaigns to modify arrangements that exacerbate their problems. The growth of such social movements achieves modification of social definitions and social policies that makes it easier for persons with disabilities to lead more normal lives.

In this chapter and the previous ones, I have tried to illustrate some of the difficulties in clearly defining the realm of mental illness, the varying conceptions of this phenomenon, competing etiological viewpoints, and some implications for possible intervention. We now turn to a review of mental health policies and the way they have evolved to the present before we examine directions for future policies.

Chapter Five

The Development
of Mental Health Policy
in the United States

In the decades following World War II, a strong coalition emerged emphasizing environmental factors as prominent contributors to mental illness and championing the importance of substituting new patterns of community care for the traditional reliance on public mental hospitals for the seriously mentally ill. In the period from approximately 1955 to 1975, this coalition vastly influenced public policy toward the mentally ill and shaped the federal role in mental health policy (Grob 1987).

Those associated with this movement often assumed that mental illness was a simple continuum from mild to severe dysfunction in contrast to a heterogeneous collection of unrelated disorders, that early intervention could prevent serious mental disorder, that population dynamics and the populations at risk were unchanging, and that use of mental health resources for outpatient psychiatric care was always more cost-effective than hospital care. These were all testable assumptions, but they were mostly accepted on faith (Mechanic 1987). In the 1960s the rhetoric of community care developed a momentum of its own, importantly shaping agendas and debates on mental health policy and broadly influencing the thinking of intellectual elites, public policy makers, and the general public (Grob 1987). In the process, many dedicated professionals and reformers lost touch with the heterogeneity of mental health problems and the tough realities of designing and implementing effective programs appropriate for the most seriously mentally ill.

Understanding the history of mental health policy, particularly in recent decades, provides a necessary perspective for understanding the forces that shaped the evolution of the mental health sector and possible points of leverage for constructive policy reform. Between 1955 and 1983, the number of mental health episodes treated in mental health specialty settings increased from 1.7 to 7 million episodes; the community hospital became the primary site for acute inpatient psychiatric care; and there was a vast growth of mental health professionals of all kinds. Despite these changes, there is persistent evidence of significant neglect of the most seriously ill long-term patients, and in the 1980s there is profound pessimism among many about our capacity to care appropriately for these patients in the community. The current negativity has been shaped in part by the excesses of ideology in the earlier decades and naive advocacy about labeling and normalization processes. These conceptions have provided a target for critics of deinstitutionalization, who focus on exaggerated claims and obvious failures of community care, proclaim the intent of deinstitutionalization as naive and counterproductive, and argue for the reestablishment of an enlarged mental hospital sector. Neither type of advocacy serves the needs of the mentally ill well or contributes to a well-informed public. By identifying some of the dominant misconceptions and defining issues more carefully, we can develop targeted and efficacious strategies that offer potential for bringing improved care to this most needy population.

In planning for the future, we can often obtain insights from the past and, therefore, we should attain some perspective on events that have already occurred and on the social, cultural, and ideological forces that have influenced them. Mental illness is not a new problem; the mentally ill have always existed in society. Methods of caring for the mentally ill have not followed a consistent developmental pattern; rather, they have been characterized by stops and starts, by advances and setbacks. Indeed, many of our present conceptions of mental illness and many current proposals were not only advocated but were also practiced a century ago. Milieu treatment, a concept widely popular today, existed in the nineteenth century in both Europe and America under the rubric of moral treatment (Bockoven 1972). Moral treatment was based on the assumption that psychiatric illness could be alleviated if patients were treated in a considerate and friendly fashion, if they had the opportunity to discuss their troubles, if their interests were stimulated, and if they were kept actively involved in life. Close relationships between staff and patients often prevailed, and patients were treated in a personal and sympathetic way. In the passage that follows, a doctor in New York State writing in 1911 describes his conception of moral treatment.

> (It) consists in removing patients from their residence to some proper asylum; and for this purpose a calm retreat in the country is to be preferred: for it is found that continuance at home aggravates the disease, as the improper association of ideas cannot be destroyed. . . . Have humane attendants, who shall act as servants to them; never threaten but execute; offer no indignities to them, as they have a high sense of honour. . . . Let their fears and resentments be soothed without unnecessary opposition; adopt a system of regularity; make them rise, take exercise and food at stated times. The diet ought

to be light, and easy of digestion, but never too low. When convalescing, allow limited liberty; introduce entertaining books and conversation. (Quoted in Deutsch 1949, pp. 91–92)

The idea of moral treatment is attributed to the French physician Philippe Pinel, who broke the pattern of harsh custodialism associated with mental institutions and substituted a program based on kindness and sympathy. It was not difficult to demonstrate that mental patients respond to sympathy and care, and Pinel had a profound influence on psychiatrists not only in Europe but also in America. Pinel's program was based on his belief that psychological factors were important causes of emotional disturbances, as were social factors and an inadequate education. Treatment of the insane, he believed, was only a form of education, and intelligent understanding associated with a minimum of mechanical restraint would bring good results.

Although moral treatment was established at institutions throughout the world, the sense of social responsibility toward the unfortunate which is more developed today was not very strong, and most patients received no better care than they had previously. Mental patients were undifferentiated from the destitute poor. When moral treatment was practiced, it was mainly available to relatively affluent persons. Dorothea Dix, who became concerned about the inhumane care received by most of the mentally ill, was able to rally influential persons to support her initiation of a reform movement that had a great effect on developments in the nineteenth century. This movement was directed toward improving the care of those mentally ill paupers who were severely punished for their condition or who received no care at all. It is ironic that this reform movement, inspired by lofty motives, led in the United States and elsewhere to the development of large custodial institutions which have set the tone for the care of the mentally ill until recently. Although some smaller institutions practicing moral treatment existed at the time, for the most part the impoverished mentally ill were excluded from them. Dorothea Dix's movement was directed toward providing a minimum amount of help, and this was a significant advance in the care of the mentally ill at the time. Events later proved that once a particular system of care had developed, it was difficult to alter it.

Even the institutions that practiced moral treatment were not immune to social changes. Social conditions accompanying the industrial revolution resulted in an increased tendency to hospitalize those who could not adapt to new circumstances (Grob 1966). While industrialization was changing the nature of work, family life, and community tolerance for bizarre behavior or incapacity, the unfortunate were exposed to great difficulties in the new industrial environment. As family structure changed, making it more difficult to contain old and disabled members within the family unit, and as the number of old people increased because of changing mortality patterns, the mental hospital often became a refuge for the old. The changing patterns of disease, particularly the increasing numbers of patients with paresis, and the dementia associated with it, resulted in more chronic and hopeless populations of patients (Grob 1983).

In New York State, 18 percent of all first admissions to mental hospitals in 1920 were diagnosed as being senile or suffering from cerebral arteriosclerosis. By 1940 they accounted for 31 percent of all admissions (Grob 1977). What was true of New York State described other states as well. In the absence of other social institutions, the mental hospital became a refuge for persons who could not cope with society on their own or for those who had no kin who could or would take responsibility for their care. Goldhamer and Marshall (1953), in studying patterns of mental hospitalization in Massachusetts over a 100-year period, could find no evidence that mental illness was increasing, but over this period admissions to mental hospitals for the aged group significantly increased. Brenner (1973), examining trends in mental hospitalization in relation to changes in the economy over a period of 127 years, found that admissions increased following periods of economic misfortune. During these periods it is the poor and dependent who fare worse, and this helps explain the large inflow to mental hospitals of poor aged and foreign immigrants who had the least capacities to care for themselves and the weakest social supports available in the community. It remains unclear whether adverse economic circumstances contributed to the prevalence of mental illness or undermined tolerance and supports for the mentally ill in the community. Whatever the case might be, economic and social instability produced large numbers of persons in need of care, and the mental hospital in the absence of other alternatives assumed this function.

With the limited facilities and resources available, mental hospitals were confronted with many more patients than they could effectively handle. The burden of their numbers made it more difficult to maintain an active program, such as moral treatment (Rothman 1971). Hospitals, limited in staff and money, dealt with these new conditions by regimentation of patients and the development of bureaucratic procedures through which large numbers of patients could be handled by limited staff (Goffman 1961). There were, of course, variations from one area to another and among different kinds of hospitals; any general depiction must leave room for the variability that existed (Grob 1973). Studies of individual hospitals provide a clearer view of some of the social forces and ideological influences that affected the structure of mental hospitals. We now turn to a review of the early history of one such hospital.

THE EARLY HISTORY OF WORCESTER STATE HOSPITAL

In a sophisticated history, Gerald Grob (1966) traces the various social forces that affected the growth and the organization of Worcester State Hospital, established in 1830 as the first state hospital for the mentally ill in Massachusetts. The interest in establishing a mental hospital in Massachusetts was encouraged by the inadequacy of informal methods of caring for the indigent and insane and was activated by vigorous, enlightened reformers who were motivated by a strong sense of religious and social responsibility. The new hospital, in its earliest perod (1833–1846), practiced moral treatment and offered its patients an optimistic and humanitarian climate. Early records of the hospital suggest considerable success at rehabilitation, not because of the efficacy of any particular psychiatric treatment, but probably as a result of the hopeful and encouraging climate, which supported the patient and inspired a feeling of being helped. Moral treatment, however, did not persist, and for most of the nineteenth century, the hospital was guided by a pessimistic psychiatric ideology that mirrored its custodial nature.

As Grob shows so well, the organization of psychiatric care was responsive to social, economic, and ideological influences in the society at large. Industrial and technological changes in Massachusetts, coupled with increasing urbanization, brought decreasing tolerance for bizarre and disruptive behavior and less ability to contain deviant behavior within the existing social structure. With the growing number of patients—the mass of them held in low esteem by the community as well as by mental hospital personnel—and many chronically ill, it was impossible to maintain the administrative and environmental attitudes necessary for moral treatment. Moreover, with a growing number of patients and limited resources, it was necessary to develop more efficient custodial attitudes and procedures. The contempt in which the hospital held its clients and the low social value accorded them by the society at large neither stimulated hospital administrators to demand greater resources to care for their patients nor encouraged the community to provide further and more intensive support.

Other forces as well led to the deterioration of the hospital. As Grob argues, new psychiatric ideologies and professionalization among psychiatrists did much to retard the care of the mentally ill. These ideologies were in part the product of psychiatrists' own attitudes and beliefs, molded by their social backgrounds and influenced by their need to maintain and increase their status. Grob believes that psychiatric insistence that the profession was scientific exerted a negative effect on mental hospitals. The emphasis on somatic factors within the traditional medical model had little to offer in the treatment of patients, and it undermined alternative approaches that could have produced improvement in patients by communicating a sense of confidence and hope (also see Bockoven 1957, 1972). Furthermore, he argues that the development of a professional psychiatric subculture erected barriers between psychiatrists and other interested groups and was used to justify the exclusion of laymen who had provided much of the impetus for the improvement of mental health care. Finally, the trend toward professionalism isolated psychiatrists from the more humanitarian and compassionate ideologies existing in the society and replaced these with a barren, alleged objectivity that offered little help or hope. Professionalization of psychiatrists thus hampered the administration of psychiatric care.

Grob's history of Worcester State Hospital provides an important cautionary tale for professionals and policy makers. The disappointment with "Great Society" programs has resulted in an ideology of futility, a loss of interest among psychiatrists in social and community programs, and a return to biological and medical approaches. The concept of disease and traditional medical care certainly plays an essential role in the care of the most severely mentally ill, but the social, organizational, and humanistic contexts of care are also crucial. Molecular biology and the neurosciences offer great promise for the future but relatively little to current patients who desperately need a broad array of care and rehabilitation services. However sophisticated our biological approaches, social and behavioral factors will continue to play an important part in the occurrence and course of mental illness and in good psychiatric care. In turning back toward biology and medical concepts, it would be tragic if psychiatry once again contributes to weakening the forces of reform and humanistic basis of care that inspires a sense of hope so important to millions.

MORE RECENT DEVELOPMENTS
IN MENTAL HEALTH POLICY

American psychiatry and mental health policy, as we know them today, are for the most part post—World War II developments. At the beginning of World War II, there were only 3,000 psychiatrists in the United States, and shortages among other treatment and research personnel in the mental health field were even more acute. Progress is reflected in the fact that there are now approximately 36,000 psychiatrists in the United States. Even more impressive increases have occurred in psychology, psychiatric nursing, psychiatric social work, and other mental health fields.

Except for their traditional role in mental hospitals, psychiatrists became most extensively involved in public policy issues during World War II, initially through their participation in selective service screening. Between January 1942 and June 1945, an estimated 1,875,000 men among the 15 million men examined were rejected for service because of alleged psychiatric disabilities. Of the men inducted, a large proportion of those later separated from the armed forces on a disability charge were discharged specifically for neuropsychiatric reasons (Felix 1967, pp. 28–29). These facts created great concern and stimulated interest in improving basic preventive and treatment services and research in the psychiatric area.

In noting the influence of such involvement, we should also point out that psychiatric participation in selective service was less successful than one might have anticipated, given the claims of its advocates. Partly because of the shortage of adequately trained professionals, partly because of the meager development of psychiatric criteria for screening, and partly because of the way selective service was administered under the pressure of manpower requirements, such screening was for the most part a failure (Ginzberg et al. 1959). Deutsch (1949) describes the situation in this way:

> It had been recommended that one psychiatrist be assigned to draft examining boards for every fifty registrants, and that a minimum of fifteen minutes be devoted to every psychiatric examination. When the many millions began to pour through selective service centers, however, these proposals became scraps of paper on the wind. Instead of fifteen minutes, an average of barely two minutes was devoted to the psychiatric examination of Army recruits. It was not unusual for a single psychiatrist to examine 200 men daily. The course of psychiatric screening throughout the war was highly irregular. In

some states and in some centers, men with long mental hospital records were rushed into the armed forces; in many centers, no effort was made to ascertain institutional histories for psychotic episodes; at others, men with histories of very mild emotional disorders were summarily rejected. The pendulum directives swung from one extreme to another during the war; at one period, practically everybody not obviously psychotic was accepted for service; at another, nobody with the slightest trace of neurosis passed the examining board. (Deutsch 1949, p. 463)

It would be totally inappropriate to evaluate the possibilities for psychiatric screening on the basis of the selective service experience. As Deutsch points out, the conditions under which these psychiatric examinations took place were totally unrealistic, and the examinations were frequently performed by general physicians with little or no training in psychiatry. However, one important observation can be gained from this experience, and it has relevance to the present. Selective service officials had a low opinion of psychiatry. When war appeared imminent, they did not give high priority to psychiatric selection. Most of the encouragement for psychiatric screening came from groups within the psychiatric profession, so psychiatrists were in no sense innocent maidens in this affair. Many of the psychiatric recommendations were absurd in light of existing knowledge and the psychiatric manpower situation. The recommendations for psychiatric screening did not show an adequate appreciation of the administrative needs of selective service and the relative priorities given to its goals—the major one was manpower procurement. Later in the war, mechanisms were devised that facilitated psychiatric screening, but the responsibility for the failure of screening must reside largely within the psychiatric profession, which encouraged the entire venture and made unrealistic claims as to what could be achieved.

In current mental health literature, programs that are promoted are commonly unrealistic in terms of manpower, the existing state of psychiatric knowledge, and organizational and community resources. All too often programs are advocated and encouraged without sufficient attention being given to their feasibility or to their consequences for social and political goals outside the realm of mental health. As psychiatry and public policy become increasingly linked, it is necessary that mental health advocates be more responsible in their recommendations and give attention not only to "ideal" psychiatric programs but also to practical ones.

POST–WORLD WAR II DEVELOPMENTS IN MENTAL HEALTH POLICY

World War II not only alerted the country to mental health needs but also provided psychiatry with opportunities to develop programs for psychiatrically disabled soldiers. Although the war brought no breakthroughs in psychiatric knowledge, it did provide individual psychiatrists with broad administrative experience and gave considerable stimulus to attempts to devise new treatment techniques that were feasible in dealing with relatively large groups of patients. If selective service did little to enhance the reputation of psychiatry, the practical response of psychiatrists in the military to very difficult psychiatric problems was impressive. They showed openness to new approaches—not always so obvious in psychiatry—and group techniques were extensively used for the first time. Army psychiatrists also experimented with the use of sedation and hypnosis. The psychiatric problems that commonly occurred alerted psychiatrists, more than ever before, to the social aspects of psychiatric care and to the effects of environment on the occurrence of mental illness. By the time the war ended, psychiatrists had gained many friends and a somewhat more receptive response among their medical colleagues.

The publicity given to psychiatric casualties and the awareness of the large manpower loss as a result of the alleged high prevalence of psychiatric defects in the screened population provided a strong impetus for development of public policy in relation to mental health. The government and informed laymen became aware of the necessity to learn more about the causes of mental illness and the means of preventing it, to assist the individual states in developing their own mental health programs, and to build a satisfactory manpower pool in the mental health area. In 1946 Congress passed the Mental Health Act, creating the National Institute of Mental Health (NIMH). The avowed intent was to have "the traditional public health approach applied to the mental health field." This program did and continues to do much to achieve the goals set for it.

POSTWAR PSYCHIATRY

The emphasis on private psychiatric care encouraged by psychoanalytic theory and practice in the 1950s and 1960s did little to facilitate the care of chronic patients in American mental hospitals, despite the overall improvement in the psychiatric manpower situation (Myers and Bean 1968). The situation improved somewhat in the 1970s, even though mental health care continued to be focused on individual psychotherapy. Many psychiatrists and psychologists continue to devote themselves to treating patients with mild and moderate problems of living. Psychodynamic ideology, which emphasizes analysis of unconscious motivation, discourages interest among many psychiatrists in the more direct and "superficial" techniques of providing support, reassurance, and direction. Unfortunately, most of the professional schools for training mental health professionals attract students and faculty primarily interested in individual psychotherapy and private practice. Even social work and nursing, which have long traditions in practicing with the most needy and disabled, have turned toward individual psychodynamics and attract students with aspirations to be private therapists. Few universities are training professional students in optimal ways to work with the most severely mentally ill, and this area has received little priority in most of our training programs. Professional psychology, which has grown rapidly in recent years, has demonstrated the least interest in the most severely impaired patients.

Although there were significant advances in the United States in manpower development and mental health research following World War II, very little of this gain was transferred to mental hospitals, and direct federal aid to the states for mental health services actually decreased during the Korean War. Although innovations were being developed—most significantly new psychoactive drugs—most states had neither the facilities and financial resources nor the personnel to implement new ideas in the mental health field. The Hoover Commission, looking into the entire issue of government reorganization, reported, "Although we believe that the federal government should gradually reduce its grants as the states take up the load for any given health activity, we conclude that the recent reduction in federal support has been too abrupt" (Hoover Commission 1955, p. 72). The commission noted that aid to the states had been significantly reduced while research support had been developing. Individual states were becoming acutely aware of their personnel and financial limitations at the same time that a tentative optimistic spirit was emerging in the mental health field because of reports of improved release rates with intensive personal care and drug therapies.

Concepts of community care were also developing during this period, stimulated by the interests of state governments reflected in the work of the Governors' Conference beginning in 1949 and the influential conferences on mental health sponsored by the Milbank Memorial Fund (Grob 1987). In 1954, New York State enacted its Community Mental Health Services Act, enabling the development of local mental health boards which could subsidize a range of services including outpatient care with state support for up to half its costs below a ceiling. By 1956, 85 percent of the population were represented by boards participating in the program.

Stimulated by these events and the interests of both the American Psychiatric Association and the American Medical Association for a Joint Commission on Mental Health and Illness, the Congress passed such legislation in 1955 (Grob 1987). When the Mental Health Study Act of 1955 was being considered, government officials no longer believed that large custodial institutions could effectively deal with mental illness. The emphasis on discussion of mental health care in the community was motivated as much by a desire to reduce hospital populations and concomitant costs as by a belief that such measures would have significant therapeutic value. In its deliberations, the Congress gave highest priority to considerations of manpower. The feeling was that already existing therapeutic knowledge could not be applied because of shortages of personnel and facilities. Government officials felt that possible remedial efforts could be increased significantly through the development of psychoactive drugs. In general, however, the experience with new drugs had not progressed to the point where they dominated the thinking of the Congress, and it is likely that the Mental Health Study Act would have been supported in their absence.

The Mental Health Study Act authorized an appropriation to the Joint Commission on Mental Illness and Health to study and make recommendations concerning various aspects of mental health policy. In 1961 the commission published its well-known report, *Action for Mental Health,* which argued strongly for an increased program of services and more funds for basic, long-term mental health research. It recommended that expenditures in the mental health field be doubled in five years and tripled in ten years. It argued for new and better recruitment and training programs for mental health workers. It suggested the expansion of treatment programs for acutely ill patients in all facilities, including community mental health clinics, general hospitals, and mental hospitals. It argued for the establishment of mental health clinics, suggesting one for every 50,000 persons in the population. It attacked the large state mental hospitals and suggested that these be converted to smaller, regional, intensive treatment centers with no more than 1,000 beds. It recommended new programs for the care of chronic patients as well as for after-care and other rehabilitation services. These were wide-ranging and ambitious demands, and they fell on receptive ears in Washington. Many of these recommendations led to action because of abundant funds and moral support from the federal government. The most far-reaching of such legislation was the new program for financing community mental health centers.

The new direction of mental health policies in the United States, however, did not flow directly from the report of the Joint Commission. *Action for Mental Health* was largely an ideological document, and, like poetry, it was sufficiently ambiguous to allow various interest groups to read what they wished into it. It is not surprising that a vigorous political battle at the federal level resulted between those psychiatrists with a public health viewpoint, who wished to develop completely new precedents for mental patient care, and those psychiatrists more within the traditional medical model, who felt that considerable federal assistance should be invested in improving the quality of mental hospitals and their capacities to provide adequate treatment to patients. Those who favored a more radical break with the past system of providing mental health services through state and federal hospitals were more influential with President John Kennedy, and the final decision was to give greatest impetus to community health centers, not mental health clinics as recommended by Joint Commission, which were to be independent of the old mental hospital system, although affiliated with it. This was a tremendously important decision and one that endorsed the viewpoint that mental illness is not inherently different from the larger range of psychological difficulties common in the community.

The implementation of the Joint Commission recommendations required more than the suggestions themselves. First, the American economy was in an excellent position, and abundant funds were available for meeting domestic needs. Second, the president himself was very much committed to the program in mental health and mental retardation, and, in contrast to some other proposed medical care programs, the mental health program did not involve any obvious group or value cleavages. Third, psychiatric drugs had changed the climate of mental health care as well as administrative attitudes, and the value of supporting mental health services seemed to be more obvious to laymen. Finally, the harmful consequences of the custodial-hospital environment had been poignantly demonstrated, and society had become increasingly aware of the unequal access to good psychiatric treatment for the rich and the poor.

The ideas of the Joint Commission were hardly new. In 1914 the Massachusetts State Board of Insanity recommended that "each hospital reach out in the community and be responsible for the mental health of the district covered by each" and advocated outpatient departments dealing with after-care, family care, and mental hygiene. These departments would take on such functions as working with discharged patients, boarding patients in foster families, and educating the public to prevent insanity (Grob 1966, p. 350). What made the report of the Joint Commission so important was not the uniqueness of its recommendations but rather the receptive climate into which they were introduced. It is possible that any reasonable set of recommendations would have been acceptable given the timing, circumstances, and mood of the people in government.

In the 1960s expenditures increased for mental health professional training, mental health services, and construction and staffing of new community mental health centers. During this period of optimism, large numbers of mental patients were released from hospitals into the community without adequate preparation, a network of appropriate services, or consideration of the social costs. Such deinstitutionalization was consistent with economic pressures on state government. Costs of caring for discharged patients could be transferred from state mental health budgets to federally subsidized programs, such as welfare and Medicaid (Scull 1977). These trends were supported by a naive optimism and ideology that the community was good and the hospital was bad. During the 1960s mental health professionals made claims of expertise that had little basis in reality. Associated with the new public health framework was a simplistic view of prevention of mental disorder, a broad increase in the boundaries of mental health concepts, and a naive political stance concerning the functions of community psychiatry in public decision making. Although the envisioned increased numbers of mental health centers, community programs, and new mental health personnel never fully materialized, the range of providers, services offered, and clients increased substantially.

The new Community Mental Health Centers (CMHCs) were to be the key to the new public health approach. Initially they were to have five essential services: inpatient care, emergency care, partial hospitalization, outpatient care, and education and consultation. In addition they were mandated to develop a continuum of care through linkages among the required services. Other services, such as pre-admission and post-discharge services for hospitalized patients, and specialized diagnostic services, were suggested but not required. As time went on the CMHCs were at the center of the debates about the nature of mental illness, and the mandated services had expanded to twelve including specialized services for children and the elderly, alcohol and drug abuse services, and followup care and transitional services for the chronically ill. The range of services grew, but a clear sense of priorities never emerged. By 1977, 650 CMHCs served almost two million people and were accessible to 43 per cent of the population (Foley and Sharfstein 1983), but the system was in peril because of the turbulent social and mental health politics of the day. Facing many competing expectations and demands, they had difficulty following a clear strategy.

The Vietnam war, its aftermath, and the disillusion with the programs of the "Great Society" resulted in the curtailment of funds for mental health programs. The Nixon years were a hostile time for mental health issues. Not only was the administration unsympathetic to mental health concerns, but existing programs for mental health centers, research, research training, and professional manpower development were phased down or out or allowed to erode with inflation. There were serious criticisms of some of these programs. It was evident that many, if not most, of the mental health centers were concentrating their efforts on ordinary problems of living rather than dealing with hard-core chronic mental patients (Chu and Trotter 1974). Massive deinstitutionalization revealed the poor planning for release of patients into the community and the inadequacy of continuing supervision and treatment. In some areas there was a backlash of community criticism of mental health policies.

It was clear by the late 1970s that the climate in which new initiatives had flourished had changed radically. It was a time for consolidation and reassessment. Despite the excesses, exaggerated claims, and naive expectations in the 1960s, much progress was evident. Outpatient care and the use of psychiatric services increased dramatically. A great shift away from public mental hospitals took place, with more acute psychiatric illness being treated in general hospitals and outpatient clinics. Behavioral techniques for treating many types of problems were commonly adopted, and treatment of disorders became more focused and diversified, breaking away from the chains of a psychoanalytic dogmatism. A vigorous civil liberties movement developed on behalf of mental patients, and patients' rights in civil commitment procedures and in other areas of care were substantially clarified and strengthened. Many patients in need were recognized and treated more quickly in the community, preventing some of the secondary disabilities associated with earlier treatment modes. Understanding of new psychoactive drugs and their adverse effects increased, allowing more sophisticated pharmacological therapy. Private and nonprofit insurance companies providing medical coverage substantially increased the scope of inpatient psychiatric benefits, and many expanded outpatient coverage as well. When all was said and done, these were no small achievements.

In the late 1960s and early 1970s, the executive branch and Congress became increasingly concerned about such problems as alcoholism and drug abuse. As funds were more limited, traditional mental health monies were tapped to launch new national efforts in these areas. Within the mental health sphere, new political constituencies developed to deal with alcohol and drug abuse problems, but what eventually emerged and still continues was an umbrella agency known by the acronym ADAMHA (the Alcohol, Drug Abuse, and Mental Health Administration) incorporating the National Institute of Mental Health (NIMH), the National Institute on Alcohol Abuse and Alcoholism (NIAAA), and the National Institute on Drug Abuse (NIDA). These agencies initially had responsibility for a variety of service programs, demonstrations, research efforts, and research and professional training programs, and they were also involved in planning and public education. ADAMHA programs were under considerable attack during the Nixon years, and the administration and the Congress were locked in battle during this period as Nixon tried to reduce and dismantle many of the programs associated with Presidents Kennedy and Johnson. By 1977, the federal government had only funded 650 of the proposed 1,500 community mental health centers at a cost of $1.5 billion, but the administration had already lost interest in continuing the program. It also was increasingly evident that these centers were not serving the most severely ill patients, but this was not the source of the administration's opposition. In any case, after the interlude of the Carter presidency, the scope and responsibility of the ADAMHA agencies were substantially reduced when the mental health center funds and other service programs were included in block grants to the states in the Reagan years. These agencies are now most fundamentally research funding agencies, and the debate continues as to whether the NIMH should be attached to the National Institutes of Health, our national health research agency.

By 1976, when Carter became president, the mental health federal programs were showing the effects of the hostility evident in the Nixon years. Also, the core concerns had changed since the social programs of the 1960s. The problems of deinstitutionalization were clearly evident and the need to develop community services for the most chronically disabled patients highly salient. Developing accessible and comprehensive community care is expensive, and the hopes that the nation, in the near future, would develop a universal system of national health insurance that protected the mentally ill were already fading in the face of medical cost inflation. There was, thus, much concern with the appropriate role of the federal government and with ways of garnering funds from various federal, state, and local programs to provide stable funding for essential community networks of care. Realizing that much depended on reimbursement possibilities, careful examination was directed to possible funding streams.

With improved epidemiological data and a renewed concern with primary medical care, there was recognition that many patients in need of mental health care are not found in psychiatric settings but in the context of general medical care. Attention was now focused on the improvement of the general physicians' recognition and management of psychiatric disorder, the availability of psychiatric consultation to general physicians, and the improvement of referral practices. Several experiments or demonstrations involving a closer integration between general medical and psychiatric services suggested that such management reduced medical utilization (Follette and Cummings 1967, Cummings and Follette 1968, Patrick et al. 1978).

In February 1977, President Carter established a Presidential Commission on Mental Health to review the mental health needs of the nation and to make recommendations. This effort, like most such commissions, was highly politicized but offered a unique opportunity because Mrs. Carter had a special interest in mental health and served as honorary chairperson of the commission. The commission made its report in 1978, addressing such issues as the organization of community services, community supports, financing, personnel, legal rights, research, prevention, and public understanding. The report argued for greater investment in mental health services, noting that although the mental health problem was one of the largest in terms of numbers of persons involved and suffering, it received only 12 percent of general health expenditures. It noted the acute need to develop community-based services, to make them financially, geographically, and socially accessible, and to make them flexible so as to serve the needs of varying social and racial groups. It argued strongly for further support for research and training, for attention to chronic mental illness, and for meeting the special needs of children, adolescents, and the elderly.

The 1978 commission, unlike its predecessor, reported in a more difficult and complex climate. Inflation was a prime concern, and health care cost increases raced ahead much faster than the economy as a whole. Government expenditures in health were already high and largely uncontrollable in part as a result of the structure of the Medicare and Medicaid programs. Policy makers appeared reluctant to make large new investments in health care initiatives, and during times of financial stringency the "haves" are reluctant to yield any ground to new areas.

Unlike the earlier initiatives of the 1960s, the commission functioned in an atmosphere of much greater fiscal constraints and with many more well-developed constituencies anxious to protect their interests. As a consequence, the report is quite general, advocates a broad array of conflicting ideas, endorses most mental health interests, and fails to face the tough question of financial priorities. Thus, it provided no clear direction among competing constituencies and may have contributed to the nasty infighting that followed in its wake about how to design appropriate legislation. As the coordinator of the President's Commission's Task Panel on the Nature and Scope of the Problems, I was clear on the difficulty of the political task of balancing competing interests, but I would have preferred a more direct course of focusing on the needs of the most severely ill. While these received much attention, other vague concepts such as prevention received equal play. In endorsing everything, the report offered no clear course of action, but it brought together a great deal of information that could serve as a vehicle for advocacy, particularly the influence of Rosalynn Carter.

The process of drafting the Mental Health Systems Act was long and tortuous, reflecting the conflicting interests involved, the competition with other Carter initiatives, and the growing fiscal constraints. After numerous efforts, a bill was presented to the Congress, which was then substantially modified in an effort to satisfy some of the strongly opposing groups that had a stake and to reach an acceptable consensus. The process reflected the difficult competing ideologies that persist in the mental health sector: those that favor comprehensive approaches versus those that focus on categorical groups; the desire of community mental health centers to retain their autonomy versus the concern of the states to hold them accountable; the concern to ensure treatment to disturbed persons in community settings versus the rights of patients to refuse care; and the goal to have the dollars follow the patient versus the concerns of hospital employees unions (AFSCME) to protect their members, etc. (Foley and Sharfstein 1983). The act was signed into law by President Carter in October, 1980.

While the legislation was being developed, the Department of Health and Human Services, at the recommendation of the President's Commission, was hard at work developing an integrated federal strategy to ensure an appropriate response to dealing with the multifaceted problems of the chronically mentally ill. This was a far-ranging effort that examined the epidemiology of severe mental illness, the range of psychiatric, medical, rehabilitative, housing, and social services available and needed, issues of personnel and recruitment, and financing reforms. The report recognized the critical importance of Medicaid, Social Security Disability Insurance, and many other federal programs, and presented an incremental approach to modifying them in a constructive way (U.S. Department of Health and Human Services 1980). The report was actually completed before the passage of the Systems Act but serves as an important analytic rationale for designing an effective national system.

The story ends sadly when the Reagan Administration, which took office one month after the passage of the act, chose not to implement it and instead began dismantling the building blocks of a national system through its "new federalism" initiative. The bulk of the federal mental health services monies, as well as funds from many other health and social programs, were returned to the states in block grants but with cuts in funding levels. Other federal programs on which the mentally ill depend lost ground or were cut back, including Medicaid, housing subsidies, and social services. Large numbers of chronically mentally ill were dropped from disability insurance by the Social Security·Administration during the disability reviews in 1980 and 1981, but with the intervention of many advocates and the federal courts, many were reinstated. The more difficult access to housing and income benefits is believed to have contributed to the enlarged population of homeless mentally ill found in every major American city.

The Reagan program that sought to reduce direct federal operation of health programs involved both a very different philosophical orientation than the Systems Act and less willingness to support expenditures for social programs. The reduction in funding made it extraordinarily difficult to maintain services, but the ideology about giving states more authority to direct mental health services within their jurisdictions had some clear merits. The federal initiatives of the 1960s typically bypassed state authority on the theory that states that had a stake in traditional mental health care were impediments to reform. Federal officials interacted directly with local service delivery systems with little involvement of state officials or concern for state priorities. Much of the hostility in negotiations of the Systems Act was a reaction to the earlier insensitivity of the federal government to state interests. And, in retrospect, it seems that the approach of the federal government contributed to the low priority given by the community mental health centers to chronic patients.

As a consequence of the changes since 1980, the federal role in providing leadership in mental health care has diminished, and the mental health policy debate has clearly shifted to the state and local arena. The National Institute of Mental Health is a much-diminished agency in policy formulation and implementation and has primarily research responsibilities. There is no early prospect in the face of the federal deficit of large new infusions of funds from the federal sector, nor is there much evidence of the willingness of most states and localities to take up the slack. Attention has shifted to ways of using existing resources in the mental health system more creatively and efficiently and obtaining entitlements to which the severely mentally ill are eligible under law. In the 1970s the mental health system came close to significantly reforming systems of services, but much of the momentum was lost in the face of economic and political change. It is inevitable that new opportunities will arise again in future years; it is essential to be well prepared to effectively take advantage of these as they occur. Much of this book speaks to this point.

THE ORGANIZATION OF STATE MENTAL HOSPITALS

Most state mental hospitals were built in the later part of the nineteenth and early part of the twentieth centuries. Many were either developed or enlarged in response to the crusade of Dorothea Dix; their construction constituted the first attempt in many areas of the country to provide attention to persons of limited resources who were mentally ill. As we learn more about the history of mental hospitals, we discover the extent of heterogeneity and the difficulty of generalization. But as the population aged and patterns of disease changed in an increasingly urbanized society, most hospitals were faced with growing numbers of chronic patients with irreversible problems who overwhelmed staff resources and gave these institutions a custodial and often harsh atmosphere. As chronic patients came to comprise an increasing proportion of the mental hospital caseload, psychiatrists shifted their work to other settings, and there was a considerable feeling of hopelessness about constructive treatment in the mental hospital. These and other influences resulted in giving mental hospitals low priority in public perceptions and financial support. This situation persisted well into the present century despite several attempts to humanize the mental hospital.

The first major humanizing influence on mental hospitals in the twentieth century was the Mental Hygiene Movement. Begun in 1908 by Clifford Beers, a former mental patient who exposed the dehumanizing aspects of mental patient care, this movement encouraged a new, humanistic ideology that stimulated some improvement in hospital conditions and public concern for the mentally ill. It did little, however, to retard the pattern of providing for the mentally ill in large and impersonal public institutions. Despite the efforts and concern of many reformers, mental hospitals maintained a custodial attitude reinforced by meager allowances for the care of psychiatric patients, limited professional staff, and dependence on untrained and unskilled manpower.

One of the most important innovations in mental patient care has been the use of psychoactive drugs, first introduced in the middle 1950s. Although these drugs do not cure patients, they do much to reduce their most disturbing symptoms; they facilitate the control of mental patients and the ability of hospital personnel to work with them. The use of drugs gave staff greater confidence in its own efficacy and helped dispel the feelings of hopelessness and apathy that had captured the mental hospital. Administrative changes were instituted, such as eliminating constraints, minimizing security arrangements, and encouraging early release. Patients under drug treatment were more tractable and cooperative, and receptivity to mental patients returning to the community increased. Finally, the feeling of hope and efficacy felt by the hospital staff was communicated to patients and the community generally and gave both renewed confidence in the ability of patients to cope with difficulties outside the hospital.

Evidence supports the contention that changes in patient retention and release patterns following the introduction of psychoactive drugs were as much the result of administrative changes in mental hospitals as they were the consequence of the drugs themselves. Some studies in English hospitals that introduced new administrative policies prior to the introduction of psychoactive drugs show that new patterns of release were observable prior to drug introduction, and they suggest that the tremendous change that took place is largely a result of alterations in administrative policies (Brown et al. 1966, Bockoven 1972, Scull 1977). Whatever the specific utility of the psychoactive drugs, the development of this new technology supported a climate of opinion and confidence making it possible to change important policies relating to patient handling and release. Whether directly or indirectly, drugs helped bring about a revolution in psychiatric care.

Despite the widespread introduction of neuroleptic drugs in the middle 1950s, many problems remained, including issues of suitable housing, subsistence, and the need to change community attitudes. It is widely assumed that deinstitutionalization began with a vengeance in 1955, the point at which inpatients in public mental hospitals reached their peak. In fact, the timing of deinstitutionalization varied greatly by state, and for the nation as a whole the pace was relatively slow, only 1.5 percent a year between 1955 and 1965 (Gronfein 1985).

Large-scale deinstitutionalization did not come until the middle 1960s, in combination with a number of changes that addressed issues of community attitudes and subsistence. Attitude change involved three strong ideological thrusts. The 1960s were a period of civil rights activity and advocacy. The young lawyers and activists for the civil liberties of the mentally ill came out of the civil rights movement and involvement with public interest law. Civil commitment was characterized by substantial abuses and was a visible target for their efforts (Ennis 1972, Miller 1976). In these initiatives they were influenced by the social science literature on the adverse effects of custodial mental hospitals and abuses of psychiatry (Goffman 1961, Szasz 1963, Wing and Brown 1970). This work provided both the ideology and much of the substance to justify an attack on involuntary hospitalization. A third aspect was psychodynamic conceptions of mental illness that were increasingly accepted in the scientific literature, the mass media, and public conceptions. Mental illness was commonly portrayed as a single continuum from mild to severe, a product substantially of sociocultural and psychosocial factors (Caplan 1964, Leighton 1967). Within this dominant ideology of environmental causation, it followed that bringing more benign influence to bear on the mentally ill would ameliorate their level of disturbance. That major mental disorders might be fundamentally different from common distress syndromes, or that poor community environments could have the same negative effects as poor hospital environments, were not considered seriously. The result was a strong anti-hospital ideology.

To successfully remove disabled people from hospitals required places for relocation, and it was not until the rapid expansion of welfare programs in the 1960s that the means became widely available. Medicare stimulated a dramatic growth of nursing home beds, and Medicaid financed the cost of nursing home residence. This not only gave the states an opportunity to transfer elderly mentally ill and demented patients receiving custodial care in hospitals to an alternative institution but also allowed transfer of significant state costs to the federal budget. The expansion of Social Security Disability Income (SSDI) in those years and the introduction of Supplemental Security Income (SSI) for those without the required work history for disability eligibility provided much of the financial support necessary to return impaired patients to a variety of community settings including families, board and care facilities, and single occupancy housing. Between 1966 and 1980 the yearly rate of deinstitutionalization averaged 6 percent. It could not have been achieved without the expansion of welfare programs.

Statistics on patients resident in mental hospitals reflect the vast changes that took place. As 1955 ended, 558,922 patients were residents in mental hospitals, but the following years show a considerable decrease in this figure. Although the number of admissions to mental hospitals rose substantially between 1955 and 1971, by the latter year, only 308,983 patients were resident in mental hospitals (President's Commission, 1978, Vol II, p. 94). Admissions dropped somewhat following 1971, and the number of resident patients continued to fall, reaching 215,573 in 1974. By the mid-1980s, inpatients in public mental hospitals fell to almost 115,000, and general hospitals had become the major site of acute psychiatric care. In 1983, there were almost three times as many admissions to general hospitals as to state mental hospitals (National Institute of Mental Health 1987b).

As a consequence of reductions in the populations of public mental hospitals and the transfer of many hopeless chronic patients to nursing homes, the public mental hospital was in many instances transformed from a custodial institution to an active treatment unit. It is, of course, difficult to describe conditions in the United States because each state maintains its own mental health system and there is great diversity in the availability of facilities, funding patterns, and relative emphasis put on different aspects of care. But overall, the professional : patient and staff : patient ratios improved enormously, and active treatment and rehabilitation programs were developed to a point where, in many instances, there was little resemblance between the hospital as it had once been and as it is now.

Despite these favorable changes, mental hospitals continue to be plagued by many of the problems and conditions that preceded these administrative and therapeutic advances. Some hospitals are still large; managing such institutions often demands organizational routines that are dehumanizing and that interfere with an individualized approach to the patient. Many patients still have very limited individual contact with professional staff, and it remains difficult to recruit well-trained psychiatrists to such institutions. Because the less severely ill are filtered off to community programs, and those more affluent and those with insurance use community hospitals, patient populations in these hospitals tend to be more chronic and more difficult to rehabilitate. Hospitals are increasingly concerned with legal issues, requiring more time for record keeping and documentation as compared with patient care. But perhaps most important is that the hospital is a poor training ground for teaching patients some degree of independence and the coping skills necessary to make a satisfactory adjustment to the community.

The statistics on the reduction of mental hospital populations, however, are somewhat misleading. Many mental patients formerly in mental hospitals have been transferred to nursing homes that may offer no active treatment and often a poorer environment than the mental hospital (Stotsky 1970, Vladeck 1980, Linn 1985). Others live in group homes, sheltered care situations, and isolated rooming houses that vary a great deal in the quality of environment, supervision, and social contact with others (Allen 1974, Segal and Aviram 1978, Lamb 1979). Still other patients are treated in general hospitals that may provide unimaginative programs based on a traditional medical model, and some are simply "dumped" in inadequate community housing in transitional housing areas with little support or assistance and are left to be victimized by criminal elements. Although deinstitutionalization has brought improved lives for many patients, residence in the community is no panacea, and it is necessary to look behind the label to assess the quality of life patients actually live in these varying contexts.

PROGRAMS OF COMMUNITY CARE

Many of the added activities that have been supported by public investment in the mental health field have been in the area of community care. The community care ideology developed from the growing realization that the mental hospital as it existed often did much to isolate patients from the community, to undermine their motivation to return, to retard skills, and, in general, to induce a level of disability above and beyond that resulting from the patient's condition. As noted earlier, the report of the Joint Commission attacked the large mental hospitals and advocated their abolition. The commission supported smaller mental hospitals providing intensive care, treatment units in general hospitals, and mental health clinics. These facilities were to be close to the patients' homes and were to keep them in touch with their families and the community. The new emphasis was on outpatient care and short periods of hospitalization when necessary. Additional alternatives were urged that fell somewhere between the total separation characterized by the mental hospital isolated from the community and outpatient care, such as day hospitals, night hospitals, halfway houses, and hostels. An understanding of the importance of maintaining patients' skills and sense of activity led to added emphasis on vocational services, sheltered workshops, and continuing employment while the patient was in the hospital. Finally, great emphasis has been given to the idea that patients should be kept in their home surroundings and that the necessary services should be provided to them and their families so that they can cope with the problems that arise.

Ideologies develop more rapidly than patterns of care, and although it was not terribly difficult to change hospital policies concerning admission and retention, there are additional obstacles in providing a system of community services that can support and buttress new hospital policies so as to ensure adequate benefits for patients. While the ideology is coherent, the services provided to patients in the community are sporadic and fragmentary, and frequently the burden that had been the hospital's has been shifted to the family. Yet in most parts of the country, no system of services aids the family in meeting crises or in dealing with the patient and the problems of care effectively. Indeed, many new initiatives are now being directed toward these ends.

THE COMPOSITION OF THE SERIOUSLY MENTALLY ILL POPULATION

Deinstitutionalization has been a rallying cry for those advocating community care and a target of their critics. Because the term is used imprecisely and is not clearly tied to particular patient populations or relocation sites (Bachrach 1976), it has little empirical utility. Deinstitutionalization is viewed as a source of many current problems and has a certain currency in the ideological debate, but the debate is more a source of heat than light.

Even prior to 1955, most inpatients in public mental hospitals returned to the community. In any given year, the net releases and deaths— the typical way of tracking inpatient occupancy—almost equaled the rate of new admissions. In 1950, for example, there were 152,000 admissions, 100,000 releases, and 41,000 deaths. The longer a patient remained in the hospital, the less the likelihood of release, but a significant proportion of new admissions returned to the community within a few months. Beginning in 1956, net releases and deaths exceeded new admissions but only by 7,952 individuals. It wasn't until 1970 that net releases (excluding deaths) actually exceeded the number of new admissions during the year (President's Commission on Mental Health 1978). Moreover, in any given year, the vast majority of patients leaving were those who were admitted relatively recently.

These simple data indicate that the deinstitutionalized population is a heterogeneous collection of varying patient cohorts (for a discussion of cohorts, see Ryder 1965). Many would have been returned to the community in the absence of policy change, and common references to the deinstitutionalized seem to refer to clients who have never been part of the long-term mental hospital population at all.

Public mental hospital populations were reduced by deaths, return of a residual group of long-term care patients to nursing homes or other community settings, substantial reduction of the average length of stay among newly admitted patients (median 23 days in 1980), and more stringent admission criteria. Of public hospital patients resident in 1955, a large proportion either have since died or have been relocated to nursing homes. Goldman, Feder, and Scanlon (1986) estimate that some 668,000 nursing home patients in 1977 had diagnoses of mental illness or dementia. This population includes transfers from mental hospitals, but most probably came to nursing homes directly from the community. Kiesler and Sibulkin (1987) estimate that as many as half of the elderly discharged from mental hospitals in the post-1964 years came to nursing homes. Nursing homes played a significant role for relocation of the elderly mentally ill but a small role for younger patients. In 1977, only about 5,500 patients under age 45 and primarily with mental illness were residing in nursing homes (Goldman, Feder, and Scanlon 1986).

The public discussion appears often to refer to the original hospitalized cohorts, but in fact the populations that alarm the community are later cohorts and mostly younger schizophrenics and substance abusers, most of whom have never been long-stay inpatients and some of whom have never had a psychiatric admission at all. As mental health services organization has changed, acute psychoses are treated typically with short inpatient admissions in community general hospitals and in reconstituted public mental hospitals. Most such patients have had entirely different histories with the mental health services system than earlier cohorts. Only some proportion of these patients would have been long-term residents of mental hospitals in an earlier era.

The amount of serious mental illness in the population, with schizophrenia as the prototype, depends on both the rate of incidence and the size of the population at risk. Much of the increasingly evident problem of serious mental illness in the community is not due to deinstitutionalization or even to changes in the way psychiatric hospitalization is used, but more to shifts in the demography of the population with large subgroups at ages with highest risk of incidence. Morton Kramer (1977) predicted these problems more than a decade ago simply by projecting demographic trends. The misattribution of the source of changes to deinstitutionalization, vaguely defined, encourages serious errors in policy making. Unless the society were prepared to maintain a massive public hospital system or alternative institutions for new occurrences of mental illness, the problem would have been evident in communities regardless of what we did.

Long-term care in aging provides an analogy. The demand for services is substantially a product of the growth of the elderly population, the increased prevalence of the oldest-old subgroup with high risks of functional disability, and the delay of mortality. Despite having enormously increased nursing home beds at large national expense, providing for 1.5 million residents, the numbers of disabled elderly in the community far outnumber those in nursing homes. Except for those most incapacitated, there is no real alternative to community care. A similar logic pertains to the criminal justice system. As the subgroups of youth at high risk of criminal activity and arrest in the population swelled, we substantially increased prison capacity. However, such capacity could not keep up with the increase in offenders, and in many localities only the most serious and persistent offenders are jailed, and many convicts are released early because of prison overcrowding.

A population of major concern to the mental health system, and to the community, are young schizophrenics and other seriously disturbed youths, who are aware of their civil liberties and hostile or indifferent to psychiatric ideologies. They are frequently uncooperative with the types of treatment made available to them, and their mental illnesses are commonly complicated by abuse of drugs and alcohol. They mix with other street people, constitute a significant minority of the homeless population, and at various points in their life trajectories are hospitalized, jailed, or live on the streets (Lamb and Grant 1982, Lamb 1984). The problems are compounded by the fact that the age groups at highest risk have increasing numbers of minority and disadvantaged youth that connect the stigma of mental illness with the social difficulties associated with color and disadvantage. This population poses difficult problems of appropriate treatment and requires approaches for establishing contact and trust that are very different from the conventional office-based mental health services. Blaming deinstitutionalization for these problems is wrongheaded since most of these patients are not appropriate clients for long-term institutional care. The barriers to designing acceptable care are not constructively addressed by simple distinctions between hospital versus community services. In contrast, they will depend on carefully developed strategies of community care.

The resistance of many young schizophrenics to traditional psychiatric treatment is not too difficult to appreciate. In addition to the general cultural values and ideologies they have assimilated, they are also typically better educated than earlier cohorts and have hopes and aspirations, however unrealistic they may be, that have been reinforced by television and other mass media and by the broader culture. Many of these youth are undergoing the typical developmental problems of late adolescence and early adulthood in addition to their impairments. It is not easy for them to accept that they have perhaps a lifelong impairment, that they require long-term medication, and that they must yield many of their hopes and expectations for the future. The denial and resistance characteristic of this situation requires mental health workers to engage in much building of trust and to approach these clients in a supportive and patient way.

HOMELESSNESS AND MENTAL ILLNESS

There have always been homeless people in large urban areas in this country, but not since the years immediately following the Great Depression has homelessness been so visible (Bassuk 1984a,b). Estimates of the number of homeless individuals in the United States have ranged from 350,000 to 3 million (U.S. Department of Housing and Urban Development (HUD) 1984, U.S. General Accounting Office 1985). However, recent attempts to systematically estimate the size of the homeless population have led to estimates close to HUD's estimates of 350,000 (Freeman and Hall 1986, Rossi et al. 1987).

The determinants of homelessness are not well understood, nor is there agreement on its permanence. The diminishing supply of low-cost housing in many cities is a contributing factor. In addition, general assistance payments and welfare stipends in most states have not kept pace with inflation, which, in combination with rising housing costs, has severely reduced the ability of low-income individuals and families to obtain housing. A third factor commonly believed to be associated with homelessness is physical and psychiatric disability. Thus, homeless people have a complex and interrelated array of problems and needs that are both medical and social in nature (Bassuk 1984a,b, U.S. General Accounting Office 1985).

In a recent study of the homeless in Chicago, more than one in three homeless people reported themselves in ill health, a rate twice as high as that found in general population surveys (Rossi and Wright 1987). More than one in four reported having a health problem that prevented their employment. Mental illness and psychiatric symptoms were major sources of disability. Almost one in four Chicago homeless reported having been in a mental hospital for stays of over 48 hours. Nearly half of the Chicago homeless exhibited levels of depression that suggested a need for clinical attention. Contacts with the criminal justice system, suggesting perhaps another kind of disability, were frequent. The cumulative incidence of these disabilities was very large, with 82 percent of the homeless reporting ill health, having been in a mental hospital or detoxification unit, having received clinically high scores on psychiatric symptom scales, or having been sentenced by a court (Rossi et al. 1987).

The Robert Wood Johnson Foundation's 19-city Health Care for the Homeless Program provides the only large data set on the health problems of the homeless (Wright 1987), with data available at the time of this writing on 118,098 clinic encounters with 42,539 homeless people. The program provides medical and social services to homeless persons without charge in clinics located in shelters, soup kitchens, and single room occupancy hotels. The demographic profile of patients cared for in these special clinics is similar to that found among the homeless nationally (Bassuk 1984a,b, Freeman and Hall 1986, Rossi et al. 1987). About one-third were homeless women; approximately 40 percent had dependent children. Over half were nonwhites. The median age was 33 years. A tenth of all patients seen in the clinics were age 15 and under.

The most frequent health problem of the homeless in the 19 cities was alcohol abuse, followed by mental illness. Approximately 38 percent of the homeless had an alcohol-related problem, and one-third had serious psychiatric symptoms and/or a history of mental illness. These estimates are roughly similar to other studies of the homeless population (Bassuk 1984a,b, Lamb 1984).

The homeless face major barriers in obtaining medical care despite their very high levels of need. Only a minority have medical insurance, Medicaid in most cases. The available evidence suggests that a substantial share of the homeless would be eligible for general assistance or could meet Social Security criteria for disability, and thus be entitled to Medicaid, Supplemental Security Income (SSI), and subsidized housing. However, actual proportions of homeless people who have these entitlements are much lower than would be expected. Recent legislation has removed some barriers to obtaining entitlements, such as the requirement of an address for receipt of SSI monthly payments. However, the process of applying for disability is a long and arduous one, and few homeless people have the persistence and the necessary help from others to follow the process through to its conclusion.

Being poor without health insurance makes access to medical care difficult (Blendon et al. 1986). The homeless must rely, in large part, on charity care provided by public hospitals and clinics. However, many of the homeless fear or reject large institutions and, except in emergencies, will not go there for medical care. They often lack transportation money to reach a centralized location. Also, the homeless are not perceived by health providers to be desirable clients. They often appear disheveled and some-times display bizarre or unusual behavior. Often their problems are not those health providers like to manage, i.e., alcoholism, mental illness, and drug abuse. Compliance with medical advice among this patient group is often low, which discourages health professionals. Thus, the barriers to access to appropriate health care for the homeless are numerous, multi-faceted, and difficult to remedy.

■   ■   ■   ■   ■

This section of our discussion has been descriptive, and although we have reviewed some of the historical elements in the evolution of mental health policy in relation to mental health services, we have not examined the issues and dilemmas that various program alternatives raise. In Chapter 8 we shall turn to such issues and explore in detail the consequences—both intended and unintended—of pursuing particular policies. Before doing this, however, we must explore in greater detail the community processes leading to definitions of mental illness and some theoretical approaches to appropriate community care.

Chapter Six

The Recognition of Mental Disorders

The extent to which mental illness is seen to exist depends on the perspectives taken and the criteria used to identify its presence. In this area it is not too difficult to play a numbers game that either maximizes or minimizes the amount of alleged mental illness by changing the criteria used. If mental illness is viewed as the presence of a clearly established disabling condition, then the estimate of its occurrence is conservative. However, if mental illness is defined as the presence of psychosomatic conditions, anxiety, or any of a wide variety of problems in living, then we can characterize a large proportion of the population as having some form of mental illness.

An early study of midtown Manhattan (Srole et al. 1962) estimated that approximately one-quarter of the more than 1,600 respondents between 20 and 59 years of age were impaired. It evaluated only 18.5 percent of the total respondent group as being healthy. Other studies have made similar observations (see Leighton et al. 1963). In a study of the prevalence of mental disorders in Kalamazoo County, Michigan (Manis et al. 1964), in which various data comparable to those collected in midtown Manhattan were obtained, the investigators demonstrated that the rates of mental illness in midtown Manhattan were not very different from those in the community they studied but were inflated by the different criteria used.

> Our interpretation is that the differences in reported rates of untreated illness arise *primarily* from lack of agreement, stated or implicit, in the criteria used to establish the cutting-point between the sick and the well. The criterion

used in the Kalamazoo community study appears to identify only the extremely ill and to underestimate total prevalence. The Baltimore procedures seem to focus on a more broadly conceived spectrum to mental illness, though they, too, admit some underestimation. The rates reported for Midtown Manhattan are apparently the consequence of a very inclusive conception of mental illness. (Manis et al. 1964 p. 89)

Plunkett and Gordon (1960), reviewing prevalence studies undertaken prior to 1960, note that percentages of the population found to be mentally ill range from less than 2 percent to as much as 33 percent (pp. 62–68). With the inadequacies of the measures used in various surveys and field studies, it seems reasonable to use such indices primarily for assessing relative differences among population groups rather than to treat the absolute levels of disorder reported as meaningful assessments (Davis 1965).

Bruce and Barbara Dohrenwend (1969) clearly illustrated the unreliability of various absolute estimates of psychiatric illness. In reviewing 25 studies of untreated cases of psychological disorder, they found that prevalence rates varied from less than 1 percent to over 60 percent of the population. Comparing epidemiological studies carried out in 1950 or earlier with those done after 1950, they found widely varying rates of pathology. The median rate in the studies after 1950 was more than seven times the one reported for the earlier studies. Because it is inconceivable that population rates have changed so radically, it is clear that these estimates reflect something other than traditionally defined psychiatric syndromes. As suggested in Chapter 3, some of the reported disability may reflect an illness behavior pattern characterized by a high level of self-awareness and a focus on bodily concerns.

By considering limited categories of mental illness, one can increase the possibility of making some reasonable estimate of morbidity. Investigators in different countries, using relatively narrow concepts of schizophrenia, agree that the prevalence of active cases varies from approximately one-quarter to 1 percent of the population (J. K. Wing 1967, L. Wing et al. 1967, National Institute of Mental Health 1985). As the concept expands, of course, the prevalence rate increases. As noted in Chapter 3, estimates range from 0.25 to 3 percent. From the point of view of public policy, questions concerning the prevalence of mental illness must be linked to decisions concerning the appropriate range of facilities that should be provided. Once we have some conception of which conditions it is reasonable to treat, we can estimate the extent of the problem we have to deal with.

Planning for psychiatric services is not vastly different from planning for general medical services. If we wish to improve the facilities available for dealing with a variety of diseases for which medical care is important, and we require estimates of community needs, we do not survey the population to determine the prevalence of common self-limited complaints. Similarly, in deciding the magnitude of psychiatric need in the population, we must not confuse the psychiatric conditions causing profound distress and disability with the prevalence of mild difficulties and mild psychophysiological complaints. I do not wish to imply that help should not be available to those who have mild difficulties, but, just as we do not confuse the common cold with heart disease, so should we not confuse psychoses or severe neurotic problems with common complaints. Estimates of the proportion of the population who are neurotic range from as little as less than five in 100 to very large proportions of the total population. Some psychiatrists who advocate a dynamic perspective go as far as to argue that everyone in the population is neurotic and that we could all benefit from a better understanding of our intrapsychic needs and repressed desires. Although such a point of view may have some value as a philosophical statement, the absence of criteria for discriminating among those more or less needy makes such positions irrelevant in the development of public policy.

In considering the issue of need, we should not be confused by the distinction between neurosis and psychosis. Although these terms—as they are used in a general sense—connote gradations of severity of illness, specific neurotic conditions cause profound distress, are incapacitating, and are amenable to effective care. It is irresponsible to confuse such conditions with those that do not cause severe discomfort, do not prevent persons from performing their social roles reasonably, and do not respond in any clear way to psychiatric intervention. While some neurotic conditions require intensive and sophisticated care and are sufficiently serious to require public policy interests, other conditions similarly labeled are trivial and are unworthy of serious concern until the more profound and disabling conditions are adequately cared for. It is extremely difficult to make adequate estimates of the need for help in the general area of the neuroses until the designation itself is more carefully defined and until the criteria for the recognition of the serious conditions within this realm are more specifically elaborated. Some progress along these lines is reflected in the elimination of the term "neurosis" from the American Psychiatric Association's *Diagnostic and Statistical Manual III,* depending instead on more specific definitions of various types of disorders usually included under this rubric.

Except in the case of clearest psychiatric conditions demanding public intervention, it is very difficult to estimate the need for facilities because the need for care is ordinarily not defined by professional criteria but rather by members of the community who decide whether to seek psychiatric care for themselves or others and under what conditions. Because definition and intervention occur within the community, we should understand the social and personal processes through which persons come to see themselves or others as suffering from a psychiatric condition and the way they come to the attention of psychiatric facilities.

MENTAL ILLNESS, ILLNESS BEHAVIOR, AND ENTRY INTO PSYCHIATRIC CARE

Every society recognizes behavior outside certain limits as deviant, and madness exists in every culture.

> Explicit labels for insanity exist in these cultures. The labels refer to beliefs, feelings, and actions that are thought to emanate from the mind or inner state of an individual and to be essentially beyond his control. . . . Almost every-

> where a pattern composed of hallucinations, delusions, disorientations, and behavioral aberrations appears to identify the idea of "losing one's mind," even though the content of these manifestations is colored by cultural beliefs. (Murphy 1976, p. 1027)

The conditions under which individuals, their significant others, and a community are sensitive to particular symptoms or behavior depend on their knowledge and beliefs and the impact of the deviance in a particular context. Whether their concept is broad or narrow, whether they intervene readily or only reluctantly, and whether they are blaming or supportive vary by time and place. As Clausen and Huffine (1975) note, however, the social definition of mental illness depends not so much on one or another symptom as on the accumulation of many inexplicable actions. These can be judged only by social context, and even clinicians in making judgments of mental processes within a narrow conception of psychiatric illness must take the context into account in evaluating the abnormality of thought and behavior.

Depending on the culture and social group, illness may be readily recognized and defined by the persons themselves or only after it becomes a social issue and others in the community demand some action. A wide range of variables affects the recognition of disorder and initiation of care (Mechanic 1978, 1982), and these are briefly described in the following list. Interestingly, these same variables apply to the definition of physical and psychological disorder.

1. The visibility, recognizability, or perceptual salience of deviant signs and symptoms.
2. The extent to which the person perceives the symptoms as serious (that is, the person's estimate of the present and future probabilities of danger).
3. The extent to which symptoms disrupt family, work, and other social activities.
4. The frequency of the appearance of deviant signs or symptoms, or their persistence, or their frequency of recurrence.
5. The tolerance threshold of those who are exposed to and evaluate the deviant signs and symptoms.
6. The information available to, the knowledge of, and the cultural assumptions and understandings of the evaluator.
7. The degree to which autistic psychological processes (perceptual processes that distort reality) are present.
8. The presence of needs that conflict with the recognition of illness or the assumption of the sick role.
9. The possibility that competing interpretations can be assigned to the symptoms once they are recognized.
10. The availability of treatment resources, their physical proximity, and the psychological and monetary costs of taking action (including not only physical distance and costs of time, money, and effort, but also stigmatization, resulting social distance, and feelings of humiliation resulting from a particular illness definition).

It may appear curious that I should attempt to group together factors affecting the recognition and the definition of both psychiatric and nonpsychiatric disorders because we know that mental patients are often brought into care through different pathways from those followed by people who suffer from general medical conditions. A large proportion of psychotics among the lower class are first recognized as mentally ill when their bizarre behavior becomes visible to community authorities; such persons are frequently brought to a psychiatric facility by police. Alcoholics and drug addicts brought into treatment often come through official routes, such as the courts, the police, or community social agencies. Despite these different pathways to care, the social processes leading to the recognition and the identification of general medical conditions and those leading to the recognition of psychiatric problems are similar. All illness is defined because the person directly concerned or others become aware that some deviation from a normal state has taken place. The community may have more tolerance for a person with a broken leg or for one who is shy and withdrawn than for the alcoholic who disturbs others or the schizophrenic who verbalizes thoughts no one can understand. The differences, however, in defining a person with a broken leg and in defining a disruptive alcoholic stem not from different social processes but rather from the manner in which these problems become manifest and from their effect on social life, social activities, and social values. If you are aware that a member of your living group has active tuberculosis and refuses to seek treatment— thus exposing you to the disease—you might choose to use official agencies to ensure that the ill person is removed from contact with you and does not threaten the public safety. What makes ordinary medical conditions different from some psychiatric ones, from the public's standpoint, are the various ways in which psychiatric disorders differ in terms of the 10 dimensions already noted.

We have no way of predicting the specific response to any condition. The definitions of normality by which deviation is judged vary among medical practitioners as well as among lay persons, especially in the area of psychiatric disorders. More frequently than not, individuals come to view themselves as ill on the basis of their own standards of functioning as well as on their previous knowledge and experience, and when marked deviations are apparent they tend to seek medical confirmation. On other occasions individuals do not recognize themselves as sick but come to accept this definition when some other person defines them as ill (for example, persons who are informed that they have hypertension or tuberculosis, although they may not actually recognize that they are ill). In some instances of mental illness, persons defined by others as sick vigorously resist this diagnosis. The definition that one is mentally ill involves a considerable change in one's self-identity, and the effects of treatment are often perceived as uncertain or harmful. Even the difference between psychiatric and nonpsychiatric conditions can be exaggerated, however, and the overlap is considerable.

The manner in which deviant feelings or behavior becomes evident may have varying disruptive effects on social life and may be associated with more or less stigma. Although some mentally ill persons withdraw from social interaction and cause no disruption in the community, others engage in visible, bizarre behavior that is threatening and frightening to others. The person whose symptoms are not disruptive is not so readily defined because the public's conceptions of health and mental illness tend to be sharply polarized. Because the behavior of mentally ill persons is viewed as markedly different from that of normal individuals, the public frequently stigmatizes persons so defined. Psychiatric conditions, as opposed to nonpsychiatric ones, tend to be more disruptive and associated with greater stigma, but we should again note that this difference is a quantitative rather than a qualitative one. We do not need to consider the social processes underlying the definitions of psychiatric and non-psychiatric conditions separately, as long as we give attention to such factors as social disruption, stigma, and resistance to accepting a definition of illness.

The ten categories pertain equally to situations in which individuals define themselves as ill and in which others regard them as "sick." Let us consider the way these categories apply to a person suffering from a self-defined depressive condition and to an alcoholic defined as a problem by the community. The recognition of a depressive illness may follow a period during which a person experiences feelings of sadness and emptiness more profound than usual, difficulty getting going, loss of interest in life, and sluggishness. Depression, however, is a fairly common symptom, and the person must recognize that this depression is more serious than previous episodes. This recognition, in turn, depends on the extent to which the symptoms disrupt activities, the persistence of the depression and associated symptoms, and tolerance for psychological pain. A self-definition of illness may depend on whether the depressed state is sufficiently profound so the person cannot get out of bed, get to work, or take on usual responsibilities and activities, and on whether the symptoms are persistent or fluctuating. It may be possible to assign competing definitions to the symptoms. If there has been some adversity, such as the death or injury of a loved one or a personal defeat in work or family life, the person may define his or her feeling state and condition as a temporary response to a frustrating and unhappy situation. But should these symptoms occur independently of adversity, the problem is likely to be viewed as coming from within the individual.

These categories can be applied equally well to definitions of alcoholics, schizophrenics, or other persons often designated by the community as mentally ill. The community is more likely to define individuals as alcoholics when their drinking is visible rather than private and when their drinking pattern extends beyond that ordinarily thought of as conventional. The definition of and response of others to such excessive drinking depend on the extent to which the drinking disrupts work, family, and other community activities and the frequency with which the person becomes drunk. If drinking leads to work absenteeism, conflict within the family, and embarrassing family situations, people are more likely to be defined as problems than if they drink themselves to sleep at night and do not disrupt family life or fail to meet social obligations. Persons in the community may have more or less tolerance for drinking and drunkenness. They may not take note of a happy drunk but may react punitively to a drunk involved in fights or driving a motor vehicle. They may react differently to drunk men and women. It is not my intent to go into each of these matters in any detail. The point is that from a conceptual view, we do not need to develop separate categories for the factors underlying the social definition of illness made by the persons themselves and for those underlying the definitions made by others (for a more complete discussion, see Mechanic 1978).

There has been considerable work directed at examining the selective processes by which individuals with various types of symptoms find their way to different types of care (Goldberg and Huxley 1980, Mechanic 1982). David Goldberg and Peter Huxley (1980) have defined four filters between a community population and an inpatient unit that can be examined in elucidating the psychiatric help-seeking process. First, there are studies at the community level, such as the ECA studies reviewed earlier, which attempt to ascertain who in the population have varying conditions and what types of help they seek. The first filter defines who in a population arrives at helpers of first contact. Most studies focus on physician use, but any type of informal or formal care seeking could be the object of inquiry. A second filter concerns whether the source of care (typically a physician) recognizes the patients' psychiatric distress, symptoms, or conditions. A third filter concerns referral to a secondary source of care, such as a mental health specialist. Depending on the illness behavior of the patient, the second filter is commonly bypassed and patients come directly to a mental health specialist, particularly in the United States. The fourth filter is admission to a psychiatric bed. This perspective can be extended to examine exchanges between acute and chronic beds, hospital beds and nursing home beds, partial-care and total-care beds, and the like, but there are limited returns in elaborating the number of filters. The number of filters to be studied, and the level of detail, depends on the policy issues of greatest importance. The more basic idea to remember is that many individual, social, cultural, and economic factors affect the exchanges among levels of care and how individuals come to pass through various selective filters.

For example, a considerable literature supports the observation that mental health status, insurance, sociodemographic variations, attitudes, social networks, other social and cultural variables, and characteristics of the health care delivery system all affect the likelihood of a mental health contact. In New Haven, the relative odds of a mental health contact of any kind within the previous six months were substantially greater among those who had a regular source of medical care (3.06 to 1), who were receptive to professionals (2.42 to 1), who were young adults (2.11 to 1), who used clinics (1.76 to 1), and who were white (1.95 to 1), unmarried (1.64 to 1), female (1.49 to 1), and had some college education (1.42 to 1) (Leaf et al. 1985). In Baltimore, unmet need for mental health care was found to be most substantial among the elderly, among nonwhites, and among those with eight or less years of education (Shapiro et al. 1985). A number of behavioral models have been developed to account for the wide variety of social, cultural, and attitudinal factors that affect the use of mental health services (Mechanic 1975, 1980, Greenley, Mechanic, and Cleary 1987). Some of these factors affect help seeking in general, while others help explain alternative choices among mental health providers (Greenley and Mechanic 1976, Greenley, Mechanic, and Cleary 1987).

Various investigators have studied the conditions under which a particular set of symptoms is viewed from a psychiatric frame of reference or from some other perspective. Charles Kadushin (1958), in interviews with 110 persons using a psychiatric clinic, attempted to ascertain how they decided to undertake psychotherapy. He found that such a decision is a five-step process: (1) persons must decide that they have a problem and that it is an emotional one; (2) they must decide whether to discuss the problem with relatives and friends; (3) they must decide at some point whether they are adequately dealing with the problem and whether to seek professional help; (4) if they choose to seek professional help, they must choose an appropriate profession from which to seek help; and (5) they must select a particular practitioner. In his clinic sample Kadushin found four characteristic ways of recognizing a problem: (1) being told by others; (2) experiencing painful physical symptoms; (3) being unhappily married; and (4) feeling unhappy in general. In a further analysis of social distance between client and professional, Kadushin (1962) found that stable interaction is most likely when there is little social distance between role partners, so that professionals who are socially close to clients are likely to be consulted. He further points out that the patient's lack of familiarity with the psychotherapist's role can also be a problem. Kadushin feels that some of these problems are alleviated through the presence of a subculture of friends and supporters of psychotherapy, and he argues that knowing others who have had psychiatric treatment, being told by one's friends to go to a psychiatrist, having one's problems noticed by others, and reading works on psychoanalysis are characteristics of those belonging to this subculture (1962, p. 530, 1966). Kadushin's analysis pertains only to some kinds of psychiatric patients; the process of defining oneself as mentally ill may vary substantially from one type of psychiatric condition to another.

If the subculture Kadushin describes exists and makes persons more receptive to particular treatment contexts, then the use of some psychiatric services may depend not so much on the seriousness of the person's condition as on whether he or she is a member of the informal subculture. A study by Scheff (1966) of users and nonusers of a student psychiatric clinic sheds some light on this issue. Scheff compared a sample of student applications for psychiatric help with a random sample of the population that had free access to this psychiatric clinic. The items on the questionnaires administered to both groups were almost identical; they had been developed from studying the problems of previous students who had applied for psychiatric help. Scheff found that the number of problems students reported was strongly related to application for psychiatric care: 59 percent of the clinic applicants had ten or more problems, while only 35 percent of the nonusers had a similar number. The most striking aspect of this result, however, is the extensive overlap between clinic applicants and the random sample in respect to the problem inventory. An equally impressive result is that religion and religious participation were more effective predictors of clinic applications than was the number of problems students had. Overall, Scheff found that the clinic sample had an overrepresentation of persons with similar social backgrounds and similar social activities.

Linn (1967), in another study of the same psychiatric clinic, provides further evidence in support of the general idea developed by Kadushin. In comparing clinic applicants with a random sample to whom clinic services were available, Linn argued that there would be an overrepresentation of applications from the group of students who were less integrated into traditional social institutions, who were more likely to identify with other students who were cosmopolitan, who were more likely to report that they had friends with socioemotional problems, and who discussed such problems with others. Linn found considerable evidence in support of these ideas. He found an overrepresentation of clinic applications among those who reported that their friends were interested in psychology, were concerned about meaning in life, and were sensitive and introspective. He found an underrepresentation of those who reported that they liked football games, were religious, and had friends who were usually well dressed (see also Bart 1968).

Although these studies were provocative, they fail to resolve several important issues. First, they fail to indicate to what extent the characteristics associated with psychiatric use reflect their correlation with symptoms as compared with patterns of seeking help. If certain patterns of behavior are associated with more symptoms, it may be the symptoms and not the behavior that results in going to a psychiatrist. Second, persons with the same problems may go to varying types of helping facilities or cope in other ways. It is not clear from these studies whether the patterns associated with going to a psychiatrist are linked with a general tendency to seek help or, more specifically, associated with going to a particular source of help.

To study this problem, my colleague James Greenley and I examined a random sample of more than 1,500 university students and others who sought psychiatric and counseling care (Greenley and Mechanic 1976, Mechanic and Greenley 1976). Although the magnitude of psychological symptoms was the most important influence in seeking help, cultural characteristics, attitudes, knowledge, and group identifications among students with comparable symptoms had an important effect on the propensity to seek care for psychological problems. We found, however, that most predictors were specific to a particular source of care. Jewish students were more likely to go to the outpatient psychiatry clinic; Catholic students were more likely to seek help from religious counselors on campus. When we took account of most types of formal help seeking, only very few characteristics differentiated those who sought help from those who did not. Women, for example, were more likely than men to seek help from general physicians, psychiatrists, and the counseling center. Students who sought help were more inclined toward introspection, were acquainted with more users of services, and had a higher reported general propensity to seek help for psychological problems. These findings support the idea that the occurrence of symptoms encourages persons to search out the meaning of their experiences and feelings. Certain orientations, such as introspection and psychological awareness, push the person toward defining the problem in a psychological context. Once the student decides to seek care, sociocultural influences, social networks, and personal values as well as knowledge of available facilities orient the student to a particular type of assistance. These results have been replicated in a large community population (Greenley, Mechanic, and Cleary, 1987).

In recent years, researchers have been giving more attention to attribution processes—the way people interpret their experiences and the causes of events. Psychological distress may be interpreted in many ways—as a psychological, social, or moral problem, for example. The schemas available in the person's social context may have major effects on the way feelings and experiences are construed (Mechanic 1972b). The women's movement is an interesting example of the emergence of widely accepted social explanations of women's distress. In earlier decades, housewives feeling a sense of malaise and unfulfillment as wives and mothers had difficulty explaining their feelings in terms other than their own inadequacies or failures. The women's movement, however, now gives support for explaining such distress less in personal terms and more as a result of inequalities, blocked opportunities, and exploitative role arrangements. The source of distress is defined outside oneself and offers different opportunities for coping.

COMMUNITY DEFINITIONS OF MENTAL ILLNESS

Many psychiatric conditions are defined not by the persons themselves but by others in the community who note bizarre behavior or failure to meet expected standards. Such labeling of a particular person as mentally ill depends on the various contingencies discussed earlier. In addition to the influences of different personal and social factors, the character of the symptoms themselves exerts a considerable effect on whether a person is defined as mentally ill. Although there are vast differences in willingness to tolerate bizarre and difficult behavior, few relatives are willing to house a patient who is suicidal, homicidal, incontinent, hallucinatory, delusional, or disoriented (Angrist et al. 1961). If the patients are sufficiently bizarre and disruptive, the probability is extremely high that they will come into care. Social definitions of illness are relevant because many serious illnesses do not develop in a particularly striking way. The ambiguity surrounding the occurrence and the severity of illness makes sociological variables important.

Although the public's conception of mental illness has been changing, there is still considerable reluctance to define a relative or friend as mentally ill and a strong tendency to normalize and to deny symptoms that become apparent. Many people still visualize mental illnesses as extreme states of disorganized behavior and as a sharp break from usual or familiar patterns. Lesser psychiatric difficulties are often viewed as physical conditions or as indications of normal variabilities in personality. When persons' symptoms are accompanied by physical indications, they are often urged to seek medical help; but should their difficult behavior be inconsistent with a physical interpretation, then it is often attributed to stubbornness or moral defects rather than to illness.

Clausen and Yarrow (1955) and their colleagues, in a unique study of mental health definitions, described five trends characterizing the process through which wives of psychiatric patients attempted to cope with their husbands' mental illness and increasingly difficult behavior: (1) the wife's first recognition of a problem depends on the accumulation of behavior that is not readily understandable or acceptable to her; (2) this recognition forces her to examine the situation and to adjust her expectations for herself and for her husband to account for his deviant response; (3) the wife's interpretation of the problem shifts back and forth from seeing the situation as normal on one occasion to seeing it as abnormal on another; (4) she tends to make continuous adaptations to the behavior of her spouse, waiting for additional cues that either confirm her definition or lead to a new one—that is, she mobilizes strong defenses against her husband's deviant behavior; and (5) finally, she reaches the point at which she can no longer sustain a definition of normality and cope with her husband's behavior. Yarrow et al. (1955) observe the following tendencies.

> The most obvious form of defense in the wife's response is the tendency to *normalize* the husband's neurotic and psychotic symptoms. His behavior is explained, justified, or made acceptable by seeing it also in herself or by assuring herself that the particular behavior occurs again and again among persons who are not ill. . . . when behavior cannot be normalized, it can be made to seem less severe or less important in a total picture than an outsider might see it. . . . By finding some grounds for the behavior or something explainable about it, the wife achieves at least momentary *attenuation* of the seriousness of it. By *balancing* acceptable with unacceptable behavior or "strange" with "normal" behavior, some wives can conclude that the husband is not seriously disturbed. . . . Defense sometimes amounts to a thoroughgoing *denial*. This takes the form of denying that the behavior perceived can be interpreted in an emotional or psychiatric framework. (Yarrow et al. 1955, pp. 22–23)

The strong tendency of relatives and the community to normalize difficult patterns of behavior until they can no longer be tolerated has relevance for public policy because it encourages long delays in seeking treatment. Awareness of such common tendencies has encouraged public health psychiatrists to support efforts toward public education. Many argue that it is first necessary to educate the public to recognize the appearance of mental illness in its earliest manifestations and to view seeking aid for these problems as appropriate. Efforts have been made in recent years to provide community facilities that are especially prepared to deal with these problems. The evidence is that such public education and the increase in access to acceptable psychiatric and other counseling facilities and practitioners have resulted in many persons with mild and moderate problems receiving care. A research group from the University of Michigan's Institute for Social Research studied public views of mental illness in 1957 (Gurin et al. 1960) and completed a similar study of over 2,000 respondents in 1976, using many of the same questions (Institute for Social Research 1979, Kulka, Veroff, and Douvan 1979, 1981). They found that over the 20-year period, use of professional help for psychological problems increased from 14 to 26 percent, although the levels of well-being in the population were approximately the same. Despite these gains, however, the fact is that seriously disturbed patients who require care do not come into treatment. Weissman and Myers (1978) in their New Haven study found that only one-quarter of the respondents studied with any diagnosis, including major depression, sought professional help for the problem in the previous year (p. 1310). Brown and Harris (1978) note comparable findings concerning depression in the Camberwell area of London. These findings have been replicated again in the ECA Studies (Leaf et al. 1985, Shapiro et al. 1985).

Families cope with mental illness in various ways. Sampson et al. (1964) found that husbands withdrew from their symptomatic schizophrenic wives, thus insulating themselves from their wives' disturbed and bizarre behavior. Contrary to popular belief, depressed women in families are not passive, but often are irritable and combative (Weissman and Paykel 1974). One way in which family members deal with such behavior is to withdraw emotionally and ignore the distressed person. Often there is a vicious cycle with the withdrawal and rejection resulting in even more depressed and disturbed behavior. Symptoms that are not physically threatening or not so bizarre that they result in social difficulties may be tolerated for years before action is taken. Treatment may be sought when the family's ability to cope breaks down because of some change in the family's internal or outside relationships. One finding of a study of children brought to a clinic, compared with children having similar symptoms but not brought into treatment, was the inability of the mother to cope and her own anxiety and depression (Shepherd, Oppenheim, and Mitchell 1966).

This failure to recognize mental illness and at times the blatant denial of it are not such simple or clear-cut issues as they may seem. Large costs may be involved in recognizing oneself, one's spouse, or one's child as mentally ill. The definitional act itself often involves major changes in the structure of interaction in the family; indeed, the recognition that a member of the family is mentally ill requires a major reorganization of the family itself. Once the definition is made and action is taken, the act is in many ways irreversible. The meanings that members of the family assign to one another have been changed, the stigma of mental illness is difficult to completely reverse, and perhaps what is most important of all, psychiatric assistance may not make any significant difference in restoring "normality" to the situation.

From a policy perspective, there is at least one other consideration. Many of these crises may be transient ones, and the usual patterns of family living may be restored without psychiatric intervention. The studies and observations on normalization are extremely biased ones. They concentrate on situations in which the *normalization process has failed and has led to further problems.* Although we have no adequate data to make an absolute judgment, these situations may constitute a small percentage of the total population of cases in which bizarre behavior occurs and normalization takes place.

In many cases early and effective treatment of disorder may reduce suffering, minimize disability and family disruption, and even prevent suicide. Excellent treatments now exist for controlling some of the worst symptoms of schizophrenia, bipolar depression, other major depressive disorders, and phobias. In many other areas, however, treatment and its value are more dubious, and there is limited benefit in encouraging persons into treatment considering the monetary and psychological costs. Although encouragement and support of persons undergoing life crises are necessary, the act of defining people's behavior as indicative of a psychiatric condition may undermine their limited self-confidence and efforts at continuing to cope in work and family life, and it may encourage a stance of dependency that leads to further disability and the acceptance of illness. The major challenge faced by new programs is to provide sustenance and help to those who are going through difficult crises without defining and structuring their problems so as to increase the probability of disability.

To some extent, the experience of the military illustrates the consequences of various alternatives. Evaluations of the use of psychotherapy in dealing with neuropsychiatric casualties indicate that the manner of providing care has a bearing on the effectiveness of the soldier. Glass (1953) reports that when psychiatric casualties were evacuated to mental health facilities during the North African and Sicilian campaigns in World War II, few soldiers were salvaged for combat duty. The psychiatrist, prior to the development of new military mental health policies, usually assumed that the patient was ill and "sought to uncover basic emotional conflicts or attempted to relate current behavior and symptoms with past personality patterns" (p. 288). This administrative policy seemingly provided patients with rational reasons for their combat failures. Both the patient and the therapist were often readily convinced that the limit of combat endurance had been reached. In contrast, when psychiatrists treated soldiers in the combat zone with such interpersonal devices as suggestion and influence, a much higher percentage of men returned to combat. Glass (1958) argued that neuropsychiatric illness was often the result of an attempt to adapt to or withdraw from dangerous combat circumstances.

> It should be recognized that both symptoms and behavioral abnormalities represent a meaningful effort at adaptation under stress. Inability to cope with threatening or dangerous situations evokes substitute behavior of an evasive or regressive pattern in an effort to reach some satisfactory compromise solution for both internal needs and external demands. Even in the bizarre types of combat psychiatric breakdown, such as mutism or uncontrolled panic flight, one can discern primitive attempts to withdraw or escape from a terrorizing environment. Less severe abnormalities, such as hysterical paralysis, self-inflicted wounds, and AWOL from battle, more readily portray their purposeful nature. In the more mild forms of combat fatigue, characterized by tremulousness, tearfulness and verbal surrender, a childish dependent adaptation is quite evident. The form or type of psychological noneffective behavior displayed in combat is not determined so much by individual personality characteristics as it is dictated either by the practical circumstances of the battle situation or by group (including medical) acceptance of such symptoms or behavior. (Glass 1958, pp. 194–95)

We can make a rough assessment of the scope and importance of social definitions in determining morbidity by evaluating the effects of changing psychiatric policies in the military. Despite the shifts in military psychiatric policy from before World War II to after the Korean War, there was an impressive consistency in the rates of admission to hospitals for armed forces personnel. This consistency suggests that changes in policy had little effect on the occurrence of psychoses requiring hospital care. The invulnerability of rates of psychosis to changing public policies is also supported by the facts that such rates are approximately the same in wartime and in peacetime and that they did not differ appreciably in the two wars under consideration. Additional evidence shows that extreme combat conditions or exposure to bombing attacks does not have any apparent effect on the rate of occurrence of psychotic conditions (Glass 1958, Group for the Advancement of Psychiatry 1960, pp. 290–91; also see the discussion of the influence of stress in Chapter 4).

In contrast, the rates of admission for psychoneurotic conditions fluctuated widely. Among army active-duty personnel, they were considerably higher in wartime than in peacetime and considerably higher in World War II than in the Korean war. The conflicting conceptions of psychoneurosis and the lack of reliability in its diagnosis allow such rates to be easily manipulated. In all overseas theaters in World War II, approximately 23 percent of all evacuations resulted from psychiatric causes; in Japan and Korea from September 1950 to May 1951, the comparable figure was only 6 percent. Military psychiatric policies during these periods appear to have had considerable influence on the rate of defined neurotic conditions.

Good evidence suggests that the much lower proportion of evacuations for psychiatric reasons in the Korean War resulted from more than the manipulation of the definition of psychoneurosis. During the Korean War, the Army developed a preventive program to retain manpower and to cut down the level of neuropsychiatric casualties. The core of the new program was to provide brief supportive treatment in the combat zone and to avoid a hospital atmosphere or one conducive to the soldier adopting a patient role. Studies of such neuropsychiatric cases returned to duty show that their performance was comparable to that of other returnees hospitalized for disease or injury or excused for administrative reasons (Group for the Advancement of Psychiatry 1960, pp. 291–92). The Navy's experience was similar to that of the Army. In the Korean War, marines were given supportive treatment close to the front; few were evacuated, and psychiatric casualty rates were one-tenth of those in World War II (Group for the Advancement of Psychiatry 1960, p. 294).

Such programs of administrative support and therapy based on viewing the soldiers' difficulties as being within the normal range under stress do not necessarily cure psychiatric problems, but they do ensure more effective behavior. Few forms of therapy presently available are curative. From the perspective of the military, the psychiatric policies pursued during and after the Korean War were less costly and more useful in promoting effective behavior than were those used in previous wars.

The military situation also sheds light on another matter discussed in Chapter 4 that must be kept in mind. Incidence of psychoses shows little responsiveness to changing conditions and administrative policies, and this suggests—although it cannot be proved—that such conditions are not part of the same continuum as psychoneurotic conditions, which appear to fluctuate widely under varying stress conditions. If we can apply the military experience to other contexts, then mental health policy in relation to chronic mental conditions of a psychotic nature must be formulated on the basis of different considerations from those given to psychoneurotic conditions and other problems of living. What is true of the incidence of psychoses is not necessarily true of their course, however. Understanding social and environmental factors helps considerably in maintenance and rehabilitation of psychotic patients.

THE COURSE OF SCHIZOPHRENIA

Clinicians have commonly viewed schizophrenia as an intractable condition with an inevitable deteriorating course. A large number of studies now refute this conception and demonstrate the possibilities for minimizing disabilities and maintaining a higher level of function than most psychiatrists believed likely. Such traditional perceptions by clinicians reflect the limited perspective through which they see patients. Their conceptions are very much influenced by the treatment failures they see over and over again and less by the larger epidemiological picture. Both epidemiological and clinical follow-up studies demonstrate that the actual course of events is more positive. These studies show extraordinary variability in adaptation and levels of functioning, and they were reviewed earlier. Our focus here is with factors that possibly explain the variable course of the disorder.

Findings from studies converge in suggesting a complex and differentiated course of illness depending on social and environmental conditions. A good illustration is the International Pilot Study of Schizophrenia, which followed 1,202 patients in nine countries (World Health Organization 1979). At two-year follow-up, 27 percent of schizophrenics had a complete recovery after the initial episode, and 26 percent had several psychotic attacks with periods of complete or partial recovery. Five-year follow-up in a subsample of American patients was highly correlated with appraisals at two years (Strauss and Carpenter 1977). Most striking in the international study is the large variation between developed and developing countries, with proportions of patients showing complete recovery varying from 6 percent in Denmark to 58 percent in Nigeria.

There was some skepticism expressed about these findings by researchers who noted that patients studied were not representative samples of schizophrenic patients in each society, and, thus, selection biases might have occurred. Thus, in a second collaborative study (Sartorius et al. 1986), efforts were made to identify representative samples of new cases of schizophrenia in each of ten countries. This was achieved by monitoring defined populations over a two-year period to identify first contacts of psychotic patients with a wide range of helping agencies including indigenous healers. Great care was taken to identify patients in different cultures by the same criteria, and, in fact, subsequent analysis showed that the symptom profiles of schizophrenic patients in varying samples were similar. Again, the investigators found that the two-year pattern of schizophrenic illness was more favorable in developing countries; while 56 percent of schizophrenics in such countries had a mild course over the two-year period, only 39 percent had comparable outcomes in the developed nations studied.

Waxler (1979), in a careful five-year follow-up study of schizophrenics in Sri Lanka, found that 45 percent were symptom-free as measured by the Psychiatric Status Schedule developed by Spitzer and colleagues. Fifty percent were rated by the psychiatrists as having adjusted normally; 58 percent were seen by their families as having normal social performance; and 42 percent had no impairment in the previous six months. Almost half of the patients were said to have worked continuously over the previous five years, according to their families. Even allowing for errors in measurement, this is an impressive outcome, and at variance with typical Western conceptions of the course of schizophrenia. Waxler carefully examined possible artifacts in her results and makes a persuasive case that her findings are indicative of important cultural differences, and she suggests a social labeling model as the best approach to understanding these differences.

Another alternative is that in rural contexts schizophrenics can more easily continue to play an economic role and can insulate themselves from interpersonal stresses and intense associations. In some cultural contexts, there may be strong mutual expectations within kinship structures that encourage efforts at functioning from the patient and more acceptance from the community (Kleinman and Mechanic 1979). Family members may be less critical of the patient, a factor associated with less exacerbation of symptomatology (Leff 1978). While some of the best outcome results have been noted in underdeveloped countries or in rural contexts in developed nations, good outcomes have also been reported from industrialized cities in Europe, suggesting a more complex process than can be explained by such gross comparisons alone. Predictors of long-term course have not been effectively identified, but continuing efforts in this area are necessary.

In the short term, expressed emotion seems to be an important prognostic factor. A growing body of research indicates that schizophrenic patients do less well in family environments characterized by negative emotional relationships and criticisms (Brown et al. 1962, 1972, Vaughn and Leff 1976, Leff 1978, Leff and Vaughn 1985). While these effects are attenuated to a considerable degree when patients are maintained on neuroleptic medications, differences in outcome persist even among medicated patients. Patients who have less face-to-face contact with relatives are also less likely to relapse in families with high expressed emotion (Vaughn and Leff 1976, Leff 1978).

The work on expressed emotion has now been examined in the context of India (Wig et al. 1987), a country that has been found to have a more favorable prognosis of schizophrenia in the World Health Organization studies. In large part, the findings in western countries have been replicated but with some intriguing differences. First, in the Indian context, hostility of significant others was the primary predictive factor. Unlike the West, criticism was often not associated with hostility, and criticism by itself was not predictive of relapse. Even more instructive was the fact that Indian relatives made fewer critical comments, fewer positive remarks, and demonstrated less overinvolvement with the patient. This was much more the case in rural areas where the traditional kinship system was stronger than among city dwellers who were more expressive. The actual mechanisms by which expressed emotion works remain unclear, but this is a very important area for further exploration.

In an intriguing analysis, James Greenley (1986) reanalyzed the original data collected by George Brown and colleagues (Brown et al. 1972). He hypothesized that the essence of the measure of expressed emotion was a type of informal social control he labeled, "high intensity interpersonal social control." Such control, Greenley argues, involves people trying to shape others' behavior "by suggesting, nagging, threatening, arguing, criticizing, playing on feelings of obligation and guilt, and so forth" (Greenley 1986, p. 25). Greenley hypothesized that if his conception is correct, expressed emotion should be associated with family fears and anxieties when they believed the patient was not ill but recalcitrant. In contrast, he reasoned, if they felt that the behavior derived from an inherent illness they would be less likely to believe that they could shape it by informal control and, thus, less likely to display high levels of expressed emotion. The analysis supported these hypotheses. Greenley's analysis does not however, explain why psychiatric patients seem so susceptible to this form of social control, since it is ubiquitous in family interactions in normal families as well.

The prognostic research on schizophrenia suggests that successful maintenance is a complex task involving a balance between maintaining a sufficient level of demand and activation to encourage motivation and functioning without excessive excitement or stimulation. If patients are left alone or isolate themselves, they often lapse into inactivity and withdrawal, and the negative features of the condition tend to become exaggerated (Wing 1978). Similarly, involving the patient too intensely in interpersonal relations or in highly stressful situations triggers vulnerabilities. The expressed emotion research also identifies an important role of medication in protecting the patient in situations of overinvolvement and criticism. Expressed emotion as measured consists mostly of negative affect, and, thus, it remains unclear to what extent and under what conditions intense positive affect can have comparable effects. Since intense involvement commonly involves both positive and negative affect, it is reasonable to speculate that schizophrenics are vulnerable to intense emotional relationships more generally, but this is yet to be convincingly demonstrated. Research work in this area has important implications for public policy as it affects intervention programs.

Chapter Seven

Coping and Social Adaptation: Implications for Mental Health Practice

After several decades of primary attention to psychodynamic aspects of various psychiatric disorders, the focus of research and application has moved to biological and genetic aspects of various psychiatric syndromes, application of principles of learning to behavior modification in varying settings, and concern with educational models for encouraging effective coping and adaptation. This chapter deals with the conceptual and empirical basis for using coping and adaptation theory as a means of individual and community intervention.

Successful adaptation at the individual level involves at least three aspects (Mechanic 1978). First, the person must have the capabilities and skills to deal with social and environmental demands; for the sake of simplicity, these are designated as coping capabilities. Coping involves not only the ability to react to environmental demands but also the ability to anticipate and plan events and the capacity to influence and control both the demands to which one will be exposed and the pace of exposure. Second, people must be motivated to act and react. Although they can escape anxiety and discomfort by withdrawing or lowering aspirations, such behavior may have high costs and is constrained by social expectations and roles. As motivation increases, the consequences of failing to achieve mastery also grow; thus, the level of motivation is an important aspect of understanding discomfort. Third, persons must be able to maintain psychological equilibrium so that they can direct energies and skills to meeting life's tasks. Ego defenses, traditionally viewed as independent from action, are more reasonably viewed as ways of facilitating performance and mastery. In extreme forms such processes of denial or projection may not facilitate coping and may even become catastrophic for personal adaptation, but in their more modest everyday manifestations, they permit coping to continue.

Individuals, however, do not behave independently of their physical and social environments, and these contribute to shaping adaptive responses. It is the fit between social structure and environmental demands and adaptive skills that determines the individual's fate. While there are those extraordinary persons who do well in any environment and under any circumstances, most of us become vulnerable when our environment changes radically and calls for entirely new adaptive responses.

Coping depends on the efficacy of the kinds of solutions for problems that we have learned in the family, in peer groups, in school, and through the mass media. These solutions may be better or worse depending on the rapidity of social change and the adaptiveness and innovativeness of the informal and formal groups that play such an important part in our lives. The kinds of motives and aspirations we have and the directions in which we channel our energies depend on the incentive systems in society and the social forms that come to be valued or condemned. Finally, the ability to maintain psychological comfort will depend not only on intrapsychic resources, but also and perhaps more importantly on the social supports available or absent in the environment. Each of these aspects will become clearer as we consider the implications of such a framework for the education and rehabilitation of the chronic mental patient and other persons with psychosocial handicaps.

As noted in earlier chapters, illness behavior is a mode of coping. It is a dynamic response to changing personal and social conditions. Illness behavior is, in part, a process through which individuals attempt to define their problem, struggle with it, and achieve some accommodation or mastery. The practitioner may help guide the process by opening constructive paths for patients, but must be careful to avoid reinforcing a maladaptive response pattern resulting from patients' fears, distorted meanings, lack of information or incorrect information, and failure to perceive viable alternatives. It is useful to separate and briefly describe some important dimensions of adaptive response that affect the ways people accommodate to serious and chronic conditions. These include the *search for meaning, social attribution,* and *social comparison.*

In any crisis the people involved attempt to assess its meaning and possible consequences. Meaning is a prerequisite for devising a coping strategy, because only through some formulation of what is occurring can a reasonable response be devised. Most life situations are sufficiently patterned so that the social context provides the necessary cues for arriving at comprehensible definitions of what is taking place, but for less common events, such as the occurrence of a psychotic episode or physical disability, the person involved may have greater difficulty arriving at a definition of the experience, its implications, and the way to respond. The subjective nature of the patient's experience often makes it difficult for the clinician to understand what the patient is experiencing, and the clinician's behavior may further alarm or isolate the patient (Davis 1963, Roth 1963, Leventhal 1975).

Patients with serious symptoms or disabilities attempt to arrive at some prognostic information concerning their problem and some indication of the way they compare with others. Because the outcomes of illness and disability are often uncertain, physicians are frequently vague and evasive in response to questions. As noted earlier, families of mental patients complain that little information is provided by psychiatrists, and they feel isolated from the treatment process. Clinicians dislike to relay what appears to be bad news, often delaying the process through which patients and their families can realistically come to terms with the problem. Patients, dissatisfied with ambiguity, may continue the search for information through other patients and other physicians. They tend to obtain a great deal of conflicting information with no one to sort and explain it to them. Patients tend to think of their own reactions to events as relatively unique. When they join self-help groups, they are often surprised and relieved to learn how typical their internal feelings and social experiences are. They come to appreciate that their reactions may be less a product of their own failures and weaknesses than of their particular situation, relieving some of the anxiety associated with the experience (Weiss 1975). It is useful to expose patients with serious chronic disease or disability to others who have experienced and coped with comparable situations. This provides a guide to the distressing experience shared by all as well as social support and encouragement during a difficult stage in the illness process (Hamburg et al. 1953, Mechanic 1978).

In the process of seeking the meaning of an illness experience, patients attempt to ascertain the causes that contributed to their current situation (*social attribution*). Their formulations shape the meaning of the situation and can open or close options for actively dealing with it or the feelings it evokes. Patients or their loved ones may suffer when they construe the problem as a result of their own negligence or interpret the illness as a threat to their self-worth. They may become sensitive to criticism or rejection in a manner that interferes with a more active and open coping orientation. Such patients and their families require continued support and reassurance that their problems do not reflect on their personal worth. Many therapists in the past have done a disservice to both patients and their families by implying that the parents were to blame for children's illnesses. Such blaming has been common in the case of autistic children and schizophrenic patients despite the lack of sound evidence of such a link.

The extent to which it is useful or damaging for patients to see themselves as instrumental in determining their own condition depends on the stage of illness and its particular characteristics. Such views of one's own instrumentality are useful to the extent that they imply a sense of efficacy and personal ability to maintain control over one's life situation. Individuals with a sense of their own coping potency are more open and confident, setting the stage for successful adaptation; they can more readily direct situations to their own advantage than others who see their fate determined by forces beyond their control. The latter view encourages a passivity and withdrawal that may be difficult to reverse once the patient finds that such avoidance reduces anxiety. To the extent, however, that individuals fail in important ways to achieve their goals and aspirations, attributing the cause of the difficulty to outside influences in contrast to one's own limitations may mitigate subjective distress at the same time that it can contribute to fresh interpersonal problems. Therapists can play an important role in guiding such attribution processes to minimize unnecessary anxiety and self-blame, while at the same time encouraging an active and optimistic stance that provides opportunities for successful adaptations reinforced by the patient's social situation.

Disability is as much a social definition as a physical status, and the outcome of a problem depends not only on the psychological state of the patient, but also on the ways clinical staff, family, employers, and friends react to the situation. They may make it more difficult to resume ordinary social roles by their overprotectiveness, stigmatization, or social exclusion of the patient. Laura Reif (1975), in a study of response to coronary heart disease, found that many such patients were defined by themselves and others as disabled despite minimal biological impairment. Responses to the postcoronary patient tended to reflect the special interests of those defining the situation as much as the physical status of the patient. Employers excluded workers from jobs they were physically capable of holding as a result of a desire to minimize possible future economic liabilities. Physicians, in order to protect their time from excessive demands of the patient and the family, were sometimes not very aggressive in encouraging a return to work despite the fact that the patient was capable of the necessary tasks. In recent years there has been a major change in attitudes about the capacity of patients with heart disease to return to work following a heart attack. Serious mental illness poses more difficult work issues, but some of the difficulties patients face in returning to work are social barriers.

The manner in which a problem or disability is defined can have major impact on possibilities for coping. Many of the social problems of the handicapped stem as much from physical and social arrangements in the community as from their own incapacities. As social definitions are modified, it is easier for persons with disabilities to fulfill conventional social roles successfully. While such social action is not directly an aspect of the therapeutic task, rehabilitation units can serve as important catalysts to bring individuals with common problems together to help identify and modify conditions in the community that hinder effective adaptation.

The way in which cause is conceptualized by both patients and clinicians can vastly affect successful coping. Dangers exist especially when refuge in illness brings significant secondary gains such as escape from threatening situations, monetary advantages, or lenient reactions from authorities. Patients obviously have significant problems, but treatment personnel have a choice as to whether they will encourage activity and realistic coping efforts or helplessness and dependence. Much traditional medical care has encouraged excessive dependency both through the way in which disability is defined and in the failure to assist the patient to develop skills to function in a meaningful way despite the primary impairment.

The process of shaping attributions concerning the nature of illness and disability is a subtle and difficult task and requires careful monitoring of the patient over time. Although attributions can be formulated to minimize patients' sense of personal responsibility for their failures, they must also be consistent with active coping. The definitions must be realistic in that they receive consensual validation on the one hand and do not encourage unrealistic expectations of the patient on the other. Attributions must be shaped to conform to a program of graded mastery experience in which successful coping is reinforced and encourages further efforts.

Patients evaluate their skills and coping capacities through a process of *social comparison*. Because of the lack of objective standards to evaluate feelings, mood, and many coping responses, they look to others in comparable situations, or to experienced treatment personnel, to obtain cues as to the meaning of ongoing events and ways to respond. How persons come to assess themselves depends very much on those around them with whom comparisons are made. In many situations, feelings and self-esteem may depend as much on this comparison process as on the objective coping capacities of the individual. In rehabilitation it is possible to guide social comparison through the informational process in a way that encourages graduated mastery of life problems. Chronically ill patients often have great faith in clinicians who assume primary responsibility for their care and who show a continuing personal interest in them. The clinician is in a powerful position to guide the comparison process through information, instruction, and social support.

A frequent failure in the care of many ill and disabled persons is the neglect of family members who, if properly informed and instructed, could have a favorable facilitative effect on the patient's rehabilitation (Aiken 1976). Families often have their own problems in coping with a sick or disabled family member and may require information and assistance from the clinical team. Family members can become a very effective extension of the clinical team by providing support for active coping, encouraging conformity with medical instructions, and facilitating through joint participation those patterns of behavior most consistent with minimizing the patient's disability. The fact is that many family members feel excluded from the care process, have difficulty obtaining needed information, and rarely receive adequate instruction as to what they might do and how to do it.

THE USE OF A COPING-ADAPTATION MODEL TO IMPROVE PATIENT FUNCTIONING

In recent years, research and analysis on the adaptive process have shifted toward studying how people come to terms with stressful life demands. Not only is more attention focused on the sociocultural and psychosocial aspects of adaptation, but approaches to treatment more commonly reflect an interest in teaching adaptive skills and helping persons construct more effective social networks to assist them in managing their difficulties and insulating themselves against further strain. The emphasis has turned from ego defense to coping in a social context, and increasingly from a medical model of rehabilitation and prevention to one that can more aptly be described as educational.

Social adaptation depends on at least five types of resources that must be activated at one time or another: (1) economic resources, (2) abilities and skills, (3) defensive techniques, (4) social supports, and (5) motivational impetus. The traditional approach that has dominated clinical medicine involves attempts to modify directly the patient's feeling state and defensive patterns, although this is probably the most difficult point of intervention. There has been no impressive evidence that such interventions have been very effective, and particularly in the case of persons with serious impairments, it seems more productive to intervene in other ways. It is undeniable that effective adjustment partly depends on the patient's psychological response to real and symbolic threats associated with the illness, and successful adaptation requires the patient to develop psychological resources that allow the control of anxiety and facilitate continued attention to the tasks of adjustment. In all probability, however, it is more productive to attempt to achieve this indirectly than through direct psychotherapeutic intervention.

An analogous model, which I believe is instructive, comes from the field of accident research. Years of effort to diminish automobile accidents through modification of the public's attitudes achieved at best only very modest results. Thinking has been redirected to developing technological and legal devices that achieve the same effects more efficiently. Greater effort is now devoted to such devices as seat belts, inflatable air bags, and improved highway design. Similarly, efforts other than those associated with attitude modification may be more effective techniques for limiting the consequences of disabilities and impairments.

Most obvious is the fact that *economic resources* lighten the load of the disabled person, diminish tangential stresses because of the ability to purchase services, and create a more comfortable environment for dealing with the primary crisis (Simmons et al. 1977). Economic resources also provide alternatives for coping that otherwise might not be available. Such resources, however, are not under the control of rehabilitation programs, and efforts must be concentrated elsewhere.

For each illness and disability, patients require specific *skills* and information to adjust effectively. While these may seem incidental to the major medical effort, they may be extraordinarily important to the patient. Skills may involve techniques for compensating for physical and psychological inadequacies, pacing oneself, preparing for anticipated embarrassing situations, and the like. To the extent that necessary skills can be clearly conceptualized and broken down into specific components, they can be more readily and effectively taught. Too frequently, vague advice such as "take it easy" or "avoid stress" substitutes for specific instructions that assist patients in meeting their personal and social goals.

While the problems of disease and disability extend far beyond the issue of coping skills, the absence of such skills or their erosion due to physical or psychological handicap exacerbates the patients' problems in assuming more ordinary social roles. It may be more difficult for them to find and maintain employment, establish functional interpersonal relationships, enjoy conventional living quarters, and manage their own affairs (Stein et al. 1975). Chronic illness inevitably involves some increased dependency, and patients must learn how to deal successfully with official bureaucracies and how to manage the good intentions or curiosity of people in the community. Particularly in the case of a visible handicap, people tend to develop an oversolicitousness and protectiveness that the patient must learn to manage firmly yet pleasantly.

A person's sense of efficacy, as well as tangible and symbolic assistance, depend on the *extent and strength of social networks.* Strengthening such networks or assisting their development where they do not exist may be much more effective than individual therapeutic approaches. There is growing evidence that the absence of group supports makes people vulnerable to environmental assaults and to other adversities. Often the mere knowledge that help is available, if needed, provides people with confidence to cope. During times of stress, in particular, we depend heavily on the assistance and moral support of others, and threat increases a need to affiliate (Schachter 1959). We still know little, however, about what types of networks best supply support without encouraging dependency or being overprotective.

It is difficult to specify clearly the components of social support (Cohen and Syme 1985). Cobb (1976) has defined it as "information leading the subject to believe that he is cared for and loved . . . , esteemed," and a member of "a network of communication and mutual obligation" (p. 300). More broadly, social support may involve nurturance, empathy, encouragement, information, material assistance, and expressions of sharing. Social supports are responsive to the need to affiliate under stress, a need that seems to be acquired very early in life and that may have a biological basis. When levels of support are sufficiently strong, they may provide the central meaning of a person's life and thus diminish the perceived impact of almost any adversity. While support provided by professionals, or even friends, may not be able to substitute for more intimate affiliative relationships (Brown et al. 1975), they may assist in coping with difficult transition periods in adaptations to illness and disability. When more intimate social supports exist, professionals may be more useful in providing assistance and information to those who are close to the ill and disabled than in trying to substitute more directly for these relationships.

Self-help and consciousness-raising groups, which have been emerging among persons with a wide variety of disabilities, are a constructive way of providing necessary information, encouragement, and tangible assistance; but such groups may not be effective as a continuing resource since they may give undue emphasis to the disability as the crucial part of the patient's identity. While some patients may require such support throughout their entire lives, others may be able to make successful adaptations that do not depend so heavily on sharing with others having similar disabilities. Normalization comes, in part, when the disability becomes more peripheral and no longer the central organizing theme in the person's life. In the short run, however, such groups are a helpful basis for the patient in understanding the problem, assessing its meaning, making realistic and comforting comparisons, and receiving tangible assistance and emotional support (Weiss 1976). These groups are almost always helpful during the acute phases of serious chronic problems and disabilities, particularly when they include patients who have successfully coped with the realistic problems and frustrations of the illness. A major function of establishing such groups early is to encourage patients at a time in their illness cycle when they are feeling hopeless. The dilemma is that what may be good for a patient at an early stage of illness may be threatening to one who has overcome the problems and is coping successfully. Participation of such patients may result in reliving the traumatic events of their illness or in encouraging continuing dependency on the disability-based group. There are, however, some who seem to receive great personal satisfaction in effectively assisting others to confront the problems of disability that they themselves have faced successfully. Such patients can be judiciously selected by the clinical team and given a special status in the rehabilitation unit.

Finally, successful social adaptation depends on a continuing willingness to remain engaged in everyday social activities and concerns (*motivational impetus*). While withdrawal is a natural and often effective means of temporarily reducing a sense of threat, its persistence becomes highly maladaptive. Withdrawal erodes social contacts and skills and feeds a sense of hopelessness. Continuing involvement with other people and significant tasks is an important aspect of maintaining an adequate psychological identity and one's social roles; above all, rehabilitation units must encourage all possible activities consistent with the patients' physical and psychological status. This is frequently not accomplished because clinical staff may find it easier to do things for patients than to tolerate the uncertainty as to whether they will take responsibility for themselves. A unit in which patients are kept active requires more monitoring and involvement of staff and makes their tasks considerably more difficult. Staff training and supervision and the maintenance of enthusiasm are essential if the unit is to maintain the necessary activity level for patients.

THE RELATIONSHIP OF THE SOCIAL ADAPTATION MODEL TO TRADITIONAL MEDICAL APPROACHES

The social process of adaptation depends on the degree of fit between the skills and capacities of individuals and their relevant supporting group structures on the one hand and the types of challenges with which they are confronted on the other. To the extent that capacities and relevant social supports are fitted well to characteristic challenges, the flow of events is routine and ordinary. The maintenance and development of mastery require that individuals face demands that are somewhat taxing but not so challenging as to defeat their coping resources. The persistent confusion between illness and illness behavior, not only in the research literature but in clinical approaches to the chronic patient, tends to obfuscate the varied alternatives available to guide the patient toward a smoother adaptation to his or her illness and to the resumption of conventional social roles.

Professionals appropriately see themselves as having a limited function in the provision of care. They are aware that they usually lack control over the environments of their patients and lack the capacity to change many of the life patterns noxious to health and successful adjustment. Both the lack of potency of the professionals in these matters and the uncertainty of knowledge encourage a retreat to the patterns of assessment and management of the patient with which therapists are most familiar and with which they feel most secure. They treat the condition and ignore the patient, bemoaning the patient's lack of cooperativeness, irrationality, and unreliability. They provide limited information on social aspects of the illness to the patient and his or her family; they frequently become inaccessible to the patient or family who have questions and problems that do not relate directly to the patient's physical status; and they worry more about physical events than the patient's social adaptation to the community or his or her level of social functioning. While the above describes physicians more than other types of mental health professionals, these issues characterize much of professional practice.

The fact is, however, that illness behavior and coping capacities may be far more influential in health outcomes than many of the biological indicators on which professionals focus. While the myocardial infarction patient may be troubled by how this illness affects his or her job and family life, the physician may focus on minor variations in cardiac output. While the schizophrenic patient's problems in the community may be greatly exacerbated by isolation and inactivity, the psychiatrist may engage in rituals, such as making slight adjustments from time to time in the patient's drug regimen. The point is not that cardiac function or drug regimen is unimportant, but rather that without attention to other matters affecting the patient's functioning and sense of well-being, treatment is relatively ineffectual.

With full awareness of the uncertainties of our knowledge in understanding the behavioral responses associated with illness, I have put emphasis on the adaptive efforts of patients and their existing social supports. In many chronic illnesses, we face situations where the basic impairment is irreversible, because of lack of effective knowledge or long-term deterioration. Achieving a reasonable quality of life for such patients will depend as much on the management of their social situations and on the skills and supports they develop as on the physical care that is provided.

Chapter Eight

The Financing and Delivery of Mental Health Services

The availability and use of mental health services depend on the financing and reimbursement system. Until fairly recently, mental health services were sharply bifurcated. The poor received little mental health care, but if sufficiently disordered or disturbing, they were maintained in public institutions with minimal active treatment. The rich bought services from private practitioners on a fee-for-service basis; if they needed hospitalization, they would receive care, at least initially, in private mental hospitals. The cost of such care was prohibitive, and even affluent patients with chronic mental illness were frequently transferred to public institutions if they did not respond to treatment after some initial period. This pattern of services allocation did not really begin to shift significantly until the 1960s with the development of community mental health centers, the extension of psychiatric outpatient facilities in hospitals, and the improvement of psychiatric benefits under private and nonprofit health insurance programs (Follmann 1970). The passage of Medicare in 1965 provided some modest psychiatric benefits to the aged, although on a more prejudicial basis than other types of medical services covered by the program. Similarly, Medicaid provided significant funds to pay for mental health services for the poor. The Medicaid program, however, organized within the welfare system (Stevens and Stevens 1974) and tied to traditional federal-state welfare relationships, has been implemented from one place to another in an uneven way. As a result of these various developments in both public and private programs, there has been a vast increase in the use of services but not in a particularly well-balanced way.

Among the changes stimulated by insurance was the expansion of general hospital inpatient beds for acute care and an enormous growth of outpatient services. In 1984, there were almost 1.7 million discharges from short-stay hospitals with a primary mental health diagnosis (Dennison 1985): 625,000 for psychoses; 392,000 for alcohol dependence; and 228,000 for neurotic and personality disorders (primarily involving depression). Average length of stay for psychiatric diagnoses was 11.9 days. The predominant pattern even for psychoses is a relatively short hospital stay to stabilize the patient's condition. The average inpatient stay in general hospitals for psychotic disorders in 1984 was only 14 days.

The growth of psychiatric services has taken place in a context of uncertainty and disagreements about the causes and appropriate treatments of mental illness and the advantages of a medical as compared with other types of intervention models. As the earlier part of this volume has indicated, disagreements continue about the appropriate boundaries for differentiating mental illness from the abundant frustrations, problems, and disillusionments that people suffer in the ordinary course of everyday life. Moreover, there is considerable controversy about appropriate models of care ranging from short-term psychotherapy to psychoanalysis, and from medication-dominated care to psychosocial models of rehabilitation. And, there are still large numbers of professionals and critics who share the view that mental illness is largely a metaphor to describe deviations from acceptable behavior and that too much focus is placed on a medical orientation to this problem. While too much emphasis is sometimes given to the medical model, a major problem in mental health care is the neglect by the mainstream medical care system of the chronically mentally ill, who have formidable medical needs. Good mental health care includes a broad array of medical, social, and rehabilitation services. But in advocating a broad orientation, we must be careful to assure that medical and psychiatric care are core components of the larger pattern of needed services.

Despite the conceptual difficulties, mental health benefits have expanded under private and nonprofit insurance plans. Estimates indicate that in 1980, mental health expenditures were 8 percent of the total health care expenditures and accounted for almost 1 percent of the gross national product. Almost 20 billion dollars were expended directly for services, and approximately another 4 billion were in the form of transfer payments to mental patients (National Institute of Mental Health 1987b). The Bureau of Labor Statistics Level of Benefits Survey shows considerable depth of inpatient mental health coverage among employees studied in firms above a minimum size (Brady, Sharfstein, and Muszynski 1986). In 1984, almost all (99 percent) had inpatient psychiatric coverage, and about half had it on the same basis as any other illness. Ninety-six percent had outpatient coverage, but only 7 percent on the same basis as other illnesses. Most common restrictions were on dollar limits and coinsurance levels (typically 50 percent). Increased coverage has contributed to the purchase of millions of additional services.

As in the general medical area, insurers tend to define as "legitimate illnesses" whatever conditions are treated by the designated experts, most typically psychiatrists. But with pressures for cost-consciousness, many insurers are carefully scrutinizing long-term therapy for individuals with psychosocial difficulties and problems in living in contrast to more serious diagnoses such as affective disorder, schizophrenia, or substance abuse. In the past, payment for services provided by psychologists and social workers was typically restricted to those working under direct supervision of physicians or receiving referrals directly from them. In recent years, psychologists have substantially freed themselves from the supervision of psychiatrists and can be reimbursed in many programs directly. Social workers typically have had difficulty in gaining recognition as independent reimbursable providers of mental health services, limiting their access to the private psychotherapy marketplace. Insurance companies have made efforts to avoid the quagmire of deciding which mental illnesses should be insurable. Instead they try to limit the number of reimbursable providers and further protect themselves by imposing relatively high coinsurance and deductibles and limiting numbers of visits, allowable fees for each consultation, and total benefits covered. In the Medicare program, coinsurance for psychiatric services was set at 50 percent in comparison to a 20 percent coinsurance for other medical services, and the maximum allowable reimbursement for psychiatric outpatient care in any year has only been $250. Legislation passed by the Congress in 1987 substantially increases this amount on a graduated basis.

THE PATTERN OF INPATIENT SERVICES

The availability of more complete insurance for inpatient care as well as the legal mandates in many states for coverage of alcohol and drug abuse services (Frisman, McGuire, and Rosenbach 1985) have contributed to the stimulation of psychiatric inpatient services in general hospitals and private psychiatric hospitals. The general hospital is now the most usual provider of acute inpatient mental health care, and private hospital beds have expanded from 2.7 percent of all inpatient beds in 1970 to 7.7 percent in 1982. The number of private hospitals increased from 150 in 1970 to 211 in 1982, and admissions grew from approximately 92,000 in 1969 to 162,000 in 1981. Full time equivalent (FTE) staff in such hospitals between 1972 and 1982 grew from 21,504 to 38,125 and patient care FTEs tripled (National Institute of Mental Health 1985, p. 49). Private psychiatric hospitals are viewed as a growth sector, and the evidence suggests that they serve primarily the insured population with less severe problems than those typically found in nonprofit or public sector beds.

The introduction of prospective hospital reimbursement under Medicare in which hospitals receive a fixed payment for care of patients classified in one of 468 diagnostic related groups (DRGs) and more stringent rate settings in such states as New Jersey (with its own DRG system), New York, Massachusetts, and Maryland have imposed some new uncertainties on the growth and future profitability of the inpatient psychiatric sector. Initially, many psychiatric units were exempt from prospective payment, but this is scheduled to change. A major difficulty is that psychiatric DRGs are very poor predictors of the intensity of resource utilization in the care of patients (Taube, Lee, and Forthofer 1984, English et al. 1986, Horgan and Jencks 1987) and, thus, the broad introduction of DRGs without a better classification is likely to have perverse effects. For example, general hospitals without psychiatric units that care for patients in "scatter beds" provide much less care per patient than those that dedicate specialized units to the care of the mentally ill. A classification system that fails to recognize these important differences can create incentives that distort care processes and reduce quality of care (Jencks, Horgan and Taube 1987).

At present, for-profit development in inpatient psychiatry focuses on areas of inpatient coverage for insured individuals with affective disorders and alcoholism, which are profitable, and concentrate new facilities disproportionately in regions of the country less subject to stringent cost regulation and competition. It is inevitable, however, that the tighter imposition of cost constraints will have significant effects on how inpatient psychiatry is carried out in both general voluntary and private hospitals. A more troubling issue is that the incentives implicit in existing forms of financing have reinforced two systems of care, one for the well insured patient, the other for those without insurance, those whose benefits have been depleted, or those who are underinsured. The latter groups include many of the chronically mentally ill.

The distribution of inpatient admissions for mental disorder varies according to type of hospital. State and county mental hospitals have the largest proportion of schizophrenic admissions and a high rate of alcohol-related admissions, these two areas accounting for three-fifths of all admissions. A similar situation characterizes the Veterans' Administration's mental hospitals, although they have fewer schizophrenics and more alcohol-related problems. Public hospitals have more patients with previous admissions indicating greater chronicity. In contrast, community general hospitals and private psychiatric hospitals have only about one-third schizophrenic and alcoholism admissions and a much larger proportion of admissions for affective disorders: 31 percent in community hospitals and 43 percent in private psychiatric hospitals (National Institute of Mental Health 1985, p. 19). The public mental hospitals are clearly dealing with the tougher and more chronic problems.

UTILIZATION OF SERVICES AND FINANCING PATTERNS

The extension of psychiatric services through expanded insurance benefits had important implications for the distribution of care. It followed and may have reinforced an existing trend toward providing services to groups in the population who needed them the least. The most comprehensive insurance coverage is frequently available to the most advantaged segments of the employed population, and even among those with comparable insurance coverage, persons with higher incomes, education, and greater sophistication use the most services (Leaf et al. 1985) despite the inverse relationship between socioeconomic status and mental health impairment (Dohrenwend and Dohrenwend 1969, 1974, Kessler 1982). One study found that insured persons with college degrees as compared with those with a grade school or less education were six times as likely to seek psychiatric care, and they used office psychotherapy visits almost ten times as often as those who were less educated (Avnet 1962). These gaps have certainly narrowed over time, but experience with educated groups receptive to psychotherapy suggests that when there are few deductibles and coinsurance provisions, they will use a large number of psychotherapy services. These patients have greater financial resources and are better able to absorb whatever cost-sharing features are involved in obtaining such care and are less inhibited from using available benefits.

Use of insurance coverage, of course, also depends on the geographic and social accessibility of care. Psychiatrists and psychotherapists are disproportionately located in urban centers and affluent areas and are socially more receptive to educated and verbal clients, resulting in different degrees of access among persons having comparable insurance benefits. Differentials in the availability of psychiatrists between metropolitan, rural, and central city areas have been as high as 20- to 30-fold (Brown 1977). Providers more available to the poor, including social workers, counselors, and other nonmedical personnel, have been excluded typically from third-party reimbursement. Which needs and services are covered depends on the professional consulted, and this results in an inconsistency in the receipt of benefits among persons with comparable problems and insurance. The affluent and sophisticated are more likely to understand the system and to make sure that they receive services from professionals eligible for reimbursement. Limitations on the definition of appropriate personnel to provide mental health care may allow the sophisticated patient to receive reimbursement for minor problems, while treatment by nonmedical personnel directed to more serious conditions may not be paid for.

It is not difficult, however, to understand the reluctance of insurers to expand the definition of reimbursable providers of mental health care in any open-ended way because such personnel significantly outnumber the approximately 36,000 psychiatrists. If there is anything we know well in the health services field, it is that the availability of supply in the absence of fee barriers dramatically affects demand. There are now very large numbers of mental health providers, including psychologists, social workers, nurses, counselors, and the like. This enormous resource could be mobilized on behalf of the most seriously mentally ill if an appropriate framework for reimbursement could be developed without opening the gateway to large numbers of additional services for those with mild and moderate mental health problems.

The present insurance structure that includes relatively complete coverage for inpatient care but much more limited coverage for outpatient treatment provides incentives for unnecessary hospital care and encourages a medical approach to mental health problems in contrast to community alternatives and educational and rehabilitative models. Such incentives turn attention away from the long-term requirements of the most impaired psychiatric patients who are in need of continuing community care services and whose needs are not covered by existing insurance programs. Insurance that reinforces traditional and expensive forms of individual treatment within a psychotherapeutic orientation also provides little opportunity for the development of innovative community options using new types of organizational arrangements and personnel. The mirage that insurance adequately provides coverage for mental health needs may erode the political support necessary to encourage the development of community mental health care for patients with chronic mental illness and high levels of impairment.

We have developed insurance programs for psychiatric benefits that limit total expenditures for psychiatric services, but also reinforce traditional, ineffective, and inefficient patterns of mental health care, inhibit innovation and use of less expensive mental health personnel, and reinforce a narrow medical view as compared with a social or educational approach to patients' psychological problems. Increased insurance coverage for mental health problems can be a major advance if we keep in mind that such benefits are only one element of a coherent mental health policy. Most existing services for impaired patients are provided by a variety of categorical programs, including mental hospitals and community mental health centers, supported by federal, state, and local authorities. Because most of the chronically disabled are poor, many of their needs are financed through welfare and other social agencies. There is a desperate need for new financial and reimbursement approaches affecting the most disadvantaged and severely mentally ill.

THE ECONOMICS OF MENTAL HEALTH CARE

In recent years, we have learned a great deal about the economics of mental health care, the effects of financial incentives on consumers, professionals, and institutions, and the cost-effectiveness of alternative ways of organizing services, but while our knowledge of the effects of insurance and copayment on the demand for mental health services has advanced, too little attention has been given to the economics of the public mental health sector or to financing of care for the most seriously mentally ill, many of whom are uninsured. The Medicaid program and its complex eligibility and administrative requirements is a continuing focus of attention in the larger health care arena, but studies of the program have not been sensitive to the special needs of the severely mentally ill and the types of Medicaid modifications that would be important to improving their care. In the next chapter, we will explore some of these issues, but let us first review some of the most important recent findings concerning insurance effects on the use of mental health services.

Not only are cost-sharing features and service limits more characteristic of mental health than other medical services, but they also appear to inhibit outpatient services even more than in other areas (Frank and McGuire 1986). McGuire (1981), for example, in a study of use of psychotherapy among more than 4,000 patients, found that this service is particularly sensitive to insurance coverage and that the effects for lower-income persons were greater than for more affluent groups. McGuire's excellent study, however, focused on patients and, thus, pertains to volume of use and not to whether help would be sought.

The best source of data on the effects of cost-sharing is the Rand Health Insurance Experiment (HIE). This study, carried out between 1974 and 1982, randomized 6,970 respondents into insurance plans with varying coinsurance requirements and, in one setting, an HMO (Group Health Insurance in Seattle). In some cases there were no coinsurance requirements (labeled the "free care" group), while in other cases families had to pay 25, 50, or 95 percent of their bills up to a $1,000 per year maximum. There were other variations (Newhouse 1974), but for our purposes what is most important is the different obligations families had to share in their costs of care. Most insurance programs in the United States have some cost-sharing, and in recent years such requirements have increased substantially in employment-related health insurance plans (Hewitt Associates 1984). Deductibles and coinsurance also play an important role in Medicare, although the Rand group did not study the Medicare age group.

In the Rand study, physician use was demonstrated to respond substantially to insurance variations. Persons in the "free" plan (no coinsurance or deductibles) accrued expenditures of about 50 percent more for ambulatory care than those with 95 percent coinsurance (Newhouse et al. 1981). Visits in these contrasting groups varied from 5.5 to 3.5 visits per person each year. This effect was found in all subgroups studied.

The Rand HIE provides an opportunity to examine use of mental health services in the context of overall medical care. In early publications, the Rand researchers reported that cost-sharing affected use of mental health services in a way comparable to its effect on other services (Wells et al. 1982), but these results were subjected to considerable controversy. Ellis and McGuire (1984, 1986) suggested that the Rand researchers underestimated the mental health coinsurance effects due to a special design feature, the maximum dollar expenditure (MDE) level for a family. Once a family reached the MDE in a particular year, services at that point became free for the remainder of the period. The probability that families in programs with different coinsurance requirements reach the MDE at varying rates may distort estimates of the size of the effects of cost-sharing on mental health expenditures.

In an extension and reanalysis of the data, stimulated by the Ellis and McGuire (1984) observations, the Rand researchers concluded that outpatient mental health use is indeed more responsive to price than other types of medical care (Keeler et al. 1986). There was a fourfold variation between extreme coinsurance groups, and those with 50 percent coinsurance and no limits on cost-sharing spent only two-fifths as much as those with "free care." Coinsurance primarily affected the number of episodes of treatment, but once a person entered care the duration and intensity varied less. Since relatively few patients seek specialized mental health care whatever their insurance levels, the per person cost in the study for such services was low. Other factors found to affect use in addition to mental health status and insurance included educational level and age (better educated persons and young adults used more), and there were also variations by site. Seattle and Massachusetts had more use than Dayton and South Carolina. The site effect is probably a product of the different availability of mental health providers in the sites and varying cultural dispositions toward mental health services in these different geographic areas.

PSYCHIATRIC CARE UNDER PREPAYMENT PLANS

The pattern of insurance benefits that has evolved under fee-for-service plans has been designed to accommodate to the existing psychiatric marketplace, which is largely organized around office-based psychotherapy. Stringent controls on the definition of reimbursable providers were necessary because psychotherapists, particularly those with a psychoanalytic orientation, would carry out long courses of "treatment" at great expense with patients who had minimal impairment. The effect of paying for such services, as noted earlier, was to subsidize disproportionately the most affluent and educated groups in the population.

An alternative model is found in many health maintenance organizations (HMOs) that maintain greater control over the referral process and the assessment of the need for services. Such programs can then provide more liberal outpatient benefits without the usual cost-sharing deterrents. Experience in a variety of such plans indicates that outpatient utilization can be maintained at reasonable levels if the primary physician plays a gatekeeper role (Follette and Cummings 1967, Cummings and Follette 1968, Goldberg, Krantz, and Locke 1970, Fullerton, Lohrenz, and Nycz 1976). These plans require the primary care physician's referral, which has a moderating effect on the claim for services. The number of psychiatrists available in the plan and the queue for service set a natural ceiling on how many services can be consumed and with what intensity. When the mental health personnel are themselves employees of the plan, when they are conscious of the cost implications of utilization, and when they have no economic incentive to prolong counseling or psychotherapy, treatment tends to be less intense and to be provided for shorter periods of time. Also, it is likely that such plans select psychiatric personnel who are more attuned to pragmatic approaches to psychiatric care and to short-term and group psychotherapy.

From an organizational view, the prepaid plan offers an advantage in that it facilitates the use of nonmedical personnel in providing mental health services. Such programs may employ psychologists and social workers and can, therefore, provide services less expensively than programs that depend entirely on psychiatrists. In contrast, most insurance policies reimburse only medical personnel and psychologists in the fee-for-service sector, creating an unnecessary dependence on the most expensive types of manpower when other mental health personnel can do as well. Capitation-type plans facilitate the provision of a broader range of services at reasonable cost, are potentially able to make use of the entire spectrum of suitable personnel, and forge a closer alliance between general medical care and more specialized mental health services.

This is not the context for a detailed review of the large and important literature on health maintenance organizations (Mechanic 1986b). Since the way health services are organized importantly affects access, costs, service mix, and health outcomes, a brief review of some recent studies of the performance of prepaid practice is appropriate, however.

There is a large literature that supports the conclusion that prepaid group practice significantly reduces costs by limiting hospital admissions by as much as 40 percent and yields an overall cost savings of 20 to 30 percent (Luft 1981, Mechanic 1979a, 1986b). These differences have been found to persist when controls for population characteristics, out-of-plan use, and other factors are considered as well. Yet these studies could not exclude the possibility of significant selection effects relating to the health status of enrollees who choose prepaid practice plans for their medical care needs. In the Rand HIE, however, families were randomized into a prepaid group practice in Seattle (Group Health Insurance). This provided an opportunity to examine the impact of this type of organization independent of selection effects.

Group Health was found to have 40 percent less admissions than the free care experimental group, although both populations faced no financial barriers to care. Overall, expenditures in Group Health were 28 percent less than in the free-care condition (Manning et al. 1984). A subsequent analysis of health status suggested that poor sick patients randomized into prepaid practice did slightly less well on outcome measures than those assigned to the fee-for-service free-care condition (Ware et al. 1986). These data are not fully convincing, but they are consistent with other studies that suggest that less educated patients have difficulties negotiating the bureaucratic barriers typical of organizational types of practice (Mechanic 1979a). Such barriers can be overcome through well-designed outreach efforts to enrollees at high risk.

Organization and financing affect mix of mental health services as well. The Rand researchers carried out analyses of the use of mental health care in the fee-for-service conditions as compared with prepaid practice. More enrollees of prepaid practice actually used mental health services than those in the "free-care" fee-for-service condition, but they were provided much less intensively. Those in prepaid practice were more likely to receive mental health services from a general medical provider, and overall mental health expenditures were only one-third of the free-care condition ($25 per year per enrollee versus $70). When prepaid enrollees saw a mental health provider, they had only one-third the number of mental health visits of the comparable fee-for-service free-care group. Group health relied more on social workers than psychiatrists or psychologists and less on individual in contrast to group or family therapies (Manning et al. 1986, Manning and Wells 1986). These results are similar to those found in nonexperimental studies.

The Rand HIE also found that when patients received mental health care from general physicians in contrast to the specialty mental health sector, the intensity and cost of services was less. More important, they found that whether patients sought care from general physicians or specialists was unrelated to mental health status at enrollment or to the level of insurance coverage. But those who visited general physicians for a mental health problem accounted for only 5 percent of total outpatient mental health expenditures because of the low intensity of mental health care provided by general physicians (Wells et al. 1987).

Since approximately half of all mental health care occurs in the general medical sector, understanding patterns and quality of such care is important. Most studies find that patients in the mental health specialty sector are more impaired on the average than those cared for by general physicians, but there is a large degree of overlap between sectors. The restricted character of the HIE sample exaggerates the extent of overlap since the population studied underrepresents the most seriously mentally ill, who would be more likely to get care from specialists. The findings, however, should alert us to the importance of carefully distinguishing between mental health visits and the content, appropriateness, and quality of care. Mental health researchers conveniently differentiate between services provided by general physicians and those provided within the specialty mental health sector. The most seriously mentally ill have complex relationships with various parts of the medical, mental health, and social services systems, and we need deeper understanding of the interacting sectors and how they affect the longitudinal care of patients.

The Rand observation of little difference in severity of problems among those seeking mental health care from the two sectors reinforces the importance of help seeking and illness behavior discussed in the previous chapter. The sociocultural attitudes and illness behavior patterns that shape patients' help seeking lead to different transactions with the health care system and different degrees of care. There is, for example, much concern about the failure of general physicians to recognize depression and manage it appropriately and the inappropriate use of psychoactive medications. From a quality point of view, different types of mental health visits are not necessarily equivalent. The cost-effectiveness of one pattern of care versus another requires careful and continuing investigation if we are to make sound policy choices.

Although, in theory, the prepaid model offers the most rational and efficient way to handle mental health problems of the most common types, and the evidence supports the notion that they provide such services efficiently, we know relatively little about how well they do in terms of outcomes in serious mental illness. The feasibility of this model has been demonstrated from an economic perspective, but it would be helpful to have a better understanding of the referral decisions made by primary care physicians, of who obtains and fails to get treatment, and of the quality of mental health care provided. The prepaid organization has an intuitive logic to it, but we need more careful study of the way the system really works, the determinants of the referral process, and the outcomes of care in relation to alternative approaches.

THE STRUCTURE OF INSURANCE AND MENTAL HEALTH BENEFITS

There is a broad consensus that a crisis exists in the financing of mental health care for the most seriously mentally ill. Traditionally a state responsibility, encompassed in institutional care, two-thirds of state mental health funds continue to finance public institutions, but most of the seriously ill are in communities, and many are uninsured. There seem to be limited solutions to the overall financing problem outside a more equitable system of entitlement that covers these highly needy individuals.

There is a common belief among the public that the Medicaid program constitutes a health safety net for those who become poor, but while the number of poor persons has increased markedly in the 1980s (a 27 percent increase in the number of Americans living at or below the poverty level between 1979 and 1984), the Medicaid program has failed to adapt to changing economic circumstances. In the average state in 1975, Medicaid eligibility covered about 71 percent of the poor, but by 1986 the threshold had dropped to 48 percent, a one-third decrease (Curtis 1986). The thresholds and cutbacks were also distributed unevenly by state. Some states regressed enormously, decreasing coverage of the poor, for example, by 63 percent in Arkansas, 60 percent in Missouri, 59 percent in Tennessee, and 65 percent in Puerto Rico. Many states showing large decreases were already in a disadvantaged situation. The consequence is that, in some states, less than one-quarter of the poor are eligible for Medicaid protection. Even in such generous states as New York, about one-third of the poor are ineligible for Medicaid including some 300,000 children (Vladeck 1986). The numbers of uninsured fluctuate and estimates vary (Bazzoli 1986), but it is commonly believed that between 1978 and 1984 the uninsured population increased by more than a third from approximately 28 to 37 million people. It is mind-boggling to reflect on the fact that we spend more than half a trillion dollars a year on health care and still continue to have such large numbers of people disenfranchised.

The nation must seek a solution to this problem, and any viable plan must incorporate the mental health needs of persons with severe mental illness. The structure of a broader entitlement program, the appropriate scope of benefits, the definition of appropriate providers, and patterns of reimbursement are all central considerations (Frank and Lave 1985, Mechanic 1987a,b). The political infighting between varying mental health professionals to protect their future interests will be vigorous, and a great deal of organization and lobbying will continue. Our concerns, however, must go well beyond the limited professional interests of psychiatrists, psychologists, or social workers. From a public perspective, we must determine the type of financing structure that is best fitted to meeting psychiatric needs, ways to ensure that the greatest benefits go to those who are more seriously impaired and least able to obtain care on their own, and ways to promote effective and efficient use of available resources for psychiatric care. The structure of the system devised will do much to establish the future form of service delivery, the types of new personnel trained, and the relationships between the mental health sector and general medical care.

One tendency in expanding care might be to extend the kinds of psychiatric coverage provided by private and nonprofit insurance plans. As we have seen, however, such insurance structures reinforce a narrow medical model and have perverse distributive effects by giving more service to the affluent than to the needy. Any effective program must have a strong focus on ways of handling the needs of chronic mental patients and on determining whether the reimbursement system facilitates or interferes with the development of necessary community services. A poorly designed financing approach may simply fix in place some of the weakest features of our existing mental health delivery system.

In designing mental health benefits, a number of issues must be resolved. First, criteria must be established to specify the types of problems that are eligible for benefits. Should such benefits be limited to diagnosed psychiatric conditions, such as schizophrenia and depression, or should they also cover marital counseling, child behavior problems, feelings of unhappiness and alienation, and life transition crises? Second, decisions must be made as to the types of institutions and practitioners that will be eligible for reimbursement. Should state and county institutions receive reimbursement for patients comparable to that received by voluntary community hospitals? How should community mental health centers, outpatient clinics, and community care programs be reimbursed? Who should be defined as reimbursable providers? Should such providers include psychologists, social workers, family counselors, and recreation therapists, and, if so, under what conditions? Should psychologists and social workers be defined as independent professionals competing with psychiatrists and other physicians, or should reimbursable services require the supervision or approval of a physician or other professional? These are emotional political issues in which physicians attempt to maintain professional dominance over other providers (Freidson 1970), while psychologists and social workers are increasingly agitating for greater autonomy and recognition as independent practitioners. Although physicians often pose the issues as if they are technical ones relevant only to their special expertise in diagnosis and use of drugs, the decisions made will have dramatic political and economic consequences for the varying professions involved.

From the patients' point of view, an important issue concerns the extent to which coinsurance and deductibles will be used. Although such cost barriers may moderate some frivolous or less important use of services, they may also keep needy patients from receiving appropriate care (Lohr et al. 1986). Such economic barriers have a disproportionate influence on the utilization behavior of the poor as compared with those more affluent. The result is that more insured benefits are used by the rich, giving them disproportionate psychiatric subsidies. Another issue concerns the imposition of total dollar or visit limits for both ambulatory and hospital coverage. Although such limits are more severe for psychiatric as compared with other types of medical services, the justification for this is solely economic. It is a means of reducing total cost, but it is not necessarily what is medically or socially desirable.

One of the most significant issues in the design of psychiatric benefits is financing the development and stable maintenance of community programs for chronic patients who need continuing care over long periods of time. By working out appropriate formulas for capitation payment (a fixed amount per patient for a specified period) for varying types of patients, it becomes possible for such programs to work out an efficient mix of therapeutic and rehabilitative personnel. Such payment schemes for chronic psychiatric patients have not been available, and community programs—particularly less traditional types of programs—have great difficulty in finding stable funding (Mechanic 1979a). The necessary financial and organizational mechanisms will take time to develop, but such development is a necessary priority.

There has been a growing interest in capitation experiments affecting the chronically mentally ill. In 1986, Congress passed provisions that allow managed care waivers in Medicaid financed mental health services to facilitate experiments allowing financial tradeoffs among types of care for patients needing a wide range of services. Such experiments would be directed to patients whose uncontrolled and unpredictable episodic use of emergency services is extremely costly and causes many crises for the system. A well-managed care system could provide more comprehensive and higher quality services at comparable cost (Mechanic and Aiken 1987). Several communities, including Philadelphia, Rochester, New York and the state of South Carolina are in the process of implementing limited capitation approaches.

Underlying many technical insurance issues that have to be resolved are a variety of important philosophical problems. First, is the care of the psychiatric patient to be seen as primarily a medical issue, or is such care more appropriately viewed within psychological, social, or educational models? Second, are boundaries of mental health care properly narrow, primarily focused on traditional types of impairment, or should public policy encourage services for a wide range of social and psychological maladjustments? Third, should needs for containment of costs limit the range of disorders covered or the definition of what providers could be reimbursed, or should cost controls be achieved through other means? Although it would be foolhardy from a public policy standpoint to reimburse any psychological service, it is equally foolish to restrict services to a narrow medical approach. My view is that although services should be broadly available, highest priority should be given to those patients who are most impaired and to those interventions that have been proven most effective. My preference would be to design an insurance program that facilitates reimbursement for care of chronic patients in community programs as well as in hospitals. Consistent with this belief, I will describe what a reasonable approach to the organization of mental health services might look like.

AN EPIDEMIOLOGICAL APPROACH TO PSYCHIATRIC NEED

Examining the way patients with a range of problems flow from the community into different service contexts is useful in assessing the dimensions of need for care (Lewis, Fein, and Mechanic 1976). Simply assessing service utilization of particular types of facilities, such as psychiatric hospitalization or outpatient psychotherapy, fails to map the variety of problems people face or their different means of coping with them. Although the epidemiological picture is incomplete because of the difficulty of adequately defining mental illness in community settings, the data available are instructive.

There are a variety of sources of community data that allow us to make some assessments of need. On the one hand, we have surveys such as the ECA studies using DSM-III criteria; on the other, we have a variety of community surveys that assess perceived need and reported symptoms. The ECA studies are an important source of data for estimating the prevalence of illness, use of services, and unmet need (Eaton and Kessler 1985). In analyzing ECA data from the Baltimore survey of the general population, Shapiro and colleagues (1985) estimate the proportion of patients with different types of disorders who received a mental health service from either nonpsychiatric physicians or specialized mental health providers. Twenty-three percent of those studied were estimated to have had a disorder during the prior six months consistent with DSM-III psychiatric criteria, but only a minority received any kind of care. In the aggregate, only 7 percent of the population who presented evidence of a recent emotional problem of any kind received a mental health service during the prior six months. The implications from such aggregate data may be arguable, but particularly disturbing is the fact that 45 percent of schizophrenics, 56 percent of those with affective disorders, and 62 percent of those with substance abuse problems and dependence received no care at all.

Leaf and his colleagues (1985), reporting on the data from New Haven, provide comparable results. Only half of those meeting DSM-III criteria for schizophrenia during the prior six months reported receiving any relevant service, and rates for other serious conditions showed even less utilization: depressive episode with grief (37 percent), alcohol or drug abuse/dependence (13 percent), manic episodes (25 percent), phobias (22 percent). Some of these conditions, such as depression and phobias, are highly responsive to treatment, and appropriate management of schizophrenia can importantly affect the course of disorder. There is clearly some difficulty with the validity of the estimates of disorder, but even allowing for much error there seems to be substantial unmet need.

Community epidemiologic studies vary a great deal in case definition, but most find a large reservoir of problems characterized by depression, anxiety, psychophysiologic discomforts, insomnia, unhappiness, and alienation (Dohrenwend et al. 1979). Although most of these problems do not constitute psychiatric disorders as conventionally defined, many of these persons suffer significantly and feel a need for assistance. At any point in time, such persons may constitute as much as one-quarter of the population, but this estimate includes both mild and more serious disturbances. Unfortunately, we have too little understanding of the natural history of these symptoms and the benefits to be gained from varying levels of support and treatment. We do know, however, that there is considerable overlap in symptoms between those treated in a variety of outpatient settings and those who receive no treatment at all.

Regardless of whether we use DSM-III criteria or psychological distress indicators, the evidence suggests that mental health problems are significantly undertreated. Many such problems may not require treatment, but the numbers of severely mentally ill who fall outside any system of services are a cause for concern. The issue is how to achieve the most effective triage and continuing responsibility for those most in need. Access to care and help seeking determine who enters the care system in the first place, but the first point of evaluation is commonly the doctor of first contact, the primary care physician.

THE ROLE OF PRIMARY MEDICAL CARE

Primary medical care is an important focus because most people have access to such services, and the vast majority of the population visit a doctor at least once a year (Robert Wood Johnson Foundation 1983). Thus effective primary care can do a great deal to support patients in distress and refer those needing more intensive and sophisticated services to appropriate professionals and facilities. Large numbers of patients coming to doctors either report or show evidence of serious psychosocial and emotional difficulties, and many physicians feel at a loss in knowing how to deal appropriately with such patients (Institute of Medicine 1979). Even the estimates from the ECA studies that 41 to 63 percent of all mental health visits occur in the primary care sector underestimate such morbidity because many patients do not define their problems in mental health terms, presenting their complaints in somatic or nonspecific ways. Physicians are, thus, often ambivalent and uncertain about appropriate treatment and referral, are commonly insecure about diagnosis and psychotropic medication, and must cope with the somatization of psychological distress and the unacceptability of mental health diagnoses to many patients.

Referral to the specialized mental health sector depends on the seriousness of the disorder, the physician's knowledge and attitudes toward mental health professionals, the availability of insurance, and the physician's perception of the willingness of the patient to accept mental health treatment. Patients' cultural background and attitudes toward the use of psychological services are significant factors affecting referral (Mechanic 1978, 1982). Studies comparing independent standardized psychiatric assessment of primary care patients to how such patients were diagnosed and managed indicate that primary care physicians commonly do not recognize psychiatric symptoms, and even less frequently make a mental health diagnosis or prescribe appropriate psychotropic medication for these patients. Also, the prevalence of such diagnoses from one physician to another is not related to accuracy as assessed independently (Goldberg and Huxley 1980). Accuracy appears to depend on the way the doctor interviews patients, personality, and academic ability; it is not related to self-assessment of psychological skills or experience.

Of those patients seen by primary care physicians, relatively few are ever referred for specialized care. Those who come or are referred to psychiatric settings tend to have more severe symptoms and social and cultural orientations that enhance their receptivity to psychiatric care (Greenley and Mechanic 1976, Greenley, Mechanic, and Cleary 1987). The majority of patients, however, receive whatever treatment they obtain from primary care physicians. Estimates vary a great deal as to the proportion of patients in general medical settings who suffer from these types of symptoms, but there is wide agreement that they constitute a considerable burden of demand on ambulatory care facilities (Andersen et al. 1977, Institute of Medicine 1979). The distress associated with these patients' problems triggers a demand for medical service (Tessler, Mechanic, and Dimond 1976), and such patients are often recipients of intensive medical and surgical care that achieve little of value. Support, reassurance, and relief of suffering through pharmacological intervention, in contrast, are of some use. Although psychoactive drugs are used extensively in medical practice (Parry et al. 1973), we do not know very much about when they are used.

Data from the National Ambulatory Medical Care Survey for 1980 and 1981 indicate that psychoactive drugs were prescribed by office-based physicians in 6 percent of all visits and in 10 percent of all visits in which a drug was prescribed (Koch 1983). The five most common diagnoses for using such drugs were neurotic disorders, essential hypertension, depression, schizophrenia, and affective psychosis. While psychiatrists were most likely to use such drugs (441 times per 1,000 visits), rates were also high in internal medicine (115 times per 1,000 visits) and general and family practice (84 times per 1,000 visits). Office-based physicians used 136 different psychotropic drugs that have different biological functions and varying types of side effects. There is a great deal of concern about the appropriate use of such drugs and allegations that primary care physicians often choose the wrong drugs or inappropriate doses in relation to the patient's symptomatology.

While experts debate whether the psychoactive drugs are used too readily or too sparingly (Gardner 1974), the implications of drug use without adequate monitoring for patients with high levels of distress are not trivial. Murphy (1975a, b) found that 71 to 91 percent of patients who committed suicide had been under the recent care of a physician. Over two-thirds of these patients had histories of suicide threats or attempts, but these suicide gestures were known to only two-fifths of the physicians who provided care for them. There was evidence that three-quarters of the patients were depressed, but this diagnosis was rarely made by nonpsychiatrists nor was the depression treated. More than one-half of those who died by overdose had an unlimited prescription of the substance ingested or had received a prescription within a week or less before their deaths.

Any effective system of primary medical care services must take account of these issues. However physicians may wish to limit their responsibilities and the scope of their work, such patients will continue to constitute a significant component of patient demand. From a public policy perspective, it would be neither productive nor economical to attempt to shift these patients to more specialized care. We have no evidence of the effectiveness of such care in most instances, and such a shift would take away scarce resources from patients with more profound disabilities who need the available specialized services. Planning to ensure that patients with distress syndromes receive supportive assistance from the general medical sector is highly desirable, however. This can be facilitated by improving the capacity of primary care practitioners to recognize more reliably such common problems as depression, alcoholism, and anxiety and by increasing their confidence in their ability to deal with such patients. Perhaps most importantly, primary care physicians must improve their pharmacological knowledge of psychoactive drugs. More effort can also be given to developing a consultant-psychiatrist role for primary care to provide backup assistance to practitioners in dealing with mental health problems (Colemen and Patrick 1978). As physicians become more organized in groups and prepaid practices, it will become possible to integrate nonphysician mental health personnel into primary care to provide counseling, supportive care, and behavior therapy and to assist in organizing and coordinating self-help and group-help efforts.

The response of the doctor to the patients' distress is affected by conceptions of etiology. To the extent that such common problems as depression and substance abuse are masked by the presentation of general physical complaints and are linked to unalterable life stresses, severe disappointments, or grave misfortunes, the physician realistically may not see himself in a good position to do very much beyond prescribing drugs to relieve symptoms. The patients' somatization may be adaptive as compared to intolerable alternatives, and it may be unproductive to undermine patients' defenses when they are unwilling or unable to deal with the conditions of their lives (Corney 1984). A cross-cultural example brings this issue sharply into focus.

In China, neurasthenia is a common diagnosis in psychiatric outpatient clinics and perhaps the most common "psychiatric diagnosis" in general medical settings. Such patients typically complain of somatic complaints characteristic of depression in Western countries but usually do not report comparable affective disturbance. Kleinman notes that psychiatrists in China routinely view neurasthenia as a "disorder of brain function involving asthenia of cerebral cortical activity" (Kleinman 1982, 1986). In a project at the Hunan Medical College, Kleinman identified 87 patients with this diagnosis who met DSM-III criteria for major depression and treated them with antidepressants. At follow-up, while a majority appeared to show significant improvement in psychiatric symptoms, there was much less effect in decreasing help seeking, maladaptive functioning, and social impairment. The patients remained skeptical of the value of the drug treatment.

Kleinman views neurasthenia as a bioculturally patterned illness experience, and he links it to extraordinary hardships in the lives of patients from which they could not escape given the harsh realities of the Chinese social system. The somatic discourse used by patients, and accepted by doctors, serves as a limited escape from involuntary and taxing life situations, and the illness idiom offers greater legitimacy than alternative escape routes (Kleinman 1986). The issue is whether modifying the Chinese doctor's concept of the clinical problem serves any constructive purpose. To the extent that the patient needs the illness, and neither the doctor nor the patient have the means to modify the harsh circumstances of the patient's life, the diagnosis, and its underlying meanings, may serve a useful purpose in providing a release, however limited, from restrictive and unalterable social conditions. The organic etiology attributed to the condition is culturally acceptable, while a diagnosis of depression or another emotional diagnosis is more suspect and more stigmatized. From one perspective, Chinese medical practice appears out-of-date; from another, it seems to fit the cultural and social conditions exceedingly well.

In Western societies, physicians have more influence than in China, and the societies offer more opportunities for life changes. Moreover, there is a strong belief in psychological phenomena and a widely shared view that it is desirable that people be in touch with themselves, views which have increasingly affected conceptions of primary medical care and the orientation of physicians to patients with psychological distress. This trend, which some physicians intuitively if not openly resist, is as much the result of a psychological ideology as it is of an established foundation of empirical results. It is undoubtedly true that some patients experience relief of physical symptoms by acknowledging their feelings and sharing them with an empathetic person. Specific forms of psychotherapy focused on interpersonal relations or cognitive orientations appear even more helpful. But it is also true that in many instances denial is an extraordinarily effective coping device and that excessive exploration of feelings and thoughts may increase negative affect and a sense of physical discomfort (Mechanic 1979b). Psychologizing medical practice has its benefits but also its risks.

The primary care physician, better aware of psychiatric morbidity, however, can use such information constructively. The practitioner can communicate an interest and willingness to listen, a cue many depressed patients feel is lacking and inhibits expression of their distress (Mechanic 1972b, Ginsberg and Brown 1982). Such information also alerts the physician to suicide and related risks and encourages greater supportiveness, vigilance, and referral when the physician is insecure. Knowledge of psychiatric syndromes and appropriate specific medication also allows more competent management. All of this can be accomplished without imposition of psychological interpretations, without undermining the patients' coping efforts, and without requiring the patient to adapt to an unacceptable definition of the problem. This is a skill highly dependent on cognitive and communication capacities, and the skillful practitioner is in a strong position to relieve the patient's symptoms, offer meaningful support, and assist in strengthening coping capacities. With trust and patience and communication of willingness to listen, even recalcitrant patients shed some of their defenses and become more amenable to influence. Much of the potential of the doctor–patient relationship, even in an age of high technology, arises from the authority of the physician and the patient's faith (Frank 1974). These assets are extraordinarily powerful and a significant force if used prudently.

Although efforts must be made to integrate more psychiatric care into the mainstream of medical care, sustained categorical efforts will be required to provide effective services to patients with chronic disorders that involve considerable handicaps. Emphasis should be given to interventions that have the highest probability of minimizing disability and reducing suffering. When care is given primarily to comfort and support, priority should be given to patients with the greatest distress and impairment. Interventions should be measured by the degree to which they enhance well-being and social functioning.

It is difficult to specify precisely the number of persons in the population who need more intensive services than those likely to be available through the general medical sector. The President's Commission on Mental Health (1978) estimated that as much as 15 percent of the population may need some form of mental health care at any time. The six-month prevalence of any disorder conforming to DSM-III criteria derived from the ECA was 18.7 percent, an estimate close to that of the Commission. Many of these patients, however, do not require care and others can do well with minimum support. But however one views the issue, the magnitude of need is large and a significant proportion of the population at some time in their lives will require assistance for such problems. For many such patients, the need for care will be a short interlude in their lives, as in the case of many reactive depressions; others, such as schizophrenics, may require continuing treatment throughout their lives and will consume considerable mental health resources. Still others, such as those with bipolar depression, alcoholism, and drug addiction, will need periodic treatment, depending on the severity of the problem. In theory, many of these patients could be cared for in general medical settings, but the practicalities make it unlikely that an adequate pattern of services for highly impaired patients can be sustained in these practices.

Although some primary care physicians with an interest in psychiatry may be able to manage chronic patients between episodes of more serious problems, the demands on primary care facilities make it inevitable that these impaired and frequently difficult patients will be inadequately monitored and neglected. Given the complexity of their problems and the intractability of their conditions, they will frustrate physicians and will suffer stigmatization by both medical and nonmedical personnel. These patients require a sustained community approach in addition to whatever medical and drug treatment they receive, and it is unlikely that an unspecialized medical context can effectively organize such services.

Whatever efforts are made to extend general insurance benefits for traditional psychiatric services must not overshadow the needs of the severely impaired patients who require services organized independently of the traditional medical sector. Such services will have to be provided largely by nonmedical personnel. Services for these patients must include diagnosis and assessment, appropriate medical care, sheltered care and preparation for limited employment, aggressive monitoring and training for community living, and continuing social supports. Although a variety of viable models have been developed in demonstration projects (Stein et al. 1975, Stein and Test 1976), we have as yet failed to develop any sustained way of financing these efforts on a continuing basis. Even under the best of conditions, such programs are difficult to organize and maintain. Without financial stability they have little chance to become established.

In sum, we might generally think of patients as having three levels of need, varying from the most prevalent conditions needing only modest interventions to those less frequent but more severe conditions requiring a wide range of medical and social services. The largest group of problems involving a lack of general well-being and a sense of psychophysiological discomfort is most properly managed within the general medical sector as a component of comprehensive medical care. A second category of more disabling conditions, such as depression, alcoholism, and severe neuroses, might best be managed through a collaborative effort involving the general medical sector but with significant assistance from psychiatric consultation and community supportive groups. The most severely impaired patients should receive highest priority for special categorical services involving medical and psychiatric assistance in addition to the entire spectrum of essential community care services.

CRITICAL PUBLIC POLICY ISSUES IN FINANCING MENTAL HEALTH SERVICES

The service model presented based on an epidemiological approach is quite different from the prevailing situation in which much outpatient care financed through insurance is traditional psychotherapy. While traditional psychotherapy may be of great value as an educational exploration of oneself, one's needs, and relationships with others, there is little evidence of its success as a mode of treatment for psychiatric disorders, although patients and their therapists often subjectively feel that improvement has occurred. As a matter of public policy, greatly extending psychotherapy services within a traditional office-based framework is an unwise allocation of scarce resources. Facilitating crisis intervention in HMOs, ambulatory clinics, and mental health centers, and short-term therapy when needed would allow the same resources to meet the needs of many more people. Although many persons in the population attuned to traditional psycho-therapies may wish to buy such services on their own, traditional psychotherapy is a poor focus for the nation's priorities in providing mental health care.

The key question is how access to mental health care for people in distress can be insured without encouraging excessive use of hospital care that is typically covered by existing insurance. If outpatient benefits are not covered, an incentive exists to use hospital care that is covered by insurance as a substitute for ambulatory or community care. If, however, ambulatory care is broadly covered by insurance, it is likely that large expenditures will be made for psychotherapy for patients who are not seriously impaired but who are socially receptive to such services. The best alternative is to provide coverage for outpatient psychiatric services within a controlled system such as a health maintenance organization in which there is no economic incentive for the practitioner to provide services that are not essential. Because relatively few people in the population belong to such programs, this alternative does not provide an overall solution for the near future. Another alternative is to provide broader coverage linked with more careful professional peer review of the need for particular types of services. Although there are some developments in this direction, the standards for ambulatory care in psychiatry are simply too diffuse and involve too much disagreement to make this a successful approach. In all likelihood, what we will see in the coming years is a combination of approaches, involving cautious extensions of outpatient benefits but accompanied by coinsurance and deductibles. There will be some growth of ambulatory psychiatric benefits in HMOs where the health care system itself is sufficiently under the organization's control, allowing the rationing of services. We will also see some modest development in peer review approaches involving standards for treatment.

The extension of traditional insurance benefits, while helpful to many people, will not substantially affect the care of the most needy chronic patients. Indeed, such efforts could create the illusion that the needs of the most severely ill are being addressed, thus reducing pressures for funding to develop an integrated community network of rehabilitative and supportive services. Expanding hospital benefits without attention to the needed network of services will promote a traditional medical response, when what is most needed for the chronic population is a wide spectrum of services for those facing a long life with impairments in work, interpersonal relationships, and the ordinary activities of daily living.

The most needy and chronic patients have been a public responsibility for more than a century. It is an illusion to believe that the private sector or the system of general medical care will give these patients high priority. The only real choice is to revitalize our public mental health systems, develop focused planning and organizational structures, and find new ways of encouraging and consolidating finances directed to this population. Doing this requires understanding of models, some tough analytic work, and many difficult choices. It is to these issues we now turn.

Chapter Nine

Central Perspectives in Formulating Mental Health Policies

The future of mental health services in the United States and elsewhere depends on the resolution of many basic scientific and practical issues. In the scientific arena, we lack understanding of most serious disorders, their basic causes, and effective interventions. Major disagreements continue as to the best way to characterize disorders, the boundaries between mental disorders and social problems, and the means to prevent, cure, or ameliorate suffering and disability. Whatever the state of our knowledge, at the practical level we must decide whom to treat, where to treat, the scope of appropriate clinicians, and how to pay for services. The purpose of this chapter is to explore some underlying issues that assist us in formulating and dealing with the policy questions.

CONCEPTS OF CHRONIC MENTAL ILLNESS

There is no agreed-on definition of chronic mental illness (CMI), but the term is usually intended to convey a history of serious acute episodes, continuing residual disability, and high levels of medical and psychosocial need. Such patients typically have serious problems in many facets of daily living including work, social relations, and family life. They are commonly unmarried or divorced, isolated from family, unemployed, and on varying forms of welfare assistance. Operationally, CMI is often defined by extended or frequent psychiatric hospitalizations and a history of repeated contact with psychiatric services and social agencies (Freedman and Moran 1984). But some in the CMI population resist or cannot access services and come to our attention primarily through the intervention of police and the criminal justice system.

The concept of chronicity refers to the time frame of illness experience in terms of duration and recurrence. As typically used in the mental health field, it conveys a sense of persistence and intractability, although we know from the studies already reviewed that patients with serious mental disorders such as schizophrenia may have very different trajectories of illness and levels of handicap. Shepherd (1987), for example, in a five-year follow-up of a representative cohort of 121 patients in an English community, assessed with standardized social and clinical measures, described four trajectories: 13 percent had one episode but no impairment; 30 percent had several episodes but with little or no impairment; 10 percent developed impairments after the first episode and had occasional exacerbations of symptoms and no full return to normality; and 47 percent had increasing impairment with subsequent exacerbations of symptoms. Depending on arbitrary definition and the relative emphasis given to symptoms and impairments, the proportion viewed as chronic might vary from 47 to 87 percent.

In developing the national plan for the chronically mentally ill, the Department of Health and Human Services adopted a definition of chronicity based on diagnosis, disability and duration.

> The chronically mentally ill population encompasses persons who suffer certain mental or emotional disorders (organic brain syndrome, schizophrenia, recurrent depressive and manic-depressive disorders, and paranoid and other psychoses, plus other disorders that may become chronic) that erode or prevent the development of the functional capacities in relation to three or more primary aspects of daily life—personal hygiene and self-care, self-direction, interpersonal relationships, social transactions, learning, and recreation—and that erode or prevent the development of their economic self-sufficiency.
>
> Most such individuals have required institutional care of extended duration, including intermediate-term hospitalization (90 days to 365 days in a single year), long-term hospitalization (one year or longer in the preceding five years), or nursing home placement because of a diagnosed mental condition or a diagnosis of senility without psychosis. Some such individuals have required short-term hospitalization (less than 90 days); others have received treatment from a medical or mental health professional solely on an outpatient basis, or—despite their needs—have received no treatment in the professional service system. Thus included in the target population are persons who are or were formerly residents of institutions (public and private psychiatric hospitals and nursing homes) and persons who are at high risk of institutionalization because of persistent mental disability (Tessler and Goldman 1982, p. 5).

The notion of chronicity speaks to the trajectory of the condition and not the diagnosis, and, thus, it is difficult to obtain accurate estimates of this population. While diagnoses such as schizophrenia encompass large proportions of chronic patients, the diagnosis itself is not a true measure of chronicity, nor are most others, except irreversible conditions such as dementia. Typically for public policy purposes, efforts are made to estimate this population based on duration of illness or treatment or by disability as measured by welfare eligibility or inability to work. While the estimates are crude, they point to the level of severe need in the population. Goldman et al. (1981) estimated the CMI population in the period 1975–1977 as varying from 1.7 to 2.4 million persons, and more recent estimates suggest a number as large as 2.78 million (National Institute of Mental Health 1987b). Between 38 and 53 percent of these individuals were patients in nursing homes with mental disorder or senility without psychosis. The vast majority of these nursing home patients, however, had little in common with the vast majority of patients in other psychiatric institutions or in the community. Even the nursing home patients with mental disorder (constituting less than half of the total nursing home patients called chronically mentally ill) were a heterogeneous group with substantially varying needs for services. The analysts making these estimates had good reason for trying to appraise the magnitude of the problem, but the aggregate number comes to be used in a way that can confuse central questions. A single number may be useful to give visibility to the issue and to mobilize public opinion, but formulation of good public policy requires careful attention to each of the many subgroups that constitute the chronic population.

CRITERIA FOR EVALUATION

Indices of cure have an unhappy history in the mental health field. As in many other areas, such indices have been distorted for administrative and propaganda purposes (Deutsch 1949). Discreditation of earlier treatment results was a source of discouragement and disillusionment in the early twentieth century, but retrospective study has shown that such debunking, like the earlier statistics, was exaggerated unnecessarily, contributing to a sense of hopelessness (Bockoven 1972). Past experience teaches that intelligent assessment of the effects of varying mental health policies must depend less on gross statistics that are easily manipulated administratively, and more on careful study of clinical and social indicators that characterize in specific terms the outcomes for patients and the community. In the last several decades, we have witnessed an enormous social change in the ways in which psychiatric patients are treated and in the contexts of care. Extreme statements—of optimism and gloom—are made on every side of the issue without detailed examination of actual outcomes for varying types of patients, their loved ones, and the community. Although detail always reveals a more ambiguous situation, social policy must arise from such ambiguity and not from idealized characterizations of reality.

The effects of varying mental health policies can be characterized and evaluated in at least three ways: (1) we can measure the subjective response of patients to various kinds of policies—whether they feel they have been helped, whether they feel they have fewer symptoms and are more able to cope; (2) we can attempt to measure their performance and the quality of their lives and those of others in the community after exposure to varying public policies; or (3) we can attempt to assess the consequences of various policies in terms of economic and administrative costs—does one policy lead to an equivalent outcome at less cost than another? All these forms of evaluation are important and compatible.

The most striking treatment change has been in the decline of long-term hospitalization and the growth of psychiatric treatment in ambulatory care settings. Although admissions are frequent, most patients remain in the hospital only briefly, and most of their care and maintenance occur in the community. Judged solely from this perspective, current practice fits quite clearly the aspirations of the Joint Commission on Mental Illness and Health (1961) and the legislation that followed.

> The objective of modern treatment of persons with major mental illness is to enable the patient to maintain himself in the community in a normal manner. To do so, it is necessary (1) to save the patient from the debilitating effects of institutionalism as much as possible, (2) if the patient requires hospitalization, to return him to home and community life as soon as possible, and (3) thereafter to maintain him in the community as long as possible. Therefore, aftercare and rehabilitation are essential parts of all service to mental patients, and the various methods of achieving rehabilitation should be integrated in all forms of services, among them day hospitals, night hospitals, aftercare clinics, public health nursing services, foster family care, convalescent nursing homes, rehabilitation centers, work services, and ex-patient groups. We recommend that demonstration programs for day and night hospitals and the more flexible use of mental hospital facilities, in the treatment of both the acute and the chronic patient, be encouraged and augmented through institutional, program, and project grants. (Joint Commission on Mental Illness and Health 1961, p. xviii)

Subsequently, we have learned what we should have known but missed in our enthusiasm for change. Community life is no panacea unless the patient's suffering is alleviated and social functioning improved. We have learned that community life, without adequate services and supports, could be as dehumanizing and debilitating as the poor mental hospital. We have learned that if the patient is sufficiently disturbed and disoriented, as many schizophrenic patients are, residence in the home or community can cause innumerable difficulties for family and others and may result in a general outcome inferior to good institutional care. We must understand more thoroughly what happens to the mental patient outside the hospital—the extent to which difficulties occur and the way they are handled. Intelligent planning of community services depends on a firm understanding of the true consequences of various policies.

An initial classic study was an experimental investigation of the prevention of hospitalization (Pasamanick, Scarpitti, and Dinitz 1967). The major intent of the study was to determine the relative value of hospital versus home treatment for schizophrenic patients under varying circumstances. The investigators randomized 152 schizophrenic patients referred to a state hospital into three groups: (1) a drug home-care group, (2) a placebo home-care group, and (3) a hospital control group. Patients treated at home were visited regularly by public health nurses and were seen less frequently by a staff psychologist, a social worker, and a psychiatrist for evaluation purposes. The study compared hospital treatment and home-care treatment by public health nurses and also compared home-care patients receiving drugs and those not receiving drugs.

Patients were involved in the study from 6 to 30 months. The investigators found that over 77 percent of the drug home-care patients remained at home throughout the study period in contrast to 34 percent of those receiving placebos. They estimated, using the hospital control group as a base, that the 57 home patients, receiving drugs saved over 4,800 days of hospitalization and that the 41 patients in the placebo group saved over 1,150 inpatient days. They also observed that members of the control group treated in the hospital required rehospitalization more frequently after they returned to the community than did the patients who were treated at home on drugs from the very start. The authors came to the following conclusion:

> This carefully designed experimental study confirmed our original hypothesis that home care for schizophrenic patients is *feasible,* that the combination of drug therapy and public health nurses' home visitations is *effective* in preventing hospitalization, and that home care is at least as good a method of treatment as hospitalization by any or all criteria, and probably superior by most. (Pasamanick Scarpitti, and Dinitz 1967, p. ix)

One aspect of the study raised some question as to whether remaining at home is an adequate measure of rehabilitation. The investigators selected patients for the study when they were referred to the state hospital for treatment. The relatives of the patients randomly selected for home treatment were informed that hospital treatment was unnecessary and that home care was more appropriate; "a due amount of persuasion" (p. 40) was used to convince the relatives to accept the patient at home. The design of the study had two consequences that differentiated those treated in the hospital from those treated at home. First, the hospital defined itself as a less appropriate context for treating the symptoms and the conditions of some patients and may have served to define different frames of reference as to what symptoms justify hospitalization among relatives of home-care and hospital-care cases. Second, by resisting the hospitalization of patients in the home-care cases, the hospital may have communicated a greater lack of willingness to help the relatives of those in the home-care group during periods of crisis than to help relatives of those in the hospital-care group. It is not unreasonable to expect that, once people are refused help of a particular sort, they are less likely to request it on the second occasion, and this tendency may explain the greater use of the hospital on subsequent occasions by patients in the hospital-treatment group. We must evaluate rehabilitation on other grounds than the frequency of hospitalization.

The investigators provided various data that reflect the psychiatric and social functioning of the patients after 6, 18, and 24 months. These data generally show considerable improvement in all groups by the sixth month, with rather little improvement thereafter. One form of treatment does not have clearly superior results in comparison to the results of others. Using the criterion of social functioning, we have little justification for choosing one form of care over another.

Finally, we should inquire into the social costs of retaining patients in the community. We can assess these costs to some extent by using data on various burdensome kinds of behavior. The investigators demonstrated that these difficult behaviors decreased substantially by the sixth month, although they occurred frequently during the initial study period. At the beginning of the study, all three groups showed an equivalent level of family and community disturbance. When the patient was removed to the hospital, the family and the community were relieved of these difficulties; when the patient stayed home, these problems continued, although they decreased through time. The data from this study did not allow assessment of how quickly the initial symptoms decreased. It was clear, however, that disturbing and troubling behavior was relieved more quickly than inadequate role performance. It should be emphasized, however, that these data on schizophrenic patients described perhaps the most disabled type of patient and cannot be readily generalized to other populations.

These data suggest that there may be considerable social cost in maintaining the patient in the community during the earliest phase of an acute episode. One alternative is to use the hospital during periods of greatest strain early in the illness episode, followed by an expeditious release. The other alternative is to provide intensive community services for patients and those who relate to them during the period when social and family costs are high. Experience in a variety of settings suggests that professional views of what families should and can do to care for disordered patients are powerful influences on behavior. It is possible to persuade families and the community to avoid hospitalization, but such a policy requires aggressive professional support for those who must cope with the social and psychological costs of such policies. In any given instance, the choice of appropriate policy depends on individual circumstances, the services available to relieve and aid in home-care situations, and, if a family setting is not appropriate, the availability of other suitable community settings.

The impact of mental illness on the family and on the psychological development of children and the resulting burden are no small matters (Kreisman and Joy 1974, Fisher, Benson, and Tessler 1986, Feldman et al. 1987). The psychological developmental theories dominant in the decades of the 1960s and 1970s commonly concentrated on family factors in contributing to mental illness and unfairly, and with little evidence, blamed families for the mental illnesses suffered by their members. Instead of using the family as a resource, therapists often isolated the family and induced feelings of guilt, often in an unconstructive way. There was far too little concern with the real difficulties of living with a seriously mentally ill person, ways of relieving the stress and burden on family members, and the necessary steps for providing community resource systems that would make community care an effective option. Some of the early studies carried out in England clearly pointed to some of the issues that had to be addressed.

An English five-year follow-up study of 339 schizophrenic hospital patients who returned to the community (Brown et al. 1966), for example, examined the behavior of patients and the impact of their behavior on relatives and the community. This study suggests that community care for schizophrenic patients involves considerable social cost. The investigators found that in the six-month period prior to the interview, 14 percent of first admissions and 27 percent of previously admitted patients showed violent, threatening, or destructive behavior. Thirty-one percent of first admissions and 49 percent of readmissions had delusions and hallucinations. Twenty-eight percent and 45 percent, respectively, had other symptoms of schizophrenia, such as marked social withdrawal, slowness, posturing, and odd behavior. Finally, 41 percent of first admissions and 47 percent of previous admissions had other symptoms, such as headaches, phobias, and depression. A significant proportion of relatives of these patients reported that the patients' illnesses were harmful to their health, affected the children adversely, created financial difficulties, and resulted in restriction of leisure activities and of the ability to have persons outside the family visit their homes. Despite these problems, approximately three-quarters of those who were living with a patient seemed to welcome the person at home, and another 15 percent were acceptant and tolerant.

One of the intentions of the investigators was to evaluate the effect of different hospital policies on patient care and functioning. They compared three hospitals, one of them known for its community care policies, and found that the functioning of patients was much the same in all three. Patients spent less time in the hospital oriented toward community care, but because they were released from the hospital before complete remission of their symptoms, they were more likely to be unemployed when they were in the community, and they experienced difficulties that led to more frequent readmissions to the hospital. Relatives of patients in the community-oriented hospital reported more problems than did relatives of patients in other hospitals.

We must view these data in perspective. Because they pertain to the most disabled category of patients, we cannot generalize the results to other psychiatric patients characterized by less social disturbance. The adequacy of a community care program depends on the adequacy of the services available outside the hospital, and in the community studied such services were not fully adequate to the task, although they were probably as good as those found more generally. This investigation does demonstrate, however, that policy changes must be evaluated in terms of their behavioral consequences and problems and not only in terms of administrative statistics.

In a related study, Grad and Sainsbury (1966) tried to compare and evaluate the effects on families of a community care service and of a hospital-centered service. They were able to evaluate outcomes in two relatively comparable communities that had these different services. The investigators measured the amount of burden incurred by relatives both on referral and three to five weeks later. Approximately two-thirds of the families with severe burdens showed some relief from the original problem regardless of the nature of the service. Among patients presenting a less severe burden, improvement was somewhat higher in the hospital-centered service (36 percent versus 24 percent). In general, the investigators found little relationship between psychiatric symptoms and the extent to which burden was relieved in the two services. They did find, however, that patients with depression caused more hardship if treated in a community service rather than in a hospital service. There were other gains in having a hospital-based service. One such gain was that the closest relative felt less anxiety and suffered less interference with social and leisure activities.

In a two-year follow-up study of the same patients, Grad (1968) found that the hospital-based service was more effective in reducing anxiety and distress among patients' relatives and created fewer financial difficulties and other problems for the family. Young men treated in the community service were much more likely than those in the hospital-based service to remain unemployed for the entire two-year period. Differences in social outcome are of large magnitude and raise important questions concerning the philosophy underlying a community-based service. After further investigation the researchers reported that patients in the community-based service were treated more superficially than were those in the hospital-based service. Grad noted the following problems in community-based services.

> Many social problems, especially those of a more subtle nature, were missed by the psychiatrists. First, their home visits were usually necessarily brief because of pressure of work; second, their interviews in accordance with their training and responsibilities and the families' expectations were patient-focused; third, the high social esteem in which doctors are held meant that family members would often either not presume to detain them by talking about their own troubles or feel relaxed enough in their presence to discuss those family trivia which often reveal social conflicts and stresses. (Grad p. 447)

Other investigations support the observation by Grad and Sainsbury (1966) that the burden of mental illness on the family is not exclusive to psychotic conditions but, indeed, may be greater in what are regarded as moderate conditions. Hoenig and Hamilton (1967), in their study of burden on the household, found that patients with personality disorders and psychogenic but nonpsychotic conditions caused a considerable amount of objective burden. Rutter (1966), in his study of the effects of mental illness on the health of children in the family, observed that the manner in which symptoms affect family interaction is more important than the nature of the symptoms themselves. While psychotic delusions and hallucinations may not have grave effects on the family if the patient is otherwise considerate and kind, neurotic conditions may lead to destructive and treacherous behavior that disrupts family life and has a profound impact on the psychological state of others in the family.

> Parental mental disorder is most likely to be followed by behavioral disturbance in the children when the parent exhibits long-standing abnormalities of personality. The "seriousness" of the illness in terms of neurosis or psychosis is probably not important, but the involvement of the child in the symptoms

of the parental illness does seem to be crucial. For example, delusions *per se* do not matter particularly but if the delusions directly involve the child and affect the parental care, it seems that the child is more likely to develop a psychiatric disorder. If the psychiatrist is to be on the alert for those disorders which are likely to have a harmful effect on other members of the family, he must inquire not only about the symptoms but also about the impact of the symptoms on other people. (Rutter p. 107)

The studies by Grad and Sainsbury (1966) and other investigators should have alerted us to the fact that changing administrative policies and modifying psychiatric procedures to a limited extent are not enough to launch a successful community care program (also see Hoenig and Hamilton 1967). Grad and Sainsbury believe that the essential ingredient in relieving burden is to assure relatives that help is available and that something can be done; this is a reasonable goal within either kind of service. This sense of control, which Grad and Sainsbury imply, has been recognized in other areas of investigation as an important factor in mediating stress response in difficult circumstances (Lazarus 1966, Rodin 1986). The investigators further suggest that for certain types of patients in particular social circumstances, home care may leave the family with many more problems than an alternative residential placement. However, because psychiatric patients are not a homogeneous group, we must study in far greater detail which social and psychological circumstances will enable patients to flourish with home care.

Despite the research evidence showing the magnitude of burden placed on many families with a mentally ill person, relatively little attention has been given to the needs of families in mental health programs. Typically, they are excluded from the treatment process, given little information, and often defined as part of the problem. Despite the burdens they face, they receive little support, inadequate information, and almost no instruction. Many therapists have a strong ideology of independence and contribute to tensions between the family and an impaired mentally ill patient who may be highly dependent on other family members. The issues are not always clear-cut or easy, but there seems to be little doubt that ideologies of therapy have done more to put blame on families than to work with them constructively to deal with extremely difficult management issues.

Families of chronically mentally ill individuals are frequently puzzled and angry about their interactions with the mental health system and mental health professionals. In situations where they have received little constructive support but are left with most of the burden, it is understandable that some have argued for slowing the deinstitutionalization process and providing more public mental hospital beds. Controlled studies demonstrate, however, that families as well as patients are much more satisfied with community care than with hospital-oriented care when there is a coherent and well-organized system of community services with a clear focus of responsibility for individual patients (New South Wales Department of Health 1983, Stein and Test 1985).

Family concerns are now represented by a large and increasingly influential national organization, the National Alliance for the Mentally Ill (NAMI), formally established in 1980. As of this time, the organization includes more than 600 local affiliates and is growing rapidly in membership, visibility, and political presence (Hatfield 1987). NAMI is an organization representing the families of the severely mentally ill who have differing points of view and no single ideology, but some particular ideas come out very strongly. First, the organization focuses on those most ill and has disdain for vague mental health ideologies dealing with the promotion of mental health that divert resources away from those who have profound needs. As two members note, "Bumper-sticker admonitions to 'hug your kid' and dance therapy classes are not of the appropriate caliber," (Howe and Howe 1987). Most NAMI members believe that severe mental illness is substantially biological in nature and strongly support the expansion of biomedical research. Many are angry at mental health professionals who blame families and exclude them from the care process, but they are not hostile to mental health treatment. Most NAMI members support better systems of community care and seek to reduce prejudice toward the mentally ill. NAMI and other newly emerging groups fill an important void in advocacy in the mental health field, an issue to which we will return later in the chapter.

THE PROCESSES OF DEINSTITUTIONALIZATION

In the discussion of the history of mental health policy, some issues relating to deinstitutionalization were raised. Here I review with greater specificity some of the forces that resulted in the reduction of public mental hospital patients from 560,000 to the approximately 115,000 who reside in such hospitals today. The intent of this discussion is to define the major forces that resulted in change. Through such understanding we have a better opportunity to define points of leverage for significant improvements in the years ahead.

Deinstitutionalization has been ambiguously defined and includes a variety of different processes (Bachrach 1976). Beginning in about 1955, and particularly in the period 1965–1980, there was a transfer of patients from traditional mental hospitals to such settings as board-and-care facilities, nursing homes, and a variety of other community living arrangements. In some instances, such release policies have led to charges of patient "dumping" and efforts on behalf of particular communities to exclude patients through restrictive zoning ordinances. In other instances it is noted that impaired patients are placed in the community without adequate support and service, only to be victimized and preyed upon by unsavory elements. Various studies have demonstrated a range of patient outcomes and levels of social functioning depending on the community, the nursing home, and the living facility involved, and on the nature of local mental health policies. It is clear that generalizations do not suffice; community mental health is as diverse as communities themselves and the implementation of local mental health policies. In some settings chronic patients receive superb community treatment and lead lives very much enriched compared with those possible in the best mental hospitals. In other contexts patients in need are neglected and exploited in an appalling fashion, function at low levels, and receive inferior or no services. Deinstitutionalization is decentralization and encompasses a wide range of experiences that result from the use of diversified settings.

The incentives for deinstitutionalization came from many quarters and had a forceful impact on social policy. The preventive and community ideology emerging from post–World War II experience established the general context, drugs provided an important and useful technology, and welfare reform made the retention of patients in the community possible. The growing economic problems faced by the states in retaining large numbers of patients in mental hospitals were particularly important, and the expansion of the welfare system provided some relief of this growing cost burden on state budgets.

Consider the factors that were operative in the period 1955–1965. Neuroleptic drugs were widely used and were extraordinarily helpful in blunting patients' most bizarre symptoms and giving professionals, administrators, family members, and the community more confidence that patients' most troublesome and frightening symptoms could be contained. They facilitated unlocking hospital wards, allowed more patient movement within the hospital, and aided discharge to the community. There are documented instances in some localities of such changes without the use of antipsychotic drugs (Scull 1977), but it is unlikely that significant reductions in hospital populations, facilitated by a combination of social forces, could have been sustained without drugs.

The phenothiazines were particularly welcomed in large public hospitals that were overcrowded and understaffed and in which hospital personnel lacked confidence in their ability to manage patients or to communicate to families or the community that such patients were controllable. The drugs changed attitudes and encouraged administrative flexibility.

The shift away from hospitals was also facilitated by a social science ideology and a body of research that supported an antihospital orientation. Moreover, young attorneys trained within the growing civil rights movement began to turn their attention to the civil liberties of mental patients and focused their attention on the abuses of civil commitment. This resulted in legal changes, making it more difficult to involuntarily hospitalize mental patients in many localities. But the key point to note is that despite the ideological environment, the emphasis on community care, the critique of hospitals, and the widespread use of drugs, the reduction of public hospital populations proceeded only slowly, approximately 1.5 percent per year between 1955 and 1965 (Gronfein 1985).

The explanation for the modest reduction of public hospital patients was the lack of an economic support base for returning patients to the community. Hospital staff had no difficulty identifying patients who could be sent to other settings but had many problems in identifying appropriate housing or assuring adequate subsistence. With the passage of Medicare and Medicaid in 1965, the introduction of SSI and the expansion of SSDI (the welfare disability programs), and with other welfare initiatives, a stronger economic and residential base for deinstitutionalization came into being. The number of public hospital inpatients began to fall rapidly, with populations decreasing an average of about 6 percent a year between 1965 and 1980 (Gronfein 1985). Medicare and Medicaid stimulated the rapid expansion of nursing home beds, which provided a custodial alternative for elderly patients with dementias and a new option for some younger psychotic patients as well. But although the newly available nursing home beds provided the alternatives, the driving force was the economic advantages for the states by transferring obligations from their own mental health budgets to the federal part of the Medicaid program.

As noted earlier, the social science community and public interest lawyers committed to civil rights and civil liberties provided the ideology that justified the retention of mental patients in the community. Both civil libertarians and social scientists were responding to the evidence of damaging consequences of long-term custodial hospitalization and the means by which people were involuntarily detained. We now turn to an examination of the way such environments affected patients.

ENVIRONMENTAL FACTORS PROMOTING EFFECTIVE PERFORMANCE

The realization that mental hospitalization could produce profound disabilities in patients above and beyond those characteristic of the condition itself was a major stimulus to the community care movement. Different investigators have described these disabilities as institutional neuroses, institutionalism, and so on (Zusman 1966). There are many indices of this syndrome, but generally it can be recognized by apathy, loss of interest and initiative, lack of reaction to the environment or future possibilities, and deterioration in personal habits. Patients who have been in custodial mental hospitals for a long time tend to be apathetic about leaving the hospitals and returning to a normal life and to lose interest in self-maintenance. They lack simple skills such as using a telephone or being able to get from one place to another on their own. For a long time observers believed that this apathy and loss of interest were consequences of psychiatric illness rather than the results of long-term residence in an institutional environment characterized by apathy and dullness.

Erving Goffman (1961) provided one of the most provocative analyses of institutional influences on patients. In Goffman's terms, the mental hospital is a total institution, and its key characteristic is "the handling of many human needs by the bureaucratic organization of whole blocks of people" (p. 6). The central feature of total institutions is the bringing together of groups of coparticipants who live in one place—thus breaking down the barriers usually separating different spheres of life—and under one authority, which organizes the different features of life within an overall plan. People are treated not as individuals but as groups and are required to do the same things together. Activities are tightly scheduled, with the sequence officially imposed from above. The various enforced activities come under a single rational plan designed to fulfill the official aims of the institution.

In depicting the atmosphere of the overcrowded Saint Elizabeth's Hospital, Goffman described the plight of mental patients in vivid terms. From his perspective, hospitalization in a mental institution leads to betrayal of the patients, deprecates their self-image, undermines their sense of autonomy, and abuses their privacy. Hospital life requires the patients to adapt in a manner detrimental to their future readjustment to community life, and their careers as mental patients are irreparably harmful to their future reputation. Goffman was sensitive to many of the deprivations of hospital life and to some of the abuses of the large mental hospital. But the view he presented was one-sided and very much organized from a middle-class perspective. Many of the deprivations Goffman points to are not experienced by all mental patients.

Many patients find their hospitalization experience a relief. The community situation from which they come is often characterized by extreme difficulty and extraordinary personal distress. Their living conditions are poor, the conflicts in their life are uncontrollable, and their physical and mental states have deteriorated. Such patients are frequently capable of harming themselves or others, or at least of damaging their lives in irreparable ways. Many patients in mental hospitals report that hospital restrictions do not bother them, that they appreciate the physical care they are receiving, and that the hospital—despite its restrictions—enhances their freedom rather than restricts it (Linn 1968; Weinstein 1979, 1983).

Although Goffman made us aware of many aspects of total institutions that can be harmful to patients, we must recognize that total institutions can have good or deleterious effects depending on a variety of factors. Total institutions—hospitals, monasteries, schools—are organizations for changing people and their identities. If clients share the goals and aspirations of the organization, their experiences in it may be worthwhile and desirable. If clients are involuntarily admitted and reject the identity the institution assigns them, residence in such an organization may be extremely stressful and lead to profound disabilities in functioning. Just as young draftees who reject the idea of military training and the authority of the military to govern their lives may find basic training a stressful experience and damaging to their self-concepts, so do hospitalized patients who feel they should not be in the hospital and who resent the regimen imposed upon them find hospitalization a stressful experience. But just as there have been many cooperative draftees, so have there been many cooperative patients, and it is incorrect to assume that the effect of the hospital on them is damaging.

Total institutions vary widely in character. They differ in their size, their staffing patterns, the organization of life within them, the pathways by which their clients arrive, and their expenditures of money, time, and effort. Goffman, in building a general model of total institutions, attributed to them all characteristics that may be specific to the hospital he studied, such as its size or staffing pattern. We have evidence that small hospitals with high personnel-patient ratios and large budgets performed their tasks better than those with the opposite characteristics (Ullmann

1967). Some mental hospitals have had deleterious effects on patients for a variety of reasons: (1) patients may have been involuntarily incarcerated in order to protect the community from them, but once they were in the hospital little of a constructive nature may have been done for them; (2) the hospital may not have made sufficient efforts to maintain the patient's interpersonal associations and skills when removed from the community, although these may deteriorate if the patient remains in the hospital for a significant period of time; (3) hospitalization may lead to the stigmatization of the patient; and (4) the hospital may require adaptations for adjustment to the ward, but such adaptations may be inconsistent with the patterns of behavior necessary to make a proper adjustment to the community. In some hospitals, for example, patients are rewarded for remaining unobtrusive and docile, or they are punished if they attempt to exercise too much initiative. Unwillingness to take initiative, however, may handicap patients when they return to the community. Not all total institutions respond in this way, and the ward staff often views the participation and the initiative of patients as signs of improving health. Our attention should focus not on whether a hospital fits the model of a total institution but rather on specifying those aspects of such institutions that affect their performance.

There are many performance variables by which hospitals may be judged. Traditionally, the major concern has been whether they protected the public and those patients in danger of harming themselves. Early studies of large mental hospitals concentrated on such issues as how hospitals with many patients can be operated by small staffs and few professional personnel. Ivan Belknap (1956) devoted considerable attention to the work system of a large hospital and to the manner in which aides in the hospital developed a reward system for the purpose of maintaining a viable patient work force. Investigators are increasingly evaluating the hospital in terms of its effects on the patients' work performance, community participation, self-esteem, sense of initiative, responsibility in performing social roles, reduction of symptoms, and understanding of themselves and their illnesses. Studies of smaller, private hospitals gave greater attention to interaction among patients and staff, communication problems, and administrative conflicts and their effects upon patients (Stanton and Schwartz 1954, Caudill 1958, Coser 1979, and for a review of this literature, see Perrow 1965). It is no longer sufficient to engage in polemics concerning the inhumane conditions of mental hospitals, although where such conditions exist, they must be fought. Instead, we must be concerned with the organization of hospitals and wards to achieve the best possible outcomes for patients.

Many investigators have observed that patients with long histories of residence in traditional mental hospitals have disability syndromes that result from apathy and lack of participation rather than from the illness condition. One term used to describe this disability syndrome is *institutionalism*. It is difficult to study because some mental health professionals do not believe that illness conditions exist, and they see all conditions as institutionally or environmentally caused. Even those who adhere to a psychiatric disease theory do not find it easy to separate the effects of the condition from those of the environment because they believe that these interact in an intricate fashion. To evaluate the nature of the institutionalism syndrome, we must look at some of the research on it.

Wing (1962), a researcher studying institutional effects on patients, argues that institutionalism is influenced by three factors: (1) the pattern of susceptibility or resistance to various institutional pressures that the individual possesses when he or she is first admitted; (2) the social pressures to which an individual is exposed after admission to an institution; and (3) the length of time the patient is exposed to these institutional pressures. To test these ideas, Wing measured the extent to which hospital schizophrenics were impaired and then attempted to evaluate how length of hospital stay affected institutionalism among patients with comparable degrees of impairment. He found that patient groups with longer lengths of stay showed a progressive increase in the proportion who appeared apathetic about life outside the hospital. Although marked symptom change did not occur over time, hopefulness and willingness to cope with life deteriorated. In such studies, of course, there is always the danger that the patient's sense of apathy affects whether he or she is released from the hospital, and thus the results may be a product of the selection process. But alongside other findings, these results support the idea that hospitals can produce a sense of apathy and hopelessness among patients. Wing and Brown (1961), in a study of three British mental hospitals, showed that different hospital environments encourage institutionalism in varying degrees. The outcome of residence depends not only on the patient's susceptibility to hospital influences and the length of exposure to such pressures but also on the nature of such influences, which may vary widely from one hospital to another.

Wing (1967) maintains that patients who are long-term residents of hospitals tend to be selected not only on the basis of their illnesses but also on the basis of their social characteristics. They often do not have strong ties with the community, family, or work, and are vulnerable because of their age, poverty, and lack of social interests and ties. Wing points out that these patients often are not concerned with the problems of personal liberty and restrictions and may find the hospital environment far preferable to community residence because this environment meets their needs and makes minimal demands on them (also see Linn 1968). Ludwig and Farrelly (1966) point to the same phenomena and argue that the problem of getting hard-core schizophrenic patients out of the hospital results in part from the patients' code of chronicity or their desire to remain there. Ludwig and Farrelly's argument is well described by the statement of a schizophrenic patient who told them, "You can't railroad me out of here."

A second aspect of institutionalism, Wing argues, is the inherent unfolding of the disease process itself.

> The bowed head and shoulders, the shuffling gait, the apathetic faces, the social withdrawal and disinterest, the loss of spontaneity, initiative and individuality described so graphically by Barton may be seen in patients who have never been in an institution in their lives. Studies of intellectual performance seem to show that the damage is often relatively sudden in onset, rather than

gradual in development as would be the case if it were the result of imposed social isolation. There is little evidence either of gradual clinical deterioration. This is not to say, of course, that the social surroundings do not affect clinical state; indeed, there is evidence to the contrary. (Wing 1967, p. 8)

The third component of institutionalism described by Wing is the influence of the institution itself, which gradually affects the patient over many years. This aspect of the syndrome is characterized by increasing dependence on institutional life and an inability to adapt to any other living situation. As Wing points out, these effects can be observed even on patients "whose premorbid personality was lively and sociable and in whom the disease has not run a severe course" (p. 9). Many earlier studies found that a large proportion of patients in mental hospitals in the United States and other countries had no serious disturbance of behavior and were kept in the hospital for largely social reasons—many of which are attributable to institutionalism (Brown 1959, Scheff 1963, Ullman 1967). Cross and his colleagues (1957), in a survey of a large mental hospital, found that most of the patients had been under care for a long time and that a majority required only routine supervision. Cooper and Early (1961) also concluded, on the basis of their survey of more than 1,000 long-term patients, that most did not require custodial care and that a majority could work. Many of the traditional practices of mental hospitals failed to encourage patients to take initiative and responsibility and contributed to the institutionalism syndrome.

In my study of two facilities for alcoholics in North Carolina, the influence of the environment was found to be extremely important in affecting the patients' attitudes toward rehabilitation (Mechanic 1961). One of the facilities studied accepted only voluntary patients and was organized around the idea of milieu therapy, making frequent use of group meetings in which patients discussed their problems with one another and with therapeutic personnel. The second facility was a custodial ward for alcoholics and drug addicts in a state mental hospital; most patients were committed to the hospital against their wishes. Patients living within these two different group atmospheres held different attitudes toward the institution and their own rehabilitation. Most patients at the voluntary facility verbalized desires for rehabilitation and a commitment to stop drinking. More than one-third of the patients at the hospital facility indicated no desire or intention to change their pattern of behavior, and the attitudes of both patients and staff toward rehabilitation could be characterized as cynical. A small group of patients on this hospital ward had entered the hospital on their own initiative to obtain assistance for their alcohol problems; they were similar in social characteristics to patients at the voluntary facility. I found that more than one-half of these patients intended to resume drinking after leaving the hospital and were pessimistic about rehabilitation. Although this was not a controlled experiment, the results strongly supported the idea that the atmosphere, group pressures, and attitudes on the ward had an important effect on the attitudes of the patients toward rehabilitation.

Many investigators have been impressed with the importance of the atmosphere of the ward on the functioning and attitudes of mental patients (Stanton and Schwartz 1954, Kellam et al. 1966), and concern with the influence of environmental atmospheres extends also to other organizations, such as schools and universities. The basic idea is that the emotional tone, tensions, attitudes, and feelings dominant on a ward affect the interactions among patients, between patients and staff, and even among staff. This interaction in turn affects the patient's motivation, attitudes, and emotional state. For many years the investigation of these ideas has been largely impressionistic because of the difficulty of measuring different ward environments and correlating these to various performance and symptom measures. Significant progress has been made in the measurement problem by Rudolf Moos.

Moos (1974) has developed a Ward Atmosphere Scale that depicts the effect of the climate of ward life on relationships, treatment, and administrative structure or system maintenance dimensions. The relationships include involvements of patients on the ward, support among patients and staff, and the degree of open expression and spontaneity. Treatment dimensions include autonomy, practical orientation, personal problem orientation, and expression of anger and aggression. Administrative structure variables include order and organization, staff control, and program clarity. Moos has used these scales to study many hospital wards in the United States and England, and the profiles of ward atmosphere can be used to examine treatment outcomes and patient adjustment. Moos has found that programs that keep patients out in the community the longest have high scores on open expression of feelings in a context emphasizing a practical orientation, order and organization, staff control, and autonomy and independence. In contrast, programs with high dropout rates tend to have little emphasis on involving patients, few social activities, and poor planning of patients' activities. Patients in such programs have little interaction and little guidance, and staff are unresponsive to criticisms or patients' suggestions.

Clearly, in acknowledging the detrimental effects of institutions on people, we should not assume that such institutional environments have not produced rehabilitative effects as well. Mental hospitals have traditionally offered patients impoverished environments and have done little to stimulate them, but this does not reflect the changes that have taken place in hospital environments and many current efforts to develop personal skills and resources and to give the patient a sense of hope (Mechanic 1967). Mental health workers have too frequently made the naive assumption that community life is always constructive, although particular family and community environments may have the same adverse effects on the patient's functioning and skills as a poor mental hospital does. The issue is not so much whether patients are resident in a hospital as it is whether the environment to which they are exposed is a stimulating and useful one for minimizing incapacities resulting from their illnesses and for maximizing their potential for living a life of reasonable quality.

Relatively few studies have examined the community contexts and environments that stimulate the patient's functioning and sense of hope and those that bring a morbid response. In an intriguing study referred to in an earlier discussion, Brown and his colleagues (1962) followed a group of schizophrenic men released from the hospital. They assessed the severity of the symptoms of these patients just before discharge and saw the patients at home with their relatives two weeks after discharge. During this home interview, they measured the amount of expressed emotion in the family. The researchers found that patients returning to a relative who showed high emotional involvement (based on measurement of expressed emotion, hostility, and dominance) deteriorated more frequently than did patients returning to a relative who showed low emotional involvement. This finding has been replicated in a variety of settings (Brown et al. 1972, Vaughn and Leff 1976, Leff and Vaughn, 1985). Earlier I noted various theoretical explanations for links between stress and schizophrenic breakdown, and it remains possible that schizophrenics cannot tolerate intense emotions of any kind. We still know too little about the types of environments that best promote control over symptoms and a reasonable level of social functioning. We do know, however, that disabled patients require incentives for activity and involvement, reinforcement for initiative and successful performance, and protection against an environment that is too demanding and too stimulating. The wide range of contexts for community care of schizophrenic patients yields a great diversity of treatment environments. Work is proceeding to describe these treatment environments and their effects in greater detail.

One such study by Segal and Aviram (1978) examined patients and proprietors of sheltered care in California. Compared to the population, sheltered care residents studied were disproportionately in the age group 50 to 65, had low education and low involvement in employment, and almost all had either never been married or come from broken marriages (95 percent). Almost all such patients were supported by welfare, with three-quarters receiving Supplemental Security Income. Although this group was only moderately symptomatic and not particularly troublesome to the community, this population constituted a highly disabled group from a social point of view and was very much dependent on the community for its support.

Segal and Aviram examined the correlates of both *external* and *internal integration* in sheltered care. The first measured the relationship of the patient to the community in terms of access and participation, the latter involved the extent to which the patient is involved in the sheltered facility and the extent to which the operator assumes responsibility for mediating the patients' needs and relationships with the community. In the sample studied, the researchers found much more internal than external integration. By far the most important factor in external integration was neighbor response, and the most important individual factor was the patients' available spending money, which could facilitate community participation. Environments high on what Moos (1974) would call "involvement" and those with a practical orientation facilitated internal integration. Positive neighbor response as reflected in their reaching out to residents also facilitated internal cohesion. In short, community social support and involvement with clients facilitated constructive participation both within the facility and in the community as a whole.

IMPLICATIONS OF COMMUNITY INSTITUTIONAL PLACEMENT

Deinstitutionalization has not only resulted in the return of many patients to the community, but has also involved major transfers of patients from traditional facilities to other community contexts, including nursing homes. From a public policy perspective, it should be apparent that providing an effective environment for mental patients is not simply a matter of whether they reside in hospitals or other types of institutions but more importantly the quality of life achieved. Although knowledge in the field of community alternatives remains to be more fully developed, we know with some certainty that inactivity, lack of participation, and dependence have an erosive effect on social functioning. Uninvolvement and excessive dependence contribute to diminished coping skills, loss of affect, and a sense of helplessness. The first requirement of any program for the long-term care of mental patients is to use the potential of patients to contribute to their own needs, to assume some responsibility for their lives, and to participate socially in a meaningful way.

The multiple settings with similar designations where patients reside allow no easy generalizations. Board and care homes, for example, are an increasingly important source of care for chronic mental patients in varying age groups, and nursing homes are a primary source of care for the mentally ill elderly. These institutions may on occasion provide superb care. More commonly, however, they provide only custodial service (Vladeck 1980), keeping patients as quiet as possible to minimize supervision. Patients in such settings are frequently on heavy doses of drugs, induced to sit for many hours each day in front of television sets and discouraged from activities that might require a larger supervisory investment from the facility. Such care contributes to an apathy syndrome.

Our review of the conditions in hospitals and other facilities that affect the functioning and quality of life of the chronically mentally ill suggest some of the requirements for high quality patient care in the community. Fortunately, some excellent models of care have been developed and they provide the groundwork for considering the policy initiatives that allow for a stronger system of community services. But, first, let us examine some of these programs and their performances when they are evaluated rigorously.

MODELS FOR COMMUNITY CARE

In recent years a variety of innovative settings and programs have been developed for the care of highly impaired patients in the community, including supervised housing, foster care, innovative board-and-care facilities, halfway houses, and patient communities. One of the most innovative of such demonstrations was a Wisconsin experiment based on a training program in community living in which an educational coping model was compared with a progressive hospital care unit (Stein et al. 1975, Stein and Test 1980a, b). An unselected group of patients seeking admission to a mental hospital was randomly assigned to experimental and control groups. Subsequent analysis found no differences on significant variables between these two groups, indicating that successful randomization had occurred. The control group received hospital treatment linked with community after-care services. The experimental group was assisted in developing an independent living situation in the community, given social support, and taught simple living skills such as budgeting, job seeking, and use of public transportation. Patients in both groups were evaluated at various intervals by independent researchers. The findings indicated that it was possible for patients who were highly impaired to be cared for almost exclusively in the community. Compared with control patients, patients in the experimental group made a more adequate community adjustment as evidenced by higher earnings from work, involvement in more social activities, more contact with friends, and more satisfaction with their life situation. Experimental patients at follow-up had fewer symptoms than the controls. This experiment demonstrated that a logically organized and aggressive community program can effectively treat even highly impaired patients in the community.

Wisconsin has had a unique mental health system for many years and Dane County, the area where Stein and Test carried out their work, is not necessarily representative of the range of community obstacles to care evident in other communities. The program, however, has been adopted in part or in its totality in other areas of the country with reports of equally promising outcomes. There has been a considerable range of successful experience with chronic patients in small and moderately sized communities, but the problems of such care in large urban areas seem especially formidable. It is in this context that the replication of the Stein and Test experiment in Sydney, Australia, is of particular interest.

In the period 1979–1981, psychiatrist John Hoult and his colleagues adopted the Wisconsin model in this large urban Australian area using a randomized controlled experiment and obtained very similar patient care and cost-effectiveness outcomes (New South Wales Department of Health 1983). Particularly notable, and consistent with the Wisconsin experience, was the extent to which patients and their families preferred the community care option. For example, at 12-month follow-up, almost two-thirds of the experimental patients were very satisfied with treatment in contrast to less than one-third of the controls. Similarly, 83 percent of relatives of project patients with whom they lived were very satisfied with treatment in contrast to 26 percent of the controls (New South Wales Department of Health 1983).

One issue the Wisconsin experiment does not speak to is the intensity of staffing essential to carry out the types of aggressive and continuing care necessary to the program. A persistent problem in many areas is the limited resources available, and the viability of the community-care model depends on a reasonable minimum of staffing. Assessing what would be an acceptable range of staffing intensity is, thus, of importance. It is notable that the Australian replication had very favorable outcomes despite a lower level of staffing than in Dane County. The demonstration was so successful that the state of New South Wales in 1983 reorganized mental health services throughout the state using the Wisconsin model (Hoult 1987).

172   *Central Perspectives in Formulating Mental Health Policies*

Family-oriented rehabilitation models based on similar principles and on the clinical research on expressed emotions have also yielded promising results in both England (Leff et al. 1982) and the United States (Falloon et al. 1984, 1985). In a controlled social intervention trial in London, schizophrenic patients having intense contact with relatives demonstrating high expressed emotion were randomly assigned to either routine outpatient care or an intervention program for patients and their families emphasizing education about schizophrenia and the role of expressed emotion in exacerbations of patients' symptoms (Leff 1982). The intervention also included family sessions in the home and relatives' groups. All patients were maintained on psychotropic drugs. After nine months, half of the 24 control patients relapsed, but only 9 percent in the experimental group did so. There were no relapses in the 73 percent of the experimental families where the aims of the intervention were achieved.

A similar experimental trial was carried out in California where family members of schizophrenics were taught about the condition and instructed in problem-solving techniques, and efforts were made to reduce family tensions (Falloon et al. 1984). Follow-up at nine months found that patients in families receiving such interventions had a much lower rate of exacerbation than those in a control group receiving clinic-based individual supportive care. Only one patient in the intervention group (6 percent) was judged to have a relapse, in contrast to eight (44 percent) in the control group (Falloon et al. 1982). A less systematic and intense follow-up after two years found that the reduction in exacerbations was maintained over the longer period (Falloon et al. 1985).

These studies represent some of the more persuasive among a much larger number of studies strongly supporting the value of community care as an alternative for hospital care (Stein and Test 1978, Kiesler 1982, Gudeman and Shore 1984, Kiesler and Sibulkin 1987). Kiesler and Sibulkin (1987), for example, have identified 14 experimental studies, most with random assignment, comparing hospital treatment to some alternative form of care. They conclude on the basis of this review that alternative care is more effective than hospitalization across a wide range of patient populations and treatment strategies.

One aspect that applies across a wide range of treatment programs includes teaching and reinforcing skills necessary for everyday living. Educational approaches within the larger medical and rehabilitation context, whatever the treatment setting, are useful components (Mechanic 1967). The emphasis on social learning has been carried to the extreme in experimental work by Paul and Lentz (1977), who have successfully used this model to resocialize patients with long histories of chronic mental illness and inappropriate behavior. Using a highly controlled treatment environment in which all staff adopt responses consistent with learning principles, concerted and continued efforts are made to shape patients' behavior so as to condition more normal responses. The approach uses instruction and direction and reinforcements through reward and punishment. The researchers have reported dramatic improvements of behavior and outcomes and demonstrate quite convincingly that even the most regressed patterns of response can be modified.

Elements of the social learning approach are used in almost all community care and social rehabilitation programs. Community care programs can never have the level of control over patients that characterizes a total institution, and our concepts of appropriate care, civil liberties and respect for the preferences of patients make it unlikely that such intensive approaches will be used extensively. These and other reasons explain the inattention given to this successful experimental program, but it is clear that social learning approaches are now an important part of the types of efforts in community care already described.

Programs for community care for chronic mental illness have not suffered from lack of innovation or evaluation. The major difficulty has been the lack of a public policy framework that facilitates the development of necessary organizational entities, allows the essential service elements and funding to be brought together, provides reimbursement for the many service components and mental health providers, and contains incentives for balancing tradeoffs between traditional medical and hospital services and a broader range of social services needed by chronic patients with large rehabilitative needs (Stein and Ganser 1983, Mechanic 1985, Talbott 1985, Mechanic and Aiken 1987). Good rehabilitation treats acute psychiatric episodes, ensures appropriate medication monitoring, maintains nutrition and health more generally, makes provision for shelter and reasonable levels of activity and participation, provides crisis support, and builds on patients' personal capacities through continuing educational efforts.

Community care involves medical and social challenges and is not inexpensive if costs are seriously assessed. A careful economic cost-benefit analysis of the Wisconsin experiment, taking into account a wide range of hidden as well as explicit costs, such as welfare payments and supervised residency costs, suggests that although such programs yield a net benefit, they are not less expensive than more conventional approaches (Weisbrod et al. 1980). Also, there are social costs in maintaining patients in the community as compared with hospital care during the more acute phases of disorder as reflected in law violations and assaultive behavior (Test and Stein 1980a, b). The prevalence of such behavior was low, but it was not inconsequential. This experiment also shows—as does experience elsewhere—that if an aggressive program does not continue, patients do not maintain the high level of functioning demonstrated (Stein and Test 1980a, b). A five-year-follow-up of the original experiment by Pasamanick and his associates (1967) also found a regression of patient functioning following the termination of the experiment (Davis et al. 1972). These studies suggest that treatment of chronic mental patients cannot be based on a short-term commitment but requires an intensive continuing effort. These programs, however, do not become institutionalized not only because they are difficult to administer and model in relation to more conventional hospital care but also because current financing of mental health services in most communities provides no basis for stability of funding for such programs.

Long-term therapy for chronic schizophrenic patients is further complicated by the fact that antipsychotic medication, which is an important component of care, often has unpleasant side effects and long-term adverse biological effects. Although antipsychotic medication is extremely helpful in controlling delusions, hallucinations, severe excitement, or withdrawal and odd behavior, it occasionally produces extrapyramidal motor reactions and, with prolonged use, tardive dyskinesia (Berger 1978). The extrapyramidal symptoms include uncontrollable restlessness, muscle spasms, and other symptoms resembling Parkinson's disease. These can be controlled by anticholinergic drugs used for treating Parkinson's disease. Tardive dyskinesia, which consists of involuntary movements of the lips, tongue, face, and other upper extremities is less reversible, more dangerous, and stigmatizing. It constitutes a serious risk for chronic patients on long-term maintenance antipsychotics. These findings on side effects complicate the treatment of chronic schizophrenic patients, particularly in community settings. First, the side effects lead patients to discontinue medication, often resulting in a relapse of their bizarre behavior. Second, both problems of patient cooperation and the real dangers of these powerful drugs require close medical supervision and monitoring of such patients. This constitutes a more strategic problem in a community than on a hospital ward and requires an aggressive and sustained administrative effort to ensure appropriate medical and rehabilitative care. Good community care is not a casual enterprise.

With cutbacks in funding, many community mental health centers depend predominantly on psychologists, social workers, and paraprofessional personnel, who can be recruited at modest salaries, restricting the use of psychiatrists to evaluate and supervise medication. Psychiatrists, working in these centers, have become increasingly isolated from responsibility for the patients' total care. Given competing and more remunerative opportunities elsewhere, many have abandoned the CMHCs serving public patients. The loss of medical responsibility for the most severely ill chronic patients, who require sophisticated diagnosis, medication, and treatment planning in addition to psychosocial services is a serious retrogressive trend (Mechanic and Aiken 1987). Good medical evaluation and supervision, as well as monitoring long-term drug needs and risks of adverse effects, are essential dimensions of care.

POINTS OF LEVERAGE

Key elements in building appropriate and effective sources of community mental health care are the organizational and financing systems and policy decisions concerning the populations and services to be covered and the types of institutions and therapists who will provide services. It is with such decisions that public policy most vitally impacts the shape of the mental health arena. Without stable funding, no innovation, however effective, is likely to be sustained for very long. Financing decisions are crucial. Such decisions must be made with sensitivity to the problems and needs of varying types of patients, understanding of services alternatives, and appreciation of the ambiguities of mental health concepts.

Mental health funds come from four major sources: third party insurance programs; state and local appropriations for mental health institutions and services; Medicaid and Medicare; and welfare benefits such as SSDI and SSI. In the previous chapter, in discussing third-party insurance, it was emphasized that many of the most needy mentally ill are not covered. Since such insurance is typically linked with stable employment, in the absence of a national insurance system it is unlikely that the extension of third-party insurance however worthy would address the special needs of the most chronic patients. Improvements in community mental health care for the most chronic patients thus depend on reforms in state mental health policy, Medicaid, and the social security disability programs.

Modifying State Mental Health Systems

Traditionally, mental illness has been a state responsibility and constitutes a significant part of state expenditures. States have invested substantially in their mental institutions, and with reduction of public inpatients many have improved their hospitals and treatment and rehabilitation programs. The vast majority of seriously mentally ill are in the community, but most states continue to be focused institutionally because of their commitments to maintain hospital improvements in a context of increased court scrutiny, because of the pressures of hospital employees and communities that depend on the financing of hospitals, and because states are reluctant to take on large new community obligations within a context of fiscal constraint. In 1981, two-thirds of state expenditures continued to support state hospitals, although the proportion varied from more than 90 percent in such states as Georgia, Iowa, and Mississippi to a minority of expenditures in California and Wisconsin (National Institute of Mental Health 1985). In the latter instances, there are strong state incentives for local government to seek alternatives to inpatient care. In Wisconsin, mental health financing encourages managed care and tradeoffs between community and inpatient care (Stein and Ganser 1983).

The problem of getting services to follow the patient is inherently more difficult in states having well-established hospital systems, communities economically dependent on hospitals, and well-organized and unionized employees. Such systems require transition plans that allow funds to follow the patient on a graduated basis, that guarantee the stability of the hospital system over some period of time, and that facilitate working closely with unions and employees in programs of scheduled attrition and retraining to the extent feasible. Concomitantly, structures need to be developed for diversion of inappropriate admissions to community programs and for intensive discharge planning commencing soon after a patient is admitted to a state hospital.

Because of the barriers in many states to a community-based system, phasing in such programs may initially require enhanced funding to build community care structures while maintaining some redundant hospital support. To the extent that such financing allows the initiation of a more rational care process, it is a wise long-term investment, although it may require considerable persuasion before state legislatures, facing resource constraints, see the wisdom of this course.

Medicaid Reform

Medicaid, the largest single national medical program affecting the long-term mentally ill, is vital to their welfare since the vast majority are poor and depend on the public system for assistance. Because the program involves federal matching grants to states that meet certain federal minimum requirements but allow states to define the range and limits of their programs within these specifications, eligibility criteria and benefits vary widely. As a consequence, only about two-fifths of the poor are covered, and many chronic patients are denied benefits. Medicaid eligibility depends on being "categorically poor"—aged, blind, disabled—or eligible for AFDC. In the case of the CMI, disability status through the Supplemental Security Income (SSI) program is the most likely route, since eligibility is linked with Medicaid benefits. The processes of obtaining benefits are dependent on geography and are often capricious. Enrolling more of the eligible mentally ill and achieving a more effective and equitable use of Medicaid dollars would contribute a great deal to improving the structure of mental health services for all impaired patients.

In 1977 it was estimated that the Medicaid program paid more than $4 billion for mental health services, constituting roughly one-quarter of all funds invested in mental health services in the United States (U.S. President's Commission on Mental Health, 1978, Vol. II, p. 579). In 1983, Medicaid accounted for $1.34 billion in expenditures in mental health organizations (Redick et al. 1986) and paid for large numbers of inpatient days in general hospitals as well. Approximately one-quarter of general hospital mental health admissions involved Medicaid payment, and in 1984 there were 1.7 million discharges of patients with such diagnoses with an average length of stay of 12 days (Dennison 1985). In short, Medicaid payment for inpatient care consumes "large bucks."

It is extremely difficult to gain effective control over the expenditure of Medicaid dollars. The program is focused on institutional services, with approximately one-half of all funds being used to reimburse nursing homes. Such funds have facilitated the transfer of large numbers of chronic patients from public mental hospitals to nursing homes, but, as we have seen, this has brought uncertain benefits. Many mental patients in nursing homes are no better off—and possibly in a worse situation—than in public mental hospitals. Transfer of patients, however, has reduced some burdens on state mental health budgets and has facilitated the upgrading of services in state and county mental institutions.

Medicaid involves 53 separate programs. Under the law, states have considerable latitude to define the scope, amount, and duration of services, and there is little uniformity. Because the Medicaid program puts pressures on state budgets, despite federal matching funds, states manipulate their costs by the way they reimburse institutions and providers. Reductions in payments to institutions and professionals lead to their refusal to serve Medicaid patients or to their providing only perfunctory services. The structure of the Medicaid program contributes to the continuation of two standards of care in many areas, despite the fact that in some localities Medicaid patients receive excellent care.

The President's Commission on Mental Health (1978) addressed various issues involving the Medicaid program and recommended more forceful control on the part of the federal government over state programming. It suggested that the federal government ensure the following: (1) states prevent discrimination on the basis of diagnosis; (2) mental health coverage be included in child health programs; (3) state programs include a reasonable amount of ambulatory services; and (4) reimbursement policies not limit the availability of services. The commission also suggested legislation to extend eligibility standards, to establish minimal mental health benefits for each state plan, and to eliminate discrimination in the allocation of services on the basis of age (U.S. President's Commission 1978, Vol. I, pp. 32–33). Many of these recommendations require new federal and state expenditures in an era of taxpayer resistance, and efforts to reduce government deficits. Although the recommendations are commendable, some do not seriously come to terms with the economic and political consequences of implementation. The recommendation that reimbursement policies not limit the availability of services would require that states pay providers approximately what they demand in the private sector. Such measures go against other developments in health care policy designed to give government greater control over reimbursement and greater ability to contain increasing costs (Mechanic 1986b).

There have been some changes in Medicaid since the President's Commission, including coverage for case-management services. But, in general, there is great resistance to extending Medicaid, although there is more openness to proposals that would reshape services in a "cost-neutral" framework. Among the issues to be addressed are how to capture funds poorly used because of services fragmentation and how to consolidate existing funding so as to achieve greater impact.

In the typical system of community services there is little ability to track mentally ill clients because of the fragmentation of service organization. Chronic patients having an exacerbation of symptoms come in or are brought to emergency rooms where they are seen by physicians unfamiliar with them, and who choose hospitalization because of the insecurities that uncertainty provokes. For example, in Philadelphia young patients using psychiatric emergency services as a point of entry to the mental health system accounted for 20 percent of the unduplicated caseload but used 60 percent of all service hours and accounted for 55 percent of all admissions (Surles and McGurrin 1987). In a well-organized community program, many of these admissions could be prevented and the patient referred to more appropriate care. About two-thirds of Medicaid mental illness bed days relate to the chronic population; more effective use of these expenditures could contribute much to revitalizing public mental health services.

At present, there are limited incentives to prevent hospitalization, and there may be pressures to fill vacant beds. Medicaid reforms could make it possible to reallocate hospital savings to community care programs within a managed care framework, which would provide the types of incentives necessary for a balanced system of care (Aiken, Somers, and Shore 1986). Demonstrations should be encouraged that allow the pooling of expected inpatient and outpatient Medicaid contributions under the control of a single accountable entity that has responsibility for a defined population of mentally ill persons. Capturing these funds not only prospectively allows careful tradeoffs in care decisions but also provides the necessary resource base to develop service components and hire appropriate personnel. To the extent that varying funding sources including state allocations to local government, local resources, and Medicaid could be managed in the same way, the potential for developing an appropriate range of integrated services becomes more possible.

Improving Disability Determination

The disability program, as it affects the mentally ill, is instructive. Based on a concept of permanent and total disability, eligibility criteria are believed to reinforce a sense of personal defeat and to be a disincentive to rehabilitation. Many mental health professionals feel ambivalent in encouraging clients to enter the disability system. Viable community care, however, depends on such support, since many severely mentally ill cannot maintain employment, are too disoriented, or behave too bizarrely to be acceptable to employers. By the mid-1970s there had been a major expansion of numbers of disabled persons receiving disability insurance, among whom the mentally ill were a major subgroup. Estimates suggest that by the late 1970s there were more than 1 half million mentally ill receiving either SSI or SSDI (National Institute of Mental Health 1987).

The growth in disability costs led to the 1980 amendments to the Social Security Act in which Congress required that states review all awards at least every three years. These reviews resulted in the loss of benefits by large numbers of severely mentally ill, among others, and subsequently to much litigation in the federal courts. It became apparent that the application of existing disability criteria seriously underestimated the incapacities of many chronic patients to work in a sustained way and stripped significant numbers of their benefits. Between 1981 and 1983 the benefits of a half million people were terminated, many of them mentally ill. Eventually, some 290,000 of those terminated were reinstated (Osterweis, Kleinman, and Mechanic 1987). New psychiatric criteria based on an integrated functional assessment were developed, which have supported the reinstatement of many patients excised from the disability rolls.

Disability determinations require considerable discretion on the part of the Social Security Administration (SSA), and success in gaining eligibility depends in no small way on how the claim is constructed, how appropriate medical and psychiatric information is obtained, and the persistence of the potential recipient. There are several levels of review and administrative law judges (ALJs) who hear appeals for the SSA reverse denials in approximately half of the cases they review (Mashaw 1983). Seriously mentally ill persons often have difficulty making an appropriate application for disability, presenting their needs in a way that increases probable success, or understanding their options when faced with denial. Because of the large numbers of mentally ill denied benefits in recent years, mental health workers and other advocates have taken an aggressive role in pursuing appeals at both the ALJ level and in the federal courts.

Expeditious attainment of disability benefits is important in order to stabilize the chronic patients' life situations and plan appropriate care. Barriers include the common delays in awarding benefits and the contradictory eligibility criteria for such benefits and access to vocational rehabilitation services. We need a better way of providing the chronic patient essential subsistence while not discouraging rehabilitation. In some localities, mental health personnel and state agencies administering disability determinations have government workers located in mental health service facilities to make the disability filing process more simple and accessible. But if the potential of this system is to be better realized, the disability system must be linked to stronger incentives for rehabilitation. This requires reconciling contradictory assumptions and eligibility requirements in these program areas.

Many provisions within the Social Security disability system speak to rehabilitation, but they clash with the requirement that recipients prove that they cannot work because of a long-lasting medical impairment. To become eligible for rehabilitation, the disabled have had to prove their work potential and their ability to benefit. Moreover, there has been little motivation for state vocational rehabilitation agencies to serve most disabled because the Social Security Administration only paid for these services when the recipient returned to work for a continuous period of nine months (Osterweis, Kleinman, and Mechanic 1987, pp. 70–71); but these patients involve a high risk of rehabilitation failure. It is thus no surprise that the rehabilitation provisions of the act are rarely used.

In 1986, the Congress extended the Vocational Rehabilitation Act. For the first time, supported work activities are permitted under the act, including transitional employment for persons with chronic mental illness. The legislation specifically includes community mental health centers among agencies encouraged to collaborate with departments of vocational rehabilitation. But vocational rehabilitation among the millions of mentally ill is still a highly underdeveloped service. As of 1984, less than 40,000 mentally ill were being served by federal and state vocational rehabilitation programs (News and Notes 1987).

THE CASE MANAGEMENT APPROACH

As communities view the challenge of developing appropriate care for the most disabled, they embrace the case-management concept. The concept has varied meanings in different contexts, but even in its legislative context involving the Medicaid program it is poorly defined. One survey of case-management concepts within Medicaid concluded that, "In concept and in practice, case-management appears to be an ill-defined process that lacks substance" (Spitz 1987, p. 69).

Case-management has a long tradition in social work, where the caseworker helped identify and mobilize a variety of community services on behalf of a client. Many of the case-management approaches used in social work for decades, such as street teams, crisis intervention, and brokering community services, are being adopted in relation to the new young chron-

ic patients and the homeless mentally ill who are less inclined toward traditional services approaches.

Case-management is loosely thought of as a solution to a wide variety
of difficult problems. But the responsibilities it is expected to bear are
alarming in the context of the realities of system disorganization and the
types of personnel given these tasks. Thinking about case-management in
the more restricted medical context, the case-manager is the primary care
physician who serves as the doctor of first contact, provides the necessary
continuing care and supervision, and makes appropriate referral for specialized medical and other services. The integrity of this role requires high-
level and broad-scope clinical judgment, linkage with the needed specialized services, and authority with other doctors and professionals and
with the patient. What is more important, it requires the authority under
reimbursement programs or existing financial arrangements to provide or
prescribe necessary services (Lewis, Fein, and Mechanic 1976).

Case-management with the chronically mentally ill population is inherently more complex. It not only requires appreciation of general medical and psychiatric needs and care, but sophistication about such varied
issues as housing, disability and welfare benefits, psychosocial rehabilitation, sheltered and competitive work programs, and issues relating to the
legal and criminal justice systems. In some systems of care, the case-manager functions as a therapist as well as a broker of services; in others the case-
manager helps define and marshall the necessary services but has no direct
therapeutic relation to the client. The scope of case-management functions, the typical caseload, the level of expected training and experience,
and the authority of the case-manager vary enormously both within and
among systems of care. Indeed, the concept is used so broadly as to have no
specific meaning at all.

In one of the few systematic studies of case-management, 417 chronically mentally ill in Texas were randomly assigned to experimental and
control groups. Each of these patients had two or more admissions to state
and/or county mental hospitals in approximately a two-year period. While
the control group could receive any but case-management services, the
experimental group were assigned to a case-management unit staffed by a
supervisor and seven case-managers with undergraduate or graduate degrees in the social sciences and an average of about four years of experience working with the mentally ill. During the study they spent about half
their time providing nonclinical services to clients and two-fifths of their
time brokering services. After 12 months it was clear that the case-management group received more services, were admitted to mental hospitals
more often, and costs were higher. While there were tendencies in favor of
the experimental group on quality of life measures, they were small and
not statistically significant (Franklin et al. 1987). This is only one study in a
large area of endeavor, but it should encourage understanding that concepts that sound appealing in theory often do not achieve their goals in
practice.

While the concept of the case-manager has intuitive appeal, it remains
unclear whether it is appropriate or realistic to assign such varied and
complex functions to individuals in contrast to more complex teams or

subsystems of care. First, there must be a clear definition of continuing responsibility; few professionals other than physicians have traditionally taken such roles. Second, given the diverse and complex functions necessary, specialization is more likely to lead to effective service. Third, case-management of these patients is clearly a longitudinal process, but the "half-life" of case-managers is short and attrition is high. Case-managers typically do not have the training and experience, control over resources, or professional standing to command resources from other organizations or even to be persuasive with them. Thus, case-management, to be effective, must be embedded in an organizational plan that defines clearly who is responsible and accountable for the care of the most highly disabled patients, has in place the necessary service elements to provide the full spectrum of needed services, and can coordinate and control diverse resources that flow into the system so that balanced decisions can be made about the expenditure of limited resources.

ORGANIZATIONAL BARRIERS

In the hospital we take shelter, activity, and basic medical supervision for granted, but each poses serious challenges for community programs of care. The closed character of hospitals allows staff to monitor patient activities carefully, to ensure medication regulation and compliance, and to induce appropriate behavior through a system of rewards. In the community, each of these areas becomes problematic and presents organizational challenges. Even approximations of these responsibilities require a level of organization and coordination absent in most community mental health service programs. Scarce resources, fragmentation of funding and service elements, lack of clear definitions of responsibility, and poorly developed career structures for the mental health professions in community care pose significant obstacles.

The Absence of a Clear Focus of Responsibility and Authority

In most of the nation's urban areas, responsibility for serving the mentally ill is fragmented among varying levels of government and categorical service agencies. There is typically little coordination among governmental sectors and providers of service, resulting in inefficiencies, duplication, poor use of resources, and failure to serve clients in need. Public mental hospital units, funded and administered by the state or county, may be poorly or not at all linked with outpatient psychiatric care or psychosocial services. Admission to and discharge from inpatient units often occurs without relation to an ongoing system of community services, or careful long-term planning of patients' needs. Agencies serving the homeless, the substance abuser, or the retarded maintain separate service systems, making it particularly difficult to help patients with multiple problems, and inpatient care under Medicaid and local medical assistance programs often function independently of outpatient care or psychosocial rehabilitation services in the community.

The precise shape of the necessary administrative structures remains unclear; different structures will fit varying political, legal, and service delivery environments. While establishment of mental health authorities implies centralization, an administrative authority could promote local diversity and program innovation. Concentration, however, can lead to less flexibility, innovation, and public support. In one city, for example, the director of a functioning authority for most of the chronic patients in that community made the strategic decision not to take over a number of smaller agencies serving some of these patients. The rationale was that each of these agencies had an enthusiastic board who served as advocate for improved care and such advocacy outweighed the advantages of his taking direct control over these agencies.

There are a variety of models for nonprofit and public authorities in such areas as transit systems, freeways, and redevelopment efforts (Walsh and Leigland 1986). Unlike authorities that can raise capital through income-producing potential, the idea of a mental health authority comes closer to state educational authorities intended to operate with more flexibility than typical government bureaucracies. The ideal is not always realized, and these agencies do develop their own bureaucratic cultures.

The relative merits of organizing mental health services through government agencies, special boards designated by statute, nonprofit voluntary groups or some hybrid of these forms remain unclear. Nor is it obvious to what degree such entities should be direct-service providers as well as planning, financing, and administrative bodies, or whether they should restrict themselves to limited administrative and regulatory functions in relation to contracting agencies. These assessments cannot be made in the abstract but must be weighed in relation to the organization and effectiveness of existing service providers, statutory requirements, and the political culture of the locality. In theory, performance contracting and the competition it implies seem advantageous to publicly organized services, but in practice the funders often become dependent on their contractees and may have few real options (Dorwart et al. 1986).

The specific strategy for governance is perhaps less crucial than the message that the mental health public sector is being revitalized. Public mental health services are in low repute among professionals, many patients, and the general public. They have typically become excessively bureaucratic, self-protective, risk-aversive, and have provided little incentive for innovation. Yet, there is little likelihood that the complex needs of the chronic mental patient will be met by the private sector. Public mental health services require greater control over resources and flexibility in operation if they are to engage the attention and energies of outstanding administrators, psychiatrists and other mental health personnel. By engaging the interest of professional communities, university training programs, and the larger public, the isolation of public-sector services can be reduced. Reasonable career structures for mental health professionals in the public sector can be developed with more opportunity to enhance the professional training and continuing education of those who work in public mental health. But achieving this will require the development of a strong and more independent entity than is now evident in most state mental health systems.

In the case of the chronically ill, there is unequivocal experience indicating that existing psychiatric treatment itself without a carefully designed system of supportive services cannot cope with the dimensions of the patient's problems or the social costs assumed by the community (Davis et al. 1972, 1974, Stein and Test 1976). No system of psychiatric insurance coverage can meet these patients' needs without resources and efforts to design programs to keep patients involved and in contact, working to the extent feasible, and associating with other people and continuing care programs. To treat these patients episodically and return them to a community without adequate programming displaces the problems without providing the instruments necessary to deal with them.

Chapter Ten

The Social Context
of Mental Health Practice:
Ethical Issues

Psychiatrists, as well as other mental health professionals, are influenced in their activities and judgments by the sociocultural context, by their personal and social biographies, by the ideologies implicit in their professional training, by the state of perspectives, theories, and scientific understanding in their disciplines, and by the economic and organizational constraints of practice settings. The practice of psychiatry involves competing roles. Although psychiatrists may select themselves into certain roles and not others, it is common for them to have multiple professional roles with varying social and ethical requirements but with no clear demarcation among them. Much of professional practice has important social control functions, and mental health practitioners are in part political actors. The conflicts in psychiatry are more sharply drawn and the boundaries of appropriate activity somewhat more hazy than in other medical disciplines.

A psychiatrist plays numerous roles, including the scientist, the physician, and the bureaucrat. While such spheres of action overlap, it is analytically useful to separate them and examine their varying aspects and the ethical dilemmas they pose.

Freidson (1970) has noted the distinction between the psychiatrist as a scientist and as a physician. The goal of the physician is action and not knowledge. The physician believes in what he or she is doing, and this is functional for both doctor and patient. The skeptical detachment of the scientist would only discourage the patient and erode the suggestive powers of the therapeutic encounter. While the scientist seeks to develop a coherent theory, the clinician is a pragmatist, depending heavily on subjective experience and trial and error in situations of uncertainty. While the scientist seeks to determine regularity of behavior in relation to abstract principles, the clinician is more subjective and suspicious of the abstract. The responsibilities of clinical work make it difficult to suspend action, to remain detached, and to lack faith that one is helping patients.

The differences between the objects of science and practice suggest different ways of proceeding in the two roles. The researcher in psychiatry must be concerned with very precise and reliable diagnosis. Only through effective distinctions among varying clinical entities can knowledge of etiology, course, and effective treatment be acquired (Mechanic 1978). Although such efforts in making finer distinctions or in identifying new conditions may be uncertain and yield no benefits for the patient, they may serve the development of scientific inquiry and understanding. Such diagnostic orientations used in a clinical context, however, may be of little use or even be dysfunctional. The labeling of questionable conditions may induce anxiety in the patient, may be stigmatizing, and may divert efforts from taking constructive action on behalf of the patient. As suggested earlier in this volume, the professionalization of psychiatry in the late nineteenth century in America and the growing assumption that mental disorders were biological in origin and required organic interventions undermined the useful activities of social reformers who devoted attention to the social context of treatment (Grob 1966). If mental disease was an unfolding of biological propensities, why worry about the social environment? The irony, of course, was that the new conception had little to offer patients and undermined helpful and constructive interventions.

Psychiatrists in their capacity as physicians have a social role that extends beyond their technical knowledge. The scope of their activities may be constrained by their conceptions of psychiatric activity, but they have limited control in defining the types of patients that seek their help. They have a social responsibility to do what they can to help patients who are suffering and seek assistance and thus cannot simply be constrained by the state of established knowledge. Psychiatrists as physicians work in part on the basis of scientific knowledge and clinical experience and in part on the basis of their social judgment of what is appropriate for the situation. As the problems faced become more uncertain and are less resolvable through existing psychiatric expertise, the psychiatrist's social biography and values have a larger impact on decision making.

Because psychiatry deals with deviance in feeling states and behavior, its conceptions run parallel to societal conceptions of social behavior, personal worth, and morality. Conceptions of behavior can be viewed from competing vantage points, and thus they are amenable to varying professional stances. In the absence of clear evidence on etiology or treatment, personal disturbance can be alternatively viewed as biological in nature, as a result of developmental failures, as a moral crisis, or as a consequence of socioeconomic, social, or structural constraints. Remedies may be seen in terms of biological restoration, moral realignment, social conditioning, or societal change. Although all of these elements may be present in the same situation, the one that the psychiatrist emphasizes has both moral and practical implications. There is no completely neutral stance. Diagnostic and therapeutic judgments have political and social implications (Halleck 1971).

In this context it is of great importance whom the therapist represents. To the extent that the therapist acts exclusively as the patient's representative and in the patient's interest as far as this can be known, the situation is relatively simple. The patient suffers and seeks assistance, and the role of the therapist is to do whatever possible to define the options available for the patient and to proceed in a manner they agree on. Such intervention may be at the biological, psychological, or social level or within a medical, psychodynamic, or educational model. The definition of the endeavor, however, is in terms of the patient's interests and needs. In real situations, failure to define options is common, and the psychiatrist's values and ideologies or practice orientations may intervene resulting in deviations from the ideal. Indeed, psychiatrists may not be conscious of their own ideologies and orientations because they are so entrenched in their own world view. Or they may proceed against the patient's wishes because they assume greater knowledge of the patient's interests. Despite these complexities, the approach is distinctive in that actions taken are for the sake of the patient and no other.

The ethic that the physician's responsibility is to the patient and no other is itself a value, as are other norms of practice such as confidentiality. The ethic arises from a commitment to individuals as compared to collectivities and is not universally shared. In the People's Republic of China, for example, psychiatric practice is a public function with primary commitment to the interests of the state and not the individual (Kleinman and Mechanic 1979). Psychiatric practice takes place openly in consultation with family members and with commune leaders. The way the patient will be handled is a public issue, and information concerning the patient's problems and management is shared with commune officials and work supervisors. While the basic content of psychiatry is seen as primarily biological, the social consequences of psychiatric advice are recognized. Professional practice cannot be divorced from existing forms of social organization.

China may seem far from American psychiatric concerns, but the issues of who the clinician represents and the proper scope of confidentiality are critical issues in the care of the chronically mentally ill. Many families of mental patients are bitter against mental health professionals, who they feel leave them uninformed and provide little help in dealing with the burden of a severely ill child or spouse. Most families are dissatisfied with the information they receive, feeling that communication is almost exclusively with the patient, isolating them from the treatment process (Hatfield 1987, Tessler et al. 1987). Effective care of chronic patients often requires communication with landlords, police, employers, and others that pushes against the traditional ethic of confidentiality that defines patient–therapist relationships.

In Western societies, psychiatrists may work as agents of individual patients or as agents of collectivities or organizations, such as families, schools, industries, courts, and the armed services (Szasz 1970). Under some circumstances, mental health professionals may retain autonomous roles in which they continue to act as agents for patients, but their organizational auspices make such roles more uncertain and more susceptible to encroachment (Halleck and Miller 1963). Couples therapy or therapy involving parents and children inevitably involves a clash of wills and interests, and the therapist is forced to take sides, though this may be reflected only in the most subtle ways. Although such therapies may involve sufficient common interest among the parties to sustain the encounter, the therapist must walk a difficult line. Therapists in such situations often see themselves as playing an autonomous role; such a role may become more tenuous as the power of the institution employing the therapist intrudes on the relationship.

When physicians work for organizations other than the patient, their loyalties are split. Although conflict of loyalties may not be a major issue in routine everyday practice, it may at any time become problematic whenever the organization and the patient have competing needs or interests. The most dramatic examples of such forms of bureaucratic psychiatry are found in totalitarian countries in which psychiatrists are state bureaucrats and may perform social control functions for the state, or in the military in which psychiatrists serve as agents of the organization. Similar pressures exist, however, whenever the psychiatrist represents some collectivity, whether it be a court, prison, school, or industrial organization. In all but the most crass cases, the psychiatrist as double agent is sufficiently ambiguous that the professional can experience feelings of neutrality and participation in the public interest. It is this comforting sense of lack of partiality that is most dangerous because it diverts attention from the dilemmas in resolving conflicts between involved parties. The use of psychiatry to discredit political dissenters or innovators is reasonably evident, even if disputed. It is the subtle social influences on psychiatric work that are more difficult to bring into the open.

SOCIAL INFLUENCES ON PSYCHIATRIC JUDGMENT

In most instances in which psychiatric judgments are made, there are no reliable independent tests to confirm or contest them. While psychiatric diagnosis focuses on disordered thought and functioning and not deviant behavior per se (Lewis 1953), judgments of disorder must be tied to social contexts and the clinician's undertaking of them based not only on clinical experience but also normal life experience. Most lay persons can recognize the bizarre symptoms associated with psychosis; it is the borderline areas that are more at issue, and at these borders it becomes more difficult to disentangle subculture, illness behavior, and psychopathology. As the subcultural situation is further from the psychiatrist's firsthand experience, the likelihood increases that inappropriate contextual norms will be applied. To the extent that the patient comes to the therapist voluntarily and seeks relief from suffering, the lack of precision in making such contextual judgments is less of a concern than when the psychiatrist acts on behalf of some other interest. Even in the former situation, however, the prestige of the therapist reinforces considerable personal power in the encounter with the patient and may reinforce one of the alternative views of the nature of the patient's problem.

The absence of procedures or laboratory tests to establish diagnoses independent of the therapist's contextual judgment makes it relatively easy for critics to insist that psychiatrists label patients on the basis of social, ethical, or legal norms and not on clearly established evidence of psychopathology (Szasz 1960, Rosenhan 1973). Although such criticisms cannot really speak to the scientific validity of the application of a disease model to the patient's suffering or deviant behavior (Spitzer 1976, Mechanic 1978), they apply to the role of psychiatrist as clinician or bureaucrat in dealing with social problems and psychological disorder. The psychiatrist who mediates conflicts between husband and wife, between parent and child, between employer and employee, and between citizens and official agencies inevitably must mix social judgments with assessments of psychopathology. When the psychiatrist acts as an agent to excuse failures at work, to obtain special preference for housing or other benefits, to obtain disability payments, to excuse deviant behavior, or in a wide variety of other arenas, he or she typically parades social judgments and personal decisions as psychiatric practice. It is therefore essential to know something about the social orientations and world views of psychiatrists.

PERSONAL AND SOCIAL BIOGRAPHIES

Psychiatrists have gone through a variety of selective screenings involving entry into medical school, into psychiatry, and into particular types of psychiatric functions, such as individual psychotherapy, hospital work, or administration. This selective process involves not only academic performance and interests but also social background, values and ideologies, and individual aspirations. Various studies show that physicians selecting psychiatry differ from students in other specialties, such as surgery or family practice, on social background, attitudes, and political orientations (Christie and Geis 1970, Colombotos et al. 1975). In their classic book, *Social Class and Mental Illness,* Hollingshead and Redlich (1958) review the dramatically varying social biographies of psychiatrists in New Haven who pursued analytic-psychological orientations as compared with those who were more directive in their approaches and depended more on organic therapies. Despite an obvious convergence in therapeutic practice, with many psychiatrists using a combination of therapies and drugs, there continues to be a distinctive selection process of mental health professionals into psychotherapy.

Therapists engaged in office-based psychotherapy are both distinctive and relatively homogeneous in their social characteristics.

> Careers terminating in the private practice of psychotherapy are populated, to a very large extent, by practitioners of highly similar cultural and social backgrounds. They come from a highly circumscribed sector of the social world, representing a special combination of social marginality in ethnic, religious, political, and social-class terms. (Henry, Sims, and Spray 1973, p. 3)

Psychotherapists coming from psychiatry, clinical psychology, and social work are more similar in social background and practice orientations to one another than to psychiatrists who are more medically inclined (Henry, Sims, and Spray 1971, 1973). Persons who become therapists, regardless of profession, perform similar activities, have comparable work styles, share many viewpoints, and have strikingly similar developmental experiences.

The implications of similarities of development and perspective among therapists are not obvious but very suggestive. Certainly it is reasonable to assume that therapists who are upwardly mobile, socially marginal, nonreligious, divorced, and politically liberal will see social and moral issues differently from more socially integrated and conventional persons, and they will communicate quite different judgments. Because therapists' personalities and orientations are important aspects of therapy, and because psychotherapy is largely an influence process (Frank 1974), the encounter inevitably involves the transmission of values. Therapists may wish to minimize personal biases, however, but they cannot help but transmit what they stand for. To the extent that this is explicit to the patient, it is less of a problem than when masked behind a professional mystique.

Greenley, Kepecs, and Henry (1979) provide data collected in 1973 from psychiatrists practicing in Chicago, some of whom were also studied in a 1962 survey (Henry, Sims, and Spray 1971). These data indicate that at least in Chicago there is strong persistence of a dominant Freudian-analytic orientation and office-based private practice. Although more psychiatrists report having an eclectic orientation, the enthusiasm of the early 1960s for social and community psychiatry has receded. It was noted as the orientation of only some 15 percent of respondents in 1973. If this study was repeated today, it would probably show the growing dominance of biological psychiatry.

There is some evidence from this survey that the social characteristics of both psychiatrists and their patients are becoming more like those of the general population, although large differences still exist. The growth of psychodynamic therapy in the United States can be viewed as a social movement, developing first among particular practitioners and patients facing certain existential dilemmas (Mechanic 1975). Psychodynamic therapies developed their roots in urban areas, with many practitioners of urban, middle-class, Jewish origins. This therapy initially attracted persons with social inclinations and characteristics similar to those of the therapists. As the movement grew, however, and therapy became more widely accepted in the culture, one would have anticipated that it would become more heterogeneous in geographic distribution and in the characteristics of both therapists and patients. The indications were that such heterogeneity was developing as psychotherapy became institutionalized, and Greenley, Kepecs, and Henry's (1979) Chicago data illustrate this trend. Comparing cohorts of psychiatrists completing residencies in different periods from before 1950 to the time of the survey, they observe a steep decline in the proportion of those with immigrant fathers, those who were Jewish, and those who were raised in a large city. Psychiatrists in 1973, as compared with 1966, reported having more women, blacks, Catholics, and poor persons as patients, and somewhat fewer Jewish patients.

The Chicago data, as well as other experience, indicate that psychiatric practice is becoming more varied and complex (Redlich and Kellert 1978). This should allow greater opportunity for patients to locate therapists who have orientations and perspectives closer to their own and should promote a healthy diversity within psychiatry itself concerning the relationship between mental health concerns and values.

THE SOCIOCULTURAL CONTEXT

The sociocultural context in which young psychiatrists develop and mature and within which they practice has a dramatic influence on their world views as well as their professional activities. Varying periods of historical time and specific cultural contexts provide different images of the nature of man, the boundaries of deviance, and the professional role of social and psychiatric intervention (Foucault 1965). In Europe, psychiatry has remained closer to general medical practice than in the United States, where psychodynamic therapies have been viewed by young psychiatrists as more prestigeful than taking care of severely disturbed or chronic patients. In the post–World War II period, psychodynamic ideas came to dominate residency programs in psychiatry and had a major effect on the way psychiatrists perceived their roles and practiced their craft. Why the United States and not Europe was the more fertile ground for psychoanalytic ideas is amenable to many interpretations; nevertheless, the fact is that it was and it resulted in a dramatic influence on views of psychopathology and treatment of patients.

During the 1960s there was great ferment in American society, characterized by social activism and an ideology that government could effectively attack social problems. This ideology had a broad sweep, and it also came to encompass conceptions of the social causes of and remedies for mental illness. Psychiatrists caught up in the ethos of the time began making grandiose claims of the potentialities for a community psychiatry. Such advocacy was not grounded in improving programming for chronic mental patients who were increasingly being returned to communities, but in claims for special societal expertise. In the words of one such advocate, "The psychiatrist must truly be a political personage in the best sense of the word. He must play a role in *controlling* the environment which man has created" (Duhl 1963, p. 73).

A major component of this new ideology was the notion that psychiatry could engage in primary prevention to limit the occurrence of mental illness. Caplan (1964) maintained that such efforts involved identifying harmful influences, encouraging environmental forces that support individuals in resisting them, and increasing the resistance of the population to future illness. The program he offered under the guise of psychiatric expertise was simply a form of social and political action. As Caplan saw it,

The mental health specialist offers consultation to legislators and administrators and collaborates with other citizens in influencing governmental agencies to change laws and regulations. Social action includes efforts to modify general attitudes and behavior of community members by communication through the educational system, the mass media, and through interaction between the professional and lay communities. (Caplan 1964, p. 56)

Caplan cites the area of welfare legislation as one that psychiatrists ought to be involved in.

In some states, the regulation of these grants [Aid to Dependent Children] in the case of children of unmarried mothers is currently being modified to dissuade the mothers from further illegitimate pregnancies. Mental health specialists are being consulted to help the legislators and welfare authorities improve the moral atmosphere in the homes where children are being brought up and to influence their mothers to marry and provide them with stable fathers. (Caplan 1964, p. 59)

Clearly Caplan wished psychiatrists to become involved in matters such as morality and values on which there were many views and differences of opinion. Caplan (1965) also saw psychiatrists extending their focus to problems of personnel selection, placement, and promotion.

If he accedes to these requests, he will find that he is using his clinical skills and his knowledge of personality and human relations and needs not only to deal with persons suspected of mental disorder, but also to predict the fitness of healthy persons to deal effectively with particular situations without endangering their mental health. He will also be exercising some influence upon the nature of the population in the organization, and hopefully he will be reducing the risk of mental disorder by excluding vulnerable candidates and by preventing the fitting of round pegs into square holes. (Caplan 1965, p. 6)

Caplan even went as far as to speculate that a psychiatrist might "exercise surveillance over key people in the community and . . . intervene in those cases where he identifies disturbed relationships in order to offer treatment or recommend dismissal" (p. 79). However, he rejected this role not because of lack of ability or knowledge on the part of psychiatrists but because it would be a distasteful role for most psychiatrists and because of political and social complications. That some psychiatrists do not find this role distasteful is evidenced by the more than 1,000 American psychiatrists who responded to an obviously biased poll by *Fact* magazine which attempted to discredit Barry Goldwater's psychological fitness to run for the presidency of the United States. A lawsuit resulted in a jury decision that Goldwater had been libeled.

Some of the concepts implicit in preventive psychiatry are unfortunate not only because they are grandiose, naive, and an obvious projection of political values, but also because they continue to divert attention from making many of the remedial efforts more consistent with existing knowledge and expertise. Preventive care during pregnancy and adequate postnatal care, still not fully available to the poor, are important in preventing mental retardation, prematurity, brain damage, and a variety of other difficulties. Family planning services and facilities for families with handicapped children are often difficult to find. The system of services in the community for chronic mental patients is at best fragmentary. By what set of values do we divert attention from these issues to pursue illusory goals? The greatest weakness of preventive psychiatry in the 1960s was the substitution of vague ideals for tangible action and a failure to specify in any clear way how psychiatric expertise could lead to the laudable goals being advocated.

The extraordinary range of roles played by psychiatrists is reflected in the work of a Harvard psychiatrist as a consultant for the Boston Patriots football team. Among his tasks were teaching techniques "to program the mind to achieve peak athletic performance" and "meeting with team members before a game to help prepare them psychologically for a competition" (Nicholi 1987). Other functions included individual therapy, drug-use prevention efforts, helping resolve conflicts among team members, and improving relations between the coach and players. It is difficult to assess what this all adds up to, but one outcome measure is that fact that Nicholi was the first physician in the National Football League to be given a game ball. The prestigious *New England Journal of Medicine,* which publishes little on chronic mental illness and rations its space in the most parsimonious way devoted more than five pages to psychiatric consultation in football.

It is essential from an ethical perspective to differentiate among varying psychiatric roles. From the role of psychiatrist as researcher, it is fully appropriate to examine the value of interpersonal interventions. Caplan (1964) maintained that various crises and transitional periods in the life span, such as entering school, having a child, going to the hospital for surgery, or moving to a new environment, pose severe stresses that may burden a person's coping capacities and entail a high risk of social breakdown. He asserted that during such periods persons had a heightened desire for help and were more responsive to it. He argued that community psychiatrists should seek out situations in which persons feel vulnerable and provide supportive help and new coping techniques. The theory argued that social breakdowns could be prevented either by intervening in the lives of people and their families during crises or by working through various professionals, such as doctors, nurses, teachers, and administrators, who naturally come into contact with people during such crises. Among the contexts Caplan suggested for such crisis intervention were prenatal and surgical wards, divorce courts, and colleges. The basic hypothesis, and one legitimate and worthy of detailed inquiry, is that it is possible to give people anticipatory guidance and emotional inoculation that help them cope with threatening events.

When the psychiatric role moves from investigation to practice, the hypothesis of crisis intervention involves major ethical dilemmas. First, although aspects of the theory are promising, it is based on a vague conceptualization that environmental trauma and the lack of coping abilities cause mental illness, a conception for which the evidence is incomplete and far from secure. Second, although such efforts may be made with laudable goals in mind, the evaluation literature attests to the fact that such programming often not only fails to achieve desired objectives, but also makes matters worse (Robins 1979a). Third, there is really very little evidence that the types of trouble-shooting preventive psychiatrists advocate, although perhaps valuable in reducing distress, have any real impact on the occurrence of mental illness or are directed at those who are likely to become mentally ill if untreated. Despite these ethical concerns, the psychiatrist could justifiably engage in such programs with interested community groups to the extent that they understand the limitations and elect to participate voluntarily. Such interventions may be viewed as any other uncertain therapy, with possible positive and adverse effects that must be balanced.

Preventive psychiatry intuitively seems enticing. After all, isn't it better to prevent illness than treat it after it occurs? Moreover, the proponents of prevention typically argue that it saves vast amounts of money, since treating severe illness is much more expensive than initial preventive care. But as we have learned so well in the area of general medical care, this argument is simplistic and often incorrect (Russell 1986, 1987). The success of prevention and potential cost savings depend on the ability to target individuals who will become more seriously ill without treatment and the cost and effectiveness of the preventive intervention. But even when we have interventions that we believe to be efficacious and that are not too costly, preventive efforts may still be a bad bargain unless we have the knowledge to target precisely. The number of people who become seriously mentally ill is a small proportion of the population. In contrast, the number of people who can be potential targets of preventive intervention is very large. Even a relatively inexpensive intervention averaged over large numbers of people can result in large aggregate costs. But many of these people get better without formal intervention. The ECA project estimated that 30 million people had a DIS-DSM III disorder and that many more millions have high levels of distress and dysfunction without such disorder. If we add additional vulnerable individuals including those under high stress, those experiencing bereavement or divorce, the unemployed, and so on, we can readily identify a target population of 100 million people. Thus, an intervention costing $100, not a particularly expensive one by psychiatric standards, would in the aggregate cost $10 billion. Think of what even a small fraction of this could do for the severely mentally ill.

Preventive psychiatry is also on shaky grounds when psychiatrists are in bureaucratic positions, providing services to those neither seeking nor desiring their assistance. The imposition of such interventions in schools, divorce courts, welfare agencies, and the like, buttressed by the coercive authority of the organization, is a serious imposition on privacy and the rights of persons to lead their lives without interference. Even if the theory were powerful and its success demonstrated, involuntary application of preventive psychiatry would raise profound ethical issues.

As the optimism of the 1960s receded, preventive psychiatry lost much of its luster, although it remains as one of many streams of psychiatric activity and much soft thinking on the issue persists. Psychiatry in the 1970s can be more generally characterized as returning to interest in the biological bases of behavior and more particularly to brain processes, microbiology, and behavioral genetics. Although psychodynamic views are highly prevalent, the field of practice is more heterogeneous than ever before, and training centers are increasingly focusing on biological re-search and a more rigorous approach to psychiatric diagnosis. This will, of course, affect the viewpoints and practice orientations of future psychia-trists. While these changes result in part from research advances in biolog-ical psychiatry and epidemiology, they also reflect changing conceptions of the potentialities of social reform in the society at large. Each cohort of psychiatrists is likely to retain a part of the social and value conceptions characteristic of its historical life cycle.

CONSTRAINTS OF PRACTICE SETTINGS

Professional practice is influenced by the social context of practice organi-zation and the manner in which payment for services is made. The influ-ence of the professional's employer on professional decision making is widely recognized and has already been discussed. I will focus here on some practice constraints that are less widely appreciated.

In the dominant forms of psychiatric therapy in the United States, the psychiatrist is a private office-based professional contracting with patients to provide services on a fee-for-service basis. Although such services may be partially covered by third-party insurance, the implicit contract is be-tween therapist and patient. Such therapy is typically organized in large time units of 45 to 50 minutes as often as every day or several times a week. Disproportionate services of this kind are purchased by the affluent or those well covered by insurance, and the therapists view themselves as responsible to their patients and not to some more abstract notion of need in the community. The form of payment in this situation—the fee for service per session—presumably creates an incentive on the part of the professional for long-term therapy beyond any point that such interven-tion would be cost effective.

An alternative model of psychiatric work is found in such entities as health maintenance organizations, community mental health centers, or the English National Health Service. In these contexts, the psychiatrist is theoretically responsible to a defined population who receive services from the organization. Because psychiatric services in these contexts cannot be made available to everyone who needs them and because the use of services has implications for the economic viability of the plan, rationing decisions must be made as to who in the population most need specialized psychiatric services and to what extent. Typically, such rationing is in part specified in the contract that patients have with the plan, such as a limitation on the number of psychiatric visits during any year. Rationing also occurs by requiring a formal referral from a primary care physician in the plan to a consulting psychiatrist. Such organizations, however, cannot sanction long-term therapy for a small number of patients at the expense of others needing services; therefore, psychiatrists are more likely to have shorter consultations, engage in short-term psychotherapy, or provide drug monitoring. Although psychiatrists with such inclinations may be drawn to these types of organizations, there is little question that organizational arrangements help shape the scope and character of psychiatric services.

Similar types of constraints operate in mental hospital practice or in community care. What can be done for a patient depends on the personnel and resources available and the number of patients requiring help. Services are frequently stretched thinly or are inadequate because demand exceeds capacity. While it is typical to bemoan the fact of inadequate financing, it is unlikely that economic opportunities will ever allow psychiatrists to provide everything possible to all patients in need. Although there are no easy ways out of the ethical dilemmas posed by the need to ration, these dilemmas suggest an ethical imperative for the mental health professions. Stated simply, such professions have an obligation to evaluate their techniques and approaches in relation to their benefits and costs, in order that the resources available can be applied in the most effective way. A prudent society cannot provide public support for long-term psychoanalysis or other psychotherapies in the absence of evidence that these approaches are more efficacious than less costly alternatives.

A NOTE ON THE CARE OF CHRONICALLY IMPAIRED PATIENTS

Deinstitutionalization and community mental health care are as much a social ideology as were earlier conceptions of the care of the mentally ill. The ideology consists of beliefs that it is desirable that individuals, to the extent possible, live independently, assume responsibility, and show a desire to adjust in some fashion to community living. The involuntary hospitalization of patients constituted a violation of cherished beliefs about individual rights, and the abuses associated with such involuntary commitment have become widely known, making it more difficult to justify civil commitment. Perhaps less widely appreciated are the pressures now placed on patients and their families to have the patient in the community and the growing tendency to refuse a hospital refuge to some highly impaired patients (Morrissey, Tessler, and Farrin 1979).

The extent to which the community should allow such refuge, and at what point, is very much tied to economic factors and the social ethos. The issue of the extent to which coercive therapies should be used to stimulate and maintain appropriate functioning does not easily yield to a consensus, and practices vary a great deal from one context to another depending on the values and commitments of professionals working with such patients. With the development of aversive techniques of control, "token economies," and other forms of behavior modification, profound questions are raised about the limits of coercion and treatment.

In sum, every aspect of psychiatric conceptualization, research, and practice is shaped by social ideologies and assumptions. Concepts of deviance, boundaries between mental disorders and other types of problems, modes of intervention, and selection of clients all vary by time and place, by the character of social structure, and by dominant social perspectives. The biography of mental health professionals and their practices are culturally shaped, and the economic system poses alternative opportunities and constraints. Because mental health professionals must work with models and because such models have broad ethical implications for every aspect of their craft, there is no way of escaping the fact that psychiatric practice is as much a moral as a medical endeavor.

Chapter Eleven

Innovations
in Mental Health Services

Historically, one of the largest problems in providing mental health services for patients with severe disorders was the absence of a reasonable range of alternatives to match diverse conditions or varying levels of disability. With the development of community mental health care and a growing emphasis on treating patients within the least restrictive alternative (Chambers 1978), there is a continuing search for good community models of care for chronic patients. We have already reviewed some examples of innovative programs. Here we focus on some of the difficulties of developing and sustaining them.

There is wide recognition of the need for solutions that provide more protection and support than is typical in outpatient therapy but do not involve the dependency or isolation characteristic of hospitalization. Although many patients can remain in the community, they are not prepared to participate fully in community activities and require considerable supervision and support. Early developments in community care were in the use of transitional communities and partial hospitalization. The British used transitional communities for the social resettlement of prisoners of war in the civilian community at the end of World War II (Wilson, Trist, and Curle 1952). They found that the readjustment of such men was difficult, and they decided to institute a program to help refit them for civilian life. They developed Civil Resettlement Units as transitional communities that facilitated the resumption of a civilian role. The purpose was to attempt to neutralize the suspicions of these men toward authority, to allow them to develop role-taking skills appropriate to civilian life but within the supportive environment of the unit, to reestablish their relationships with the home society, and to help them structure their personal goals. Men who went through the program made a better adjustment than did men with comparable experiences who did not.

The halfway house and the community hostel are transitional communities increasingly used in the care of the mentally ill. The halfway house, located within the community, is a relatively small unit housing between 5 and 20 persons. The patients, who share a common situation, provide emotional support for one another; additional supervisory personnel are usually also available. The halfway house is an intermediate solution in that patients who are not prepared to return home or to their jobs or who are too insecure to make their own living arrangements can live in a supportive environment with others who understand their problems, who are tolerant of their difficulties, and who provide emotional support. The hostel, which is frequently used in European countries for housing former mental patients, provides similar support. Both halfway houses and hostels facilitate the relocation in the community of patients who have no relatives or friends willing to assume responsibility for their care. Similarly, these facilities provide therapeutic personnel with an option if they feel that family living arrangements are inappropriate for the patient. These transitional communities also facilitate a later readjustment in which ex-patients may try to live completely on their own.

Partial hospitalization refers most frequently to night and day hospitals. The day hospital provides a program for mental patients who live at home or at some other lodging but who spend their days at the hospital. Such institutions relieve the burden on the family and also help keep patients active and involved by providing them with support and other therapeutic services. They allow the patient to retain ties with the community, but they also reduce the psychological and social costs for the community and the patient. When day hospitals began in the United States, they were used as halfway institutions for patients who had been hospitalized. They are now used largely in lieu of hospitalization (Kramer 1962). The night hospital is for patients capable of fulfilling work responsibilities but requiring a treatment and supportive program. Through the night hospital, patients maintain productive functioning in the community at the same time that they are able to take advantage of a hospital program.

Intermediate programs are organized in many ways. Some are associated with public mental hospitals, others with state departments of mental health. Some are run by the Veterans Administration, others by private mental hospitals or psychiatry departments in general hospitals. Some of these institutions develop independently; others are integrated with a variety of social services for mental patients. Among the more important of such services are sheltered workshops and retraining facilities, after-care programs, and ex-patient clubs. The sheltered workshop provides work opportunities and learning experiences under supervision but does not expose patients to the competitive situation of a normal job. It may allow them to develop their confidence so that they can undertake employment in the community, or it may offer them work opportunities when they might otherwise be unemployed and without any useful activity. Often, however, the work is boring and repetitive, and patients sometimes complain of being mixed with other persons with visible disabilities. After-care programs provide support and help for patients who have moved back to the community but are faced with loneliness, isolation, and other social and psychological difficulties. Ex-patient clubs meet some of the same needs, giving persons the support of fellow ex-patients and helping to alleviate the isolation experienced by many who return to the community. Accompanying these changes have been modifications within the hospitals themselves, such as the institution of patient government and the elimination of many of the custodial aspects of the hospital, such as locked doors.

There are numerous examples of viable and creative community alternatives for chronic patients. Fairweather and his colleagues (1969) established a community group living situation for chronic posthospital patients that included the organization of a janitorial service that responded to community needs for such services. As the project continued, supervision over patients was relaxed, and the patients took more responsibility. In comparing this program with traditional after-care, the investigators found patients in this program to have greater productivity without loss in the area of psychosocial adjustment, and even during periods of maximum supervision, the experimental programs were considerably less expensive than the traditional services. The Fairweather Lodge program has been adopted in various contexts: In Austin, Texas, for example, chronic patients in a Lodge have responsibility for cleaning the Texas legislature facilities, and even severely ill patients have been self-supporting. Several innovative community service programs have been developed in Denver, Colorado (Polak 1978), in which hospitalization is avoided and problems are dealt with through home visits and systems intervention. During periods of crisis or when no adequate permanent home is available, patients are placed in carefully selected families and are supported by clinical supervision, instruction of home sponsors, and clinical home visits. Families taking such patients receive a per diem payment for room, board, and client care. Other programs train and use community members to assist chronic patients in daily life activities (Weinman and Kleiner 1978). Some communities have established patient apartment complexes, clubs, and recreation centers for the chronically disabled and lonely, and a variety of sheltered work situations (Stein and Test 1978).

In recognizing the development of new treatment situations, we should note that these are not typical of mental health services around the country, and although there are many halfway houses, day and night hospitals, sheltered workshops, and the like, many communities still provide few of these facilities, while large communities may have selected facilities but not the entire array. Ideally, every community should have a wide range of services so that mental health professionals can consider the magnitude of patients' illnesses and disabilities in fitting them to the appropriate service.

MAINTENANCE OF CHRONIC PSYCHIATRIC PATIENTS

In Chapter 7, I described a general coping-adaptation approach that could serve as a useful perspective in organizing programs for patients in the community. Much of the treatment of mental patients in the past was based on a view of people as sponges—absorbing developmental and environmental stimuli—rather than being based on a perspective that viewed them as active agents molding and affecting, to some extent, the conditions to which they are exposed. Much of our psychological vocabulary is phrased in terms of intrapsychic responses to environmental stress rather than in terms of active strivings and social performance. Although all scientific activity must ultimately be based on a deterministic model of some form, social activity is a product of the manipulation and arrangement of symbols. The scope of the symbolic environment in a complex and dynamic society—and even in simple ones—is so vast and so rich that people have considerable opportunity to affect the direction of their lives. We can, therefore, gain some advantage by conceptually specifying for psychiatric purposes the active problem-solving aspects of human adaptation, their relationship to the social structure, and their bearing on the rehabilitation of chronic patients.

In considering the meaning of the concept of social and psychological stress, we realize that this term refers to neither stimuli nor reactions in themselves but rather to a discrepancy between a problem or challenge and an individual's capacity to deal with or to adapt to it. This definition makes clear the importance of skill and performance components as well as of psychological defenses. Coping, as I use the term, is the instrumental behavior and problem-solving capacity of a person to meet demands and goals. It involves the application of acquired skills, techniques, and knowledge. The extent to which a person experiences discomfort in the first place is often a product of the inadequacy of such skill repertoires. In contrast to coping, defense (as I am using the term) is the manner in which a person manages his or her emotional and affective states when discomfort is aroused or anticipated. Most psychodynamic and psychological work deals with defense and not with coping. Implicit within traditional psychological approaches is the idea that the links between abilities and performance are obvious or irrelevant and that only the psychodynamics of intrapsychic response remain problematic.

Many clinicians who work with the psychiatrically disabled emphasize psychological barriers and techniques and give too little attention to the strategies and techniques people use to deal with tasks and other people. This emphasis is implicit in their psychological bias and in their entire orientation to the patient. Instead of exploring the nature of the patient's difficulties that lead him or her to seek care or others to insist upon removal from the social situation, clinicians frequently emphasize early development and relationships. Too often therapy designed to change patients is undertaken without giving careful consideration to the situation and problems to which they must return, the skills they will require, and the attitudes and feelings about their disabilities among significant others. Although many problems in accomplishing difficult tasks or in dealing with the social environment may not realistically be amenable to intervention, mental health workers can help improve patients' coping effectiveness either by changing or modifying their level of instrumental efforts or by helping to alter the social conditions under which they live so that their skills are more adequate and their problems less of a handicap.

Irrespective of whether psychiatric conditions are a consequence of neurological, psychological, genetic, or other problems, various social factors can have important effects on the course of a disability. Rehabilitation in contrast to treatment is frequently concerned with manipulating and regulating the context of the illness rather than the illness itself to achieve the best possible outcome given the practical limits of the nature of the condition and the situational contingencies. Rehabilitation is well advanced in physical medicine; experts have developed ingenious devices that allow persons with serious disabilities to overcome them and to live useful lives. In comparison, the mental health area offers a more difficult and uncertain situation, and experts continue to grope for a feasible model by which rehabilitation may be furthered (Watts and Bennett 1983, Shepherd 1984).

A rehabilitation approach is based on the premise that the person's injury, defect, or condition is irreversible because of the present state of knowledge and medical technology. The basic concern, then, is to provide techniques for changing living situations so that the condition, injury, or defect results in the least possible disability. Devices that change some aspect of the people and provide them with new skills include artificial hands, seeing eye dogs, and artificial talking devices for those who have cancer of the larynx and can no longer speak. These new tools help overcome the disability, and a period of training allows patients to adapt to their use. Disability can also be contained by controlling the environment in various ways. People who have disabling conditions can continue to meet role expectations through the use of special equipment that allows them to continue to do their jobs. A homemaker confined to a wheelchair can use kitchen appliances of different height and construction. The operating principle of such rehabilitation attempts is to change the skills and environment of a person so that an irreversible physical condition results in the least possible disability and disruption of patterns of living.

Rehabilitation does not imply that it is desirable to contain disability in contrast to reversing illness conditions. Unfortunately, in many areas we lack the necessary knowledge and the technology to do this, and under such conditions it is important to help people cope within the limits of their condition. Although this point is very obvious, in the area of psychiatric illnesses, where the knowledge to reverse the basic conditions is frequently lacking, rehabilitation efforts devoted to helping individuals live with their conditions are sometimes criticized as defeatist. However, until we have a better understanding of the etiology, course, and treatment of most mental illnesses, it may be more reasonable to attempt to contain disability in this area than to pursue cures without any real knowledge of the ways they are to be achieved.

Because there is little agreement on approaches for community care programs, the decision to provide a program in no sense specifies what is to be undertaken. At one extreme stand those who visualize community care as nothing more than the extension of the various forms of psychotherapy to new categories of people. More commonly, community care is visualized as a form of social work in which a trained practitioner helps the patient and the family weather crises by applying some knowledge of group and psychodynamic functioning or by the practitioner serving as an ombudsman, helping to bail the patient and the family out of difficulty with official agencies. I suspect that all these approaches supply a certain degree of support and help that mental patients do not ordinarily receive. But they do not necessarily either correspond to the magnitude of the disability these patients often experience or encourage patients to strive more actively to improve their capacities to cope with their environment. I do not want to belittle any support and sustenance offered to these patients because the most elementary forms of such help are so frequently absent from their lives, and we know that even contact with unskilled but sympathetic workers can do much to keep them functioning in the community. If we are to meet our responsibility to the mentally ill and their families, however, we must aspire to achieve and accomplish much more than this.

As we consider various alternatives for rehabilitation programs, an educational approach often seems better fitted to the needs of community care than do traditional medical approaches. Successful functioning results in large part from the way people learn to approach problems and to the practice they obtain through experience and training. Patients frequently lack information, skills, and abilities that are important in satisfactorily adapting to community life. Although improving the patient's capacity to make a satisfactory adjustment to the community is in no way a cure, the acquisition of new and relevant skills can inspire hope and confidence and can increase involvement in other aspects of a treatment program as well. An educational approach focuses more attention and emphasis on the patient's current level of social functioning and less on his or her past, and it encourages detailed and careful assessment of the way the patient behaves in a variety of nonhospital contexts.

Successful social functioning depends on a person's ability to mobilize effort when such effort is necessary, on the manner of organizing and applying such efforts, on psychological and instrumental skills and abilities, and on supports in the social environment. Although social support is well developed within most community care programs, the other facets of social functioning have been relatively neglected.

The mobilization of effort, assuming some level of involvement, may be facilitated by developing personal and social controls that reinforce and encourage good work habits. Traditionally in the care of the mentally ill in America, patients defined as sufficiently sick to require institutional care were defined as too deteriorated to perform in work roles. Instead, they were frequently allowed to sink into an apathetic stupor while their work skills atrophied. Although the attitude toward the work of mental patients has become more reasonable, such persons are often regarded as too sick to pursue meaningful tasks, and a very limited scope of such activity is available to the patient in many treatment contexts. The assumption that mental illness is totally incapacitating is reinforced by programs that fail to keep active those aspects of social functioning that can be sustained. Yet, the ability to continue performing meaningful tasks while under treatment can do much to raise patients' confidence in themselves and to encourage persistence in coping efforts.

Organization of effort involves (1) the way persons anticipate situations; (2) the way they seek information about them; (3) the extent to which they plan, prepare, and rehearse them in a psychological and social sense; (4) the way they test problem solutions; (5) the way they consider and prepare alternative courses of action should the situation require it; and (6) the way they allocate time and effort. When one begins to look at this problem in the case of chronic mental patients, it is astonishing how poorly their efforts are organized. In general psychiatric practice, the ineffectual organization of effort is often seen as a byproduct of the patient's condition and not as a basic component of it. Although such ineffectual performance may be an attribute of the illness, improvement in functioning may be valuable for the patient's self-confidence and mental state generally.

One of the difficulties all psychiatric programs face is the inability to obtain a comprehensive view of the way the patient behaves in a variety of meaningful social contexts. Because it is usually impractical for mental health workers to follow the patient closely within the community, they must depend either on informants or on information gleaned from observations of the patient's behavior in the clinical context. The clinical context is a highly artificial one, however, and may produce problems of coping very much unrelated to those that confront the patient in the community (Rapoport 1960). As clinical contexts are constructed so that they are more characteristic of actual living conditions, more accurate assessment of patients and the provision of programs fitted to their needs become possible. To return to the work example, it is valuable to develop sheltered work contexts that more realistically approximate community work contexts. This goal has been achieved to some extent in settings that provide realistic contexts for evaluation and instruction and in which mental health facilities have been able to contract meaningful work of substantial variety (Furman 1965).

In one sense a clinic might be viewed as a school in which the educational program, like a good tutorial program, takes into account the social, educational, and psychological needs of the student. From at least one perspective, mental patients suffer from inadequate and misguided socialization experiences; they have failed to acquire the psychological and coping skills necessary for reasonable social adjustment. Such failures may be the product of inherited capacities, brain damage, impoverished childhood circumstances, inadequate training for dealing with stress, or a variety of other causes. The source of the difficulty, however, may not be so important as the question of whether or not it can be remedied with an appropriate program.

One can visualize various advantages in using an educational model in contrast to a medical one. Successful social functioning requires some ability to act as one's own agent, and one of the disadvantages of the medical model is the tremendous dependence the chronic patient develops on physicians, nurses, social workers and other mental health workers, and on the institution as a physical entity. An educational model is likely to encourage higher expectations concerning personal responsibility and initiative, and its goals are specific in contrast to the diffuseness of general psychiatric approaches. Moreover, the educational model is a familiar one in our society. One of the persistent problems in the expansion of mental health care to new populations is the difficulty of reaching working-class people. Although all social strata may not equally share esteem for education, this model is one that persons from all social segments know and have experienced, and working-class people who aspire to a better life for themselves and their children have increasingly defined education as an essential means. Such a model may appeal to the working-class patients who feel more comfortable with it than they do with modern psychodynamics. Patients share in the educational process to a greater extent than they do in traditional medical approaches, and they are more likely to accept the goals toward which they are moving. Although patients also share in psychodynamic therapies, the goals are more diffuse and less relevant to the specific problems patients face than are the goals of the educational approach. The active role of the client toward well-defined and understandable goals within the educational model can stimulate a sense of control over one's life, self-confidence, and competence and can encourage activity toward self-improvement (Johnson, Hanson, and Rothaus 1967).

There has been considerable experience and research, particularly in England, in the area of industrial rehabilitation (Wing 1967). In various studies the results of training moderately handicapped, chronic schizophrenics who wanted to leave the hospital were reasonably good. Even older patients who were made resistant to rehabilitation showed some benefit from the program. Hospitals that prepare their patients for industrial rehabilitation show better results than those that do not. As Wing points out, Industrial Rehabilitation Units provide conditions difficult to devise in mental hospitals, such as a realistic industrial setting, a majority of non-institutionalized workers, and specific training in work habits. Although one should be careful not to exaggerate the results of such training and although some of the improvement noted may be the result of the attention these patients receive, the experience with such programs is reasonably promising and is particularly so when they are supplemented with other services.

My own experience in sponsoring a research clerical service within a day hospital connected with the Maudsley Hospital in London supports the experience of others who have developed work programs for chronic mental patients. At the time the research clerical unit was set up, industrial work, such as soldering equipment and wiring electric pianos, was available to patients, but the hospital was having difficulty finding sufficient clerical work to maintain an office unit. Many of the patients were chronic schizophrenics and severely handicapped, and I suspect there was some doubt that the hospital could run a successful office unit. At the time, I was having considerable difficulty staffing a very large office operation for a national study, and after pricing the work commercially I made arrangements with Dr. Douglas Bennett and his staff to set up the clerical operation within the hospital. Patients typed and duplicated questionnaires, addressed letters and envelopes, and even signed my name on various correspondence with my permission. An editing system was devised whereby all work completed by one patient was checked by a second one, and further sample checks were made by me and by the occupational therapist in charge of the work operation within the hospital. The hospital received the commercial rate for the various jobs done, and the patients were compensated for their work at the legally allowed rates. Although I did not systematically study the project itself, it is my distinct impression that the quality of the work was superb and that the rate of error was lower than that which I can reasonably expect from graduate research assistants at universities. The clerical work situation has now been routinized at this day hospital and has been highly successful.

It was also my impression and that of others who were in a position to observe the project that the patients received gratification not only from their earnings but also from the work. It provided them with tasks that allowed them to use their skills in a way that they and the staff defined as meaningful. Although the performance was not very good from the point of view of efficiency (the average time for the production of each unit was much higher than it would have been commercially), when the patients were allowed to work at their own pace, the quality of performance was high. Mental health facilities that would like to contract such work would probably have to price the job rather than provide services on an hourly basis. Or they might pay an hourly wage subsidized in part through the rehabilitation program. In any case it seems clear that maintaining such a unit even within a mental hospital is a feasible goal and one that provides meaningful tasks to help keep patients active and involved.

No doubt working under sheltered conditions confronts the patient with a somewhat different situation from that presented by working within the community. For many patients, a sheltered situation is a temporary expedient until their psychological state improves and they regain confidence. Other patients, if they work at all, probably require a sheltered situation. The opportunity for the handicapped patient to work in the community depends on various contingencies, such as the state of the employment market and welfare legislation. When manpower is short, employers are more willing to tolerate inefficient workers and those with bizarre mannerisms than they are when manpower is abundant. Similarly, some countries like England have laws that require employers to hire a certain proportion of disabled persons, and such legislation increases opportunities for the absorption of disabled persons into the work force. Indeed, efficiency is not the most noble of all values, and employers have a responsibility to society and human welfare as well as to the maintenance of profit.

In our society a high value is placed on independent employment, and for many patients this is a realistic goal. Many highly skilled patients have lost their self-confidence, but through sheltered work and social support they can graduate to an independent job. Others may never be fully independent but can perform useful and high quality work when there are supportive services available for both patient and employer. Employers will take risks in sectors of the economy where labor shortages exist, but with appropriate preparation employers will cooperate in even less favorable labor markets.

Some community programs, for example, contract with employers to provide a certain number of jobs for clients in the program who are able to work. The care system makes a commitment that workers will come to work and perform at a reasonable level and that in emergencies staff members will fill the jobs to meet the commitment. In well-run programs, employers learn that many patients with psychiatric illness are more reliable and perform better than recruits from the labor pool employers typically rely on, and employers find such arrangements in their interest. Initially, employers are insecure about the mentally ill. It is important that they feel they can get immediate help when a mental health problem develops at the workplace.

A major difficulty is that many of the jobs for patients are in service industries that offer poor working conditions, such as kitchens, laundries, and restaurants. Many psychiatric patients are well educated and have a high level of skill but suffer great insecurities in the work context. It is more difficult to return these patients to suitable work since most programs concentrate on less educated and less skilled workers, who are the more typical clients. Expectations are higher in these jobs and employer tolerance is lower because employers typically recruit from a more stable labor force than in work demanding few skills.

It is worth noting that mental symptoms are often independent of work skills, and many handicapped patients are good and reliable workers. Some of the most handicapped patients, even during periods of acute symptoms, can work in some settings, as experience in Fairweather Lodges have demonstrated. These work settings typically do not involve direct contact with the public, and thus social reactions do not become a barrier to allowing the patient to continue working. Much more can be accomplished in work settings with the mentally ill, but work rehabilitation funding is essential to organize and carry out these programs. Program barriers to rehabilitation embedded in the incentives in the Social Security system discussed earlier need to be addressed.

The education model in contrast to the medical model may also be useful in that it makes the problems of patients appear more reasonable to the uninformed, and it may help minimize the stigma attached to the patients' difficulties. Despite a vast educational campaign, the concept of mental illness still carries the connotation of insanity. By emphasizing the normal potentialities of the mental patient, the educational approach may decrease social distance between treatment personnel and patients and between mental health and community contexts. Others probably find mental patients more acceptable when their problems are described in interpersonal terms (as problems of living and of interpersonal relations) in contrast to being described as illnesses of the mind.

In the long run, of course, little is achieved by changing the labels we use without changing our practices. The proper organization of an educationally oriented rehabilitation program depends on the attitudes and ap-

proaches of mental health workers. To the extent that they nurture patients' dependency responses, encourage sick-role reactions, and serve
patients rather than motivate them to serve themselves, educational efforts
are limited. An educational approach must start with the assumption that
most mental patients either have or can develop the capacities to meet their
own needs; through sympathetic attention, encouragement of motivation,
and scheduling and reinforcement of mastery experience, we may be able
to set the stage for patients' improvement in social and psychological
functioning.

The foregoing considerations of an educational approach in dealing
with disabled patients are based on the assumption—by no means
proved—that a significant part of the psychological discomfort persons
experience results from failures in social functioning. If skills and mastery
can be developed so that persons respond appropriately to difficult events
in their environment, the experience of successful performance and mastery may in itself help resolve much of the suffering and distress of many
mental patients. It requires no elaboration that such general comments do
not apply to every patient. One of the greatest defects of current efforts in
mental health rehabilitation is the administrative assumption that the same
care can be given to those within a broad and diverse spectrum of social
and psychological disabilities. If mental health clinics are to deal seriously
with the magnitude of the problems they face, they must develop diversified and flexible services that more realistically approach the needs of their
clients.

PROBLEMS IN THE DIFFUSION OF MENTAL HEALTH INNOVATIONS

As some of the examples given suggest, there have been many innovative
developments in community mental health care. Such new ideas face considerable difficulty in becoming widely accepted and used, and these programs often face problems in finding stable funding even in areas in which
they do develop. Such new service programs are frequently outside existing reimbursement schemes, such as nonprofit and private insurance,
Medicare, and Medicaid. In order to become established, these programs
must attract special developmental funds or hospital improvement grants
from federal or state government or must receive financial backing from
local government. Because local government is reluctant to increase expenditures for what might become expensive programs attracting new clients,
achieving financial stability is an uphill battle.

The organization of new types of community care requires a shift
from traditional and accepted bureaucratic procedures. Such programs
must be especially attentive to community acceptance, the employment
market, the welfare and social services system, housing, relationships with
police and other community agencies, and intraprofessional relationships
and rivalries. The professional working in community care has a less for-

mal role than in an institution. Such a person must be a facilitator, coordinator, and integrator. These professionals must be tolerant of more fluid roles and relationships and must be able to work on a more equal basis with a wide range of other mental health professionals and community participants. Individuals must engage in definition and redefinition of tasks as they deal with others in related programs in the network of services. The professional, in a sense, becomes a broker who must negotiate among varying interests and agencies, and effectiveness resides in the ability to get things done and not in a traditional authority structure or special degrees.

It is not too difficult to understand why successful innovations are not readily replicated. Funding arrangements are often difficult. Unusual leadership is often necessary. The excitement and rewards in being an innovator are not as great for those who copy what has been done elsewhere and require giving up the security of defined roles and relationships and the comfort that comes from achieving certainty and control over the work environment. There is a great inertia in the existing pattern of professional services. A change in direction requires a leader who can communicate to others the sense of excitement in a new venture and who has the organizational skills to bring the necessary people and organizations together. In the absence of a strong incentive—such as available funding—it is extraordinarily difficult to build the necessary momentum.

Even in innovative programs that become established, maintaining momentum is a difficult challenge. The patients to be cared for are chronic and difficult and often intractable. While something new generates excitement and enthusiasm, people eventually get tired. They seek to regularize their work patterns and control uncertainties in their environment. Even new roles tend to become bureaucratized with attempts to define responsibilities and turfs more precisely. Over time, unless leadership is very strong, personnel tend to become more cynical, more smug about their failures, less sensitive to their clients, and less committed to their jobs. In the jargon of the professional world, they "burn out." Moreover, the leaders who develop these programs—being innovators—move on to other challenges leaving a gap in administration. If such a program is lucky enough to attract a talented administrator who can help institutionalize its innovativeness, it may have a good prognosis, but often the most talented personnel drift away to other programs as their talents and successes are recognized.

In sum, the diffusion of innovation in service patterns is a difficult challenge and one not easily achieved. New types of services and organizational arrangements are highly fragile and unstable and require a great deal of community support. While traditional services, such as hospitals, outpatient clinics, and nursing homes, are integrated into community organizational and financial arrangements, new care programs must sell their care, convincing community leaders that they are effective, efficient, and worthy of support. Such new community programs not only require public relations but face competition from conventional services that are reluctant to give up existing funding or community support. Developing effective programs requires not only initiative and technical competence but also a good sense of community politics.

INNOVATIONS IN HOUSING

Housing the severely mentally ill in large cities, while typically not thought of as a mental health issue, is one of the most critical problems faced by mental health services. It is unreasonable to anticipate that community care programs can provide adequate mental health services to patients living on the street, in large shelters for the homeless, or in dangerous and unsuitable housing. Housing is not a formal responsibility of the mental health sector, but the sector neglects this problem at its peril.

Causes of homelessness among the mentally ill have already been reviewed. Much of the difficulty is the scarcity of housing and the competition among needy groups for the available housing units. Other problems include fear and prejudice toward the mentally ill in many neighborhoods, community resistance to group homes and other sheltered housing arrangements, and a profound lack of understanding about mental illness among those typically responsible for housing development and assignment.

Federal efforts to create new housing opportunities have diminished in recent years, and the emphasis is away from public housing to private sector development. Public housing support is thus concentrated in helping eligible clients pay rent in the community housing marketplace. These subsidies, however, are far too few to meet the necessary demand, and many eligible mental patients who have the capacity to live independently in dwellings scattered throughout the community find it impossible to get the necessary assistance.

But even if such assistance were available, scattered-site independent housing is not suitable for some severely mentally ill patients who require help and supervision and for others who must progress slowly to independent living situations. Thus, good community care requires a broad spectrum of housing opportunities ranging from those with varying levels of supervision to independence. In many communities there is strong community resistance to the establishment of group homes, board and care facilities, supervised apartments, and other special projects directed to housing the mentally ill. Gaining community support presents some difficult dilemmas (Dear and Taylor 1982). On the one hand, a mental health program can inform a neighborhood that it plans to locate a group house in their vicinity and seek to gain cooperation. Such prior information provides an opportunity for opponents to mobilize political resistance (Hogan 1986a, b), which can end the project. On the other hand, the strategy of quietly establishing the facility without the neighborhood's awareness can result in bitter confrontations and isolation of the facility from the neighborhood. Often, however, the quiet establishment of a facility has so little effect that when neighbors learn of its existence, they accept it. Problems arise when patients with bizarre mannerisms wander on others' property or make their presence obvious. Resistance is much less in urban commercial zones where residents are much less involved in neighborhoods. Such locations may be advantageous if they are close to services and facilities patients need, but too often these sites are chosen as paths of least resistance, independent of any advantages of the location.

Varying mental health programs have demonstrated considerable ingenuity in teaching patients "house-making" skills and working with landlords to gain their acceptance and support. There is a wide range of self-help and group-support mechanisms including pairing successful patient residents with new community care patients and graduating levels of independence among varying types of residences with different levels and intensity of professional supervision.

THE ORGANIZATION OF THE DEVELOPING MENTAL HEALTH PROFESSIONS

The community mental health movement has created many new roles and opportunities in the mental health field. The relationship among professions and the specific responsibilities of each group are very much in flux; each professional group is feeling its way, and the relationships among them are sensitive and changing. Many professions, such as psychiatry and social work, are undergoing tremendous internal change, while others, such as recreational therapy, are searching for an appropriate role. Each of the groups is not only responsive to the circumstances of its work situation but is also attuned to the definitions of prestige and activity within its own professional structure. The concept of the harmonious mental health team must be considered and understood in light of the conflict and competition inevitable among these various professional groups.

Rushing (1964), in a study of the relationships among mental health professionals within a university hospital psychiatric unit, noted that the adherence of professional persons to their own standards may lead to rigid and inflexible responses to the immediate hospital situation. He noted that social workers had difficulty adapting to the educational needs of the hospital, while psychologists, who realized that their primary role in the hospital was to administer psychological tests, still tended to identify with academic teaching and research roles. The result was that the daily work situation required responses inconsistent with professional images and led to resentment and conflict. As Rushing (1964) so nicely pointed out, despite the talk about team effort and equality, each of the professional groups strove to achieve prestige, which is a precious commodity within organizations; if some have more, others have less.

> A community of equals is a fiction, particularly a community composed of several different groups. Despite their proclamations to the contrary, it is not likely that psychiatrists will accept their "ancillaries" as their status equals—at least most will not. Consequently, it is probably best to dispense with a myth which "ancillaries" recognize as such. Conflict between myth and reality, especially when the conflict is recognized, may create unnecessary strain. (Rushing 1964, pp. 258–59)

Although community care contexts provide more opportunities for new and expanded roles for various mental health professionals than traditional institutional contexts, the relationship among such professionals is a major political issue. Physicians continue to want control over other professional groups operating in the health arena, take measures to avoid direct competition, and continue to be able to command great legitimacy in the public's perceptions, allowing them to charge higher fees than other professionals providing comparable services. In recent years psychologists have been somewhat successful in achieving legitimization of their independent professional roles and in obtaining eligibility as reimbursable providers under some health insurance programs for private therapeutic services. Social workers, in contrast, have had more difficulty in legitimizing an independent therapeutic role outside their traditional base in community social agencies. In fact, many psychiatrists, psychologists, and social workers provide similar types of psychotherapeutic services that would be difficult to distinguish on the basis of professional origins (Henry, Sims, and Spray 1971). Although psychiatrists can legally prescribe drugs and the other professionals cannot, their functioning as psychotherapists is often indistinguishable from that of psychologists and social workers. Freidson (1970) has noted that for medicine more generally, professional control resides with those groups that can gain acceptance of their special and unique competence and contribution from the public. Such legal dominance by psychiatry makes it difficult for competing professionals to fulfill their potential.

In recent years new developments in mental health care other than in the area of drug treatment have come substantially from nonmedical disciplines. Behavior therapy and its applications are largely based on psychological research, and its practical use was primarily stimulated by psychologists. Crisis intervention techniques have a long history in social work, and the practical management of patients now so relevant for community care has been a traditional concern among social work agencies. The emphasis on interactional and group therapies is based on research and applications in the social and behavioral sciences and not in medicine. As behavioral and social techniques are used increasingly in patient management, such professions as psychology can claim special expertise more credibly, and the growing strength of clinical psychology derives not only from good politics but also from the growing acceptance of behavioral therapies in the treatment of psychiatric disorders.

THE FUTURE OF INNOVATIVE MENTAL HEALTH SERVICES

Developing innovative services and allowing them to take root require both a mechanism by which such services can be financed and an incentive structure that allows an efficient mix of varying types of mental health personnel. The present modes of financing not only favor traditional services but also encourage competition and friction among existing mental health professionals. One possible approach is to develop contracts with community organizations to provide and coordinate a total pattern of care for chronic patients who meet certain eligibility criteria on a capitation basis—that is, so much per patient per month. Organizations providing the entire range of medical and social services could be given incentives to develop a total integrated pattern of service that substitutes less expensive services when appropriate for more expensive hospital and professional services. Existing financial arrangements encourage the most expensive types of care that are eligible for reimbursement as compared with less expensive services that are not eligible. An organization working on a fixed budget has incentives to use a variety of services that may be more economical than traditional care. A service organization paid in this way also has a disincentive for increasing patient dependency on medical care in areas in which the patient can assume reasonable responsibility. The incentive structure influences the organization to encourage patient independence and responsibility which, from existing evidence, is consistent with sound rehabilitation. Any such approach, however, must protect against any inclination to withhold necessary services or to provide less than adequate service because of economic and budgetary limitations.

In sum, developing innovative approaches has not been a major problem in the mental health arena. It has frequently been difficult to obtain careful evaluation of varying innovations and to distinguish between those that were truly effective as compared with those that were mere fads. Once particular approaches have been found to be superior to conventional services, it has often been difficult to achieve their widespread adoption because of reimbursement rules, conflicting interests between traditional programs and new innovations, and the pattern of traditionally organized professional relationships. Innovation requires more than having a good idea. It necessitates understanding of financial aspects of care and the political organization of service agencies and professional relationships. It also requires the leadership to attract people to new roles and tasks and to stimulate their motivation and commitment.

Chapter Twelve

Mental Illness,
the Community,
and the Law

Mental illness creates a variety of problems for the community as well as for the families of the mentally ill. Mentally ill persons may be a nuisance in the community and may disrupt normal social activities; they may be dangerous or frightening. They may be so depressed, disoriented, or deluded that their presence in the community poses serious risks to their own health and welfare. A person with a psychotic depression may be a serious suicide risk, and persons suffering from extreme states of agitation and confusion may undertake actions that seriously harm their own and their families' welfare. Public policies have developed for removing mentally ill persons considered dangerous from the community and providing them with treatment or custody.

The community must determine the conditions under which exposing the mentally ill person to involuntary procedures violates rights and humanitarian principles. It must define when a person is to be regarded as mentally incompetent or when a person accused of a crime should be excused from responsibility because of mental illness. Indeed, under what conditions should a person be regarded as competent to stand trial? The community must also consider under what conditions and by what criteria a person should be deemed competent to make a contract, to make a will, to get married, to have custody of children, or even to drive an automobile. Policies and procedures must be established that define these competency situations (Allen et al. 1968, Brooks 1974). Governmental agencies must specify the conditions under which mentally ill persons (1) are kept from holding sensitive government positions, (2) are denied adoption rights, and (3) are to be provided with health and welfare services. All these issues cannot be dealt with in this chapter, but some significant questions and dilemmas underlying the response of the social system to problems of mental illness will be discussed.

The difficulty in establishing clear-cut and coherent policies should be apparent; many issues pertaining to the identification, etiology, and care of mental illness remain cloudy. Although one may for legal purposes arbitrarily attempt to define mental illness, mental competence, dangerous behavior, and fitness to stand trial, if the behavioral knowledge underlying such concepts is deficient, the application of these labels inevitably tends to be ambiguous and inconsistent. Courts and community agencies must muddle through these difficulties and deal with such problems in the best way they can. Despite the difficulty in defining and predicting dangerous behavior, members of the community cannot disregard such patterns of behavior. Even though psychiatrists do not agree on the nature and scope of mental illness, the law cannot be oblivious to such matters.

One of the major issues underlying the approach of the community to the mentally ill is whether or not such persons can exercise judgment and thus be held responsible for their actions. Social life proceeds on the assumption that people's activity is rationally motivated and that they should be held responsible in most circumstances for the consequences of their behavior. At the same time we add certain qualifications to such assumptions; in the case of some accidents, for example, we presume the person did harm without intent and was not negligent within the legal meaning of the term. Much debate in the mental health area concerns the point in mental functioning at which it becomes appropriate to assume that persons are not responsible for their behavior, are unable to exercise judgment, or are incapable of making decisions relevant to their own welfare. To translate these problems into concrete policy questions, we must in some fashion resolve the following issues: (1) At what point is it reasonable to treat patients involuntarily for a psychiatric condition on the assumption that they are unable to appreciate their need for such care? (2) At what point are persons because of mental illness so unable to appreciate the circumstances of their positions that they must be presumed to be legally incompetent or be assessed as unfit to stand trial when charged with a crime? (3) At what point are we to excuse persons from responsibility for unlawful acts on the assumption that their mental state at the time they acted absolved them from responsibility for such acts?

When the state acts to deprive mental patients of their freedom because of mental illness, a number of salient legal issues become relevant to the care of such patients. Do they have a *right to treatment* and, if so, what is the nature of this right? Do they have a right to refuse treatment and, if so, under what conditions? If the law requires that interference in the patient's life follows the least restrictive alternative, how can such alternatives be defined, and what constitutes more and less restrictive ones?

Similarly, in therapeutic work many issues arise as to the obligation of the therapist to the patient as compared with the public or other parties. Is the principle of confidentiality between patient and therapist sacrosanct, or does the therapist have an obligation to inform others of personal dangers to them that might be revealed in therapy? If the psychiatrist is examining or treating a patient under the custody of a court, a correctional institution, an employer, or some other third-party are there legal obligations to inform the client of possible conflicts of interest? What are the requirements for informed consent in both therapy and investigation? What are the legal implications of using aversive therapies without informed consent? What constitutes psychiatric malpractice?

Although there are many legal and ethical issues affecting almost every aspect of psychiatric practice, some have greater consequences than others for large numbers of patients. In this chapter attention is given primarily to legal issues of great importance for social policy in mental health care, such as involuntary civil commitment and the right to treatment. While the uses of psychiatry in corrections, or such civil matters as testimonial capacity are not unimportant, discussing a few issues in some detail will be more useful than attempting to survey the wide range of issues in the law and mental health area. Brooks (1974) and Stone (1975) provide more thorough examinations of these areas.

THE PROBLEM OF INVOLUNTARY HOSPITALIZATION

Persons suffering from mental illness frequently fail to recognize that they are mentally ill and require treatment. They may be unwilling or reluctant to accept psychiatric assistance and to cooperate in their care. On the assumption that such patients may constitute a threat to others or to themselves, all states provide legal channels for their involuntary commitment to a psychiatric facility.

Although the state of Virginia enacted a law for the involuntary commitment of mental patients in 1806, for the most part the incarceration of the mentally ill was informally administered until the middle of the nineteenth century. During that period considerable concern arose over the unjustified commitment of sane people to mental institutions, and in 1845 Chief Justice Lemuel Shaw of the Massachusetts Supreme Court established the precedent that individuals could be restrained only if dangerous to themselves or others and only if restraint would be conducive to their restoration. This principle has been the foundation of most state statutes. Although such statutes were instituted to protect the rights of sane individuals, they were sometimes used as vehicles to deprive patients who may be suffering from psychiatric conditions of their civil liberties, even when these patients in fact were not serious threats to themselves or to others in the narrow meaning of these words.

Relatives of patients and others in the community often demand their removal because they feel their behavior is dangerous or extremely disruptive. Such patients often threaten suicide or violence, engage in destructive

behavior, or demonstrate grossly bizarre and disturbing symptoms. Some
cases leading to hospital admission are cited below (adapted from Brown et
al. 1966).

> Mr. A. C. refused to eat the food provided and had various delusions—for
> example, that people were poisoning him. Before his admission his mother
> said that he became wild, throwing things about and threatening his parents.
> (p. 47)

> Mr. A. D. was found wandering by the police. His parents reported that
> before he left his home he had been breaking up furniture in the house. (p.
> 47)

> Two weeks before coming to the hospital Mr. A. G. said that he had met God.
> His mother reported that he had been wild in manner. He read the Bible all
> night and was excitable and restless. He couldn't sleep and walked into his
> mother's room at night and wanted to talk to her. He said he wanted to sit on
> her lap—and why didn't she kiss him like her husband. (p. 47)

> Mr. A. I. had become a social nuisance. He had been walking around at night,
> and accusing his neighbors of controlling and interfering with his body. (p.
> 48)

One has to consider only his or her own response to persistent behavior of
this kind to appreciate why people in the community often demand that
mentally ill persons be involuntarily committed to hospitals when they are
unwilling to seek help on their own.

In 1969 the state of California passed the Lanterman-Petris-Short
Act, which radically revised civil commitment laws, and every other state
eventually made changes influenced by California and the *Lessard* v.
Schmidt decision in Wisconsin, which severely limited and focused the
grounds for involuntary detention of the mentally ill and introduced
rigorous due process procedures. These modifications made the substantive criteria for civil commitment more specific, requiring some combination of mental illness and either dangerousness or incapacity to care for
oneself. Also, duration of commitment was specified and made more brief,
and due process guarantees used in criminal cases were extended to civil
commitment procedures (Lamb and Mills 1986).

Although practices from one area to another remain highly variable,
the use of civil commitment has declined substantially. As Stone (1975)
noted:

> Psychiatrists who once committed people because it was the easiest thing to do
> are increasingly diffident. Courts are apt to be more scrupulous in reaching
> their decisions; lawyers are more frequently involved in preventing confine-
> ment; and hospitals are more fastidious about their own role. (Stone 1975, p.
> 43)

When hospitalization in public hospitals was the dominant mode of care,
involuntary hospitalization was the conventional form of admission. With
changes in patterns of hospitalization and legal reform, the situation has

dramatically changed. A special NIMH study of legal status of admissions in 1980 showed that public hospitals continue to be the most common setting for involuntary admissions. Although accounting for only 31 percent of all inpatient admissions in 1980, these hospitals were the source of 64 percent of all involuntary commitments. While 58 percent of admissions to state and county mental hospitals were involuntary, only 15 percent of admissions to private psychiatric hospitals and 8 percent of psychiatric admissions to nonpublic general hospitals had this status (Rosenstein et al. 1986).

Those challenging involuntary commitment took great heart from the Supreme Court decision in the Donaldson case. This case, brought as a right-to-treatment suit, was actually decided quite narrowly by the Court, which ignored the broad right-to-treatment claim. Instead, the Court ruled that the state could not continue to confine involuntarily a mentally ill person who was not dangerous to himself or others, was not receiving treatment, and who was capable of surviving safely outside the hospital (Stone 1984). The case involved Kenneth Donaldson, a patient in Chatahoochee State Hospital in Florida from 1957 to 1972, who had refused medication and electroshock treatment, claiming at times to be a Christian Scientist, but who received no other treatment. Donaldson had been diagnosed as a chronic paranoid schizophrenic, and his efforts to gain release and his assertion that he would write a book about his confinement were interpreted as part of his paranoia (see his book, Donaldson 1976). Hospital officials took neither his efforts nor those of other caretakers in the community to gain his release seriously and confined him to a ward for the criminally insane and denied him ground privileges despite lack of evidence of dangerous behavior. Ultimately, a jury awarded Donaldson $38,500 in compensatory and punitive damages, deciding against two hospital doctors who had confined him involuntarily.

The changes in state civil commitment statutes brought about by civil liberties activism in the mental health field are now viewed by some critics as having gone too far. These critics allege that present procedures are unduly restrictive, denying necessary care to many individuals and contributing to the criminalization of mental illness and to the problem of the homeless mentally ill wandering our city streets. As one critic has argued, "The right to liberty has become an excuse for failing to address, even failing to recognize the needs of thousands of abandoned men and women we sweep by in our streets, in our parks, and in the train and bus stations where they gather for warmth" (Appelbaum 1987). There is now renewed interest in commitment criteria based on the need for care and treatment. Both strong civil libertarian and *parens patriae* (the state as parent) positions contend to sway the views of state legislatures and judges.

At one extreme we find various civil liberties advocates who believe that our rights are so precious and mental health criteria so uncertain that there is never any justification for depriving persons of their rights, even when they are believed to be dangerous to themselves or others (Szasz 1963, Ennis 1972, Miller 1976). Although such critics may recognize that some persons may suffer as a result of this view, the benefits of pursuing such a policy course, they believe, are much greater than in following alternative policies that have major costs in terms of erosion of liberty rights. At the other extreme are many psychiatrists who believe that the greatest value is the treatment of mentally ill patients, whether they recognize the need for such treatment or not, and that the law should provide the professional with appropriate latitude. Such psychiatrists often understate the uncertainties of psychiatry, overestimate the efficacy of psychiatric treatment, and show little awareness of our civil liberties traditions. There are many intermediate positions, and it seems clear that a sound policy falls somewhere between the two extremes.

Before considering alternative policies, I should emphasize that the use of civil commitment reflects the need of society to deal with troublesome problems when the community demands action. The problems themselves cannot be defined away. To the extent that the law tightens opportunities for civil commitment, other mechanisms may be used more frequently to deal with troublesome patients, such as arrests for minor legal infractions. Many of the pressures for mental hospital beds for the elderly, to choose a different example, were relieved through the expansion of nursing home beds that provided an alternative residence. The key point is that the processes of civil commitment operate in a community context. The community pressures that encourage commitment do not disappear simply because legal procedures have been tightened. If hospitalization is difficult to achieve in troublesome cases, such mentally ill persons are more likely to be jailed. While there is no direct or simple relationship between civil commitment procedures and criminalization, the two are certainly linked.

The changes that took place in civil commitment procedures in the 1960s and 1970s were not only a response to social ideologies, but also a reaction to obvious abuses of the *parens patriae* approach. Civil commitment has had four goals: (1) protecting society from dangerous mental patients; (2) protecting the mentally ill from harming themselves; (3) providing mental health care to those who need it but may not appreciate the need; and (4) relieving families and communities from persons who may not be dangerous but who are bizarre and troublesome and disrupt everyday life. As states modified their procedures, they gave emphasis to the concepts of danger to self and others and downplayed treatment and convenience goals. Moreover, the criteria for danger were sharpened and narrowed, and courts increasingly rejected broad theoretical notions in contrast to the imminence of danger. As a consequence it became more difficult in many localities to commit patients whom psychiatrists believed to be in grave need of treatment.

It is essential to understand the context in which these changes came about. In the 1950s and 1960s, when deinstitutionalization forces were developing, commitment processes were informal and highly paternalistic. Typically, the alleged mentally ill person was engaging in visible, bizarre behavior, difficult to understand, unpredictable, and in violation of usual expectations and social patterns. Such behavior causes anguish to the family and frightens those around the disturbed individual. Frequently such a person engaged in disruptive behavior, which brought him or her into contact with the police or personnel from social agencies, who initiated proceedings. When an application was filed, there was in fact a strong presumption that the person in question required hospitalization.

Because judges were often busy and assumed that such patients were likely to require detention and treatment, many considered it pointless to conduct a thorough hearing. It was generally assumed that the patient was mentally ill, or the occasion for the commitment would not have arisen. Moreover, those who were the object of these procedures were commonly mentally ill, peculiar, or eccentric, and their unusual behavior and mannerisms could readily be seen as indicators of a need for treatment. Judges then, much more than now, had limited knowledge of mental illness and accepted the broad authority of physicians, relying on their judgments. Judges, thus, seldom allowed their own observations to supersede the recommendations of medical examiners, and in this context a full legal hearing appeared to be a waste of time and not conducive to the patient's mental state (Scheff 1964 a,b). Thus the commitment process often had the form of due process of law but was actually vacuous because the decision was frequently predetermined.

Because persons faced with civil commitment were entangled in social conflicts with family or community members, it was assumed that custody and treatment at the very worst would do no harm. As Scheff (1964b) noted in his studies of civil commitment in Wisconsin in the early 1960s, this bias was based on premises of doubtful validity.

1. The condition of mentally ill persons deteriorates rapidly without psychiatric assistance.
2. Effective psychiatric treatments exist for most mental illnesses.
3. Unlike surgery, there are no risks involved in involuntary psychiatric treatment; it either helps or is neutral, it can't hurt.
4. Exposing a prospective mental patient to questioning, cross-examination, and other screening procedures exposes him to the unnecessary stigma of trial-like procedures, and may do further damage to his mental condition.
5. There is an element of danger to self or to others in most mental illness. It is better to risk unnecessary hospitalization than the harm the patient might do himself or others. (Scheff 1964b, p. 411)

Each of these premises was at best a half-truth. In many instances psychiatric assistance had dubious value, and involuntary incarceration could do more harm than could be justified by the effectiveness of existing therapies. Moreover, involuntary hospitalization could harm individuals' self-concepts and self-confidence as well as injure their social standing. We have already noted some of the harmful effects of mental hospitals on patients and adverse effects from psychoactive drugs. Although these therapies may be necessary, they are not without undesirable consequences, and their involuntary use raises serious issues. In arguing against due process of law in legal proceedings affecting the mentally ill, psychiatrists frequently maintain that such procedures expose patients to unnecessary indignities damaging to their mental condition. Legal procedures, however, if carried out in a dignified manner, should not necessarily expose patients to indignities. Szasz (1961) stated the argument well:

> I believe it is possible that such a hearing is traumatic for a person, as it is alleged to be. However, I feel even more strongly that to be placed in an institution without explanations of how one got there, why one got there, and for how long one will be confined, is even more traumatic. The question is not simply whether a given person is "mentally ill" and whether a hearing is "traumatic"—but rather what are our choices as to how we might deal with this person. If in the name of their allegedly traumatic experience we do what we now do—that is, confuse the patient and deprive him of the opportunity to effectively resist the commitment procedure—then I am 100 per cent against it. . . . I think if a hearing is conducted with humanity and with sensitivity, I don't see anything traumatic about it. (Szasz 1961, p. 266)

Involuntary commitment in earlier decades had been used to deal with persons who were deviant from prevailing social norms and who posed difficult dilemmas for parents, other relatives, co-workers, and community members. This type of case particularly aroused those concerned with civil liberties and illustrated ways in which such procedures could abrogate constitutional rights. Some of these issues are illustrated by a 1967 case involving a 22-year-old veteran of the armed services living in a manner that can be described as "beatnik" in the vicinity of the University of Wisconsin in Madison (Simmonds 1967).

After returning home from the armed services, this young man lived for a short time with his parents in northeastern Wisconsin. Contrary to his parents' values, he did not seek employment, stayed out at night, and did not communicate with his wife, who was living in England at the time. These behaviors distressed and worried his parents. In September, he moved to Madison and lived with various friends, both male and female. He did not communicate with his parents or his wife. In January his parents came to Madison, presumably to encourage him to change his pattern of living, only to experience an angry and unhappy confrontation.

The parents, distressed by the unconventional behavior of their son, consulted their family physician, who agreed to sign an application to commit him without an examination, even though he had not seen the young man for several years. The parents then consulted the institutional placement coordinator for Dane County; he called the doctor and gave him a choice of immediate arrest or a court order giving notice of a hearing under the state Mental Health Act. The physician chose to have the man arrested as a person "dangerous to himself and others and in need of immediate hospitalization." The coordinator sent the application to the doctor, who provided alleged medical reasons to justify the decision. A judge signed the application at once and relayed the papers to the sheriff for service. One afternoon, without warning, two officers apprehended the youth and locked him up. His friends brought the matter to the attention of the Wisconsin Civil Liberties Union, which challenged the legality of the procedure followed.

It is instructive to consider the evidence provided by the doctor to justify the decision that the young man was dangerous to himself and others and in need of immediate hospitalization.

He has seemed very "different" since he returned from the service in July, 1966. He has seemed very touchy, and critical of everything including his parents. On occasions he has very high opinions of himself and unbelievable plans, such as a job with the University of Wisconsin Engineering Department in research with a Dodge Camper provided, then the idea of entering international law. Since July he has had periods of depression and periods of manic exhilaration. . . .

That the patient is in need of hospitalization and is irresponsible and dangerous to self and others, so as to require immediate temporary detention by reason of his coming to Madison in September of 1966. He has not communicated with his parents or his wife in England. On January 21, 1967, his parents came to Madison, found him living in an apartment strewn with beer cans, shades pulled, with several "Beatnik" type people. He used foul and threatening language to his parents. He made definite threats towards his mother. (Simmonds 1967, p. 13)

Even if we assume the validity of the alleged facts, nothing in the statement established that the youth was, in fact, mentally ill, a danger to himself or others, or in need of immediate temporary detention. The statement does attest that the youth was leading an unconventional life, was violating the moral beliefs of his parents, and was unresponsive to their exhortations to change his pattern of living. Given his age, however, he had every right to do so. Consistent with the ruling of the judge, who granted a writ of habeas corpus, we must conclude that the commitment procedure used was a violation of constitutional rights and that it deprived the young man of liberty without due process of law. The alleged expert medical knowledge that provided justification for detention was based on hearsay and not on an examination of the patient, and the evidence used to justify his detention as a person "dangerous to himself and others and in need of immediate hospitalization" was inadequate and deficient. If the youth had not had the assistance of an attorney, he would probably have been involuntarily kept in the hospital as long as the psychiatric staff thought necessary.

The issue was not whether the youth in question had psychiatric difficulties. If we take psychiatric surveys seriously, a significant proportion of our total population has psychiatric difficulties, yet we would not seriously suggest that most such persons require forced treatment. The issues are whether under the circumstances it was proper for the young man to be subjected to involuntary commitment and whether there was a sufficient evaluation of the facts or adherence to the legal requirements for such a commitment. Dubious use of the emergency provisions of the Mental Health Act, apprehension without notice, and irresponsibility on the part of the physician raised grave concern over the manner in which the commitment laws were applied. Many persons affected by this procedure were not so fortunate in having friends who could intervene on their behalf, and the violation of their rights often did not become visible to the community.

The process described did not require a villain. The actions of each of the parties involved, although perhaps ill-advised, were probably based on commendable motives. The parents could not understand their son's lifestyle and may have been inclined to see it as a sign of mental aberration.

The doctor, acting as an agent of the family, probably perceived the situation similarly and wished to help the family in dealing with the problem. Officials, such as the institutional placement coordinator and the judge, probably operated with a strong presumption that such deviance was indicative of mental illness and were willing to cooperate with the parents and their doctor. In short, the process actually encouraged a shifting of responsibility and a willingness on the part of various actors to cooperate in what was viewed as a reasonable decision by neglecting the niceties of due process.

This case also illustrates the way in which conflicts of interests and values can raise the issue of mental illness. Children often reject their parents' values and patterns of behavior and pursue courses of action and modes of living that threaten and distress parents. The children may be sufficiently alienated so that discussions become altercations and lead to the use of foul and abusive language. Parents often threaten their children, and children, protecting their independence, may state their position in an emotionally threatening and unpleasant manner. When such conflicts occur, aggrieved parties sometimes characterize the behavior of their adversaries as mental illness. Such conflicts, however, occur not uncommonly and are hardly grounds for the use of involuntary commitment procedures.

It was abuses of this kind that encouraged the efforts of activist lawyers in the litigation resulting in the landmark Wisconsin decision and in the legal efforts supported by the American Civil Liberties Union (Ennis 1972). In 1969, the California Lanterman-Petris-Short Law was purposely designed to create obstacles to discourage the practice of commitment and, particularly, long periods of confinement (Segal and Aviram 1978, p. 47). The law made criteria for involuntary commitment more stringent and created financial incentives to stimulate local government to provide alternative care to the large state institutions. The legislation established a series of graduated categories that required more evidence of impairment or danger to justify longer periods of involuntary hospitalization. Continuing review of such decisions was also required, making it difficult to follow the past practice of committing patients indefinitely. Some psychiatrists believe that such changes do not allow the community to be properly protected, and patients are now allowed to "die with their rights on" (Treffert 1973). Although such a claim is excessive and supported more by emotionalism than by evidence, there is indication that the California changes, as well as those in many other states, did not achieve all that was hoped for. The new statute was successful in reducing the amount and duration of hospitalization, but many mentally ill patients did not get adequate community-care services, and others were dealt with through the criminal justice system (Stone 1975). While the legislation made it substantially more difficult to deprive people of their freedoms involuntarily because of mental illness and vague allegations of danger, it did not create sufficient support for community systems of care. This experience shows that the welfare of patients depends more on excellent systems of care than on legal definitions, but improved protections of patients' rights are not to be taken as unimportant.

Many lawyers involved in the area of patient rights feel strongly that mental patients facing involuntary confinement, depriving them of precious liberties, ought to have the same procedural rights as those available to criminal defendants. In the *Lessard* decision in 1972, the court found that mental patients faced with civil commitment have rights to timely notice of the charges, notice of right to a jury trial, aid of counsel, protection against self-incrimination, and assurance that the evidence on which a claim of dangerousness is made be established "beyond a reasonable doubt." Although some judges now conscientiously try to apply these procedural guidelines, others largely ignore them. Application of these rights in concrete cases can be enormously difficult and may depend on professional assistance, which may not be available. Even with the best of legal intentions there remains a large gap between legal theories and realities (Warren 1982).

Among civil libertarians there emerge two distinct views. Such critics as Szasz (1963) simply argue that individual freedom is the highest good and must be protected. From this position it matters little whether psychiatry is capable of reliable or poor judgments, whether its treatments are effective, or whether decisions are highly selective. It is the value of liberty that is the essential consideration and not any empirical fact about psychiatry. In contrast, Miller (1976) makes his case on the fragility and unreliability of psychiatric judgments of dangerousness, the large discrepancies between commitment laws and their implementation, the farce of many commitment procedures, and the selective social outcomes from one jurisdiction to another. In his view,

> the basis for police power commitment should be physical violence or potential physical violence which is imminent, constituting a "clear and present" danger, and based on testimony related to actual conduct. Any such commitment should be subject to mandatory review within two weeks. (Miller 1976, p. 73)

Miller argues quite forcefully that social danger and the damage to property should not be grounds for commitment and that the mentally ill subjected to commitment procedures should have most of the rights of criminal defendants, including formal notice, the right to face accusers and cross-examine them, notice of a right to trial by jury, and the right to counsel. Moreover, Miller argues that there should be no provisions for "psychiatric emergencies," that stuporous or passive people should be treated as are the unconscious in medical emergencies, and that persons threatening violence should be dealt with in the context of criminal law.

While there is much in Miller's analysis and advocacy that is compelling, there is also a certain unwillingness to face the hard issues and a glibness that is easier to sustain in the abstract than in the reality. As Miller, in anticipating his critics, notes,

> Concern will be expressed about the person who wanders the streets, eats from garbage cans, and lives a degrading life. Someone will remember the eccentric who gives his money away on the streets or walks about with thou-

sands of dollars sewn inside the lining of his coat. Others will object to sick people being held in jails instead of hospitals. Possibly the strongest outcry will be against those provisions which call for full due process and adversary proceedings within the courtroom. In the larger context, these objections will have little merit (Miller 1976, p. 137).

But do they really? Are there responsibilities on the part of the community to intervene when individuals seriously injure themselves and their loved ones, short of violence, but deny a need for help? Perhaps not, but the issue is too difficult to be dealt with simply by the glib assertion that our concepts and knowledge are vague and too easily subject to abuse.

While Miller's argument depends on demonstrating variability and inconsistencies in civil commitment, such demonstrations are unclear. One can show such variation in almost every area of medical endeavor, including reliability of diagnosis, admission to hospitals, surgical intervention, length of hospital stay for given procedures, use of laboratory and specialized diagnostic facilities, and prescription of medications. Certainly, the logical conclusion is not that these facilities and procedures are worthless. Sometimes they are used well and effectively and other times badly; sometimes they are overused and at other times underutilized. Medical practice improves when we can identify more precisely the conditions under which certain decisions are appropriate.

Is, then, civil commitment or involuntary treatment ever justified in the absence of imminent physical danger? Improving due process encourages a more responsible stance from both physicians and the courts, but it hardly solves the problem of coping with many difficult dilemmas that some mentally ill persons present for themselves, their families, and community members. Although there is strong rhetoric supporting management of disturbing patients within the context of the criminal law, this is neither in the patient's interest nor consistent with humanitarian concerns. The grounds for commitment should be narrow, the protections for the alleged mentally ill rigorous, and the use of less restrictive alternatives exhausted. There are, however, patients who fail to recognize a problem and cause great pain and anguish for others and damage to themselves. If they are sufficiently disturbing, they will be dealt with by the community in one way or another. What we really seek is not a sense of righteousness that may come from knowing that we have avoided the use of police powers, but some sense that we have found a constructive response to a painful problem, one that protects the future life chances of the disturbed patient.

One can argue that a certain amount of suffering is a price we must pay to protect our liberties and that many mental patients should be handled within the context of criminal law. But as one gets closer to the human dilemmas that bizarre and disoriented persons can cause for families and communities, one appreciates the need for continuing to explore humane alternatives that allow intervention without threatening the rights of most mentally ill persons, who need no such forceful interference in their lives. The difficulty lies in knowing where to draw the line and establishing uniform criteria in which the community can have confidence.

Stone (1975) suggested a five-step procedure through which assessments might be made as to the appropriateness of civil commitment: (1) reliable diagnosis of a severe mental illness, (2) assessment as to whether the person's immediate prognosis involves major distress, (3) availability of treatment, (4) the possibility that the illness impaired the person's ability to make a decision as to whether he or she was willing to accept treatment, and (5) assessment as to whether a reasonable person would accept or reject such treatment. Stone argues that involuntary confinement is justified when there is convincing evidence of a serious illness causing suffering for which treatment is available, where the patient's refusal of treatment is irrational, and where a reasonable person in possession of all faculties under the circumstances would accept such treatment. He calls this the Thank You Theory, implying that patients looking back on the experience would be grateful for state intervention.

> This is the Thank You Theory of Civil Commitment: it asks the psychiatrist to focus his inquiry on illness and treatment, and it asks the law to guarantee the treatment before it intervenes in the name of parens patriae. It is radical in the sense that it insists that society fulfill its promise of benefit when it trenches on human freedom. It is also radical in that it divests civil commitment of a police function; dangerous behavior is returned to the province of criminal law. Only someone who is irrational, treatable, and incidentally dangerous would be confined in the mental health system. (Stone 1975, p. 70)

Although Stone's Thank You Theory is appealing, it depends on trust in the integrity and reliability of psychiatric assessment and treatment, areas of continuing controversy. Many people weigh the values involved differently and would not want to trade off some patients' civil liberties for treatment that psychiatrists contended was valuable. Those who favor civil commitment primarily as a means to get dangerous and troublesome people off the streets might find Stone's approach disturbing, in that it separates the social control function from civil commitment. Stone's approach, however, is valuable because its main intent is to assist patients who may not appreciate their own needs rather than to assist the community. The Thank You Theory attempts to struggle with the central dilemmas underlying commitment rather than simply to take an ideological position.

In 1983, the American Psychiatric Association suggested a model state law on civil commitment (Stromberg and Stone 1983) substantially influenced by the thinking underlying the Thank You Theory. A central part of the proposal is to extend the *parens patriae* grounds for commitment to cover cases where the person is likely to suffer substantial mental and physical deterioration and lacks the capacity to make an informed decision. A commitment would occur if a severely mentally ill person would be likely to suffer or continue to suffer severe and abnormal mental, emotional, or physical distress associated with substantial deterioration of prior ability to function independently. While the intent of the drafters is to bring into treatment many of the mentally ill now languishing on the streets, the criteria are sufficiently ambiguous to be successfully applied to other populations of patients, and in the words of one of its critics is "extremely broad and ultimately incoherent" (Rubenstein 1985). As with so many other attempts, such language as "substantial deterioration" is difficult to apply clearly and consistently (for a useful debate on the issues, see Appelbaum 1985).

While the language of commitment statutes is not unimportant, and while litigation and court decisions are an important part of defining and improving our procedures, it is a mistake to depend too substantially on them. Many wise people have addressed the language of civil commitment procedures, but no language, however astutely drafted, can compensate for the deficiencies of mental health care. Almost all of the existing statutes have language sufficiently broad to allow judges to commit patients they believe should be hospitalized. Dangerousness is open to varying interpretations, as is the notion of grave disablement, both common features of many state laws. The problem is less in the specification of legal criteria and more in the conflicting views among psychiatrists, lawyers, the mentally ill and society at large, and the overall inadequacy of mental health services. No language games can adjudicate these real conflicts. Moreover, while the courts may establish reasonable principles, the inadequacies of both the mental health and criminal justice systems results in a large gap between theory and reality (Warren 1982). As one very experienced forensic psychiatrist noted, "My experience suggests that no matter how clear or detailed a law is, judges, police, attorneys, and bureaucrats often ignore or have no knowledge of its fine points. These officials, especially judges, who are often not accountable to anyone, routinely do what they think is best for the patient or what they think the law intends without regard to what the law really says" (Zusman 1985, p. 978).

Civil commitment is part of a larger structure of mental health care, and changes in procedures, without concomitant changes in other areas, are likely to have unanticipated consequences. A study of such legal changes following the murder of an elderly couple in Seattle by a 23-year-old neighbor, who earlier in the day had been denied voluntary admission to a state hospital, illustrates the issue (Pierce et al. 1986). Like every other state, Washington had tightened its civil commitment procedures in the period following *Lessard* in Wisconsin. But in 1979, the legislature, in response to public pressure, revised its criteria for commitment to expand the definition of grave disability to allow commitment of persons noncompliant with medication regimens and at risk of severe deterioration. The act also added "danger to property" as a danger criterion. Admissions increased substantially in the locality of the murder even before the law was changed, suggesting the robustness of the earlier criteria. In another part of the state less affected by the murder publicity, admissions dramatically increased but only following the legal changes. Thus, it seems that strong public opinion and legal changes can have their independent effects. But the effects were not what policy makers intended or anticipated. In both instances, hospital capacity did not increase, and the involuntary commitments displaced those seeking voluntary admission. This is particularly ironic in the light of the fact that the murderer who activated public opinion on this issue had sought to enter the hospital voluntarily but had been refused.

The fact is that we often have applicable legal mechanisms but lack the conditions or motivation to implement them in any meaningful way. Outpatient commitment is a case in point. Many states have made provision for commitment in a less restrictive environment, but the procedures appear to be infrequently used in most localities (Miller 1985). Clinicians seem to have little knowledge about the conditions under which such procedures should be used, and there is little evidence of close collaboration between clinicians and representatives of the legal system. There seems to be much confusion about the necessary conditions for outpatient commitment, the responsibilities of the mental health system in these cases, the applicability of patient rights honored in the hospital context, and the powers and discretion of judges when they use this mechanism. The only research studies depict experience in the state of North Carolina, an innovating state in outpatient commitment, and they illustrate both the potential and complexity of implementing this legal mechanism successfully. Much depends on the attitudes and cooperation of mental health professionals and the quality of mental health and social services in the community. When the mental health system is receptive, this new mechanism can work well (Hiday and Goodman 1982, Hiday and Scheid-Cook 1987b).

Other legal alternatives for protecting persons who lack the capacity to care for themselves include guardianship and conservatorship arrangements, but such mechanisms are poorly understood and rarely used. California specifically provides a conservatorship arrangement for individuals gravely disabled as a consequence of mental illness, and the court assigns a conservator for one-year renewable periods. The conservator has the legal power to manage the person's affairs including hospitalizing the individual when required, deciding on living arrangements, and managing the individual's money. Two highly experienced professionals familiar with this mechanism in California view it as an important therapeutic instrument when the conservators have appropriate backgrounds relevant to understanding chronic mental illness (Lamb and Mills 1986).

None of these mechanisms, however, can prosper in an impoverished and fragmented community care system. The abuses in the use of civil commitment in earlier periods were in part motivated by a desire to take action when there were few decent community alternatives for mentally ill people. With changes in mental health policies and more stringent criteria for civil commitment, many patients who would have been hospitalized remain in the community. Most are probably better off, but others continue to suffer seriously from their problems and to lead unhappy and pitiful lives. The potentialities exist for developing a wide variety of alternatives that are capable of assisting the patient without unduly disrupting whatever positive ties remain in the community. We have done poorly in developing needed assistance particularly for the long-term chronic patient—the type of patient who is a prime candidate for civil commitment. Without alternatives, the community will find some way of dealing with the mentally ill who are difficult, disturbing, and frightening that will often not be in the interests of the patient. If civil commitment presents an affront to the concept of individual freedom and personal integrity, less restrictive but more effective alternatives must be developed and encouraged, in addition to improvements in due process. In the final analysis, the future for the mentally ill depends far more on how we meet their needs than the form, or even the content, of due process.

A NOTE ON THE CONCEPT OF DANGER

The concept of dangerousness is inherent in many judgments concerning civil and criminal commitments, but the concept itself, despite continuing efforts to provide clarification, is extraordinarily fuzzy (Brooks 1978, 1984). Lay people in making such judgments tend to focus on bizarre and inexplicable behavior that frightens them, but such behavior is not correlated substantially or at all with violence and harm. Unfortunately, professional predictions of dangerousness are little better than lay judgments, and the clarity of the concept leaves much to be desired.

Violence is commonplace in our society. Most persons who engage in violent, destructive, or other harmful behaviors are not mentally ill unless the behaviors are defined as criteria for judging illness, which would be tautological. All of us pose some risks to others—by the way we live, the way we drive, the extent to which we take precautions to avoid accidents, and so on. Psychiatrists' conceptions of danger include a tendency toward personal violence, such as attacks on persons or property. A businessperson who sells defective products or a manufacturer who fails to report a known safety defect in a product may do far more harm to others than a mentally ill person but would not usually be included within the psychiatric conception. We tend not to think of white-collar crime as dangerous in a psychiatric sense because it follows logically from our assumptions about motivation and is easy to understand within the context of our commercial and materialistic values.

Another aspect of psychiatrists' concepts of dangerous and injurious behavior involves deviant forms of behavior contrary to the social patterns of the community as they understand them. An adult who obtains sexual gratification from fondling small children is likely to be thought of as dangerous, while the manufacturer who knowingly sells products harmful to public health and safety is thought of as selfish or greedy. Very little systematic knowledge allows psychiatrists to predict realistically when a patient is dangerous (Cocozza and Steadman 1978). They must depend on their clinical judgment and a variety of clinical impressions. Although the research literature is scanty on the prediction of dangerous behavior and includes many methodological problems, the evidence suggests that at best only a minority of patients adjudged dangerous actually commit acts of violence when released (Stone 1975). Both laypersons and psychiatrists might be able to predict danger better than chance, but such predictions will involve large numbers of false positives. If we are to detain dangerous persons successfully, we would also have to detain large numbers of persons who in fact were not dangerous. Because very few people actually commit dangerous crimes, trying to use preventive detention would mean that for every dangerous person detained, numerous innocent people would also be deprived of their liberties although they did not violate any law. No sane social policy can follow such a course.

Contrary to popular conceptions, studies suggest that in the aggregate mental patients are no more dangerous than others (Rappeport 1967, pp. 72–80) or, if they are, the differences are very small allowing little success in prediction (Stone 1975). The best predictor of dangerousness, whether patients are mentally ill or not, is prior unlawful and dangerous behavior (Monahan 1981), and psychiatrists tend to use such criteria in making their predictions (Cocozza and Steadman 1978). The fact is that if prior behavior is the criterion, anyone can make the judgment. Even with prior behavior as a standard, predictions would lead to a high proportion of false positives. The Supreme Court has accepted prior convictions as a basis for withholding bail in some cases, but the issue remains as to what types of prior criminal behavior justify "preventive detention" in the period awaiting trial.

It seems reasonably clear why the general public views the mentally ill as more dangerous than objective studies indicate. The bizarre behavior of many mentally ill is difficult to understand and appears unpredictable and uncontrollable. Moreover, the news media give prominence to the former-mental-patient status of those who commit serious crimes. Such attributions are unlikely to be made when persons who have been mentally ill demonstrate great achievements or achieve high honors, although many do (Scheff 1984).

Some mentally ill persons are dangerous, however, and the probability is better than average that certain subgroups have a higher propensity than others to engage in violent and irrational behavior. Beyond the use of the history of past behavior, most criteria used by psychiatrists are highly uncertain. Although their utility is unproven, other criteria frequently used are the repression of normal aggression and the presence of deep feelings of rage, a sense of helplessness and feeling trapped, the presence of paranoid delusions or hallucinations, especially when these imply violence, and the admission of patients that they find it difficult to control their antisocial urges. Some psychiatrists feel that aggression, particularly that associated with the excessive use of alcohol and drugs, is very dangerous; others give attention to subcultural factors such as the readiness to express aggression (Rappeport 1967).

The validity of clinical conceptions of danger and violence has not been established, and there is every reason to believe that violence is specific to situation and context and not simply an attribute of a person. To the extent that this is true, prediction of dangerousness will always be an uncertain activity. Yet, persons are deprived of their freedom on the basis of an alleged risk of high danger, and thus there is an obligation to clarify our understanding and examine whether or not such decisions are really justified. If danger is mostly related to specific contexts, then we must better identify the types of contexts that elicit violence and determine ways to minimize them. We also need to be clearer on the distinction between symbolic and real dangers. For example, persons who engage in various deviant patterns of sexual satisfaction, such as the peeper, the exhibitionist, or the child molester, are presumed dangerous by the community because people do not understand such patterns of behavior and find it difficult to conceive that any but a highly irrational person can behave in that way. In contrast, people are much less aroused by drunken drivers, in part because it is much easier for them to comprehend how a "normal" person like themselves can be in such a situation.

One consequence of the efforts to tighten commitment laws has been the attempt to be more explicit in defining danger. The *Lessard* decision, for example, required that such a finding be based on a "recent act, attempt, or threat to do substantial harm." As Brooks (1978) has noted, even this effort to clarify language begs the question of what type of act and with what recency, as well as what constitutes an attempt or threat. In practice, psychiatrists and judges read into these definitions whatever they wish, and there is a failure to distinguish between real menace and substantial nuisance and imposition. How should judges deal, as Brooks (1978) asks, with a manic person who depletes family resources and exposes them to financial hardship, or a hysterical person who continually calls others on the phone in the middle of the night, night after night? It appears that what judges and psychiatrists do is less determined by the precise definitions and more by the state of community opinion and pressures at the time. When a psychotic man killed two persons in New York City following the Statue of Liberty celebration, psychiatrists began to detain more patients and psychiatric emergency rooms and hospitals filled to capacity. The law did not change to make detention easier, but public opinion changed, making psychiatrists feel that they would be held responsible for releasing dangerous mentally ill persons. Thus they became much more cautious. This phenomenon was illustrated by the experience in the state of Washington discussed earlier (Pierce et al. 1986).

In areas other than the law, our society needs assessments of whether persons are reliable or whether there is a considerable risk that they may engage in dangerous behavior. The armed forces must have some assurance that the handling of nuclear weapons and other dangerous tasks are not allocated to unstable persons. Businesses and industrial firms are concerned that persons in positions of considerable responsibility are able to perform their tasks without endangering others or the company. A schizophrenic pilot is probably too inattentive to fly an airplane safely, and, indeed, such inattentiveness may risk the lives of a great many people. There are attempts to assess psychologically and psychiatrically the mental stability of potential employees for particular jobs, although the adequacy of these screening programs is in doubt. Concern even extends to the threat that high public officials who are psychiatrically disabled may harm the public because of their illness, but as yet no one has found an adequate way to balance these risks against the political risk of surveillance of mental health and the risks inherent in the imprecise character of psychiatric selection procedures. Much more research and conceptual sophistication are needed in these areas, but it seems unlikely that we can ever fully resolve the fundamental dilemmas.

THE RIGHT TO TREATMENT

The significance of right-to-treatment concepts depends on the range of application. Although lawyers have made efforts to apply the concept to mental health care generally, whatever effectiveness this legal theory has demonstrated thus far has been in relation to persons involuntarily de-tained in public institutions. Involuntary commitments have substantially diminished, but significant numbers of mentally ill continue to be involuntarily detained presumably because they are in need of treatment, but once detained little real treatment is available. Initially, right-to-treatment theories were directed at remedying the horrendous conditions common in many public institutions. With deinstitutionalization, improvements in many public hospitals, and the reluctance of the Supreme Court to accept the legal theory that patients enjoy such a constitutional right, some of the momentum has been lost, but as I will illustrate there are some unanticipated problems with devising a remedy applicable to only one part of the mental health system.

Although there were early precedents in right-to-treatment decisions (Stone 1975, pp. 83–96), a major breakthrough came in 1971 in *Wyatt* v. *Stickney*, in which the federal district court in Alabama held that involuntarily committed patients "unquestionably have a constitutional right to receive such individual treatment as will give each of them a realistic opportunity to be cured or to improve his or her mental condition" (Mechanic 1974, p. 233). The court found that the defendant's treatment program was deficient because it failed to provide a humane psychological and physical environment and a qualified staff in sufficient number to administer adequate treatment and individualized treatment plans. In the judgment of the court, "to deprive any citizen of his or her liberty upon the altruistic theory that the confinement is for humane therapeutic reasons and then fail to provide adequate treatment violates the very fundamentals of due process" (Mechanic 1974, p. 233).

On the urging of litigants, the court established a large number of standards, which it defined as "medical and constitutional minimums," mandating changes in staffing, physical resources, and treatment processes. If the implementation of such standards alleviates the horrible conditions that were documented as prevalent, they obviously contribute to fairness and decency. It is not clear, however, that the standards promulgated were particularly wise in achieving the best outcomes in relation to cost that would be possible if such resources were used as part of an overall mental health strategy, including both inpatient and community care of the mentally ill. The nature of legal advocacy required an approach that focused on the involuntary hospital patient because the "handle" was the argument that the deprivation of liberty for humane therapeutic reasons without the provision of treatment was a violation of due process of law. This need for a strategy required the litigants to view the mental health system narrowly and to focus their attention on only one aspect of care, allowing the possibility of displacement of the problem to other parts of the mental health system not so easily addressed by litigation.

The hospital standards promulgated had a variety of limitations. They tended to reinforce a medical model of treatment and highly stratified roles among health professionals at the same time that health experts were increasingly becoming aware of the limitations of professional dominance and rigidly enforced roles. They encouraged the allocation of resources to hospital care in contrast to a network of community facilities more appropriately fitted to the management of mental health problems in the community. They demanded that expensive and scarce medical resources be devoted to the parts of the mental health system in which they may be least effective in treatment and thus yield a low benefit-cost outcome. Perhaps most dangerous of all is that such standards encourage an indiscriminate dumping of patients in the community without providing an adequate network of community care that facilitates social functioning and alleviates the social costs for families and community members of having highly disabled persons residing in the community.

There are no definitive data on the full consequences of the right-to-treatment decisions, even in Alabama where such major court rulings were applied on a large scale. There is evidence, however, that large numbers of patients were released from Alabama hospitals following these decisions. The number of releases was larger than would have been expected on the basis of existing trends in adjacent states (Leaf 1978a,b). Right-to-treatment decisions assisted, if they did not affect directly, efforts to increase Alabama's mental health budget and the staffing patterns in psychiatric institutions. It is difficult to come to any conclusion other than that the *Wyatt* decision contributed to a climate that brought greater support and investment for mental health facilities and programs in Alabama. Although we have only modest knowledge about the fate of patients who were released to either the community or nursing homes, indications are that they had varying experiences, some not conducive to a high quality of social functioning. Many remained institutionalized in the community or in nursing homes, but, on balance, the result seems positive (Leaf 1978a). Because of the middle-class bias of public interest lawyers, it is almost inconceivable to them at this time that any patients could be better off in hospitals given their inadequacies. Study of the situation of some chronic mental patients, however, suggests that lower-status and highly disabled patients sometimes find it more comforting to have residence in institutions than in the community (Ludwig and Farrelly 1966). Once patients are released to the community, they are no longer protected by right-to-treatment decisions, and they are at the mercy of prevailing conditions and resources in the community, which are often minimal and may be more inadequate than those available in a hospital program.

The right-to-treatment theory supported by Judge Frank Johnson in Alabama received little support in *Donaldson*, which was initially brought as a right-to-treatment case. Instead, the Supreme Court decided the case on the much more narrow ground that the state could not detain without treatment nondangerous persons capable of surviving in the community on their own. It was clear that the majority of the Supreme Court was not ready to support the theory of a constitutional right to treatment. While Chief Justice Burger in his concurring opinion made clear his strong opposition to the assertion of a new right, his opinion has apparently not deterred judges in lower courts from proceeding on this theoretical basis (Stone 1984, p. 117). Some judges, in response to public interest lawyers' litigation, have even extended this right to community care, but it is not clear to what degree activist courts can direct state governments on how to establish priorities and allocate limited public resources.

It seems clear that there is at least an accepted constitutional right to minimal standards for the mentally retarded. In *Youngberg and Romeo*, the

Supreme Court established that committed retarded patients had a right to "conditions of reasonable care and safety, reasonable nonrestrictive confinement conditions, and such training as may be required by these interests." Federal courts have extended the concept of minimum rights to include treatment to prevent clinical deterioration among committed patients, but it is too early to assess how far these legal theories can be successfully extended (Lamb and Mills 1986).

In many localities impaired patients have been dumped in communities without adequate financial, social, or treatment resources. Many live with other deviants in "welfare hotels" in disorganized areas, frequently find themselves in substandard facilities in the community run for profit by operators who provide few treatment resources, or are without homes at all. Given the poor conditions to which they are exposed, these patients frequently experience an exacerbation of symptoms and insecurities and, given their limited coping capacities, face horrendous life problems. In the case of schizophrenic patients, it is recognized that aggressive care is required if they are not to regress (Davis et al. 1972), but under most community circumstances, such care is not available and former patients simply become lost in the community.

Establishing a right to treatment cannot be seen independently of these other trends. If we do not consider the mental health system as a whole, we may find that by putting pressure on one aspect of the system, we create more intense problems in other areas. A major limitation of the litigation approach is the difficulty of viewing the system as a whole in contrast to seeking particular constitutional remedies.

Thus it is difficult to be too confident about the benefits gained through right-to-treatment decisions. Fair and effective rehabilitation for mental patients depends on the entire framework of medical and mental health care and decisions made through the legislative process. The publicity accompanying right-to-treatment litigation helps make inadequate conditions of mental health care more salient to legislators and may arouse the sympathies of the public. It also contributes to eliminating some obvious abuses of institutional care. The concept of right to treatment really means adequate or acceptable treatment and not all that science or knowledge allows. To the extent that this legal approach focuses attention on the lack of treatment or unacceptable care, it is a justified strategy. Beyond this, we need a means to examine treatment in all contexts, not only the hospital, so that we can use our resources most beneficially for all patients wherever they are.

RIGHT TO REFUSE TREATMENT

Malpractice standards based on the common law encompass the illegality of a physician treating patients without their consent, except under conditions where consent cannot be reasonably expected, as in medical emergencies. This is an important principle, but the courts have traditionally allowed mental hospitals to treat mental patients involuntarily. In pursuing right-to-refuse-treatment litigation in mental hospitals, lawyers have adopted a constitutional rather than a malpractice approach (Stone 1981).

Right-to-refuse-treatment efforts began in the 1970s with measures to protect involuntary patients in quasi-criminal institutions from experimental drug treatment and psychosurgery (Brooks 1979, Stone 1984), but it was only later that these suits were extended to medications where much of the controversy has focused. Two major cases, *Rennie* in New Jersey and *Rogers* in Massachusetts, have accounted for much of the contentious debate over the regulation of psychiatric treatment.

As Stone (1981) has conceded, whatever the theory, it is clear that there must be a right to refuse treatment from a legal perspective, but the real issue is "how it can be implemented in a way that takes into account both the rights of patients and their needs" (p. 360). An additional question is how to achieve an appropriate balance between regulatory efforts and the use of limited psychiatric resources in an efficient and meaningful way.

The declaration of a right to refuse treatment has no substantial statistical effect. Relatively few patients actually refuse treatment, and the protracted litigation has direct influence on a limited number of cases. But the assertion of the right probably contributes to communication and negotiation with patients about their treatment regimen and induces psychiatrists in institutions to be more respectful of patients' concerns about their treatment (Lamb and Mills 1986). An alleged cost of such regulation is its effect on the morale and perspectives of psychiatrists, who are said to view such requirements as intrusions on their ability to care for patients appropriately and, as a result, become apathetic about providing proper treatment (Stone 1981). The difficulty appears to be less in the principle itself and more in the way psychiatrists may define the situation and limit their own efforts to treat.

In *Rennie*, the federal district court in New Jersey accepted the view that involuntary medication with neuroleptic drugs was an invasion of constitutionally protected privacy. Later, the circuit court of appeals changed the constitutional rationale to "protection from harm." The Massachusetts federal district court accepted the further theory, based on the First Amendment guaranteeing free speech and thought, that the administration of neuroleptic drugs alters the mind and thus interferes with the constitutionally protected right. The Massachusetts decision was viewed by psychiatrists as particularly offensive and nonsensical and as an affront to the necessary discretion of clinicians (Stone 1981). There is no basis in the belief that neuroleptic drugs affect the mind in the sense accepted in the *Rogers* decision. This view was later rejected by the circuit court of appeals.

While these decisions have instituted some checkpoints on psychiatric discretion, they do not prevent psychiatrists from administering medications in emergencies. In a later decision in a Wisconsin case (*Stensvad* v. *Reivitz*), the United States District Court upheld a Wisconsin provision allowing an involuntarily committed patient in a criminal commitment to be medicated without consent (Lamb and Mills 1986). Considerable discretion remains, and hospital practice is believed not to have been much affected. To the extent that these cases have motivated more thoughtfulness in the use of medication, better communication with patients, and greater awareness of how particular medications and dosage may be particularly troublesome for the patient, they probably contribute to better patient care and the type of consideration one would expect in any decent medical encounter.

These cases and the court judgments reflect the fact that many medications have serious adverse effects and may cause permanent disability, as in the case of tardive dyskinesia with the use of neuroleptics. Mental hospitals neither attract the best clinicians nor represent the ideal context for a sensitive therapeutic relationship. There is no indication that the formal procedures prescribed by the courts are frequently used, leading some psychiatrists to argue that this is all a "tempest in a teapot." In contrast, others believe that the assertion of a right to refuse treatment and establishing procedures to review refusals serves as a deterrent to arbitrary and insensitive care and indirectly contributes to a more humane treatment context. The evidence remains unclear, but the basic point is not. Treatment should always take place so as to give credence to the patient's wishes and reactions. Good care requires not only prescribing the right medication, but calibrating and scheduling it so that it interferes to the smallest possible extent with the patient's sense of well-being. Indeed, there may be possibilities of selecting among different drugs, varying means of administration, and alternative schedules. Moderating the arbitrariness of care thus moves us in the right direction, unless there is contrary evidence that the regulatory process has either resulted in inability to treat patients who need care or diverted significant resources from patient care to support regulatory mechanisms.

INCOMPETENCY TO STAND TRIAL

The well-known use of the insanity defense is relatively infrequent in comparison to the decision that a person charged with a crime is incompetent to stand trial. The reasoning behind such a determination is that defendants must cooperate in preparing their cases and must assist in their defenses. If they lack the capacity to understand the proceedings because of a mental disease or mental deficiency, it is unfair to persist with a trial because this would deprive them of rights accorded all defendants.

Although in extreme cases such provisions pose no great difficulty, in many instances the concept of competency is a murky one. The law regards all ordinary persons as having similar capacities to appreciate the proceedings against them and to assist in their defense, but actually persons vary as greatly in their intelligence and understanding as court proceedings vary in their complexity. Thus ordinary "normal" persons under "normal" conditions may have more or less capacity to assist in their defense. Mental incompetency pertains, however, not to this normal range but to a lack of capacity caused by mental defects or mental illness.

We face here some of the same issues we have faced before. How is one to develop standards for determining when a defendant lacks capacity to understand the situation and to assist the lawyer? Are we to regard such capacity as inherent in the individual regardless of the difficulty of the case or the necessity of cooperation? Or are we to view it not as an absolute state but as being relative to the defendant's own prior abilities and capacities?

Are we to define a lowered capacity because of mental illness in a defendant of ordinarily high intelligence and deep understanding as incompetence when we define the understanding of a normal person of average intelligence as competence? Persons whose usual performance is impaired may still outperform others who are fulfilling their highest capabilities.

The resolution of the issue depends on the way lawyers, judges, and psychiatrists view mental illness and on conceptions of the link between mental illness and competence. Although this matter has not been studied in any detailed way, clearly the response of courts on this issue is highly variable. Theoretically, the defense, the prosecution, or the judge may raise the issue of the defendant's fitness to stand trial. Each may raise the issue for different motives and on the basis of different understandings of the concepts involved. As with commitment proceedings, much may depend on the determinations offered by psychiatric experts called to testify as to the competence of the defendant. For example, in the case of *Aponte* v. *State,* in New Jersey, the following psychiatric views were offered to support the determination of incompetence as stated in the summary of Chief Justice Weintraub:

> Dr. Brancale testified Aponte's illness has its peaks and valleys. He said, "this man certainly knows his attorney, knows the psychiatrists that have examined him, and remembers the date and knows he is on trial. But underneath all of this I do not think there is a real comprehension of the dilemma." He conceded that Aponte answered questions "at a reasonably intellectual level" and the answers were "responsive," although the witness added, "I think he was beginning to get irrelevant material in there. " . . .
> Dr. Brancale, on the trial judge's interrogation, said Aponte "intellectually" comprehended his situation, but not "emotionally," that his answers were "intelligently responsive," but "emotionally he is not involved in this in any way whatsoever"; that he could consult with counsel "in a limited way, or in the limited framework of intelligence." In summary, the doctor stated his "guarded" view was that "Intellectually, and as the Judge asked me, he can answer questions intelligently and at the same time his emotional disturbance is such that he would not give or be able to present an adequate defense or help his lawyer because his emotions would not allow him to do so." (Katz et al. 1967, p. 568)

The circumstances in this case were not simple. The defendant was alleged to have murdered a 13-year-old boy for rather bizarre motives, and these circumstances themselves would lead many laymen to view the defendant as mentally ill. Two psychiatric experts who testified on his behalf believed him to be schizophrenic with homicidal and suicidal tendencies, although they believed he was legally sane. Psychiatric experts testifying for the state found the defendant to be lacking in mental illness from a psychiatric perspective and sane from a legal point of view. Such a difference of opinion among experts about the presence or absence of mental illness is a frequent occurrence in adversary proceedings. Chief Justice Weintraub on review came to this conclusion:

> Aponte's testimony itself gives no evidence that he could not fairly stand trial. We find therein nothing to suggest that he is unaware of his position. His

memory was precise with respect to the homicide and his conduct before and since. His testimony was vivid. He was responsive. (Katz et al. 1967, p. 568)

In this case the defense attorney probably felt that a judgment of incompetence to stand trial would be in the interest of his client. Such judgments can be made for a wide variety of reasons. Sometimes participants feel that this is the most humanitarian route for dealing with the situation. On other occasions the anger of the community is so aroused against the defendant that his or her attorney wishes to delay the trial as long as possible to allow the public interest and emotions to dissipate, or the attorney may just want time to prepare the case more carefully.

We should also note some of the difficulties relating to psychiatric testimony in such cases. In the testimony in support of the defense in the *Aponte* case, the psychiatric judgment was based not on cognitive understanding or on the actual behavior of the defendant in assisting his attorney but rather on the defendant's emotional appreciation of his circumstances. Intuitively we can grasp what the psychiatrist means by emotional appreciation in particularly selected cases, but we have no clear criteria for making such judgments. There is great disparity of opinion among psychiatrists on such judgments, and the basis of these judgments is frequently unclear. Thus, conceptually, one may posit discrepancies between a person's cognitive and emotional responses, but from a practical standpoint such judgments are difficult to make, and it is not clear how large a discrepancy is necessary before one can reasonably argue that it is improper for the defendant to stand trial or that it is inappropriate to regard him or her as responsible.

The rule for assessing competence in most jurisdictions is based on a standard used in federal cases approved by the Supreme Court in *Dusky* v. *United States* (Winick 1983). Under this test it must be ascertained whether the defendant "has sufficient present ability to consult with his lawyer with a reasonable degree of rational understanding—and whether he has a rational as well as factual understanding of the proceedings against him." One can readily see the room for discretion in assessing what is reasonable and the demarcation between factual and rational understanding. Indeed, the distinction itself is murky. More detail is provided by the American Law Institute's Model Penal Code, but the elaboration, while conveying clearly the types of competence expected, introduces further ambiguity through such concepts as "mental capacity to appreciate."

If patients are found to be incompetent, they are usually sent to a hospital for care and treatment until such time as they are capable to stand trial. Typically, many were kept in such hospitals for periods beyond the maximum sentence for the alleged crime, and some have been kept for life. Studies of practices in the 1960s suggested that this mechanism was often used as a way of removing patients from the community for an extended period (Hess and Thomas 1963). In California, following reforms in civil commitment processes, large numbers of mentally ill persons were processed through the criminal system, charged with minor violations, found incompetent to stand trial, and then incarcerated (Stone 1975, p. 207).

This was an area of extraordinary abuse. In 1972, the Supreme Court in *Jackson* v. *Indiana* insisted that commitments made on the basis of incompetency to stand trial must be for treatment aimed at restoring the necessary capacity. It was the intention of the court to end the practice of using the incompetency mechanism to achieve indeterminate incarceration. The Court held that a defendant committed on this basis "cannot be held more than a reasonable period of time necessary to determine whether there is substantial probability that he will attain that capacity in the foreseeable future." "Reasonable" has since been defined by the courts as varying from 6 to 18 months. Following this period, if competence is not restored, the ordinary civil commitment procedures are required. As of the early 1980s, it has been suggested that these requirements are commonly violated in many jurisdictions and that many of the constitutional rights stated by the Supreme Court in this area remain theoretical (Winick 1983). As Winick (1983) notes: "Neither judicial decision nor the statutory pronouncements of the legislature are self-executing. Incompetent defendants often are unaware of their rights or lack the initiative or resources to assert them. Defense counsel all too frequently neglect their incompetent clients once they have been committed" (p. 28).

It would be difficult to attempt to make sense of the results of the incompetency process in terms of the substance of the concepts used. Instead, we must recognize that this process, like the commitment process, has been used to deal with a variety of situations that confront the community and, despite a landmark decision by the Supreme Court more than 15 years ago, is still probably abused. If mentally ill persons believed to be dangerous commit minor offenses, they may at best be put in custody for a short time under usual proceedings and be released when they have served their sentences or their civil commitment expires. Such a person deemed incompetent to stand trial, however, has been kept in a mental hospital for an indefinite period. As civil commitment became more difficult a judgment of incompetency to stand trial until recent years has allowed for the indefinite detention of persons believed to be dangerous, those who cannot take care of themselves, or those who are public nuisances. The motives underlying this process, however, were not as clear as the discussion suggests. Many such defendants were clearly mentally ill, and lawyers and judges may have felt that a determination of incompetence was in their best interest. Critics of the process feel that this legal provision has effectively allowed the community to deny persons their legal right to a trial, to a determinate sentence, and to due process of law.

THE INSANITY DEFENSE

In statistical or even practical terms, the insanity defense is far less important than most other issues we have considered, but there is no issue in law and psychiatry that elicits comparable emotion and debate. This issue is a morality play and the warring ground for proponents of varying ideologies reflecting opposing stances on the longstanding controversy about free will and determinism. While these concerns are not absent from other legal issues we have reviewed, the insanity defense focuses important conflicts of values that involve core assumptions about the nature of mankind and society. These conflicts periodically reach the boiling point when triggered by a particularly salient event. Such a recent event was the attempt by John Hinckley to assassinate President Reagan and his subsequent trial. Indeed, in the view of one important observer, the acquittal of Hinckley by reason of insanity "shook public confidence in the American criminal justice system" (Stone 1984, p. 77).

There are many reasons to lack confidence in our criminal justice system, but it is not obvious why the Hinckley verdict should have this effect. As Alan Stone (1984) noted, the "verdict was fully compatible with the psychiatric testimony, the applicable legal test, and the burdens of proof" (p. 78), and in this sense it was legally just. But the fact is that, despite Hinckley's obvious serious mental illness, many Americans wanted him held accountable and punished for his deed, and the lawyers, psychiatrists, politicians, and social commentators once again went through their periodic ritual of proposing new tests and procedures to assess legal insanity, and some advocated the abolition of the plea itself (Brooks 1985). These periodic exercises are doomed to failure because playing with words cannot resolve fundamental philosophical issues on which the public is divided. The discussion of the insanity defense cyclically repeats itself, but there is really little new. Depending on public sentiment, the rules can be written and applied more or less restrictively, but they cannot resolve basically contradictory philosophies.

Stone (1975) notes that there were only 11 successful insanity pleas in New York State during the 1960s. But with the community psychiatry movement of the 1960s and 1970s, changing attitudes toward the mentally ill, and a greater permissiveness in social thinking overall, many jurisdictions adopted a more lenient test of insanity and even the interpretation of more traditional tests were broadened. Changes both in the tests and the social context led to increased use of the insanity defense. Indeed, Hinckley was tried under a broadened test (the ALI test), which we will soon review and which has been adopted by many jurisdictions.

Psychiatric testimony and the conflicting views of psychiatrists are easily made to look ludicrous in the context of ideological disputes: "psychiatry is an easy target no matter how excellent the expert psychiatric witnesses may be" (Stone 1984, p. 78). These problems become more severe as the climate of greater leniency encouraged lawyers to attempt more extreme—some bizarre—defenses by extracting diagnostic labels from the DSM-III, such as "pathological gambling" and "post-traumatic stress" disorders. These defenses impress observers as having little credibility as grounds for diminished responsibility, but they are increasingly used. In the killing of Harvey Milk, a city official in San Francisco, the defense, in arguing for diminished capacity, a permissable California plea, made the argument that junk food affected the defendant's mental functioning. This argument, which the media publicized and derisively labeled the "Twinkie Defense," did little to put psychiatry in a favorable light (Perr 1985).

Tests for Insanity

When a person is charged with having committed a crime, the assumption that he or she is sane prevails unless it can be determined that by reason of insanity or mental defect the person is not legally responsible for the wrongful conduct with which he or she is charged. A prevalent criterion, in one form or another, is still the M'Naghten rule, dating back to a case decided in Great Britain in 1843. The rule states:

> that every man is to be presumed to be sane, and . . . that to establish a defense on the ground of insanity, it must be clearly proved that, at the time of committing the act, the party accused was labouring under such a defect of reason, from disease of the mind, as not to know the nature and quality of the act he was doing; or if he did know it, that he did not know he was doing what was wrong. (Goldstein 1967, p. 45)

In addition to M'Naghten, several states use the irresistible-impulse rule, which establishes as a criterion for legal insanity that defendants have a mental disease which prevents them from effectively controlling their conduct.

The rules used in establishing legal insanity have aroused heated controversy over the years. Many psychiatrists argue that they fail to take account of contemporary psychiatric knowledge and tend to be rigid, unrealistic, and harsh (Glueck 1963). They maintain that the determination of sanity should depend on whether and to what extent the defendant is suffering from a mental disease or defect. The United States Court of Appeals for the District of Columbia under the leadership of Chief Judge D. L. Bazelon applied for a time a new rule applauded by many psychiatrists. The Durham rule stated that "an accused is not criminally responsible if his unlawful act was the product of mental disease or mental defect." Judge Bazelon hoped that this new rule would permit psychiatrists to testify more fully and easily concerning the defendant's mental condition (Bazelon 1967).

Although it was Judge Bazelon's intent to allow the psychiatrist to explain how the person came to engage in the behavior at issue, in reality the new ruling did little to improve the quality of psychiatric testimony. The Durham rule provided no criteria for defining mental illness or for establishing the conditions under which an unlawful act could be said to be a product of such disease. Psychiatrists continued to come into court stating dogmatic judgments rather than explaining in a meaningful way how knowledge of behavior could result in a better decision. Psychiatric experts responded expediently in terms of their own professional needs and desires. Many observers opposed Durham because they feared the rule was too lenient, would be used too frequently, and would undermine legal accountability. In their view the concept of sickness was expanding, pushing out moral blame. Results are not always as one might anticipate. The court in the District of Columbia dealt most commonly with cases from St. Elizabeths, a large federal hospital. Faced with a large patient population and unwilling to take on larger burdens, psychiatrists from the hospital staff used a very strict interpretation when they testified in the D.C. court (Arens 1967).

A great deal of attention is given to the language of varying tests. Such language is often important in focusing criteria, but the general climate of opinion is also of great importance. There is little information on how varying tests affect jury decisions; depending on the composition of the jury, the education and sophistication of the jurors, and their own philosophical orientations, the instructions given to the jury may be more or less important. As in the case of judges' decisions, the law establishes some constraints, but its interpretation depends on perceptions, notions about fairness, and philosophical predilections.

Underlying the debate concerning responsibility is a philosophical dispute between those with rehabilitation perspectives and those with punishment perspectives; the latter maintain that it is necessary for the legal system to encourage a strong sense of responsibility by punishing wrongdoing and attempting to deter violations of the law. Those with rehabilitation perspectives think that deviant behavior is more appropriately regarded as sickness than as badness and that treatment is more appropriate than punishment. If persons violate society's codes because of their own tragic human condition, they argue, the proper road to rehabilitation is sympathy and care, not imprisonment. Such persons wish to give psychiatrists a large role in the determination of responsibility.

Between the traditional M'Naghten rule and the Durham formulation lies the following recommendation of the American Law Institute (Donnelly et al. 1962), which is increasingly used in varying jurisdictions.

> A person is not responsible for criminal conduct if at the time of such conduct as a result of mental disease or defect he lacks substantial capacity either to appreciate the criminality of his conduct or to conform his conduct to the requirements of law. (Donnelly et al. 1962, p. 750)

The ALI rule clearly establishes that mental disease or defect does not include abnormalities manifested only by repeated criminal or otherwise antisocial conduct. The definition is intended to limit the inclusiveness of the concept of mental illness by excluding persons generally characterized as psychopaths.

Over the years certain assumptions, not always consistent, have been made concerning the meaning of particular words within these rules and the manner in which they are to be construed. Thus, for example, does "knowing the nature and quality of one's act," in the M'Naghten rule, refer only to the ability to cognitively know the law or may it be construed to pertain as well to the ability to emotionally appreciate the meaning of the law? Much of the controversy over these rules is in part based on the breadth of interpretation given to certain words. It is not our role here to consider the various legal constructions that can be applied to the language of these various rules, although such matters are important. It is more appropriate to consider the basic issues of public policy underlying them.

As noted earlier, one of the arguments in favor of modification of the traditional insanity defense is that treatment is more meaningful and valuable than punishment as a response to deviant behavior. Implicit in this argument is the notion that a determination of insanity and subsequent treatment in a mental hospital are more humane and constructive than imprisonment. But some observers contest this assumption (Szasz 1963, 1965). Given the stigma of mental illness, they maintain that psychiatric hospitalization is not necessarily more humane or useful to society and the individual than imprisonment. Logically, the issues of responsibility and treatment need not be tied together. There is no reason, as Szasz (1963) maintains, why correctional institutions cannot institute sound psychiatric programs directed to providing therapeutic help to inmates. Similarly, the fact that an institution is called a hospital does not guarantee that it provides a therapeutic program or a humane environment.

Further, we have the thorny issues of when is mental illness sufficiently severe to assume that it is unreasonable to hold a person with such a condition responsible for his or her behavior, and how does one reasonably link the state of a person's personality with a specific wrongful act. We have already noted the uncertainty of the concept of mental illness. Psychiatrists disagree among themselves on the meaning and applicability of the concept. Such disagreement applies to the assessment of individual patients and also extends to theoretical conceptions of the phenomenon itself. Some psychiatrists regard mental illnesses as particular, identifiable syndromes akin to those found in the ordinary practice of medicine. To others, mental illness is a dynamic concept characterizing the individual's psychological and social adjustment. A few psychiatrists even contend that no concept of mental illness can be judged independently of the norms of conduct set by the community. To some psychiatrists, mental illness is a limited concept applicable only to a small proportion of problems; others use the concept in such a general fashion that they can maintain that almost everyone in some sense is mentally ill. Although such uncertainty may not be an insuperable barrier in the clinical setting, it is hardly tolerable in legal circumstances, where the concept must be used for making dispositions of persons who have offended the rules of society.

Although jurists and psychiatrists may not fully agree on where to draw the line, such matters in any case are appropriately left to judges and juries. The role of the psychiatrist in legal proceedings as an expert witness is to inform the fact-finder who must make the decision—the judge or the jury. In the case of the insanity defense the psychiatrist is asked to offer information relevant to the decision-making process. Too frequently psychiatrists themselves provide testimony in relation to their understanding of the prevailing legal rule rather than attempting to depict in the clearest way possible the psychological state and social circumstances of the defendant. Since the determination of responsibility is properly the function of judges and juries, psychiatrists should provide useful information to them and not attempt to answer the question of responsibility.

The determination of insanity is a social judgment; it is not a scientific issue or one which allows any reasonably scientific assessment. The rationale underlying the use of the psychiatrists as expert witnesses is that they have experience with and opportunity to observe the mentally ill and are thus in a good position to inform the jury and judge concerning possible psychological contingencies affecting the defendant's actions. The judgment of whether it is reasonable to regard the defendant as responsible for his or her behavior cannot be made on technical or scientific grounds. If, for example, a schizophrenic patient is apprehended committing a crime and when arrested is seen to be in a hallucinogenic state, one would be tempted to attribute the unlawful behavior to schizophrenia. However, most hallucinating schizophrenics do not commit crimes, and many nonschizophrenics do. Thus, the fact that schizophrenia is a concomitant of the unlawful act in no sense establishes any causal relationship between them. In some cases, of course, a link is obvious, as when a mental patient hears voices which tell him or her to commit an irrational and meaningless offense. But in such circumstances one hardly needs a psychiatrist to make the necessary observations or to decide whether they are believable.

Basically, psychiatrists assess such situations in a manner not too different from that of a layman. They establish a link between an offense and an illness by observing the irrationality of the act itself, which they then attribute to the illness from which the patient appears to be suffering. They have an advantage over the ordinary layman in that their familiarity with mental illness tends to give them better insights into how a morbid psychological state can become linked with a particular irrational pattern of behavior. But other professionals such as psychologists, social workers, and nurses have similar special experience that may be informative to those who must make the decision. The courts should attempt to obtain the best description possible of all the circumstances surrounding the case, and perhaps they can best obtain this description if expert witnesses refrain from stating at all whether they believe the defendant to be responsible. Under such circumstances the issue can be properly left to the judge and the jury, who can consider, given the circumstances of the defendant when the act was committed, whether it is appropriate to regard him or her as responsible for it.

Another alternative, which has been adopted by the English, as well as by some American jurisdictions, is to ascertain whether the person is guilty of the unlawful act with which he or she is charged. If the defendant is found guilty but mentally ill, this condition is taken into account in sentencing. Under the law the defendant may be sent to a hospital rather than to a prison but may not be kept there longer than the maximum sentence for the crime for which he or she has been found guilty. This procedure overcomes the danger that a defendant found insane will be held in a hospital for life or for a period exceeding the one that he or she would have served in prison if the defendant was found to be sane.

As a final note, we must be careful not to confuse the legal issues of dealing with mentally ill violators with what really goes on in the courts (Donnelly et al. 1962, Skolnick 1966, Blumberg 1967). As in the general administration of the criminal law, courts do not operate in practice as they do in theory. Talented psychiatrists and lawyers seek to avoid such proceedings, and the courts deal with such cases in a hurried fashion. Careful legal procedures under such conditions are often disregarded.

Civil commitment, right to treatment, right to refuse treatment, incompetency to stand trial, and the insanity defense are examples of a large number of complex legal issues affecting the fate of the mentally ill. As treatment procedures change, as our concept of rights expands, and as we become more aware of less visible abuses, a history of litigation develops in neglected areas, sometimes resulting in the development of new standards. The questions are often complex; they require research and understanding that is often lacking; and they involve professional judgments that remain uncertain. Often they raise issues of balancing the welfare of the individual with that of society and the needs of present with those of future generations.

We are increasingly sensitive about research carried out with patients, particularly those who are in institutions or other coercive situations and where there are questions about their ability to give informed consent. We face ticklish problems about a patient's right to refuse treatment, particularly when the patient is psychotic and out of touch and when failure to provide treatment creates a range of problems and costs for the facilities involved and perhaps other patients. Does a patient have rights to insist on more expensive as compared with less expensive treatment approaches, and, if so, does the state have a responsibility to pay when the patient is indigent? How does one deal with refusal of treatment when the treatment itself is built into the institutional environment as with token economies, therapeutic communities, and education for community living?

It is foolish to consider any of these issues as simple or clear-cut. Certain principles, however, are helpful in examining them and in reaching pragmatic decisions. First, whenever possible, it seems desirable to maximize the individual's right to avoid coercion. This principle is best achieved by offering choices and options. Second, when there is a conflict between the needs of individuals and the needs of an organization or society, preference should always be given to the needs of the individual unless the reasons not to are very compelling. The individual as compared with society is weak; large organizations or the community can absorb costs in uncertain situations more readily than individuals. Preference must, I believe, be given to individual needs. Last, but perhaps most essential, is the value of providing good and humane alternatives. To the extent that we do so, the requirement even to consider legal coercion is minimized.

References

AIKEN, LINDA H., "Chronic Illness and Responsive Ambulatory Care," in *The Growth of Bureaucratic Medicine: An Inquiry into the Dynamics of Patient Behavior and the Organization of Medical Care*, pp. 239–51, by David Mechanic. New York: Wiley-Interscience, 1976.

AIKEN, LINDA H., STEPHEN A. SOMERS, AND MILES F. SHORE, "Private Foundations in Health Affairs: A Case Study of the Development of a National Initiative for the Chronically Mentally Ill," *American Psychologist*, 41 (1986), 1290–95.

ALLEN, PRISCILLA, "A Consumer's View of California's Mental Health Care System," *Psychiatric Quarterly*, 48 (1974), 1–13.

ALLEN, RICHARD C., ELYCE ZENOFF FERSTER, AND HENRY WEIHOFEN, *Mental Impairment and Legal Incompetency*. Englewood Cliffs, N.J.: Prentice-Hall, 1968.

AMERICAN PSYCHIATRIC ASSOCIATION, *Diagnostic and Statistical Manual of Mental Disorders (Third Edition-Revised)* (DSM–III–R) Washington, D.C., 1987.

ANDERSEN, RONALD, ANITA FRANCIS, JOANNA LION, AND VIRGINIA S. DAUGHETY, "Psychologically Related Illness and Health Services Utilization," *Medical Care*, 15 (1977 supplement), 59–73.

ANGRIST, SHIRLEY, MARK LEFTON, SIMON DINITZ, AND BENJAMIN PASAMANICK, "Tolerance of Deviant Behaviour, Posthospital Performance Levels, and Rehospitalization," *Proceedings of Third World Congress of Psychiatry*, Vol. 1 (Montreal 1961), 237–41.

ANTHONY, JAMES C., et al., "Comparison of the Lay Diagnostic Interview Schedule and a Standardized Psychiatric Diagnosis," *Archives of General Psychiatry*, 42 (1985), 667–75.

APPELBAUM, PAUL, "Special Section on APA's Model Commitment Law," *Hospital and Community Psychiatry*, 36 (1985), 966–89.

———, "Crazy in the Streets," *Commentary*, 83 (1987), 34–39.

ARENS, RICHARD, "The Durham Rule in Action: Judicial Psychiatry and Psychiatric Justice," *Law and Society Review*, 1 (1967), 41–80.

AVNET, HELEN HERSHFIELD, *Psychiatric Insurance: Financing Short-Term Ambulatory Treatment*. New York: Group Health Insurance, 1962.

BACHRACH, LEONA L., *Deinstitutionalization: An Analytical Review and Sociological Perspective.* Washington, D.C.: U.S. Government Printing Office, DHEW Publication No. (ADM) 76–351, 1976.

BACK, KURT W., *Beyond Words: The Story of Sensitivty Training and the Encounter Movement.* New York: Russell Sage Foundation, 1972.

BANDURA, ALBERT, *Principles of Behavior Modification.* New York: Holt, Rinehart and Winston, 1969.

BART, PAULINE B., "Social Structure and Vocabularies of Discomfort: What Happened to Female Hysteria?" *Journal of Health and Social Behavior,* 9 (1968), 188–93.

BASSUK, ELLEN, et al., "The Homeless Problem," *Scientific American,* 251 (1984a), 40–45.

———, "Is Homelessness a Mental Health Problem?" *American Journal of Psychiatry,* 141 (1984), 1546–49.

BATESON, GREGORY, DON D. JACKSON, JAY HALEY, AND JOHN WEAKLAND, "Toward a Theory of Schizophrenia," *Behavioral Science,* 1 (1956), 251–64.

BAYER, RONALD, AND ROBERT L. SPITZER, "Neurosis, Psychodynamics, and DSM-III: A History of the Controversy," *Archives of General Psychiatry,* 42 (1985), 187–96.

BAZELON, DAVID L., "Justice Stumbles over Science," *Trans-Action,* 4 (1967), 8–17.

BAZZOLI, GLORIA J., "Health Care for the Indigent: Overview of Critical Issues," *Health Services Research,* 21 (1986), 353–93.

BECK, AARON T., *Cognitive Therapy and the Emotional Disorders.* New York: International Universities Press, 1976.

BECKER, HOWARD S., *Outsiders: Studies in the Sociology of Deviance.* New York: Free Press, 1963.

BELKNAP, IVAN, *Human Problems of a State Mental Hospital.* New York: McGraw-Hill, 1956.

BERGER, PHILIP A., "Medical Treatment of Mental Illness," *Science,* 200 (1978), 974–81.

BLENDON, ROBERT, et al., "Uncompensated Care by Hospitals or Public Insurance for the Poor," *New England Journal of Medicine,* 314 (1986), 1160–63.

BLEULER, MANFRED, *The Schizophrenic Disorders: Long-Term Patient and Family Studies,* (translated by S. M. Clemens). New Haven: Yale University Press, 1978.

BOCKOVEN, J. SANBOURNE, "Some Relationships between Cultural Attitudes toward Individuality and Care of the Mentally Ill: An Historical Study," in *The Patient and the Mental Hospital: Contributions of Research in the Science of Social Behavior,* eds. Milton Greenblatt, Daniel J. Levinson, and Richard H. Williams, pp. 517–26. New York: Free Press, 1957.

———, *Moral Treatment in Community Mental Health.* New York: Springer-Verlag, 1972.

BORUS, JONATHAN F., MARGARET C. OLENDZKI, LARRY KESSLER, et al., "The 'Offset Effect' of Mental Health Treatment on Ambulatory Medical Care Utilization and Charges," *Archives of General Psychiatry,* 42 (1985), 573–87.

BRADY, JO, STEVEN S. SHARFSTEIN, AND IRWIN L. MUSZYNSKI, "Trends in Private Insurance Coverage for Mental Illness," *American Journal of Psychiatry,* 143 (1986), 1276–79.

BREIER, ALAN, AND JOHN STRAUSS, "Self-Control in Psychotic Disorders," *Archives of General Psychiatry,* 40 (1983), 1141–45.

BRENNER, M. HARVEY, *Mental Illness and the Economy.* Cambridge: Harvard University Press, 1973.

BROOKS, ALEXANDER D., *Law Psychiatry and the Mental Health System.* Boston: Little, Brown, 1974.

———, "Notes on Defining the 'Dangerousness' of the Mentally Ill," in *Dangerous Behavior: A Problem in Law and Mental Health,* ed. C. Frederick, pp. 37–59. Rockville, Md.: National Institute of Mental Health, 1978.

———, "The Impact of Law on Psychiatric Hospitalization: Onslaught or Imperative Reform." *New Directions for Mental Health Services,* 4 (1979), 13–35.

———, "Defining the Dangerousness of the Mentally Ill: Involuntary Civil Commitment," in *Mentally Abnormal Offenders,* eds. M. Craft and A. Craft, pp. 280–307. London: Balliere Tindall, 1984.

———, "The Merits of Abolishing the Insanity Defense," *Annals of the American Academy of Political and Social Science,* 477 (1985), 125–36.

BROWN, BERTRAM S., "The Federal Government and Psychiatric Education: Progress, Problems, and Prospects," *New Dimensions in Mental Health.* Washington, D.C.: U.S. Government Printing Office, DHEW Publication No. (ADM) 77–511, 1977.

BROWN, GEORGE W., "Social Factors Influencing Length of Hospital Stay of Schizophrenic Patients," *British Medical Journal,* 2 (1959), 1300–302.

————, "Mental Illness," in *Applications of Social Science to Clinical Medicine and Health Policy*, eds. Linda H. Aiken and David Mechanic, pp. 175–203. New Brunswick, N.J.: Rutgers University Press, 1986.

BROWN, GEORGE W., et al., "Influence of Family Life on the Course of Schizophrenic Illness," *British Journal of Preventive and Social Medicine*, 16 (1962), 55–68.

————, *Schizophrenia and Social Care: A Comparative Follow-Up Study of 339 Schizophrenic Patients*. New York: Oxford University Press, 1966.

BROWN, GEORGE W., AND J. L. T. BIRLEY, "Crises and Life Changes and the Onset of Schizophrenia," *Journal of Health and Social Behavior*, 9 (1968), 203–14.

BROWN, GEORGE W., J. L. T. BIRLEY, AND JOHN K. WING, "Influence of Family Life on the Course of Schizophrenic Disorders: A Replication," *British Journal of Psychiatry*, 121 (1972), 241–58.

BROWN, GEORGE W., T. K. J. CRAIG AND TIRRIL HARRIS, "Depression: Distress or Disease? Some Epidemiological Considerations," *British Journal of Psychiatry*, 147 (1985), 612–22.

BROWN, GEORGE W., MAIRE NÍ BHOLCHÁIN, AND TIRRIL HARRIS, "Social Class and Psychiatric Disturbance Among Women in an Urban Population," *Sociology*, 9 (1975), 225–54.

BROWN, GEORGE W., AND TIRRIL HARRIS, *Social Origins of Depression: A Study of Psychiatric Disorder in Women*. New York: Free Press, 1978.

CAPLAN, GERALD, *Principles of Preventive Psychiatry*. New York: Basic Books, 1964.

————, "Community Psychiatry—Introduction and Overview," in *Concepts of Community Psychiatry: A Framework for Training*, ed. Stephen E. Goldston, pp. 3–18. Washington, D.C.: U.S. Government Printing Office, 1965.

CARSTAIRS, G. M., "The Social Limits of Eccentricity: An English Study," in *Culture and Mental Health: Cross-Cultural Studies*, ed. Marvin K. Opler, pp. 373–89. New York: Macmillan, 1959.

CAUDILL, WILLIAM, *The Psychiatric Hospital as a Small Society*. Cambridge: Harvard University Press, 1958.

CHAMBERS, DAVID L., "Community-Based Treatment and the Constitution: The Principle of the Least Restrictive Alternative," in *Alternatives to Mental Hospital Treatment*, eds. Leonard I. Stein and Mary Ann Test, pp. 23–39. New York: Plenum, 1978.

CHEUNG, FANNY M., AND BERNARD W. K. LAU, "Situational Variations of Help-Seeking Behavior Among Chinese Patients," *Comprehensive Psychiatry*, 23 (1982), 252–62.

CHRISTIE, RICHARD, AND FLORENCE L. GEIS, *Studies in Machiavellianism*. New York: Academic Press, 1970.

CHU, FRANKLIN D., AND SHARLAND TROTTER, *The Madness Establishment*. New York: Grossman Publishers, 1974.

CIOMPI, LUC, "Natural History of Schizophrenia in the Long Term," *British Journal of Psychiatry*, 136 (1980), 413–20.

CLAUSEN, JOHN A., "Mental Disorders," in *Contemporary Social Problems: An Introduction to the Sociology of Deviant Behavior and Social Disorganization*, eds. Robert K. Merton and Robert A. Nisbet, pp. 127–80. New York: Harcourt Brace Jovanovich, 1961.

————, "Mental Disorder," in *Handbook of Medical Sociology*, 3rd ed., eds. Howard E. Freeman, Sol Levine, and Leo G. Reeder, pp. 97–112. Englewood Cliffs, N.J.: Prentice-Hall, 1979.

————, "Stigma and Mental Disorder: Phenomena and Terminology," *Psychiatry*, 44 (1981), 287–96.

CLAUSEN, JOHN A., AND MARIAN RADKE YARROW, eds., "The Impact of Mental Illness on the Family," *The Journal of Social Issues*, 11 no. 4 (1955).

CLAUSEN, JOHN A., AND CAROL L. HUFFINE, "Sociocultural and Sociopsychological Factors Affecting Social Responses to Mental Disorder," *Journal of Health and Social Behavior*, 16 (1975), 405–20.

CLAUSEN, JOHN A., NANCY G. PFEFFER, AND CAROL L. HUFFINE, "Help-Seeking in Severe Mental Illness," in *Symptoms, Illness Behavior and Help-Seeking*, ed. David Mechanic, pp. 135–55. New Brunswick: Rutgers University Press, 1982.

CLEARY, PAUL, AND DAVID MECHANIC, "Sex Differences in Psychological Distress among Married People," *Journal of Health and Social Behavior*, 24 (1983), 111–21.

CLONINGER, C. ROBERT, et al., "The Principles of Genetics in Relation to Psychiatry," in *Handbook of Psychiatry 5: The Scientific Foundations of Psychiatry*, ed. M. Shepherd, pp. 34–66. New York: Cambridge University Press, 1985.

COBB, SIDNEY, "Social Support as a Moderator of Life Stress," *Psychosomatic Medicine*, 38 (1976), 300–14.

COCOZZA, JOSEPH J., AND HENRY J. STEADMAN, "Prediction in Psychiatry: An Example of Misplaced Confidence in Experts," *Social Problems*, 25 (1978), 265–76.

COHEN, SHELDON, AND S. LEONARD SYME, *Social Support and Health.* Orlando: Academic Press, 1985.

COLEMAN, JULES V., AND DONALD L. PATRICK, "Psychiatry and General Health Care," *American Journal of Public Health*, 68 (1978), 451–57.

COLOMBOTOS, JOHN, CORINNE KIRCHNER, AND MICHAEL MILLMAN, "Physicians View National Health Insurance: A National Study," *Medical Care*, 13 (1975), 369–96.

CONTE, HOPE R., et al., "Combined Psychotherapy and Pharmacotherapy for Depression," *Archives of General Psychiatry*, 43 (1986), 471–79.

COOPER, A. B., AND D. F. EARLY, "Evolution in the Mental Hospital: Review of a Hospital Population," *British Medical Journal* 1 (1961), 1600–1603.

CORNEY, ROSLYN H., "The Effectiveness of Attached Social Workers in the Management of Depressed Female Patients in General Practice," *Psychological Medicine*, (1984), monograph supplement 6.

COSER, ROSE LAUB, *Training in Ambiguity: Learning Through Doing in a Mental Hospital.* New York: Free Press, 1979.

CRANDELL, DEWITT L., AND BRUCE P. DOHRENWEND, "Some Relations Among Psychiatric Symptoms, Organic Illness, and Social Class," *American Journal of Psychiatry*, 123 (1967), 1527–38.

CROSS, K. W., et al., "A Survey of Chronic Patients in a Mental Hospital," *British Journal of Psychiatry*, 103 (1957), 146–71.

CUMMINGS, NICHOLAS A., AND WILLIAM T. FOLLETTE, "Psychiatric Services and Medical Utilization in a Prepaid Health Plan Setting: Part II," *Medical Care*, 6 (1968), 31–41.

CURTIS, RICK, "The Role of State Governments in Assuring Access to Care," *Inquiry*, 23 (1986), 277–85.

DAVIS, ANN E., SIMON DINITZ, AND BENJAMIN PASAMANICK, "The Prevention of Hospitalization in Schizophrenia: Five Years After and Experimental Program," *American Journal of Orthopsychiatry*, 42 (1972), 375–88.

DAVIS, ANN, BENJAMIN PASAMANICK, AND SIMON DINITZ, *Schizophrenics in the New Custodial Community: Five Years After the Experiment.* Columbus: Ohio State University, 1974.

DAVIS, FRED, *Passage Through Crisis: Polio Victims and Their Families.* Indianapolis: Bobbs-Merrill, 1963.

DAVIS, JAMES A., *Education for Positive Mental Health: A Review of Existing Research and Recommendations for Future Studies.* Chicago: Aldine, 1965.

DEAR, MICHAEL J., AND S. M. TAYLOR, *Not on Our Street.* London: Pion, 1982.

DENNISON, CHARLES F., "1984 Summary: National Discharge Survey," *Advanced Data From Vital and Health Statistics*, No. 112, DHHS Publication No. (PHS) 85–1250. Hyattsville, Md.: National Center for Health Statistics, 1985.

DEUTSCH, ALBERT, *The Mentally Ill in America: A History of Their Care and Treatment from Colonial Times*, 2nd ed. New York: Columbia University Press, 1949.

DOHRENWEND, BARBARA SNELL, AND BRUCE P. DOHRENWEND, eds., *Stressful Life Events: Their Nature and Effects.* New York: Wiley-Interscience, 1974.

———, *Stressful Life Events and Their Contexts.* New Brunswick, N.J.: Rutgers University Press, 1981.

DOHRENWEND, BRUCE P., "Some Issues in the Definition and Measurement of Psychiatric Disorders in General Populations," in *Proceedings of the 14th National Meeting of the Public Health Conference on Records and Statistics*, pp. 480–89. Washington, D.C.: National Center for Health Statistics, Health Resources Adminsitration, 1973.

———, "Sociocultural and Social-Psychological Factors in the Genesis of Mental Disorders," *Journal of Health and Social Behavior*, 16 (1975), 365–92.

DOHRENWEND, BRUCE P., AND BARBARA SNELL DOHRENWEND, *Social Status and Psychological Disorder: A Causal Inquiry.* New York: Wiley-Interscience, 1969.

———, "Psychiatric Disorders in Urban Settings," in *American Handbook of Psychiatry*, 2nd ed., Vol. 2., ed. Silvano Arieti, pp. 424–47. New York: Basic Books, 1974a.

———, "Social and Cultural Influences on Psychopathology," *Annual Review of Psychology*, Vol. 25, pp. 417–52. Palo Alto, Calif.: Annual Reviews, Inc. 1974b.

DOHRENWEND, BRUCE P., et al., "What Psychiatric Screening Scales Measure in the General Population, Part I: Jerome Frank's Concept of Demoralization," unpublished manuscript, 1979.

———, *Mental Illness in the United States: Epidemiological Estimates.* New York: Praeger, 1980.

DOLAN, LAWRENCE W., *Recent Trends in the Evolution of State Psychiatric Hospital Systems.* New Brunswick, N.J.: The Rutgers-Princeton Program in Mental Health Research, 1986.

DOLLARD, JOHN, AND NEAL E. MILLER, *Personality and Psychotherapy: An Analysis in Terms of Learning, Thinking, and Culture.* New York: McGraw-Hill, 1950.

DONALDSON, KENNETH, *Insanity Inside Out.* New York: Crown Publishers, 1976.

DONNELLY, RICHARD C., et al., *Criminal Law.* New York: Free Press, 1962.

DORWART, ROBERT A., et al., "The Promise and Pitfalls of Purchase-of-Service Contracts," *Hospital and Community Psychiatry*, 37 (1986), 875–78.

DUHL, LEONARD J., ed., *The Urban Condition: People and Policy in the Metropolis.* New York: Basic Books, 1963.

EATON, WILLIAM W., LARRY G. KESSLER, eds., *Epidemiologic Field Methods in Psychiatry: The NIMH Epidemiologic Catchment Area Program.* Orlando, Fla.: Academic Press, 1985.

ELDER, GLEN H., JR., *Children of the Great Depression: Social Change in Life Experience.* Chicago: University of Chicago Press, 1974.

ELLIS, RANDALL P., AND THOMAS G. MCGUIRE, *Cost-Sharing and Demand for Ambulatory Mental Health Services: Interpreting the Results of the Rand Health Insurance Study.* Boston, MA: Boston University, Department of Economics, 1984.

———, "Cost-Sharing and Patterns of Mental Health Care Utilization," *Journal of Human Resources*, 21 (1986), 359–79.

ENGLISH, JOSEPH T., et al., "Diagnosis-Related Groups and General Hospital Psychiatry: The APA Study," *American Journal of Psychiatry*, 143 (1986), 131–39.

ENNIS, BRUCE J., *Prisoners of Psychiatry: Mental Patients, Psychiatrists, and the Law.* New York: Harcourt Brace Jovanovich, 1972.

ERIKSON, KAI T., *Wayward Puritans: A Study in the Sociology of Deviance.* New York: John Wiley, 1966.

ESSEN-MÖELLER, E., "Individual Traits and Morbidity in a Swedish Rural Population," *Acta Psychiatrica et Neurologica Scandinavica Supplementa*, 100 (1956).

ESTROFF, SUE, *Making It Crazy: An Ethnography of Psychiatric Clients in an American Community.* Berkeley and Los Angeles, Calif.: University of California Press, 1981.

FAIRWEATHER, GEORGE W., DAVID H. SANDERS, HUGO MAYNARD, DAVID L. CRESSLER, WITH DOROTHY BLECK, *Community Life for the Mentally Ill: An Alternative to Institutional Care.* Chicago: Aldine, 1969.

FALLOON, IAN, R. H., et al., "Family Management in the Prevention of Exacerbations of Schizophrenia: a Controlled Study," *New England Journal of Medicine*, 306 (1982), 1437–40.

———, *Family Care of Schizophrenia.* New York: Guilford Press, 1984.

———, "Family Management in the Prevention of Morbidity of Schizophrenia," *Archives of General Psychiatry*, 42 (1985), 887–97.

FELDMAN, RONALD, et al., *Children at Risk: In the Web of Parental Mental Illness.* New Brunswick, N.J.: Rutgers University Press, 1987.

FELIX, ROBERT H., *Mental Illness: Progress and Prospects.* New York: Columbia University Press, 1967.

FISHER, G. A., P. R. BENSON, AND R. C. TESSLER, "Family Response to Mental Illness: Developments Since Deinstitutionalization," paper presented at the annual meeting for the Society of Social Problems, New York, 1986.

FOLEY, HENRY A., AND STEVEN SHARFSTEIN, *Madness and Government: Who Cares for the Mentally Ill?* Washington, D.C.: American Psychiatric Press, 1983.

FOLLETTE, WILLIAM, AND NICHOLAS A. CUMMINGS, "Psychiatric Services and Medical Utilization in a Prepaid Health Plan Setting," *Medical Care*, 5 (1967), 25–35.

FOLLMANN, JOSEPH F., JR., *Insurance Coverage for Mental Illness.* New York: American Management Associations, Inc., 1970.

FOUCAULT, MICHEL, *Madness and Civilization: A History of Insanity in the Age of Reason.* New York: Pantheon, 1965.

FRANK, GEORGE H., "The Role of the Family in the Development of Psychopathology," *Psychological Bulletin*, 64 (1965), 191–205.

FRANK, JEROME D., *Persuasion and Healing: A Comparative Study of Psychotherapy*, rev. ed. New York: Schocken Books, Inc., 1974.

FRANK, RICHARD G., AND JUDITH R. LAVE, "The Impact of Medicaid Benefit Design on Length of Hospital Stay and Patient Transfers," *Hospital and Community Psychiatry*, 36 (1985), 749–53.

FRANK, RICHARD G., AND THOMAS G. McGUIRE, "A Review of Studies of the Impact of Insurance on the Demand and Utilization of Specialty Mental Health Services," *Health Services Research*, 21 (1986), 241–65.

FRANKLIN, JACK L., et al., "An Evaluation of Case Management." *American Journal of Public Health*, 77 (1987), 674–78.

FREEDMAN, RUTH I. AND ANN MORAN, "Wanderers in a Promised Land: The Chronically Mentally Ill and Deinstitutionalization," *Medical Care Supplement*, 22 (1984).

FREEMAN, HOWARD E., AND OZZIE G. SIMMONS, *The Mental Patient Comes Home*. New York: John Wiley, 1963.

FREEMAN, R. B., AND B. HALL, "Permanent Homelessness in America?" National Bureau of Economic Research, Working Paper No. 2013, unpublished, 1986.

FREIDSON, ELIOT, *Professional Dominance: The Social Structure of Medical Care*. New York: Lieber-Atherton, 1970.

FRIED, MARC, "Effects of Social Change on Mental Health," *American Journal of Orthopsychiatry*, 34 (1964), 3–28.

FRIEDMAN, MEYER, AND RAY H. ROSENMAN, *Type A Behavior and Your Heart*. New York: Knopf, 1974.

FRISMAN, LINDA K., THOMAS G. McGUIRE, AND MARGO L. ROSENBACH, "Costs of Mandates for Outpatient Mental Health Care in Private Health Insurance," *Archives of General Psychiatry*, 42 (1985), 558–61.

FROMM, ERICH, *The Sane Society*. New York: Holt, Rinehart and Winston, 1955.

FULLERTON, DONALD T., FRANCIS N. LOHRENZ, AND GREGORY R. NYCZ, "Utilization of Prepaid Services by Patients with Psychiatric Diagnoses," *American Journal of Psychiatry*, 133 (1976), 1057–60.

FURMAN, SYLVAN S., *Community Mental Health Services in Northern Europe*. Washington, D.C.: U.S. Government Printing Office, Public Health Service Publication No. 1407, 1965.

GARDNER, ELMER A., "Implications of Psychoactive Drug Therapy," *The New England Journal of Medicine*, 290 (1974), 800–801.

GINSBERG, SUSANNAH M., AND GEORGE W. BROWN, "No Time for Depression: A Study of Help-Seeking among Mothers of Preschool Children," in *Symptoms, Illness Behavior and Help-Seeking*, ed. David Mechanic, pp. 87–114. New Brunswick: Rutgers University Press, 1982.

GINZBERG, ELI, JAMES K. ANDERSON, SOL W. GINSBURG, AND JOHN L. HERMA, *The Ineffective Soldier: Lessons for Management and the Nation*, 3 vols. New York: Columbia University Press, 1959.

GLASS, ALBERT J., "Psychotherapy in the Combat Zone," in *Symposium on Stress*, pp. 284–94, Washington, D.C.: Army Medical Service Graduate School, Walter Reed Army Medical Hospital, 1953.

————, "Observations upon the Epidemiology of Mental Illness in Troops During Warfare," in *Symposium on Preventive and Social Psychiatry*, pp. 185–98. Washington, D.C.: U.S. Government Printing Office, Walter Reed Army Institute of Research, 1958.

GLUECK, SHELDON, *Law and Psychiatry*. London: Tavistock, 1963.

GOFFMAN, ERVING, *Asylums: Essays on the Social Situation of Mental Patients and Other Inmates*. Garden City, N.Y.: Doubleday (Anchor), 1961.

GOLDBERG, DAVID, AND PETER HUXLEY, *Mental Illness in the Community: The Pathways to Psychiatric Care*. New York: Tavistock Publications, 1980.

GOLDBERG, IRVING D., GOLDIE KRANTZ, AND BEN Z. LOCKE, "Effect of a Short-Term Outpatients Psychiatric Therapy Benefit on the Utilization of Medical Services in a Prepaid Group Practice Medical Program," *Medical Care*, 8 (1970), 419–28.

GOLDHAMER, HERBERT, AND ANDREW W. MARSHALL, *Psychosis and Civilization: Two Studies in the Frequency of Mental Disease*. New York: The Free Press, 1953.

GOLDMAN, HOWARD H., ANTOINETTE A. GATTOZZI, AND CARL A. TAUBE, "Defining and Counting the Chronically Mentally Ill," *Hospital and Community Psychiatry*, 32 (1981), 21–27.

GOLDMAN, HOWARD H., JUDITH FEDER, AND WILLIAM SCANLON, "Chronic Mental Patients in Nursing Homes: Re-Examining Data from the National Nursing Home Survey," *Hospital and Community Psychiatry*, 37 (1986), 269–72.

GOLDSTEIN, ABRAHAM, *The Insanity Defense.* New Haven, Conn.: Yale University Press, 1967.

GOTTESMAN, IRVING I., "Schizophrenia and Genetics: Where Are You? Are You Sure?," in *The Nature of Schizophrenia: New Approaches to Research and Treatment*, eds. L. Wynne et al., pp. 59–69. New York: Wiley, 1978.

GOTTESMAN, IRVING I., AND SHIELDS, JAMES, *Schizophrenia: The Epigenetic Puzzle.* New York: Cambridge University Press, 1982.

GRAD, JACQUELINE C., "A Two-Year Follow-Up," in *Community Mental Health: An International Perspective*, eds. Richard H. Williams and Lucy D. Ozarin, pp. 429–54. San Francisco: Jossey-Bass, 1968.

GRAD, JACQUELINE C., AND PETER SAINSBURY, "Evaluating the Community Psychiatric Service in Chichester: Results," *Milbank Memorial Fund Quarterly*, 44 (1966), 246–78.

GREENLEY, JAMES R., "Social Control and Expressed Emotion," *Journal of Nervous and Mental Disease*, 174 (1986), 24–30.

GREENLEY, JAMES R., AND DAVID MECHANIC, "Social Selection in Seeking Help for Psychological Problems," *Journal of Health and Social Behavior*, 17 (1976), 249–62.

GREENLEY, JAMES R., JOSEPH C. KEPECS, AND WILLIAM H. HENRY, "A Comparison of Psychiatric Practice in Chicago in 1962 and 1973," unpublished manuscript, Department of Psychiatry, University of Wisconsin, Madison, 1979.

GREENLEY, JAMES R., DAVID MECHANIC, AND PAUL D. CLEARY, "Seeking Help for Psychological Problems: A Replication and Extension," *Medical Care*, 25 (1987), 1113–28.

GROB, GERALD N., *The State and the Mentally Ill: A History of Worcester State Hospital in Massachusetts, 1830–1920.* Chapel Hill: University of North Carolina Press, 1966.

———, *Mental Institutions in America: Social Policy to 1875.* New York: Free Press, 1973.

———, "Rediscovering Asylums: The Unhistorical History of the Mental Hospital," *The Hastings Center Report*, 7 (1977), 33–41.

———, *Mental Illness and American Society, 1875–1940.* Princeton: Princeton University Press, 1983.

———, "The Forging of Mental Health Policy in America: World War II to New Frontier," *Journal of the History of Medicine and Allied Sciences*, 42 (1987), 410–46.

GRONFEIN, WILLIAM, "Incentives and Intentions in Mental Health Policy: A Comparison of the Medicaid and Community Mental Health Programs," *Journal of Health and Social Behavior*, 26 (1985), 192–206.

GROUP FOR THE ADVANCEMENT OF PSYCHIATRY, *Preventive Psychiatry in the Armed Forces: With Some Implications for Civilian Use.* New York: Group for the Advancement of Psychiatry, Report No. 47, 1960.

GUDEMAN, JOHN E., AND MILES F. SHORE, "Beyond Deinstitutionalization: A New Class of Facilities for the Mentally Ill," *New England Journal of Medicine*, 311 (1984), 832–36.

GURIN, GERALD, JOSEPH VEROFF, AND SHEILA FELD, *Americans View Their Mental Health.* New York: Basic Books, 1960.

HAGNELL, OLLE, *A Prospective Study of the Incidence of Mental Disorder.* Stockholm: Svenska Bokförlaget Norstedts-Bonniers, 1966.

HALLECK, SEYMOUR L., AND MILTON H. MILLER, "The Psychiatric Consultation: Questionable Social Precedents of Some Current Practices," *The American Journal of Psychiatry*, 120 (1963), 164–69.

HALLECK, SEYMOUR L., *The Politics of Therapy.* New York: Science House, 1971.

———, *The Treatment of Emotional Disorders.* New York: Aronson, 1978.

HAMBURG, DAVID A., CURTIS P. ARTZ, ERIC REISS, et al., "Clinical Importance of Emotional Problems in the Care of Patients with Burns," *New England Journal of Medicine*, 248 (1953), 355–59.

HARDING, COURTENAY M., JOSEPH ZUBIN, AND JOHN S. STRAUSS, "Chronicity in Schizophrenia: Fact, Partial Facts or Artifact?," *Hospital and Community Psychiatry*, 38 (1987), 477–86.

HARDING, COURTENAY M., GEORGE W. BROOKS, AND TAKAMARU ASHIKAGA, et al., "The Vermont Longitudinal Study of Persons with Severe Mental Illness: I. Methodology, Study Sample, and Overall Status," *American Journal of Psychiatry*, 144 (1987a), 718–26.

———, "The Vermont Longitudinal Study of Persons with Severe Mental Illness: II. Long-

Term Outcome of Subjects Who Retrospectively Met DSM-III Criteria for Schizophrenia," *American Journal of Psychiatry,* 144 (1987b), 727–35.

HARRIS, TIRRIL, GEORGE BROWN, AND ANTONIA BIFULCO, "Loss of Parent in Childhood and Adult Psychiatric Disorder: The Role of Social Class Position and Premarital Pregnancy," *Psychological Medicine,* 17 (1987), 163–83.

HATFIELD, AGNES, ed., *Families of the Mentally Ill: Meeting the Challenges,* New Directions for Mental Health Services, No. 34. San Francisco: Jossey-Bass, 1987.

HENRY, WILLIAM E., JOHN H. SIMS, AND S. LEE SPRAY, *The Fifth Profession: Becoming a Psychotherapist.* San Francisco: Jossey-Bass, 1971.

_____, *Public and Private Lives of Psychotherapists.* San Francisco: Jossey-Bass, 1973.

HESS, JOHN H., AND HERBERT E. THOMAS, "Incompetency to Stand Trial: Procedures, Results, and Problems," *American Journal of Psychiatry,* 119 (1963), 713–20.

HESTON, LEONARD L., "Psychiatric Disorders in Foster Home Reared Children of Schizophrenic Mothers," *British Journal of Psychiatry,* 112 (1966), 819–25.

HEWITT ASSOCIATES, *Company Practices in Health Care Management.* Lincolnshire, Ill., 1984.

HIDAY, VIRGINIA, AND RODNEY GOODMAN, "The Least Restrictive Alternative to Involuntary Hospitalization, Outpatient Commitment: Its Use and Effectiveness," *Journal of Psychiatry and Law,* 10 (1982), 81–96.

HIDAY, VIRGINIA, AND TERESA SCHEID-COOK, "The North Carolina Experience with Outpatient Commitment: A Critical Appraisal," paper presented at the International Congress of Law and Psychiatry, Montreal, 1986.

HOENIG, J., AND MARIAN W. HAMILTON, "The Burden on the Household in an Extramural Psychiatric Service," in *New Aspects of the Mental Health Services,* eds. Hugh Freeman and James Farndale, pp. 612–35. Elmsford, N.Y.: Pergamon Press, 1967.

HOGAN, RICHARD, "It Can't Happen Here: Community Opposition to Group Homes," *Sociological Focus,* 19 (1986a), 361–74.

_____, "Gaining Community Support for Group Homes," *Community Mental Health Journal,* 22 (1986b), 117–26.

HOLLINGSHEAD, AUGUST B., AND FREDERICK C. REDLICH, *Social Class and Mental Illness: A Community Study.* New York: John Wiley, 1958.

HOOVER COMMISSION, *Task Force Report on Federal Medical Services,* February 1955.

HORGAN, CONSTANCE M. AND STEPHEN F. JENCKS, "Research on Psychiatric Classification and Payment Systems," *Medical Care,* 25 Supplement (1987), 522–36.

HOULT, JOHN, "Replicating the Mendota Model in Australia," *Hospital and Community Psychiatry,* 38 (1987), 565.

HOWE, CAROL, AND JAMES HOWE, "The National Alliance for the Mentally Ill: History and Ideology," in *Families of the Mentally Ill: Meeting the Challenges,* New Directions for Mental Health Services, No. 34, ed. A. B. Hatfield, pp. 23–33. San Francisco: Jossey-Bass, 1987.

HUBER, G., G. GROSS, AND R. SCHEUTTLER, *Schizophrenia.* Berlin: Springer-Verlag, 1979.

INSTITUTE OF MEDICINE, *Mental Health Services in General Health Care.* Washington, D.C.: National Academy of Sciences, 1979.

INSTITUTE FOR SOCIAL RESEARCH, *Newsletter,* pp. 4–5. Ann Arbor: University of Michigan, 1979.

JAHODA, MARIE, *Current Concepts of Positive Mental Health.* New York: Basic Books, 1958.

JENCKS, STEPHEN F., CONSTANCE HORGAN AND CARL A. TAUBE, "Evidence on Provider Response to Prospective Payment," *Medical Care* 25 Supplement (1987), 537–41.

JOHNSON, DALE L., PHILIP G. HANSON, AND PAUL ROTHAUS, "Human Relations Training as a Response to a Need for Effective and Economical Psychiatric Treatment," in *New Aspects of the Mental Health Services,* eds. Hugh Freeman and James Farndale, pp. 381–91. Elmsford, N.Y.: Pergamon Press, 1967.

JOINT COMMISSION ON MENTAL ILLNESS AND HEALTH, *Action for Mental Health.* New York: Science Editions, 1961.

JONES, KENNETH R., AND THOMAS VISCHI, "Impact of Alcohol, Drug Abuse, and Mental Health Treatment on Medical Care Utilization: A Review of the Research Literature," *Medical Care Supplement* 17, No. 12 (1979).

KADUSHIN, CHARLES, "Individual Decisions to Undertake Psychotherapy," *Administrative Science Quarterly,* 3 (1958), 379–411.

————, "Social Distance Between Client and Professional," *American Journal of Sociology,* 67 (1962), 517–31.

————, "The Friends and Supporters of Psychotherapy: On Social Circles in Urban Life," *American Sociological Review,* 31 (1966), 786–802.

KALLMAN, FRANZ J., "The Genetic Theory of Schizophrenia," in *Personality in Nature, Society, and Culture* (2nd ed.), eds. Clyde Kluckhohn and Henry A. Murray, pp. 80–99. New York: Knopf, 1953.

KATZ, JAY, JOSEPH GOLDSTEIN, AND ALAN M. DERSHOWITZ, *Psychoanalysis, Psychiatry, and Law.* New York: Free Press, 1967.

KEELER, EMMETT B., et al., *The Demand for Episodes of Mental Health Services* (R-3432-NIMH). Santa Monica, Calif.: Rand Corporation, 1986.

KELLAM, SHEPPARD G., JUNE L. SCHMELZER, AND AUDREY BERMAN, "Variation in the Atmospheres of Psychiatric Wards," *Archives of General Psychiatry,* 14 (1966), 561–70.

KENDELL, R. E., I. F. BROCKINGTON, AND J. P. LEFF, "Prognostic Implications of Six Alternative Definitions of Schizophrenia," *Archives of General Psychiatry,* 36 (1979), 25–31.

KESSLER, RONALD C., "A Disaggregation of the Relationship Between Socio-Economic Status and Psychological Distress," *American Sociological Review,* 47 (1982), 752–64.

KESSLER, RONALD C., AND NEIGHBORS, HAROLD W., "A New Perspective on the Relationships among Race, Social Class, and Psychological Distress," *Journal of Health and Social Behavior,* 27 (1986), 107–15.

KETY, SEYMOUR, "Concluding Comments," in *The Nature of Schizophrenia: New Approaches to Research and Treatment,* eds. L. Wynne et al., pp. 156–57. New York: Wiley, 1978.

————, "The Interface between Neuroscience and Psychiatry," in *Psychiatry and Its Related Disciplines,* eds. R. Rosenberg, F. Schulsinger and E. Strömgren, pp. 21–28. Copenhagen: World Psychiatric Association, 1986.

KIESLER, CHARLES A., "Mental Hospitals and Alternative Care," *American Psychologist,* 37 (1982), 349–60.

KIESLER, CHARLES A., AND AMY E. SIBULKIN, *Mental Hospitalization: Myths and Facts about a National Crisis.* Newbury Park, Calif.: Sage Publications, 1987.

KLEINMAN, ARTHUR, "Neurasthenia and Depression: A Study of Somatization and Culture in China," *Culture, Medicine and Psychiatry,* 2 (1982), 117–90.

————, *Social Origins of Distress and Disease: Depression, Neurasthenia and Pain in Modern China.* New Haven: Yale University Press, 1986.

KLEINMAN, ARTHUR, AND DAVID MECHANIC, "Some Observations of Mental Illness and Its Treatment in the People's Republic of China," *The Journal of Nervous and Mental Disease,* 167 (1979), 267–74.

KLERMAN GERALD L., et al., *Manual for Short-Term Interpersonal Psychotherapy (IPT) of Depression.* New York: Basic Books, 1984.

KOCH, HUGO, "Utilization of Psychotropic Drugs in Office-Based Ambulatory Care, National Ambulatory Medical Care Survey, 1980 and 1981," *Advanced Data,* No 90. DHHS Publication No. (PHS) 851250. Hyattsville: National Center for Health Statistics, 1983.

KOHN, MELVIN L., "Social Class and Schizophrenia: A Critical Review and a Reformulation," *Schizophrenic Bulletin,* 7 (1973), 60–79.

————, *Class and Conformity: A Study in Values,* 2nd ed. Chicago: University of Chicago Press, 1977.

KOHN, MELVIN L., AND JOHN A. CLAUSEN, "Social Isolation and Schizophrenia," *American Sociological Review,* 20 (1955), 265–73.

KOLATA, GINA, "Manic-Depression Gene Tied to Chromosome II." *Science,* 235 (1987), 1139–40.

KOLB, LAWRENCE C., *Modern Clinical Psychiatry,* 9th ed. Philadelphia: Saunders, 1977.

KORBASA, SUZANNE C., "Stressful Life Events, Personality, and Health: An Inquiry into Hardiness." *Journal Personality and Social Psychology,* 37 (1979), 1–11.

KRAMER, BERNARD M., *Day Hospital: A Study of Partial Hospitalization in Psychiatry.* New York: Grune and Stratton, 1962.

KRAMER, MORTON, *Psychiatric Services and the Changing Institutional Scene, 1950–1985.* National Institute of Mental Health, Series B., No. 12. Washington, D.C.: U.S. Government Printing Office, (ADM) 77–433, 1977.

KRAMER, MORTON, SEYMOUR PERLIN, FRANK KIESLER, ISADORE TUERK, AND PAUL V.

LEMKAU, "General Discussion," in "Psychiatric Epidemiology and Mental Health Planning," eds. Russell R. Monroe, Gerald D. Klee, and Eugene B. Brody. *Psychiatric Research Reports,* 22 (1967), 357–64.

KREISMAN, DOLORES, AND VIRGINIA JOY, "Family Response to the Mental Illness of a Relative: A Review of the Literature," *Schizophrenia Bulletin,* 10 (1974), 34–57.

KRINGLEN, EINAR, "Adult Offspring of Two Psychotic Parents, with Special Reference to Schizophrenia," in *The Nature of Schizophrenia: New Approaches to Research and Treatment,* eds. L. Wynne et al., pp. 9–24. New York: Wiley, 1978.

KULKA, RICHARD A., JOSEPH VEROFF, AND ELIZABETH DOUVAN, "Social Class and the Use of Professional Help for Personal Problems: 1957 and 1976," *Journal of Health and Social Behavior,* 20 (1979), 2–17.

⸻, *Mental Health in America. Patterns of Help-Seeking from 1957 to 1976.* New York: Basic Books, 1981.

LAMB, H. RICHARD, "The New Asylums in the Community," *Archives of General Psychiatry,* 36 (1979), 129–34.

⸻, ed., *The Homeless Mentally Ill: A Task Force Report of the American Psychiatric Association.* Washington, D.C.: American Psychiatric Association, 1984.

LAMB, H. RICHARD, AND ROBERT W. GRANT, "The Mentally Ill in an Urban County Jail," *Archives of General Psychology,* 39 (1982), 17–22.

LAMB, H. RICHARD AND MARK J. MILLS, "Needed Changes in Law and Procedure for the Chronically Mentally Ill." *Hospital and Community Psychiatry,* 37 (1986), 475–80.

LANGNER, THOMAS S. "A Twenty-Two Item Screening Score of Psychiatric Symptoms Indicating Impairment," *Journal of Health and Human Behavior,* 3 (1962), 269–76.

LANGNER, THOMAS S., AND STANLEY T. MICHAEL, *Life Stress and Mental Health: The Midtown Manhattan Study.* New York: The Free Press, 1963.

LAZARUS, RICHARD S., *Psychological Stress and the Coping Process.* New York: McGraw-Hill, 1966.

LAZARUS, RICHARD S., AND SUSAN FOLKMAN, *Stress, Appraisal and Coping.* New York: Springer-Verlag, 1984.

LEAF, PHILIP J., "Legal Intervention into a Mental Health System: The Outcomes of *Wyatt* v. *Stickney,*" unpublished Ph.D. dissertation, Department of Sociology, University of Wisconsin, Madison, 1978a.

⸻, "The Medical Marketplace and Public Interest Law: Part II. Alabama After Wyatt: PIL Intervention into a Mental Health Services Delivery System," in *Public Interest Law: An Economic and Institutional Analysis,* by Burton A. Weisbrod in collaboration with Joel F. Handler and Neil K. Komesar, pp. 374–94. Berkeley: University of California Press, 1978b.

LEAF, PHILIP J., et al., "Contact with Health Professionals for the Treatment of Psychiatric and Emotional Problems," *Medical Care,* 23 (1985), 1322–37.

LEFF, JULIAN, "Social and Psychological Causes of Acute Attack," in *Schizophrenia: Toward a New Synthesis,* ed. John Wing, pp. 139–65. New York: Grune and Stratton, 1978.

LEFF, JULIAN, et al., "A Controlled Trial of Social Intervention in the Families of Schizophrenic Patients," *British Journal of Psychiatry,* 141 (1982), 121–34.

LEFF, JULIAN, AND VAUGHN, CHRISTINE, *Expressed Emotion in Families.* New York: Guilford Press, 1985.

LEIGHTON, ALEXANDER, "Is Social Environment a Cause of Psychiatric Disorder?" in "Psychiatric Epidemiology and Mental Health Planning," eds. Russell R. Monroe, Gerald D. Klee, and Eugene B. Brody. *Psychiatric Research Reports,* 22 (1967), 337–45.

LEIGHTON, DOROTHEA C., JOHN S. HARDING, DAVID B. MACKLIN, ALLISTER M. MACMILLAN, AND ALEXANDER H. LEIGHTON, *The Character of Danger: Psychiatric Symptoms in Selected Communities.* New York: Basic Books, 1963.

LEMERT, EDWIN M., *Social Pathology: A Systematic Approach to the Theory of Sociopathic Behavior.* New York: McGraw-Hill, 1951.

LEVENTHAL, HOWARD, "Findings and Theory in the Study of Fear Communications," in *Advances in Experimental Social Psychology,* Vol. 5, ed. Leonard Berkowitz, pp. 119–86. New York: Academic Press, 1970.

⸻, "The Consequences of Depersonalization during Illness and Treatment: An Information-Processing Model," in *Humanizing Health Care,* pp. 119–61, eds. Jan Howard and Anselm Strauss. New York: Wiley-Interscience, 1975.

LEWIS, AUBREY, "Health as a Social Concept," *British Journal of Sociology*, 4 (1953), 109–24.

LEWIS, CHARLES E., RASHI FEIN, AND DAVID MECHANIC, *A Right to Health: The Problem of Access to Primary Medical Care*. New York: Wiley-Interscience, 1976.

LIDZ, THEODORE, *The Family and Human Adaptation: Three Lectures*. London: The Hogarth Press, 1963.

LINK, BRUCE G., AND FRANCIS T. CULLEN, "Contact with the Mentally Ill and Perceptions of How Dangerous They Are." *Journal of Health and Social Behavior*, 27 (1986), 289–303.

LINN, LAWRENCE S., "Social Characteristics and Social Interaction in the Utilization of a Psychiatric Outpatient Clinic," *Journal of Health and Social Behavior*, 8 (1967), 3–14.

―――, "The Mental Hospital in the Patient's Phenomenal World," unpublished Ph.D. dissertation, Department of Sociology, University of Wisconsin, Madison, 1968.

LINN, MARGARET W. et al., "Nursing Home Care as an Alternative to Psychiatric Hospitalization." *Archives of General Psychiatry*, 42 (1985), 544–51.

LOHR, KATHLEEN N., et al., *Use of Medical Care in the Rand Health Insurance Experiment: Diagnosis- and Service-Specific Analyses in a Randomized Controlled Trial*, (R-3469-HHS). Santa Monica, Calif.: Rand Publications, 1986.

LUDWIG, ARNOLD M., AND FRANK FARRELLY, "The Code of Chronicity," *Archives of General Psychiatry*, 15 (1966), 562–68.

LUFT, HAROLD S. *Health Maintenance Organizations: Dimensions of Performance*. New York: Wiley-Interscience, 1981.

MACCOBY, ELEANOR E., "The Choice of Variables in the Study of Socialization," *Sociometry*, 24 (1961), 357–71.

MANIS, JEROME G., MILTON J. BRAWER, CHESTER L. HUNT, AND LEONARD C. KERCHER, "Validating a Mental Health Scale," *American Sociological Review*, 28 (1963), 108–16.

―――, "Estimating the Prevalence of Mental Illness," *American Sociological Review*, 29 (1964), 84–89.

MANNING, WILLIAM G., et al., "A Controlled Trial of the Effect of a Prepaid Group Practice on Use of Services," *New England Journal of Medicine*, 310 (1984), 1505–10.

―――, *Use of Outpatient Mental Health Care: Trial of a Prepaid Group Practice Versus Fee-For-Service* (R-3277-NIMH). Santa Monica, Calif.: Rand Corporation, 1986.

MANNING, WILLIAM G., AND KENNETH B. WELLS, "Preliminary Results of a Controlled Trial of the Effect of a Prepaid Group Practice on the Outpatient Use of Mental Health Services," *Journal of Human Resources*, 21 (1986), 293–320.

MARKS, ISAAC M., *Fears and Phobias*. New York: Academic Press, 1969.

―――, "Research in Neurosis: A Selective Review — I. Causes and Courses," *Psychological Medicine*, 3 (1973), 436–54.

MASHAW, JERRY L., *Bureaucratic Justice: Managing Social Security Disability Claims*. New Haven, Conn.: Yale University Press, 1983.

McCORD, JOAN, "A Thirty-Year Follow-Up of Treatment Effects," paper presented at the meetings of the American Association of Psychiatric Services for Children, 1976.

McGHIE, ANDREW, AND JAMES CHAPMAN, "Disorders of Attention and Perception in Early Schizophrenia," *British Journal of Medical Psychology*, 34 (1961), 103–16.

McGUFFIN, P., A. E. FARMER, AND I. I. GOTTESMAN, "Modern Diagnostic Criteria and Genetic Studies of Schizophrenia," in *Search for the Causes of Schizophrenia*, eds. H. Hafner et al., pp. 143–156. Berlin: Springer-Verlag, 1987.

McGUIRE, THOMAS, *Financing Psychotherapy: Costs, Effects, and Public Policy*. Cambridge, Mass.: Ballinger, 1981.

MECHANIC, DAVID, "Relevance of Group Amosphere and Attitudes for the Rehabilitation of Alcoholics," *Quarterly Journal of Studies on Alcohol*, 22 (1961), 634–45.

―――, "Some Factors in Identifying and Defining Mental Illness," *Mental Hygiene*, 46 (1962a), 66–74.

―――, *Students Under Stress*. New York: Free Press, 1962b.

―――, "Therapeutic Intervention: Issues in the Care of the Mentally Ill," *American Journal of Orthopsychiatry*, 37 (1967), 703–18.

―――, "Social Class and Schizophrenia: Some Requirements for a Plausible Theory of Social Influence," *Social Forces*, 50 (1972a), 305–9.

―――, "Social Psychologic Factors Affecting the Presentation of Bodily Complaints," *New England Journal of Medicine*, 286 (1972b), 1132–39.

―――, *Politics, Medicine, and Social Science*. New York: Wiley-Interscience, 1974.

———, "Sociocultural and Social-Psychological Factors Affecting Personal Responses to Psychological Disorder," *Journal of Health and Social Behavior*, 16 (1975), 393–404.

———, *The Growth of Bureaucratic Medicine*. New York: Wiley-Interscience, 1976.

———, *Medical Sociology*, 2nd ed. New York: Free Press, 1978.

———, *Future Issues in Health Care: Social Policy and the Rationing of Medical Services*. New York: Free Press, 1979a.

———, "Development of Psychological Distress Among Young Adults," *Archives of General Psychiatry*, 36 (1979b), 1233–39.

———, ed., *Symptoms, Illness Behavior, and Help-Seeking*. New Brunswick, N.J.: Rutgers University Press, 1982.

———, "Mental Health and Social Policy: Initiatives for the 1980's," *Health Affairs*, 4 (1985), 76–88.

———, "Health Care for the Poor: Some Policy Alternatives," *Journal of Family Practice*, 22 (1986a), 283–89.

———, *From Advocacy to Allocation: The Evolving American Health Care System*. New York: Free Press, 1986b.

MECHANIC, DAVID AND LINDA H. AIKEN, "Improving the care of of Patients with Chronic Mental Illness," *New England Journal of Medicine*, 317 (1987), 1634–38.

MECHANIC, DAVID, AND JAMES R. GREENLEY, "The Prevalence of Psychological Distress and Help-Seeking in a College Student Population," *Social Psychiatry*, 11 (1976), 1–14.

MECHANIC, DAVID, PAUL D. CLEARY, AND JAMES R. GREENLEY, "Distress Syndromes, Illness Behavior, Access to Care and Medical Utilization in a Defined Population," *Medical Care*, 20 (1982), 361–72.

MILLER, KENT S., *Managing Madness: The Case Against Civil Commitment*. New York: Free Press, 1976.

MILLER, ROBERT D., "Commitment to Outpatient Treatment: A National Survey." *Hospital and Community Psychiatry*, 36 (1985), 265–70.

MISCHLER, ELLIOT G., AND NANCY E. WAXLER, "Family Interaction Processes and Schizophrenia: A Review of Current Theories," *Merrill-Palmer Quarterly*, 11 (1965), 269–315.

MONAHAN, JOHN, *The Clinical Prediction of Violent Behavior*. Rockville, Md.: National Institute of Mental Health, 1981.

MOOS, RUDOLF H., *Evaluating Treatment Environments: A Social Ecological Approach*. New York: Wiley-Interscience, 1974.

MORRISSEY, JOSEPH P., RICHARD C. TESSLER, AND LINDA L. FARRIN, "Being 'Seen But Not Admitted': A Note on Some Neglected Aspects of State Hospital Deinstitutionalization," *American Journal of Orthopsychiatry*, 49 (1979), 153–56.

MURPHY, GEORGE E., "The Physician's Responsibility for Suicide: I. An Error of Commission," *Annals of Internal Medicine*, 82 (1975a), 301–4.

———, "The Physician's Responsibility for Suicide: II. Errors of Omission," *Annals of Internal Medicine*, 82 (1975b), 305–9.

MURPHY, H. B. M., "Social Change and Mental Health," in *Causes of Mental Disorders: A Review of Epidemiological Knowledge*, pp. 280–329. New York: Milbank Memorial Fund, 1961.

MURPHY, JANE M., 'Psychiatric Labeling in Cross-Cultural Perspective," *Science*, 191 (1976), 1019–28.

MYERS, JEROME K., AND LEE L. BEAN, *A Decade Later: A Follow-Up of Social Class and Mental Illness*. New York: John Wiley, 1968.

MYERS, JEROME K., et al., "Six-Month Prevalence of Psychiatric Disorders in Three Communities," *Archives of General Psychiatry*, 41 (1984), 959–67.

NATIONAL CENTER FOR HEALTH STATISTICS, HEALTH RESOURCES ADMINISTRATION, *Health Resources Statistics: Health Manpower and Health Facilities, 1975*. Washington, D.C.: U.S. Government Printing Office, DHEW Publication No. (HRA) 76-1509, 1976.

———, "Office Visits to Psychiatrists: National Ambulatory Medical Care Survey, United States, 1975–76," *Advance Data from Vital & Health Statistics*, National Center for Health Statistics, Number 38, DHEW Publication No. (PHS) 78–1250, August 25, 1978.

———, "1985 Summary: National Ambulatory Medical Care Survey," *Advance Data from Vital and Health Statistics*, No. 128, DHHS Pub. No. (HS) 87-1250. Hyattsville, Md.: Public Health Service, Jan. 23, 1987.

NATIONAL INSTITUTE OF MENTAL HEALTH, *Mental Health, United States 1985*. Washington, D.C.: U.S. Government Printing Office, DHHS Pub. No. (ADM) 85-1378, 1985.

————, *Task Force on Nursing Summary Report*, February 9, 1987a.
————, *Mental Health, United States 1987*, Manderscheid, R. W., and Barrett, S. A., eds., DHHS Publication No. (ADM) 87-1518. Washington, D.C.: U.S. Government Printing Office, 1987b.
NEWHOUSE, JOSEPH, "A Design for a Health Insurance Experiment," *Inquiry*, 11 (1974), 5–27.
NEWHOUSE, JOSEPH, et al., "Some Interim Results from a Controlled Trial of Cost-Sharing in Health Insurance," *New England Journal of Medicine*, 305 (1981), 1501–507.
NEW SOUTH WALES DEPARTMENT OF HEALTH, *Psychiatric Hospital Versus Community Treatment: A Controlled Study*. Sydney, Australia (HSR 83-046), 1983.
NEWS AND NOTES, "Psychiatry Leads Specialties in Proportion of Women Practitioners, APA Survey Shows." *Hospital and Community Psychiatry*, 37 (1986), 1167–68.
NEWS AND NOTES, "New Vocational Rehabilitation Act Expands Work, Training Opportunities for Mentally Ill." *Hospital and Community Psychiatry*, 38 (1987), 212–13.
NICHOLI, ARMAND M., JR., "Psychiatric Consultation in Professional Football," *New England Journal of Medicine*, 316 (1987), 1095–100.
ØDEGAARD, Ø., "Discussion of 'Sociocultural Factors in the Epidemiology of Schizophrenia,'" *International Journal of Psychiatry*, 1 (1965), 296–97.
PARRY, HUGH J., MITCHELL B. BALTER, GLEN D. MELLINGER, IRA H. CISIN, AND DEAN I. MANHEIMER, "National Patterns of Psychotherapeutic Drug Use," *Archives of General Psychiatry*, 28 (1973), 769–83.
PASAMANICK, BENJAMIN, FRANK R. SCARPITTI, AND SIMON DINITZ, *Schizophrenics in the Community: An Experimental Study in the Prevention of Hospitalization*. New York: Appleton-Century-Crofts, 1967.
PATRICK, DONALD L., JEFF EAGLE, AND JULES V. COLEMAN, "Primary Care Treatment of Emotional Problems in an HMO," *Medical Care*, 16 (1978), 47–60.
PAUL, GORDAN L., AND ROBERT J. LENTZ, *Psychosocial Treatment of Chronic Mental Patients*. Cambridge, Mass.: Harvard University Press, 1977.
PEARLIN, LEONARD I., AND JOYCE S. JOHNSON, "Marital Status, Life-Strains and Depression," *American Sociological Review*, 42 (1977), 704–15.
PERR, IRWIN N., "The Insanity Defense: The Case for Abolition." *Hospital and Community Psychiatry*, 36 (1985), 51–54.
PERROW, CHARLES, "Hospitals: Technology, Structure, and Goals," in *Handbook of Organizations*, ed. James G. March, pp. 910–71. Skokie, Ill.: Rand McNally, 1965.
PHILLIPS, DEREK L., AND KEVIN J. CLANCY, "Responses Biases in Field Studies of Mental Illness," *American Sociological Review*, 35 (1970), 503–15.
PIERCE, GLENN L., et al., "The Impact of Public Policy and Publicity on Admissions to State Mental Health Hospitals." *Journal of Health Politics, Policy and Law*, 11 (1986), 41–66.
PLUNKETT, RICHARD J., AND JOHN E. GORDON, *Epidemiology and Mental Illness*. New York: Basic Books, 1960.
POLAK, PAUL R., "A Comprehensive System of Alternatives to Psychiatric Hospitalization," in *Alternatives to Mental Hospital Treatment*, eds. Leonard I. Stein and Mary Ann Test, pp. 115–37. New York: Plenum, 1978.
QUINTON, DAVID, AND MICHAEL RUTTER, "Family Pathology and Child Psychiatric Disorder: A Four-Year Prospective Study,." in *Longitudinal Studies in Child Psychology and Psychiatry: Practical Lessons from Research Experience*, ed. R. Nichol. New York: Wiley, 1984a.
————, "Parents with Children in Care: Intergenerational Continuities," *Journal of Child Psychology and Psychiatry*, 25 (1984b), 231–50.
RAPOPORT, ROBERT N. *Community as Doctor: New Perspectives on a Therapeutic Community*. Springfield, Ill.: Chas. C. Thomas, 1960.
RAPPEPORT, JONAS R., ed., *The Clinical Evaluation of the Dangerousness of the Mentally Ill*. Springfield, Ill.: Chas. C. Thomas, 1967.
REDICK, RICHARD W., et al., *Specialty Mental Health Organizations, United States, 1983–84*. Rockville, Md.: National Institute of Mental Health, 1986.
REDLICH, FREDERICK C., AND DANIEL X. FREEDMAN, *The Theory and Practice of Psychiatry*. New York: Basic Books, 1966.
REDLICH, FREDERICK C., AND STEPHEN R. KELLERT, "Trends in American Mental Health," *American Journal of Psychiatry*, 135 (1978), 22–28.

REGIER, DARREL A., et al., "The NIMH Epidemiologic Catchment Area Study," *Archives of General Psychiatry*, 41 (1984), 934–41.

REICH, THEODORE, et al., "Genetics of the Affective Psychoses," in *Handbook of Psychiatry 3: Psychoses of Uncertain Actiology*, eds. J. K. Wing and L. Wing, pp. 147–59. New York: Cambridge University Press, 1985.

REID, DONALD D., "Precipitating Proximal Factors in the Occurrence of Mental Disorders: Epidemiological Evidence," in *Causes of Mental Disorders: A Review of Epidemiological Knowledge*, pp. 197–216. New York: Milbank Memorial Fund, 1961.

REIF, LAURA J., "Cardiacs and Normals: The Social Construction of a Disability," unpublished Ph.D. dissertation, University of California, San Francisco, 1975.

ROBERT WOOD JOHNSON FOUNDATION, *Special Report: Updated Report on Access to Health Care for the American People*. Princeton, N.J.: Robert Wood Johnson Foundation, 1983.

ROBINS, LEE N., *Deviant Children Grown Up: Sociological and Psychiatric Study of Sociopathic Personality*. Baltimore: Williams & Wilkins, 1966.

――――, "Evaluation of Psychiatric Services for Children in the United States," in *Roots of Evaluation*, eds. J. K. Wing and H. Hafner. London: Oxford University Press, 1973.

――――, "Alcoholism and Labelling Theory," in *The Labelling of Deviance: Evaluating a Perspective*, ed. Walter R. Gove, pp. 21–33. New York: Halsted Press, 1975.

――――, Longitudinal Methods in the Study of Normal and Pathological Development," in *Psychiatrie de Gegenwart*, Vol. 1, 2nd ed., eds. K. P. Kisker, J. E. Meyer, C. Müller, and E. Stromgren, pp. 627–84. Heidelberg: Springer, 1979a.

――――, "Follow-Up Studies of Behavior Disorders in Children," in *Psychopathological Disorders of Childhood*, 2nd ed., eds. Herbert C. Quay and John S. Werry. New York: Wiley, 1979b.

――――, "Continuities and Discontinuities in the Psychiatric Disorders of Children," in *Handbook of Health, Health Care and the Health Professions*, ed. David Mechanic, pp. 195–219. New York: Free Press, 1983.

――――, "Epidemiology: Reflections on Testing the Validity of Psychiatric Interviews," *Archives of General Psychiatry*, 42 (1985), 918–24.

ROBINS, LEE N., et al., "Lifetime Prevalence of Specific Psychiatric Disorders in Three Sites," *Archives of General Psychiatry*, 41 (1984), 949–58.

――――, "The Diagnostic Interview Schedule," in *Epidemiologic Field Methods in Psychiatry*, eds. W. W. Eaton and L. G. Kessler, pp. 143–70. New York: Academic Press, 1985.

RODIN, JUDITH, "Aging and Health Effects of the Sense of Control." *Science*, 233 (1986), 1271–76.

RODIN, JUDITH, AND ELLEN J. LANGNER, "Long-Term Effects of a Control-Relevant Intervention with the Institutionalized Aged." *Journal of Personality and Social Psychology*, 35 (1977), 897–902.

ROSENHAN, DAVID L., "On Being Sane in Insane Places," *Science*, 179 (1973), 250–58.

ROSENSTEIN, MARILYN J., et al., "Legal Status of Admissions to Three Inpatient Psychiatric Settings, United States, 1980," *Mental Health Statistical Note*, 178, Surveys and Reports Branch. Rockville, Md.: National Institute of Mental Health, 1986.

ROSENTHAL, DAVID, *Genetic Theory and Abnormal Behavior*. New York: McGraw-Hill, 1970.

ROSSI, PETER H., AND JAMES D. WRIGHT, "The Determinants of Homelessness," *Health Affairs*, 6 (1987), 19–32.

ROSSI, PETER H., et al., "The Urban Homeless: Estimating Composition and Size," *Science*, 235 (1987), 1336–1341.

ROTH, JULIUS A., *Timetables: Structuring the Passage of Time in Hospital Treatment and Other Careers*. Indianapolis: Bobbs-Merrill, 1963.

ROTHMAN, DAVID J., *The Discovery of the Asylum: Social Order and Disorder in the New Republic*. Boston: Little, Brown, 1971.

RUBENSTEIN, LEONARD, "APA's Model Law: Hurting the People It Seeks to Help." *Hospital and Community Psychiatry*, 36 (1985), 968–72.

RUBENSTEIN, MARK, AND RICHARD SIMONS, "The Schizophrenic Disorders," in *Understanding Human Behavior in Health and Illness*, 2nd ed., eds. Richard Simons and Herbert Pardes, pp. 612–25. Baltimore: Williams and Wilkins, 1981.

RUSHING, WILLIAM A., *The Psychiatric Professions: Power, Conflict, and Adaptation in a Psychiatric Hospital Staff*. Chapel Hill: University of North Carolina Press, 1964.

RUSSELL, LOUISE, *Is Prevention Better Than Cure?*. Washington, D.C.: The Brookings Institution, 1986.
———, *Evaluating Preventive Care: Report on a Workshop*. Washington, D.C.: The Brookings Institution, 1987.
RUTTER, MICHAEL, *Children of Sick Parents: An Environmental and Psychiatric Study*. New York: Oxford University Press, 1966.
———, "Relationships Between Child and Adult Psychiatric Disorders," *Acta Psychiatrica Scandinavica*, 48 (1972), 3–21.
RYDER, NORMAN B., "The Cohort as a Concept in the Study of Social Change," *American Sociological Review*, 30 (1965), 843–61.
SAMPSON, HAROLD S., SHELDON L. MESSINGER, AND ROBERT D. TOWNE, *Schizophrenic Women: Studies in Marital Crisis*. New York: Atherton Press, 1964.
SARTORIUS, NORMAN, et al., "Early Manifestations and First-Contact Incidence of Schizophrenia in Different Cultures," *Psychological Medicine*, 16 (1986), 909–28.
SCHACHTER, STANLEY, *The Psychology of Affiliation: Experimental Studies of the Sources of Gregariousness*. Stanford: Stanford University Press, 1959.
SCHEFF, THOMAS J., "Legitimate, Transitional, and Illegitimate Mental Patients in a Midwestern State," *The American Journal of Psychiatry*, 120 (1963), 267–69.
———, "Social Conditions for Rationality: How Urban and Rural Courts Deal with the Mentally Ill," *The American Behavioral Scientist*, 7 (1964a), 21–24.
———, "The Societal Reaction to Deviance: Ascriptive Elements in the Psychiatric Screening of Mental Patients in a Midwestern State," *Social Problems*, 11 (1964b), 401–13.
———, "Users and Non-Users of a Student Psychiatric Clinic," *Journal of Health and Human Behavior*, 7 (1966), 114–21.
———, *Being Mentally Ill: A Sociological Theory*. Chicago: Aldine, 1966 (second edition, 1984).
SCULL, ANDREW T., *Decarceration: Community Treatment and the Deviant*. Englewood Cliffs, N.J.: Prentice-Hall, 1977.
SEGAL, STEPHEN P., AND URI AVIRAM, *The Mentally Ill in Community-Based Sheltered Care: A Study of Community Care and Social Integration*. New York: Wiley-Interscience, 1978.
SEILER, LAUREN H., "The 22-Item Scale Used in Field Studies of Mental Illness: A Question of Method, a Question of Substance, and a Question of Theory," *Journal of Health and Social Behavior*, 14 (1973), 252–64.
SELIGMAN, MARTIN E. P., *Helplessness: On Depression, Development, and Death*. San Francisco: W. H. Freeman and Company Publishers, 1975.
SEWELL, WILLIAM H., "Infant Training and the Personality of the Child," *American Journal of Sociology*, 58 (1952), 150–59.
SHAPIRO, SAM, et al., "Utilization of Health and Mental Health Services: Three Epidemiological Catchment Area Sites," *Archives of General Psychiatry*, 41 (1984), 971–78.
———, "Measuring Need for Mental Health Services in a General Population," *Medical Care*, 23 (1985), 1033–43.
SHEPHERD, GEOFF, *Institutional Care and Rehabilitation*. London: Longman, 1984.
SHEPHERD, MICHAEL, "Formulation of New Research Strategies on Schizophrenia," in *Search for the Causes of Schizophrenia*, eds. H. Hafner et al., pp. 29–38. Berlin: Springer-Verlag, 1987.
SHEPHERD, MICHAEL, A. N. OPPENHEIM, AND SHEILA MITCHELL, "Childhood Behavior Disorders and the Child-Guidance Clinic. An Epidemiological Study," *Journal of Child Psychology and Psychiatry*, 7 (1966), 39–52.
SHEPHERD, MICHAEL, BRIAN COOPER, ALEXANDER C. BROWN, AND GRAHAM KALTON, *Psychiatric Illness in General Practice*. London: Oxford University Press, 1966.
SIMMONDS, JAMES A., "An Examination of Procedures for Commitment to a Mental Hospital: The Case Behind Bill 388-A," *Newsletter of the Wisconsin Psychiatric Institute*, University of Wisconsin (1967), 11–14.
SIMMONS, ROBERT G., SUSAN D. KLEIN, AND RICHARD L. SIMMONS, *Gift of Life: The Social and Psychological Impact of Organ Transplantation*. New York: Wiley-Interscience, 1977.
SKINNER, B. F., *Beyond Freedom and Dignity*. New York: Knopf, 1971.
SMITH, G. RICHARD, JR., ROBERTA A. MONSON, AND DEBBY C. RAY, "Psychiatric Consultation in Somatization Disorder: A Randomized Controlled Study," *New England Journal of Medicine*, 314 (1986), 1407–13.

SPITZ, BRUCE, "A National Survey of Medicaid Case-Management Programs." *Health Affairs,* 6 (1987), 61–70.

SPITZER, ROBERT L., "More on Pseudoscience in Science and the Case for Psychiatric Diagnosis," *Archives of General Psychiatry,* 33 (1976), 459–70.

SPITZER, ROBERT L., AND JEAN ENDICOTT, "Medical and Mental Disorder: Proposed Definition and Criteria," in *Critical Issues in Psychiatric Diagnosis,* eds. Robert L. Spitzer and Donald F. Klein. New York: Raven Press, 1978.

SROLE, LEO, THOMAS S. LANGNER, STANLEY T. MICHAEL, MARVIN K. OPLER, AND THOMAS A. C. RENNIE, *Mental Health in the Metropolis: The Midtown Manhattan Study.* New York: McGraw-Hill, 1962.

STANTON, ALFRED H., AND MORRIS S. SCHWARTZ, *The Mental Hospital: A Study of Institutional Participation in Psychiatric Illness and Treatment.* New York: Basic Books, 1954.

STAPP, JOY, et al., "Census of Psychological Personnel: 1983," *American Psychologist,* 40 (1985), 1317–51.

STEIN, LEONARD I., MARY ANN TEST, AND ARNOLD J. MARX, "Alternatives to the Hospital: A Controlled Study," *The American Journal of Psychiatry,* 132 (1975), 517–22.

STEIN, LEONARD I., AND LEONARD J. GANSER, "Wisconsin System for Funding Mental Health Services," in *New Directions for Mental Health Services: Unified Mental Health System,* ed. J. Talbott, pp. 25–32. San Francisco: Jossey-Bass, 1983.

STEIN, LEONARD I., AND MARY ANN TEST, "Training in Community Living: One-Year Evaluation," *The American Journal of Psychiatry,* 133 (1976), 917–18.

———, eds., *Alternatives to Mental Hospital Treatment.* New York: Plenum, 1978.

———, "Alternatives to Mental Hospital Treatment I. Conceptual Model Treatment Program and Clinical Evaluation," *Archives of General Psychiatry,* 37 (1980a), 392–97.

———, "Alternatives to Mental Hospital Treatment III. Social Cost," *Archives of General Psychiatry,* 37 (1980b), 409–12.

———, eds., *The Training in Community Living Model: A Decade of Experience,* New Directions for Mental Health Services, No. 26. San Francisco: Jossey-Bass, 1985.

STEVENS, ROBERT, AND ROSEMARY STEVENS, *Welfare Medicine in America A Case Study of Medicaid.* New York: Free Press, 1974.

STONE, ALAN A., *Mental Health and Law: A System in Transition.* Rockville, Md.: Center for Studies of Crime and Delinquency, National Institute of Mental Health, DHEW Publication No. (ADM) 75–176, 1975.

———, "The Right to Refuse Treatment." *Archives of General Psychiatry,* 38 (1981), 358–62.

———, *Law, Psychiatry, and Morality.* Washington, D.C.: American Psychiatric Press, 1984.

STOTSKY, BERNARD A., *The Nursing Home and the Aged Psychiatric Patient.* New York: Appleton-Century-Crofts, 1970.

STRAUSS, JOHN S., "The Functional Psychoses," in *Psychiatry in General Medical Practice,* eds. Gene Usdin and Jerry Lewis, pp. 279–302. New York: McGraw-Hill, 1979.

STRAUSS, JOHN S., AND WILLIAM T. CARPENTER, "Prediction of Outcome in Schizophrenia: III. Five-Year Outcome and Its Predictors," *Archives of General Psychiatry,* 34 (1977), 159–63.

STROMBERG, C. D., AND ALAN STONE, "A Model State Law on Civil Commitment of the Mentally Ill," *Harvard Journal on Legislation,* 20 (1983), 275–96.

SULLIVAN, HARRY STACK, *The Interpersonal Theory of Psychiatry.* New York: W. W. Norton & Co., Inc., 1953.

SURLES, RICHARD C. AND MARTIN C. McGURRIN, "Increased Use of Psychiatric Emergency Services by Young Chronically Mentally Ill Patients," *Hospital and Community Psychiatry,* 38 (1987), 401–05.

SUTHERLAND, NORMAN S., *Breakdown.* Briarcliff Manor, N.Y.: Stein & Day, 1977.

SZASZ, THOMAS S., "The Myth of Mental Illness," *The American Psychologist,* 15 (1960), 113–18.

———, "Constitutional Rights of the Mentally Ill," hearings before the Subcommittee on Constitutional Rights of the Committee on the Judiciary, United States Senate, 87th Congress, 1st Session. Washington, D.C.: U.S. Government Printing Office, 1961, pp. 251–72.

———, *Law, Liberty, and Psychiatry: An Inquiry into the Social Uses of Mental Health Practices.* New York: Macmillan, 1963.

———, *The Ethics of Psychoanalysis.* New York: Basic Books, 1965.

————, *Ideology and Insanity: Essays on the Psychiatric Dehumanization of Man.* New York: Doubleday (Anchor), 1970.

————, *The Myth of Mental Illness: Foundations of a Theory of Personal Conduct,* rev. ed. New York: Harper and Row, 1974.

TALBOTT, JOHN A., "The Fate of the Public Psychiatric System," *Hospital and Community Psychiatry,* 36 (1985), 46–50.

TARRIER, NICHOLAS, CHRISTINE VAUGHN, MALCOLM H. LADER, AND JULIAN P. LEFF, "Bodily Reactions to People and Events in Schizophrenics," *Archives of General Psychiatry,* 36 (1979), 311–15.

TAUBE, CARL, EUN S. LEE, AND RONALD N. FORTHOFER, "DRGs in Psychiatry: An Empirical Evaluation," *Medical Care,* 22 (1984), 597–610.

TAUBE, CARL, LARRY KESSLER, AND M. FEUERBERG, "Utilization and Expenditures for Ambulatory Medical Care During 1980," *National Medical Care Utilization and Expenditure Survey Data Report* No. 5, DHHS Publication No. (PHS) 84-2000. Washingon, D.C.: Government Printing Office, 1984.

TESSLER, RICHARD, DAVID MECHANIC, AND MARGARET DIMOND, "The Effect of Psychological Distress on Physician Utilization: A Prospective Study," *Journal of Health and Social Behavior,* 17 (1976), 353–64.

TESSLER, RICHARD, AND DAVID MECHANIC, "Psychological Distress and Perceived Health Status," *Journal of Health and Social Behavior,* 19 (1978), 254–62.

TESSLER, RICHARD, AND HOWARD H. GOLDMAN, *The Chronically Mentally Ill: Assessing the Community Support Programs.* Cambridge: Ballinger Publishing Company, 1982.

TESSLER, RICHARD, et al., "Stages in Family Response to Mental Illness: An Ideal Type," *Psychosocial Rehabilitation Journal,* 10 (1987), 3–16.

TEST, MARY ANN, AND LEONARD I. STEIN, "An Alternative to Mental Hospital Treatment: II. Social Cost," unpublished paper, Department of Psychiatry, University of Wisconsin, Madison, 1979.

TOUSIGNANT, MICHAEL, GUY DENIS, AND REJEAN LACHAPELLE, "Some Considerations Concerning the Validity and Use of the Health Opinion Survey," *Journal of Health and Social Behavior,* 15 (1974), 241–52.

TREFFERT, DAROLD A., "Dying with Their Rights On," *The American Journal of Psychiatry,* 130 (1973), 1041.

TSUANG, MING T., ROBERT F. WOOLSON, AND JEROME A. FLEMING, "Long-Term Outcome of Major Psychoses: I. Schizophrenia and Affective Disorders Compared with Psychiatrically Symptom-Free Surgical Conditions," *Archives of General Psychiatry,* 36 (1979), 1295–1301.

TURNER, R. JAY, AND MORTON O. WAGENFELD, "Occupational Mobility and Schizophrenia: An Assessment of the Social Causation and Social Selection Hypotheses," *American Sociological Review,* 32 (1967), 104–13.

ULLMANN, LEONARD P., *Institution and Outcome: A Comparative Study of Psychiatric Hospitals.* Elmsford, N.Y.: Pergamon Press. 1967.

U.S. DEPARTMENT OF HEALTH AND HUMAN SERVICES, *Toward a National Plan for the Chronically Mentally Ill,* Report to the Secretary — 1980, DHHS Publication No. (ADM 81-1077). Rockville, Md.: Department of Health and Human Services, 1980.

U.S. DEPARTMENT OF HOUSING AND URBAN DEVELOPMENT (HUD), *A Report to the Secretary on the Homeless and Emergency Shelters.* Washington, D.C.: Office of Policy Development and Research, 1984.

U.S. GENERAL ACCOUNTING OFFICE, *Homelessness: A Complex Problem and the Federal Response.* Washington, D.C.: General Accounting Office, 1985.

U.S. PRESIDENT'S COMMISSION ON MENTAL HEALTH, *Report of the Task Panel on the Nature and Scope of the Problems,* Vol. I, Vol. II Appendix. Washington, D.C.: U.S. Government Printing Office, 1978.

VAUGHN, CHRISTINE E., AND JULIAN P. LEFF, "The Influence of Family and Social Factors on the Course of Psychiatric Illness: A Comparison of Schizophrenic and Depressed Neurotic Patients," *The British Journal of Psychiatry,* 129 (1976), 125–37.

VLADECK, BRUCE, *Unloving Care: The Nursing Home Tragedy.* New York: Basic Books, 1980.

————, "The End of Health Insurance," *President's Letter,* New York: United Hospital Fund, 1986.

WALSH, ANNMARIE AND JAMES LEIGLAND, *Public Authorities and Mental Health Programs.* Washington, D.C.: Institute for Public Administration, 1986.

WARE, JOHN E., JR., et al., "Comparison of Health Outcomes at a Health Maintenance Organization with Those of Fee-For-Service Care," *Lancet,* 14 (1986), 1017–22.

WARREN, CAROL, *The Court of Last Resort: Mental Illness and the Law.* Chicago: University of Chicago Press, 1982.

WATTS, FRASER N., AND DOUGLAS H. BENNETT eds., *Theory and Practice of Psychiatric Rehabilitation.* New York: Wiley, 1983.

WAXLER, NANCY E., "Is Outcome for Schizophrenia Better in Non-Industrial Societies? The Case of Sri Lanka," *Journal of Nervous and Mental Disease,* 167 (1979), 144–58.

WEINMAN, BERNARD, AND ROBERT J. KLEINER, "The Impact of Community Living and Community Member Intervention on the Adjustment of the Chronic Psychotic Patient," in *Alternatives to Mental Hospital Treatment,* eds. Leonard I. Stein and Mary Ann Test, pp. 139–59. New York: Plenum, 1978.

WEINSTEIN, RAYMOND, "Patient Attitudes toward Mental Hospitalization: A Review of Qualitative Research," *Journal of Health and Social Behavior,* 20 (1979), 237–58.

————, "Labeling Theory and the Attitudes of Mental Patients: A Review," *Journal of Health and Social Behavior,* 24 (1983), 70–84.

WEISBROD, BURTON A., MARY ANN TEST, AND LEONARD I. STEIN, "Alternatives to Mental Hospital Treatment II. Economic Benefit - Cost Analysis," *Archives of General Psychiatry,* 37 (1980), 400–402.

WEISS, ROBERT S., *Marital Separation.* New York: Basic Books, 1975.

————, "Transition States and Other Stressful Situations: Their Nature and Programs for Their Management," in *Support Systems and Mutual Help: Multidisciplinary Explorations,* eds. Gerald Caplan and Marie Killilea, pp. 213–32. New York: Grune and Stratton, 1976.

WEISSMAN, MYRNA M., AND EUGENE S. PAYKEL, *The Depressed Woman: A Study of Social Relationships.* Chicago: University of Chicago Press, 1974.

WEISSMAN, MYRNA M., AND GERALD L. KLERMAN, "Sex Differences and the Epidemiology of Depression," *Archives of General Psychiatry,* 34 (1977), 98–111.

WEISSMAN, MYRNA M., AND JEROME K. MYERS, "Affective Disorders in a U.S. Urban Community: The Use of Research Diagnostic Criteria in an Epidemiological Survey," *Archives of General Psychiatry,* 35 (1978), 1304–11.

WELLS, KENNETH B., et al., *Cost-Sharing and the Demand for Ambulatory Mental Health Services* (CR-2960-HHS). Santa Monica, Calif.: Rand Corporation, 1982.

————, "Cost-Sharing and the Use of General Medical Physicians for Outpatient Mental Health Care," *Health Services Research,* 22 (1987), 1–17.

WHEATON, BLAIR, "The Sociogenesis of Psychological Disorder: Reexamining the Causal Issues with Longitudinal Data," *American Sociological Review,* 43 (1978), 383–403.

————, "Models for the Stress-Buffering Functions of Coping Resources." *Journal of Health and Social Behavior,* 26 (1985), 352–64.

WHITE, KERR L., "Evaluation of Medical Education and Health Care," in *Community Medicine: Teaching, Research, and Health Care,* eds. Willoughby Lathem and Anne Newbery, pp. 241–70. New York: Appleton-Century-Crofts, 1970.

WIG, N. N., M. H. BEDI, A. GHOSH, et al., "Expressed Emotion and Schizophrenia in North India," *British Journal of Psychiatry,* 151 (1987), 156–173.

WILSON, A. T. M., E. L. TRIST, AND ADAM CURLE, "Transitional Communities and Social Reconnection: A Study of the Civil Resettlement of British Prisoners of War," in *Readings in Social Psychology,* rev. ed., eds. Guy E. Swanson, Theodore M. Newcomb, and Eugene L. Hartley, pp. 561–79. New York: Holt, Rhinehart & Winston, 1952.

WING, JOHN. K., "Institutionalism in Mental Hospitals," *British Journal of Social and Clinical Psychology,* 1 (1962), 38–51.

————, "Rehabilitation of Psychiatric Patients," *The British Journal of Psychiatry,* 109 (1963), 635–41.

————, "The Modern Management of Schizophrenia," in *New Aspects of the Mental Health Services,* eds. Hugh Freeman and James Farndale, pp. 3–28. Elmsford, N.Y.: Pergamon Press, 1967.

————, *Reasoning About Madness.* Oxford: Oxford University Press, 1978.

WING, JOHN K., AND GEORGE W. BROWN, "Social Treatment of Chronic Schizophrenia: A

Comprehensive Survey of Three Mental Hospitals," *Journal of Mental Science,* 107 (1961), 847–61.

————, *Institutionalism and Schizophrenia: A Comparative Study of Three Mental Hospitals, 1960–1968.* Cambridge: Cambridge University Press, 1970.

WING, JOHN K., J. L. T. BIRLEY, J. E. COOPER, P. GRAHAM, AND A. D. ISAACS, "Reliability of a Procedure for Measuring and Classifying 'Present Psychiatric State,'" *The British Journal of Psychiatry,* 5113 (1967), 499–515.

WING, JOHN K., AND ANTHEA M. HAILEY, eds., *Evaluating Community Psychiatric Service: The Camberwell Register, 1964–1971.* London: Oxford University Press, 1972.

WING, JOHN K., JOHN E. COOPER AND NORMAN SARTORIUS, *Measurement and Classification of Psychiatric Symptoms.* Cambridge: Cambridge University Press, 1974.

WING, LORNA, JOHN K. WING, ANTHEA HAILEY, et al., "The Use of Psychiatric Services in Three Urban Areas: An International Case Register Study," *Social Psychiatry,* 2 (1967), 158–67.

WINICK, BRUCE J., "Incompetency to Stand Trial: Developments in the Law," in *Mentally Disordered Offenders: Perspectives from Law and Social Science,* eds. J. Monahan and H. J. Steadman, pp. 3–38. New York: Plenum, 1983.

WITKIN, MICHAEL J., et al., "Specialty Mental Health System Characteristics," in *Mental Health, United States: 1987.* DHHS Publication No (ADM) 87-1518. Washington, D.C.: Government Printing Office, 1987.

WOLPE, JOSEPH, *Psychotherapy by Reciprocal Inhibition.* Stanford: Stanford University Press, 1958.

WORLD HEALTH ORGANIZATION, *Report of the International Pilot Study of Schizophrenia,* Vol. I. Geneva: World Health Organization, 1973.

————, *Schizophrenia: An International Follow-up Study.* Geneva, New York: John Wiley, 1979.

WRIGHT, JAMES D., *The National Health Care for the Homeless Program: The First Year.* Amherst, Mass.: Social and Demographic Research Institute, University of Massachusetts, unpublished report to the Robert Wood Johnson Foundation, 1987.

WYNNE, LYMAN, RUE CROMWELL, AND STEVEN MATTHYSSE eds., *The Nature of Schizophrenia: New Approaches to Research and Treatment.* New York: Wiley, 1978.

YARROW, MARIAN RADKE, CHARLOTTE GREEN SCHWARTZ, HARRIET S. MURPHY, AND LEILA CALHOUN DEASY, "The Psychological Meaning of Mental Illness in the Family," *The Journal of Social Issues,* 11, (1955), 12–24.

ZUSMAN, JACK, "Some Explanations of the Changing Appearance of Psychotic Patients: Antecedents of the Social Breakdown Syndrome Concept," *Milbank Memorial Fund Quarterly,* 44 (1966, Part 2), 363–94.

————, "APA's Model Commitment Law and the Need for Better Mental Health Services," *Hospital and Community Psychiatry,* 36 (1985), 978–80.

Name Index

Subject Index

Achievement patterns, 67
Action for Mental Health, 89–90
Adaptation (*see also* Coping)
  resources for, 127–29
  through search for meaning, 123–24
  through social attribution, 123, 124–26
  through social comparison, 123, 124, 126
Adjustment, mental illness as failure in, 5
Adolescent problems, schizophrenia and, 66
Affective disorders, 10 (*see also* Depression)
  genetic components, of, 65
  prevalence of, 18–19
After-care programs, 199
Agencies, 6
Aggression, 59, 67
  concept of danger and, 229
Aging, long-term care in, 101
Alcohol, Drug Abuse, and Mental Health Administration (ADAMHA), 92–93
Alcohol abuse:
  environmental influences on treatment of, 167
  government focus on, 92
  among the homeless, 103
  labeling theory and, 78
  recognition of, 110
ALI (American Law Institute) rule for testing insanity, 241
Ambulatory care, 150
  growth of, 155
American Psychiatric Association, 17
Antisocial behavior, 67
  epidemiology of, 59–60
Anxiety responses, 71
Apathy syndrome (*see* Institutional neuroses [institutionalism])
Aponte v. *State*, 236–37
Army Neuro-Psychiatric Screening Adjunct, 47
Attribution, social, adaptation through, 123, 124–26
Authority, mental health, 181–83

Behavior disorders, epidemiology of, 59–60
Behavior modification, 32, 69
Behavior therapy, 211 (*see also* Learning theory)
  components of, 72
  criticisms of, 71–72
  effectiveness of, 72
  self-control extension of, 72
Biology (*see also* Genetics)
  advances in, 34
  mental illness and, 33–34, 65
Bipolar disorders, 19 (*see also* Depression)
Bizarre behavior, 2, 5
Brain, biological mechanisms and mental illness, 65

Capitation-type health plans, 138–39, 142–43
Care (*see also* Community care; Service, mental health)

barriers to, 55–56
  utilization of, 50–56
Case-management approach to community care, 8, 179–81
CATEGO, 21
Causes of mental illness (*see* Etiology of mental disorders)
Child-rearing practices, 67
Children:
  depression and raising of, 57
  institutional care of, 68
Child therapeutic services, 69–70
China, neurasthenia in, 147–48
Chronically mentally ill, 152–54
  case-management with, 180
  community alternatives for, 199
  community care for, 82, 173
  disability benefits for, 178–79
  ethical issues involving, 195–96
  federal studies of, 94–95
  financing of care for, crisis in, 140–43
  insurance programs and, 149, 175
  maintenance of, innovations in, 200–207
  Medicaid eligibility of, 176
  population of:
    composition of, 100–102
    estimates of, 153–54
  primary care physicians and, 149
  professional neglect of, 132
  treatment of:
    insufficient, 144–45
    training for, 88
Chronicity, concept of, 153–54
Civil liberties activism, commitment statutes and, 217–18
Civil Resettlement Units, 197–98
Civil rights movement, deinstitutionalization and, 97
Clerical services, staffed by mentally ill, 204–5
Clubs, ex-patient, 199
Cognitive therapy for depression, 32
Coinsurance, outpatient services and, 137–38
Collective mobilization, 79–80
Commitment, 215–28
  appropriate, procedure for determining, 225
  based on incompetency to stand trial, 237–38
  concept of danger and, 228–30
  individual freedom and, 223
  model state law on, 225–26
  outpatient, 227
  parens patriae approach to, 217, 218, 225
  psychiatric judgments and, 218, 223
  social contexts of, 218–20
  Thank You Theory of, 225
  in violation of individual rights, 220–22
Community(ies) (*see also* Epidemiology, psychiatric)
  approach to mentally ill, 214
  definitions of mental illness, 114–19
    tendency to normalize deviant behavior and, 114–16.

political and professional dominance of, 211
professionalization of, negative effects of, 85
social influences on judgment of, 187–88
sociocultural context and, 190–94
Psychiatry (*see also* Developmental models of mental illness)
development in the United States, 12
manpower shortage in, 87–88
postwar, 88–96
preventive, 39, 190–94
psychodynamic orientation of, 11–13, 190
scope and function of, 43–44
in selective service, 86–87
training in 1980s for, 13
Psychoactive drugs (*see* Drug[s])
Psychodynamic therapy (*see* Psychotherapy [psychodynamic therapy])
Psychologists, clinical, 7, 8
legitimization achieved by, 211
Psychology, clinical, 9
behavioral orientation of, 13
Psychoneurosis, incidence during war, 118
Psychosis:
affective, 10
neurosis vs., 107
Psychosocial development perspective on etiology of mental disorders, 65–70
Psychotherapy By Reciprocal Inhibition (Wolpe), 70–71
Psychotherapy (psychodynamic therapy), 8, 11–13, 190
diversification of, 31–32
federal funding of, 150
person-environment fit and, 32
as social movement, 189

Rand Health Insurance Experiment (HIE), 137, 139–40
Reaction formation, 4
Reaction patterns:
defined, 4
exaggerations of, 69–70
Referrals, 53, 55–56
HMOs and, 138
from primary care physicians, 145–46
Rehabilitation:
community care programs for, 201–2
educational approach to, 202
family-oriented, for schizophrenia, 172
goals of, 201
industrial, 204
Social Security disability system and, 179
through work, 204–6
Reinforcement schedules, 71 (*see also* Behavior therapy; Learning theory)
Rennie case, 234
Repression, 70
Residues, 4
Resilience, stress and, 58–59
Rogers case, 234

Schizophrenia, 10, 19
approaches to and theoretical conceptions of, 22–25

course of, 119–21
criminal behavior and, 243
debate over nature of, 26–27
diagnosis of, 20–21
early peer relations and adolescent problems and, 66
emotional intensity and, 64, 120–21, 169, 172
environment and, 64–65
epidemiology of, 46
family and, 64–66, 120–21
family-oriented rehabilitation models for, 172
heredity theory of, 62–63
hospitalization vs. home treatment for, 155–57
incomplete care for, 144
life events and, 64–65, 74
prognosis of, 21–22
socioeconomic status and, 56–57
among the young, 101–2
Schizophrenics, reentry into community, 158
Selective service, psychiatric participation in, 86–87
Self-control, 72
Self-help groups, 128–29
Service, mental health (*see also* Help seeking)
ambulatory clinics, 150
applicants for, characteristics of, 112–13
bifurcation of, 131
child therapy, 69–70
education model of, 202–7
entry into, 107–14
fee-for-service model of, 194
financing and delivery of, 131–51
critical public policy issues in, 150–51
epidemiological approach to psychiatric need and, 143–45
mix of services and, 139
pattern of inpatient services and, 133–34
prepayment plans, 138–40
primary medical care and, 145–50
service utilization and, 134–36
structure of insurance and mental health benefits, 140–43
growth of, 131–32
inequalities in, 11–12
innovations in, 197–212
future of, 211–12
in housing, 209–10
in maintenance of chronic psychiatric patients, 200–207
in organization of professionals, 210–11
problems in diffusion of, 207–8
insurance and, 132–33
in the military, 117–19
need for, estimating, 107
planning for, 106–7
rationing of, 194–95
use of, factors affecting, 111–12
Sex, depression and, 57–58
Sheltered care, external and internal integration in, 169
Sheltered workshops, 198–99, 205
Skills, adaptational, 127
Social adjustment, mental illness as failure in, 5
Social control, high intensity interpersonal, 121
Social functioning (*see* Functioning, patient)
Social Security, disability determination, 178–79
Social Security Act, 1980 amendments to, 178
Social Security Disability Income (SSDI), 98